Professional Issues in Software Engineering

Professional Issues in Software Engineering

Third edition

Frank Bott
Allison Coleman
Jack Eaton
Diane Rowland

Taylor & Francis
Taylor & Francis Group

LONDON AND NEW YORK

11185

First published in 1991 by Pitman Publishing
First published by UCL Press Limited as a second impression 1994
Second edition 1995
Second impression 1996
Reprinted 1998

First published by Taylor & Francis 2001
11 New Fetter Lane, London EC4P 4EE

Simultaneously published in the USA and Canada
by Taylor & Francis Inc,
29 West 35th Street, New York, NY 10001

Reprinted 2001, 2003, 2004

Taylor & Francis is an imprint of the Taylor & Francis Group

© 2001 M. F. Bott, J. A. Coleman, J. Eaton, D. Rowland

The rights of Frank Bott, Allison Coleman, Jack Eaton and
Diane Rowland to be identified as authors of this work have been
asserted in accordance with sections 77 and 78 of the Copyright,
Designs and Patents Act 1988.

Typeset by Keyword Publishing Services Ltd.
Printed and bound in Great Britain by St Edmundsbury Press Ltd,
Bury St Edmunds, Suffolk

Every effort has been made to ensure that the advice and information
in this book is true and accurate at the time of going to press.
However, neither the publisher nor the authors can accept any legal
responsibility or liability for any errors or omissions that may be made.

British Library Cataloguing in Publication Data
A catalogue record for this book is available from the British Library

Library of Congress Cataloging in Publication Data
Professional issues in software engineering / Frank Bott ... [et al.].
  – 3rd ed.
     p. cm.
  Includes bibliographical references and index.
  1. Software engineering.   1. Bott, Frank.

QA 76,758, P76 2000
005.1'068'–dc21   00-037780

ISBN 0-7484-0951-3

Contents

Preface

It is widely recognized that a professional engineer needs to be aware of a range of issues much wider than the mere technical knowledge necessary to practice the chosen engineering discipline. The Engineering Council, for example, requires that the formation of a professional engineer should include, amongst other things,

> Technical decision making and its commercial and economic implementation;... knowledge of government legislation affecting work, e.g. safety, health, environmental requirements; an understanding of the principles of management and industrial relations; some knowledge of trade unions and their organization; an understanding of the engineer's responsibility to the profession, to the community and to the environment.[1]

This book addresses topics such as these in the context of software engineering. When the first edition was written, there was little published about them that was aimed at the practising engineer, although, of course, they were all the subject of much specialized writing. Furthermore, it was only in a very few areas, such as data protection, that there was material aimed at the software engineer; such material as was aimed at the practising engineer was typically aimed at the very different fields of production and manufacturing.

Ten years and two editions later, this situation has changed little. Continuing changes, both in information technology and in the regulatory and professional context within which it operates, make a new edition of the book desirable, while the success of the previous editions and the generous reception they received from reviewers make such an effort worthwhile.

The most obvious of the changes that affect the book is the development of the Internet and the World-Wide Web. It is hard to believe that, only five

1. *Standards and routes to registration* (SARTOR), 2nd edn (London: The Engineering Council, 1990).

years ago, the question of covering issues related to the Internet simply did not arise. Intellectual property is the area most obviously affected but its ramifications can be seen in many other areas. Electronic commerce is a closely related area that we would have liked to cover. Unfortunately, the legal situation is so confused at present that any discussion would have been misleading and out of date by the time the book was published.

But the Web has had a second and more subtle effect on the book. The book is based largely on the authors' professional experience and their personal researches. The Web has made our work much easier by making many of the primary sources for the book readily available. We have thus been able to consult a much wider range of primary sources – codes of conduct and statements of policy from a range of professional bodies in several countries, statutes, both of the United Kingdom parliament and various states in the United States of America, international agreements, and so on – than was possible when preparing earlier editions. What is more, we can reasonably refer to these documents, secure in the knowledge that the interested reader can gain access to them without undue difficulty.

The passing of the Data Protection Act 1998, implementing the "Framework" European Directive on data protection (1992) is less momentous than the development of the Internet. Nevertheless, it is a important and substantial change to the law relating to data protection, which will have a significant effect on the practices of many software engineers. It has led to a complete rewriting of Chapter 12.

Chapter 1 has also been very substantially extended. First, the decision, in June 1998, by the Texas Board of Professional Engineers to recognize software engineering as a branch of engineering and to license suitably qualified and experienced practitioners has most important long-term implication for the software engineering profession. It also makes the legal status of the engineering profession in the United States a matter of interest to British software engineers. Accordingly, we have included a fairly lengthy section on this topic. Secondly, a growing concern with ethics in software engineering has led us to include substantial new sections on professional codes of conduct and their interpretations, as well as some more general background material on ethics. In this connection, we are grateful to the British Computer Society for allowing us to include its Code of Conduct as an appendix. There are many differences not only of detail but also of philosophy between the various professional codes of conduct; the BCS Code is, in the view of the authors, one of the best in the engineering field.

It is appropriate to repeat here a word of warning from the preface to the first edition. The purpose of this book is to explain the central principles and issues in the areas covered, not to give a professional knowledge of those areas. Any one topic covered would require several volumes for a comprehensive coverage so that what is said here is, inevitably, introductory and much is omitted. Just as you would not regard a lawyer who had read a book on computing and written a couple of Visual Basic programs as competent to design the software for an air traffic control system, so you must not regard yourself as a competent lawyer, accountant or other professional on the strength of having studied this book.

The book has its origins in a course which has been given for many years to final year honours students in Computing and Software Engineering at the University of Wales, Aberystwyth. We are grateful to our students and colleagues for their comments on parts of the text; the book has benefited greatly from such contributions but any faults that remain are, of course, solely our responsibility.

Frank Bott
Aberystwyth
December 1999

List of cases

Adsett v K. & L. Steelfounders and Engineers Ltd [1953] All ER 97

Associated British Ports v Transport and General Workers Union [1989] IRLR 291, 305

Bevan Investments v Blackhall and Struthers No 2 [1973] 2NZLR 45

Blackpool and Fylde College v National Association of Teachers in Further and Higher Education [1994] IRLR 227

Bollinger v Costa Brava Wine Co. [1980] Ch 262

British Gas Trading Ltd v Data Protection Registrar (1998)

British Leyland v Armstrong [1986] AC 577

Bulmer v Bollinger [1974] FSR 334

Cantor Fitzgerald International v Traidton (UK) Ltd (1999) (unreported)

CCN Systems Ltd and CCN Credit Systems Ltd v Data Protection Registrar (1991)

Coco v Clark [1969] RPC 41

Cole v Trafford [1918] 2KB 523

Computer Associates v Altai 23 USPQ 2d 1241 (1992)

Cox v Riley [1986] 83 Cr. App. R. 54

Cubby Inc. v Compuserve Inc. (776 F Supp 135)

Donoghue v Stevenson [1932] AC562

Edwards v National Coal Board [1949] 1 KB 704

Elton John v Richard James (1985) (unreported)

Erven Warnink v Townend [1979] AC 731

Faccenda Chicken v Fowler [1987] Ch.117

Foreningen of Arbejdsledere I Danmark v Daddy's Dance Hall 324/86, [1998] ECR 739

Gilbert O'Sullivan v Management Agency and Music Ltd [1985] 3 All ER 351

Godfrey v Demon Internet Ltd

Greaves v Deakin [1980] AC 477 at 495

IBCOS Computers Ltd v Barclays Bank Highland Finance Ltd [1994] FSR 275, 289

Innovations (Mail Order) Ltd v Data Protection Registrar (1993)

John Richardson v Flanders [1993] FSR 497

John Walker v Henry Ost [1970] RPC 489

Lee v Nursery Furnishing Ltd [1945] 61 TLR 263

Table of statutes

Arbitration Act 1996
Companies Acts 1948, 1985 & 1989
Companies (Single Person Private Limited Companies) Regulations 1992
Computer Misuse Act 1990
Consumer Protection Act 1987
Control of Substances Hazardous to Health Regulations
Copyright Act 1911
Copyright Act 1956
Copyright and Rights in Databases Regulations 1997
Copyright (Computer Programs) Regulations 1992
Copyright, Patents and Designs Act 1988
Criminal Damage Act 1971
Data Protection Act 1984
Data Protection Act 1998
Defamation Act 1996
Design Right (Semi-Conductor Topographies) Regulations 1989, 1992, 1993
Disability and Discrimination Act 1995
Duration of Copyright and Rights in Performance Regulations 1995
Employment Act 1980
Employment Act 1982
Employment Act 1988
Employment Rights Act 1996
Factories Act 1937 241
Factories Act 1961
Finance (No. 2) Act 1992
Forgery and Counterfeiting Act 1981
Health and Safety at Work etc Act 1974
Human Rights Act 1998
Industrial Relations Act 1971
Insolvency Act 1986
Interception of Communications Act 1985
Official Secrets Act 1989

Chapter 1

The engineering profession

Terms like *profession*, *professional* and *professionalism* carry a whole variety of meanings; in some contexts they are simply descriptive (e.g. a professional writer), in some they are commendatory (a professional piece of work), and in some they are pejorative (a professional foul). Furthermore, there is a subtle difference between the activities included in the term *the professions*, which is[1] usually taken to include a rather limited range of employments in the Church of England, the law, medicine and the armed forces, and the use of the term *profession* in phrases such as "the engineering profession" or "the medical profession". In this chapter we shall try to give a precise meaning to this latter usage, particularly in the context of the engineering profession.

The legal (and social) status of the engineering profession is markedly different in different countries. In particular, the position in the USA is very different from that in the UK and the changes now in progress there will have the effect of integrating software engineering into the legal framework governing the engineering profession as a whole. Accordingly, Section 1.5 is devoted to a description of the situation in the USA.

We shall also discuss the obligations and privileges which membership of a profession carries and the way in which individuals qualify for membership; in particular, we shall consider some of the ethical issues that arise in software engineering and the ways in which these may be addressed.

1.1 What makes a profession?

Chambers 20th Century Dictionary defines profession, in the sense in which we are interested, as:

> . . . an employment not mechanical and requiring some degree of learning; a calling, habitual employment; the collective body of persons engaged in any profession; . . .

---

1. Or was: the term is falling out of favour, probably because the idea is no longer felt to be a useful one.

Parts of this definition are clearly too wide: grave digging may be regarded as an habitual employment for some people but anyone who described it as a profession would be in danger of being suspected of irony.

To come closer to characterizing what is meant by profession in normal usage, we may take the last part of the definition (*the collective body . . .*) and ask what it is that those bodies which are commonly thought of as professional have in common. At least within the UK, three characteristics become apparent:

- the collective body controls entry to the profession;
- the collective body is self governing and self regulatory, in the sense that it establishes and enforces a code of conduct on its members;
- the collective body is established either by a Royal Charter or by statute (Act of Parliament) which defines the extent of its authority and requires it to undertake certain duties and responsibilities.

If we take these characteristics as defining a profession, we see that solicitors, barristers, doctors, dentists, accountants, surveyors, architects, engineers and many others fall within the definition; so too do one or two less obvious groups such as physicists.

An interesting case is that of school teachers. Most school teachers consider their calling a profession but, until very recently, it fell outside the definition given above; entry to school teaching depended on recognition by the Department of Education and Science, a government body, rather than by an independent chartered body and there was no independent body which laid down a code of conduct – this was largely a matter for the teachers' employers. This is about to change. The Teaching and Higher Education Act 1998 provided for the establishment of a General Teaching Council for each of England, Wales, and Northern Ireland. (Such a council has existed in Scotland since 1965.) The councils will be responsible for setting up and maintaining a register of teachers, for promulgating a code of conduct, and for removing from the register teachers who seriously breach the code or who are demonstrably incompetent; the councils will also have a significant influence over the training of teachers. With a few minor exceptions, registration with the appropriate council will be essential for any practising school teacher. The General Teaching Council for England will come into being in September 2000. It will be made up of 25 elected teachers, nine teachers appointed by organizations representing teachers, 16 members appointed by other interested bodies, such as the Commission for Racial Equality and the Confederation of British Industry, and 13 members appointed by the Secretary of State for Education and Employment, two at least of whom must represent parents' interests. This will put teachers in the same position as doctors and dentists, as a profession subject to statutory control, i.e., control laid down by Act of Parliament.

In contrast to the councils governing professions subject to statutory control, a professional body must already be in existence before it can seek recognition through a Royal Charter. The decision to grant a Royal Charter to a professional body is taken primarily on the grounds of the public interest – is it in the public interest that the activities of the group of practitioners which the body represents should be regulated and, if so, is the professional body a fit, proper and appropriate instrument to do this? This raises subsidiary questions about how representative of practitioners in the field the body is, and the extent to which its members can claim to be a coherent group. A Royal Charter is only granted after extensive investigations; although it confers some privileges, it imposes many responsibilities which the body must be willing and able to accept.

There are some important but subtle differences between the professions. It is a criminal offence, for example, to claim to be a medical doctor, a veterinary surgeon, a dentist, an optician, a solicitor, or an insurance broker without being registered with the appropriate statutory body. If anyone is found to be committing this offence, the police will normally take action and the Crown Prosecution Service will prosecute. On the other hand, while you are not, for example, allowed to claim to be a Chartered Engineer or a Member of the British Computer Society unless you are, it is up to the Engineering Council or the BCS, as the case may be, to take action in the courts; they cannot rely on the authorities to take action. (This is a practical difference between a profession established by statute and one established by Royal Charter.) And there is nothing to stop you claiming merely to be an engineer or physicist – even if you have no qualifications whatsoever[2]! In such a case, you might commit an offence by claiming to be an engineer in order to commit a fraud but not by claiming to be an engineer merely to enhance your standing with your neighbours.

The previous paragraph concerns the protection of professional *titles*; this is quite separate from the question of *licence to practise*. Some, but not all, of the activities of some of the professions mentioned above can only be carried out by registered members of the profession. Thus no person may practise dentistry unless registered with the General Dental Council and no unqualified person may act as a solicitor or prepare certain specified documents. Perhaps surprisingly, however, unqualified persons are not debarred from practising medicine as such, although there are a number of activities, such as supplying prescription-only drugs, that they are not allowed to carry out and certain appointments, in particular in the National Health Service, that they cannot hold. There is no statutory control of the right to practise as an engineer in Britain.

---

2. This is the position in the UK. In the USA and some European countries, it is a criminal offence to call oneself an engineer without possession of the appropriate qualifications. See Section 1.5.

1.2 Structure of the engineering profession

The engineering profession has a two-tier structure. At the first level, there are the engineering institutions, that is, the chartered professional bodies, each of which covers a single or several closely related engineering disciplines. Examples are the Institution of Electrical Engineers, the Institution of Mechanical Engineers and the British Computer Society. Each institution has its own rules regarding membership and its own codes of practice and conduct.

The British Computer Society (BCS) is the engineering institution which is the most natural one for software engineers to join. However, the Institution of Electrical Engineers (IEE) also welcomes software engineers, particularly those whose interests incline towards safety critical systems or control systems, and offers an extensive programme of relevant professional activities. The BCS and the IEE collaborate in many areas, for example the publication of the *IEE Proceedings–Software*, the leading European journal in the field of software engineering.

Individual institutions represent the interests of engineers practising in their field and are frequently consulted by Government as a source of expert and impartial advice. The BCS, for example, is consulted on such issues as safety critical systems, the legal protection of software, data protection, and the law relating to misuse of computers. Institutions' public activities are not, of course, limited to responding to requests for advice. Their charters impose a variety of duties on them, including the advancement of knowledge in their field, the maintenance and improvement of standards of practice, and the advancement of education.

The second-level body in engineering is the Engineering Council, a chartered body which recognizes certain engineering institutions as its "Nominated Bodies". This means that the Engineering Council is satisfied that their standards of membership meet its requirements. In this way, the Engineering Council acts as an "umbrella" body and represents the interests of the engineering profession as a whole. It is consulted on matters which affect the entire profession, such as the organization of engineering education.

An important function of the Engineering Council is to maintain, through the Board for Engineers' Registration, the national register of qualified engineers and technicians[3], which currently contains some 290,000 names. The register is divided into three sections: Chartered Engineers, Incorporated Engineers, and Engineering Technicians. Chartered Engineers are considered

---

3. The Engineering Council and many of the professional engineering institutions feel that the use of the term *engineer* instead of *technician* (as in "we're waiting for an engineer to mend the washing machine") has much to do with the low status that engineers enjoy in the UK. It is ironic, therefore, that the Board of Engineers' Registration should be responsible for the registration of technicians.

to be qualified to develop new technology, to apply existing technology in novel ways and to take responsibility for large, high-risk projects. They are currently expected to be educated to honours degree level, as well as having appropriate professional experience. With a few exceptions, any full or "corporate" member of an engineering institution is entitled to be registered as a Chartered Engineer and thus to use the designatory letters CEng. There are two other registers, one for Incorporated Engineers and one for Engineering Technicians, entitled to use the letters IEng or Eng Tech, as appropriate. The minimum educational qualification required for IEng is that of a BTEC Higher National Certificate and for Eng Tech a BTEC National Certificate. For those entering higher education in 1999 or later, these requirements have been strengthened; see Section 1.4.1 below.

Registration as a Chartered Engineer is the ultimate recognition of professional engineering status; in particular, it generally allows the engineer to be recognized as qualified to practise elsewhere in Europe. This done through FEANI (*Fédération Européene d'Associations Nationales d'Ingénieurs*, European Federation of National Engineering Associations), an umbrella organization which, amongst other activities, maintains a register of European Engineers, who are entitled to use the title Eur Ing (as a prefix, in continental style, rather than as a suffix as would be normal in Britain). Chartered Engineers are normally entitled to register as European Engineers with FEANI.

The European Directive 89/48/EEC regulates the mutual recognition of professional qualifications within the European Union; it came into force in 1991. It provides, in general, that engineers (and other professionals) who wish to have their qualifications recognized by a member state other than that in which they obtained the qualifications may be required either to serve a period of adaptation or to sit an examination (called an aptitude test). However, in answer to a question asked by a Member of the European Parliament to the European Commission, it has been formally stated that the Commission considers that "an engineer who has obtained the title of Eur Ing should not normally be required to undertake an adaptation period or sit an aptitude test". This means effectively that, subject to registration with FEANI, possession of Chartered Engineer status guarantees recognition elsewhere within the European Union. Twenty countries belong to FEANI and the Eur Ing title indicates recognition of professional status by the professional bodies in all of them; legal recognition, however, applies only in the countries of the European Union. In many of these countries, there is statutory protection of the title of engineer and in some it confers a licence to practise.

1.3 Development of the engineering profession

The term "engineer" was first used in the sense of a military engineer, concerned with the building of engines of war and other military construction. It was in the eighteenth century that the term "civil engineer" began to be used to distinguish engineers who were concerned with civil rather than military construction. It was also in the eighteenth century that the first formal groupings of engineers began to appear. The first was the French *Corps des Ponts et Chaussées* (Group for Bridges and Roads), founded in Paris in 1716; a society of civil engineers was formed in England later in the century. It was also in Britain that the first engineering grouping that aimed to represent the profession, and thus to be a professional body in the modern sense, was formed. The Institution of Civil Engineers was founded in 1818; it was fortunate in persuading the doyen of British civil engineers, Thomas Telford, to become its first president and it was as a result of his efforts that the institution received its royal charter in 1828. The Institution of Mechanical Engineers was founded in 1847, the Royal Institution of Naval Architects in 1860, the Institution of Gas Engineers in 1863, and the Institution of Electrical Engineers in 1871. Many others followed – there are now 42 chartered engineering institutions. The British Computer Society was founded in 1957 and received its Royal Charter in 1984. Like most of the institutions, it started life as a learned society, seeing itself primarily as a vehicle for the exchange of views and the dissemination of knowledge among people with a shared interest in computing; it subsequently developed the concern for education and the promulgation of good practice which characterizes a professional institution.

The large number of engineering institutions did not make it easy for the engineering profession to formulate and promulgate views on matters affecting the profession as a whole. There was no uniformity in the requirements for membership of the different institutions, and employers, to whom the issue of qualifications might be expected to be important, had no say in institutional qualification procedures, except through any personal membership of an institution that they might have. It was to address these problems that 13 of the largest chartered institutions began a long process of negotiation which led, in 1962, to the formation of the Engineering Institutions Joint Council. This body itself gained a Royal Charter in 1965 and changed its name to the Council of Engineering Institutions (CEI).

The CEI achieved much. In particular, it established the three tiers of engineering qualifications and the registration mechanisms for them and gained acceptance of these from all the institutions. However, it failed to make the qualifications respected by the general public or by employers, and it failed to get itself recognized as the voice of the engineering profession. In 1977, the then Labour government announced the setting up of a committee of enquiry into the engineering profession, chaired by Sir Monty Finniston, a distinguished engineer and industrialist. Its terms of reference were wide and it was asked to review and make recommendations about the requirement for engineers in industry, the role of the engineering institutions, and the advantages and disadvantages of statutory registration and licensing of engineers; it was specifically asked to review the arrangements in other major industrial countries. The committee reported in 1979, by which time a Conservative government was in power. The report of the committee is universally known as the Finniston Report[4].

The Finniston Committee visited Canada, the United States, Japan, France, West Germany (as it then was), Denmark, Sweden and the Netherlands; its report contains the statement:

> In every overseas country at which we looked the status of engineers and engineering was high; it attracted high quality entrants and was accorded a priority in social and industrial affairs that is generally lacking in the UK.

The position has not changed substantially in the 20 years since the committee reported and similar comments continue to be made.

Finniston found that, in all the countries visited, the mechanism for registering engineers involved the state and, in most cases, there was provision for organized input from employers. It was only in the UK that this process was left entirely to the profession. However, the committee concluded:

> On balance we take the view that the priority and status given to engineering in other countries depends largely on deep-seated cultural factors. Registration may serve to institutionalize and confirm these factors but it cannot of itself fundamentally alter them.

In other words, whatever changes may be made to the registration procedures, much more is needed if engineers and engineering are to achieve in the UK the status and prestige that they enjoy elsewhere.

The Finniston Report came out in favour of statutory registration of engineers through the establishment of a *statutory* Engineering Authority (i.e. a body established by Act of Parliament); the authority would have had powers which included maintenance of the registers of qualified engineers, membership of which would be open to everyone who satisfied its requirements, without any requirement for membership of one of the professional institutions. It did not recommend statutory licensing of engineers, except in areas where safety was involved. It recommended the introduction of the BEng and MEng degrees, although under significantly different conditions to those under which they were finally introduced.

Although the Finniston Report was accepted by the government, many of its 80 recommendations were ignored and others were adopted only in a modified form. (Many of them were in the form of general exhortations to

---

4. *Engineering our future*, Report of the Committee of Inquiry into the Engineering Profession, Cmnd 7794 (HMSO, January 1980).

employers and to schools and were, in fact, incapable of being given real government backing.) The government was not disposed to introduce legislation to establish a statutory authority and the individual institutions, for obvious reasons, strongly opposed the proposal that institutional membership should not be necessary for registration. The result was the Engineering Council, established by Royal Charter, not by Act of Parliament, and with a continuing requirement for membership of a professional engineering institution in order to be registered.

The Engineering Council has proved a more effective body than the CEI. In collaboration with the institutions, it has developed initiatives to promote the profession among young people; it has contributed to the development of the teaching of technology in schools; it has launched its own code of conduct and a codes of professional practice on risk and on engineers and the environment; it has established a much more uniform standard of professional competence for engineers throughout the profession; and it has contributed in a wide variety of ways to engineering education. Not surprisingly, however, given the weakness that was built into it from the start, it has not succeeded in overcoming the fragmentation of the profession. There are still 42 engineering institutions recognized by the Council; there is a lot of waste and duplication; and there is still much mutual distrust among the individual institutions.

Recognizing these problems, the Council of Presidents of all the institutions set up, in January 1992, a steering group under the chairmanship of Sir John Fairclough, Chairman of the Engineering Council, on the unification of the engineering profession. The steering group produced its first report[5] in April 1993. The report foresaw the eventual merging of the institutions into a single body but, in the short to medium term, envisaged a new relationship between the Engineering Council and the institutions. This new relationship would involve grouping the institutions into a small number of "colleges" and more democratic elections to the governing body of the Engineering Council. These proposals have now been adopted but we are still a long way from having a single institution.

Brief mention should be made of the Royal Academy of Engineering. This is an élite body, made up of distinguished engineers, who are entitled to use the designatory letters FEng. It is intended to be comparable with the Royal Society and the British Academy. Like them, it receives some government funding to encourage high-quality research in engineering and to support certain other initiatives. By its very nature, however, it has little impact on the practising engineer. Its establishment is, however, one more

---

5. *Engineering into the millennium* (The Engineering Council, 10 Maltravers Street, London WC2R 3ER, 1993).

element in the struggle to enhance the prestige of engineering in the United Kingdom.

1.4 Professional qualifications

Entry to almost all professions requires an appropriate educational qualification followed by appropriate professional experience. Within this basic pattern there is a great deal of diversity. In some cases, the educational qualification must be gained from an accredited academic course (see below); in some cases, it can be gained wholly from such a course or partly from such a course and partly from examinations run by the professional body; and in some cases the final qualification must come from the examinations run by the professional body.

Most candidates for membership of the engineering institutions have graduated from accredited courses and the qualification resulting from successful completion of the course fulfils the educational requirement for membership; accredited courses must be of honours degree standard (but see Section 1.4.1 below). However, for candidates who have not been able to qualify by this route, the Engineering Council itself runs examinations covering a very wide range of engineering topics; it is then open to the individual institutions to state their requirements for membership in terms of papers to be taken and grades to be attained.

At this point, it is as well to clarify what is meant by membership of a professional body. There are usually several grades of member but these can be divided into two categories, professional and non-professional grades. The professional or corporate grades (typically Member and Fellow) are occupied solely by members who have met the body's educational requirements and have satisfied its requirement for professional experience; to a very large extent the members in these grades run the institution and its constitution requires that all positions of authority are occupied by such members. The non-corporate grades (Associate, Licentiate, Affiliate, Student, etc.) may be occupied by people from a variety of categories, such as:

- students on accredited courses;
- graduates who are in the course of completing their period of qualifying experience;
- professionals from other disciplines whose work is related to that of the institution;
- persons with approved qualifications and experience at a lower level than is required for professional membership.

The last of the above categories is particularly important in some branches of engineering where many technicians are highly qualified although not at graduate level. As already mentioned, the Engineering Council recognizes this by the two levels of registration below CEng. It should be remarked that not all corporate members of, for example, the British Computer Society necessarily qualify as Chartered Engineers; they must also satisfy the Engineering Council's definition of what constitutes an engineer.

1.4.1 Course accreditation

The normal procedure by which an engineering institution accredits a degree course starts with a written submission from the department offering the course to the Institution. Among other things, this submission describes the objectives of the course, the syllabus, the entry requirements, the methods of assessment, the facilities available and the qualifications of the staff teaching the course.

If the written submission is *prima facie* acceptable, then arrangements are made for a party, consisting of academics and industrialists who are professional members of the Institution, to visit the department to discuss the course with both staff and students and to inspect the facilities and student project work. Following this visit, the Accreditation Committee of the Institution receives a report from the visiting party and, on this basis, decides whether accreditation should be granted. The maximum period for which accreditation can be granted is five years but a lesser period may be granted if the course is not felt to be wholly satisfactory; in some cases accreditation may only be granted on condition that certain changes are made, or it may be refused completely.

Although the preparation of the written submission requires a lot of work and the visit is always looked forward to with some trepidation, most departments find that the accreditation process is very valuable. First, the need to review objectives, syllabuses and other aspects of the course at least every five years is a valuable discipline. Secondly, exposing even the best of courses to assessment by group of external experts will always produce valuable comments and suggestions. (Universities are nowadays required to have their own internal course review procedures but these procedures do not necessarily have substantial input from external experts and, as a result, may be concerned more with regulations than with content.)

It was stated earlier that the appropriate educational base for a Chartered Engineer was an accredited honours degree. For students entering higher education at the start of the 1999/2000 academic year or later, the position is different. With the substantial expansion of the numbers entering higher education in the United Kingdom during the 1980s and 1990s, the Engineering Council became concerned about the standards achieved by students awarded honours degrees. A particular concern was that, on entry to such courses, many students had a very limited knowledge of mathematics and physics; the result was that much of the first year was devoted to remedial teaching of such topics and, as a consequence, the level of engineering knowledge attained at the end of a three year honours degree course was much less than it had been when the accreditation system had been set up. There was also concern about the general intellectual level of many of the students on the new courses and about the danger of UK engineering qualifications not being recognized internationally. These concerns led the Engineering Council to revise substantially its criteria for accreditation. There are two major changes, which are being phased in over a number of years.

First, only four-year degrees (usually MEng degrees) will normally be accredited as fulfilling the educational requirements for registration as a Chartered Engineer. Three-year degrees may be awarded partial CEng accreditation or may be accredited for Incorporated Engineer status. A person holding such a degree may fulfil the educational requirements for CEng by completing "a matching section". Precisely what constitutes a matching section is not altogether clear but an appropriate Master's degree or appropriate training as part of an employer's scheme would both seem acceptable.

The second change is that, in order for a course to be accredited, the entrants to the course must meet certain standards. Put simply, for full CEng accreditation, 80 per cent of the entrants to the course must have an A-level points score[6] of at least 24; for partial accreditation, 80 per cent must have an A-level score of at least 18 points.

Other changes include strengthening and formalizing the requirements for initial experience and for the professional review that evaluates this.

These changes to the educational requirements for CEng are matched by corresponding changes to the requirements for IEng. An accredited three-year degree is now required as the basic requirement for registration as an incorporated engineer; an alternative is an HNC or HND with a suitable "matching section".

1.4.2 The engineering applications requirements

The Finniston Report recommended that the education and professional training of a Chartered Engineer should include four essential elements known as Engineering Applications, EA1 to EA4. These are:

---

6. A-level is the United Kingdom School Leaving Examination. Like the Abitur in Germany and the Baccalauréat in France, it is a public examination, centrally administered; there is no comparable system in the United States, although a few individual states do have something similar. It is usually taken in three subjects and the passing grades are A, B, C, D, and E. The points score is computed on the basis of 10 points for an A, 8 for a B, 6 for a C, 4 for a D, and 2 for an E, although these weights are expected to change in the near future. The Engineering Council's concern is more readily appreciated when it is realized that the average points score for many accredited engineering degree programmes during the 1990s has been as low as 4 or 5.

EA1 an introduction to the properties, fabrication and use of materials;

EA2 application of engineering principles to the solution of practical problems based upon engineering systems and processes;

EA3 a structured introduction to industry under supervision and involving a range of practical assignments;

EA4 specific preparation for a first responsible post and a period carrying responsibility in that post with decreasingly close supervision.

This recommendation was adopted by the Engineering Council; EA1 and EA2 are required to be covered by any accredited course, while EA3 and EA4 must be satisfied during the qualifying period of professional experience.

The EA requirements, particularly EA1, are, inevitably, couched in very general terms and individual engineering institutions must interpret them in a way appropriate to their own speciality. The BCS suggests the following interpretation of EA1, for example,

> An introduction to good engineering practice and to the representation, meaning, modelling and processing of data by means of programs and the machines which execute them.

Provided that it is undertaken in a suitable engineering context, the major individual project which normally forms part of the final year of an honours degree course in engineering is usually seen as being the major element in meeting the EA2 requirement.

1.4.3 The BCS Professional Development Scheme

The assessment of professional experience is much more difficult than the assessment of educational qualifications since the nature of the experience can vary so widely from one individual to another, depending on the environment in which the experience is gained. In the late 1980s, in an effort to provide a framework within which the experience can be recorded and classified, the BCS introduced its Professional Development Scheme (PDS).

Participants in the PDS are issued with a log book when they enter the scheme. This log book is used to record their work experience and training. They are regularly interviewed by a senior colleague who must normally be an MBCS; he or she will sign the log book to confirm the accuracy of the entries made since the last interview and make recommendations for future training and experience designed to develop the participant's career.

An essential part of the PDS is the *industry structure model*. This imposes a matrix structure on employment within the industry. The columns of the matrix represent different *streams* of experience; thus one column represents application programming, another represents telecommunications, and so on. The rows of the matrix represent different levels of work, from trainee upwards. Each entry in the matrix is known as a *cell*. For each cell, there is a description of the experience and training that a person should have had before entering the cell, a description of the work that a person in the cell is expected to carry out and recommendations for training to be received while working in the cell. In principle, and very largely in practice, any job in the industry can be assigned to a cell.

While it would be undesirable to lay down mechanistic criteria (so many months at such and such a level, so many at the next level, etc.) for assessing whether an applicant's professional experience is sufficient to meet the requirements for professional membership, the combination of the log book and the industry structure model provide a useful framework within which an applicant's experience can be assessed. Many large employers have adopted the scheme as a basis for their own career development programmes.

1.4.4 International recognition

We have already mentioned the possibility of registration as a European Engineer and the recognition that this brings in the countries whose national engineering associations are part of FEANI. Following a very substantial exchange of information and detailed examination of procedures and regulations, an important step towards wider international recognition was taken in the late 1980s, when the national engineering associations of Australia, Canada, Ireland, New Zealand, and the United States signed what is known as the Washington Accord.

The signatories to the Accord recognized that the academic requirements for qualifying as a professional engineer are substantially equivalent in all six countries and that their accreditation procedures are comparable. Each signatory therefore agreed to "make every reasonable effort to ensure that the bodies responsible for registering or licensing professional engineers in its country or territory accept the substantial equivalence of engineering academic programs accredited by the signatories to the agreement." It was not possible for the national engineering associations to guarantee this acceptance because, in some countries, as we shall see below, this acceptance depends on statutory licensing boards.

It is important to realize that the Washington Accord applies only to the *academic* requirements for qualifying as a professional engineer. Thus an accredited degree from Britain should be sufficient to exempt you from the educational requirements in the other countries but this does not mean that the possession of CEng will exempt you from the other requirements, of professional experience or public examinations, for example, that may be necessary to become a fully qualified professional engineer there. Efforts are proceeding to try to extend the Washington Accord to cover mutual recognition of professional registration and to widen the group of signatories. (Hong

Kong has recently been added to the original group of six countries.) This is likely to be a long process.

1.5 The engineering profession in the United States

The engineering profession is much more highly regarded in the USA than in the United Kingdom and is subject to strict statutory legislation, going further than what the Finniston Report recommended. The title of engineer is protected and the practice of engineering is restricted. Very similar legislation exists in Canada.

1.5.1 Licensing of engineers

In the first quarter of the 20th century almost all states of the Union enacted legislation to restrict the practice of engineering and the use of the title "engineer" to persons who were licensed by a state engineering licensing board. These boards were set up with a statutory duty to regulate admission to the engineering profession by licensing professional engineers who meet specific criteria. The declared aim was to safeguard life, health and property and to promote the public welfare. The details differ from state to state but are substantially similar; the same statutes usually cover land surveyors and often architects.

Typically, a state's statutes define what is meant by practising as a professional engineer in very broad terms, so as to include both the use of the term engineer, either alone or qualified by terms such as "professional" or "consulting", and carrying out or offering to carry out engineering activities. The flavour of these definitions is shown by the following extract from the statutes of the State of Missouri:

Statute 327.181 Practice as professional engineer defined

Any person practices [*sic*] in Missouri as a professional engineer who renders or offers to render or holds himself out as willing or able to render any service or creative work, the adequate performance of which requires engineering education, training and experience in the application of special knowledge of the mathematical, physical, and engineering sciences to such services or creative work as consultation, investigation, evaluation, planning and design of engineering works and systems, engineering teaching of advanced engineering subjects or courses related thereto, engineering surveys, and the inspection of construction for the purpose of assuring compliance with drawings and specifications, any of which embraces such service or work either public or private, in connection with any utilities, structures, buildings, machines, equipment, processes, work systems, or projects and including such architectural work as is incidental to the practice of engineering; or who uses the title "professional engineer" or "consulting engineer" or the word "engineer" alone or preceded by any word indicating or implying that such person is or holds himself out to be a professional engineer, or who shall use any word or words, letters, figures, degrees, or titles or other description indicating or implying that such a person is a professional engineer or is willing or able to practice engineering.

As is often the case, the desire to avoid loopholes and ambiguity has led to such complexity that it is very difficult to tease out the meaning of this excessively long sentence. Furthermore, there is an element of circularity in it (an engineer is someone who practises engineering). Nevertheless, it is clear that those who drafted the statute were trying to cast their net as wide as possible – it clearly implies, for example, that those teaching engineering in higher education are regarded as practising engineering. The last part of the sentence makes it clear that that those who choose to call themselves software engineers will be regarded as practising engineering. What is less clear is whether the same applies to those who call themselves programmers or, say, system designers and who are doing precisely the same sort of jobs as those who call themselves software engineers. In other words, the *title* of software engineer is reserved but it is not clear whether the *function* is reserved.

Following a definition of engineering, the statutes typically provide that no one may practise as a professional engineer unless they are registered and that a company offering engineering services to the public must do so through the medium of a registered professional engineer. Further, no company may use the word engineer or engineering in its name unless it employs at least one registered professional engineer. Anyone breaking these provisions is guilty of a criminal offence.

The statutes then lay down the criteria for registration. These normally include successful completion of an accredited degree course of at least four years duration, passing eight-hour examinations (fortunately split into two four-hour sessions!) in the fundamentals of engineering and in the principles and practice of engineering, and four years of approved experience. The examination in the fundamentals of engineering is normally taken at around the same time as the degree is completed and that in the principles and practice of engineering at the end of the period of professional experience. The syllabuses and examination procedures are co-ordinated by the National Council of Examiners for Engineering and Surveying, so that uniform standards and quality are maintained across the whole of the USA. (Canadian licences are not accepted in the USA precisely because registration in Canada does not involve passing the examination in the principles and practices of engineering.)

The engineering licensing boards are statutory bodies with strictly limited functions and are thus very different from the professional engineering institutions in the UK.

1.5.2 The position of software engineering

The definitions of engineering enshrined in the statutes of the various states cannot be taken to include software engineering unless they are stretched well beyond what is reasonable. The examination in the principles and practices of engineering can be taken in 36 different branches of engineering but software engineering is not one of these. On the other hand, the restrictions on the use of the words "engineer" and "engineering" are quite clear. The resulting position is absurd: the only people who are formally allowed to describe themselves as software engineers are those who are licensed in some other branch of the discipline and a company can only describe itself as a software engineering company if it employs at least one professional engineer licensed in another branch.

The use of the term "software engineering" had become widespread by the mid-1990s; the situation was further complicated by the fact that suppliers such as Sun Microsystems and Microsoft were awarding qualifications with titles like "certified systems engineer" or "network engineer" to those who could demonstrate suitable skills and knowledge in the use of their equipment. Initially, the licensing boards attempted seriously to oppose the use of the term software engineering. According to Capers Jones[7], Tennessee actively prohibits the use of the term in business literature and advertising, while Texas forced universities to stop offering degrees in software engineering. In such circumstances, however, the licensing boards cannot resist the tide of usage. It was therefore inevitable that, rather than try to prevent the use of the term "software engineering", the licensing boards should seek to regulate it.

The Texas Board of Professional Engineers was the first licensing board to approve the registration of software engineers, in June 1998. At that point there were no appropriate examinations in fundamentals of engineering and principles and practices of engineering available for them to take. Because Texas, uniquely amongst the states of the Union, allows the examination requirements to be waived in the case of practitioners of sufficient experience, it has been possible for some software engineers to be registered more or less immediately. The National Council of Examiners for Engineering and Surveying is planning to offer licensing examinations. It can be expected that, as soon as the exams are available, most other states will follow Texas in approving the registration of software engineers.

---

7. Capers Jones, "Legal status of software engineering", *IEEE Computer*, May, 98–99, 1995.

The Texas decision was not an isolated event. Rather, it was the natural consequence of several years of discussion and activity within and among the relevant professional bodies.

1.5.3 Professional bodies and accreditation in the USA

The United States possesses a range of professional engineering societies comparable to that in the UK. In particular, there are two organizations that carry out many of the functions performed by the IEE and the BCS in the UK. The Association for Computing Machinery (ACM) may be thought of as comparable to the BCS, while the Institution of Electrical and Electronic Engineers (IEEE) compares loosely with the IEE, its Computer Society corresponding to the IEE's Informatics Division. Both the IEEE and the ACM publish a range of journals covering theory and practice in all aspects of IT; they are the most prestigious and the most widely read of academic and professional publications in the field. The IEEE Computer Society and the ACM collaborate extensively on matters connected with the software engineering profession, through joint committees and task forces, such as the one that produced the Software Engineering Code of Ethics that will be discussed later. The IEEE–ACM Joint Steering Committee for the Establishment of Software Engineering as a Profession, meeting from 1993 to 1998, was the primary force that led to the Texas board's decision to register software engineers.

Accreditation of engineering courses in the United States is only indirectly a matter for professional bodies. Instead, it is undertaken by a body called the Accreditation Board for Engineering and Technology (ABET). ABET is a federation of 28 professional engineering and technical societies. So long as software engineering was not regarded as an engineering discipline from the point of view of registration, it was not considered to fall within ABET's remit. Instead, courses in computer science and software engineering were considered by the Computer Sciences Accreditation Board (CSAB); this is a body set up jointly by the ACM and the IEEE Computer Society. In 1998, an agreement was reached between ABET and CSAB, leading to the ACM and the IEEE Computer Society becoming part of the ABET federation and to the CSAB becoming a constituent part of ABET.

American licensing and accreditation practice in engineering requires the definition of a "body of knowledge" that registered practitioners must possess. The IEEE-CS and the ACM are also working together to produce a definition of this[8].

---

8. A preliminary version can be found at the web site http://www.lrgl.uqam.ca.

1.5.4 Certification of engineering artefacts

One of the duties that is reserved for registered engineers is the certification of engineering products. Wherever an engineering project could potentially affect public safety, it must be certified at various stages by a registered engineer. Thus, for example, a dam would need to be certified at the end of the design stage to ensure that all proper issues have been addressed in producing the design and that the design is safe; on completion, a registered engineer would need to certify that it had been constructed correctly in accordance with the design; and a registered engineer would need to inspect it at regular intervals during its life and certify that it is still safe.

The licensing of software engineers means that this same requirement for certification can now be imposed on the software element of safety critical systems. The issue of what it means to certify software is a matter of increasingly active debate. The topic is discussed further in Chapter 10.

1.6 Ethics and software engineering

Ethics is the study of right and wrong in relation to human actions. It includes *meta-ethics*, that is, study of the general principles from which ethical systems can be built; *moral theory*, that is, the ethical systems themselves, consisting of the criteria and procedures that can be applied to decide whether individual actions are right or wrong; and *practical ethics* or *applied ethics*, that is, the application of ethical systems to the analysis of particular situations, including such specialized areas as business ethics and medical ethics.

There are few, if any, ethical issues that are peculiar to software engineering. Nevertheless, the availability of technology and its speed and effectiveness mean that many ethical questions present themselves in a particularly acute form. The obligation to keep an individual's medical records confidential has long been recognized and accepted; we would criticize the management of a hospital that allowed the key to the room containing all the manual records to hang on a convenient hook outside the door when no staff were on duty. When a bank president who serves on a medical commission uses technology to identify all sufferers from cancer who hold loans from his bank and then forecloses on those loans, he is clearly in breach of the obligation of confidentiality[9]. However, it is information technology that has made the offence possible. What concerns us, then, is not the issue of confidentiality

---

9. "RMs need to safeguard patient records to protect hospitals", *Hospital Risk Management*, September, 129–140, 1993. Cited by Ross Anderson in his report "Security in clinical information systems", published by the British Medical Association in January 1996. The whole of this report is worth reading as it shows well the subtle interplay of ethical and technical issues. It is available on the World-Wide Web at http://www.cl.cam.uk/users/rja14/#med.

of medical records but the moral responsibility of the system developers who have left the metaphorical key hanging outside the door, that is, who developed a medical records system that did not contain access controls to make such an action impossible.

There is an important difference between morality and law. Not everything that is wrong needs to be made illegal, nor is everything that is illegal necessarily immoral. Not infrequently, it happens that some real or imaginary problem associated with IT (the London Ambulance System[10], pornography on the Internet, software theft, hacking, etc.) gets taken up by the media and generates a sort of crisis. It is important that IT professionals should be capable of thinking clearly about such situations, since they are the people who understand them and know what is and is not possible. There is often pressure for legislation that is hard to resist even though it may be unnecessary or ill-advised.

1.7 Strands in ethical thinking

Ethics has been studied for many thousands of years and there are written records of what people have thought and argued about for much of this period. This material does not become obsolete. What was written in Greece 2,500 years ago or in China 5,000 years ago can be just as relevant to our ethical dilemmas as what was written last year. This means that an ethical debate about issues that seem essentially modern often turns out to depend on fundamental attitudes that have been the subject of discussion since the start of recorded history. In this section, we shall, very briefly and simplistically, review some of the important ideas of meta-ethics that seem particularly relevant to the ethical problems facing the software engineer.

1.7.1 Rules and consequences

One view of morality that has been popular at many times in the past, although it is somewhat out of favour at present, is that bad actions can be avoided and good actions ensured simply by following a set of rules. The most widely known such set of rules is probably the Ten Commandments, found in the Old Testament, which form part of the common heritage of Christianity, Judaism and Islam.

---

10. This was a *cause célèbre* in the early 1990s. In commissioning its command and control system, the London Ambulance Service ignored more or less every canon of good management and good procurement practice. The prime contractor was ignorant of the difficulties of systems of this type. The system failed catastrophically within three days of being brought into service, with the result that the ambulance service was very badly disrupted. The disaster is discussed further in Section 10.4.

If we leave aside the Commandments that are specifically religious, we see that the rest constitute a set of rules that are not a bad basis for behaviour in a fairly simple society. However, it is difficult to see what they contribute to the debate about employers reading employees' e-mail or, indeed, to debate about many other contemporary issues. Through two millennia Christian theologians have tried to build ethical systems based on Christian teaching that are appropriate to the needs of the society they live in. As society evolves, each generation has to reconsider its moral teaching. This leads inevitably to tension and conflict between progressives and conservatives and is as evident in Judaism and Islam as it is in Christianity.

Naïve popular moralists and preachers often try to reduce morality to a single simple rule such as *Do as you would be done by is the surest method that I know of pleasing*[11]. In more modern language we might express this as: *Treat others in the way you would like to be treated*. While superficially attractive, it fails even on the level of interpersonal relationships. *Love thy neighbour as thyself* is a more sophisticated expression of this idea and has much to commend it on the level of interpersonal relationships but it is still manifestly incapable, by itself, of resolving ethical problems at the level of society as a whole.

The problem with rule-based morality is that, in an ethically difficult situation, there are usually several different possible actions that might be taken and each of them breaks one or more rules or is otherwise undesirable.

An alternative to a rule-based morality is *consequentialism*. Consequentialists believe that general rules are not specific enough to guide actions and that the primary factor in judging an action must be its consequences. This means, of course, that we must have some mechanism for deciding whether the consequences are good or bad. Such a mechanism is often provided by *utilitarianism*. This doctrine was first enunciated by Francis Hutcheson (1694–1746) in the form: *That action is best, which procures the greatest happiness for the greatest numbers*[12]. In this form, it falls down, if in no other way, on the unavoidable mathematical fact that you cannot, in general, maximize two functions at the same time. (Politics provides many good topical examples.) A more defensible statement was given by John Stuart Mill (1806–1873) in the form: *Actions are right in proportion as they tend to promote pleasure or happiness*[13].

If the doctrine of consequentialism is to be useful, we must not try to see too far ahead. Essentially, we should only concern ourselves with consequences that are reasonably foreseeable. Otherwise, the network of cause and effect becomes so complex that everyone is responsible for everything and the notion of moral responsibility becomes so diluted as to be meaningless.

---

11. Usually attributed to the Earl of Chesterfield (1694–1773).
12. More usually cited in the words of Jeremy Bentham (1748–1832) who wrote "The greatest happiness of the greatest number is the foundation of morals and legislation".
13. J. S. Mill, *Utilitarianism*, 1863.

(For rather similar reasons, it is customary to rule out or, at least, limit the amount of consequential damages payable if one party to a contract fails to fulfil its duties under the contract. If a new payroll system is three months late, it is reasonable to expect the supplier to pay the additional costs associated with having to retain the old system. It is not reasonable to expect him to pay the damages awarded to the employee who was injured when the old line printer fell on her, even though this would not have happened if the new system had been delivered on time.)

Consequentialism and rule-based morality can be regarded as in some ways complementary. It is quite possible to accept that the foreseeable consequences of an action are often an important element in judging it, without accepting that they must always be the primary factor. And one can accept rules on the grounds that complying with them is the best way of achieving good consequences. Thus it is perfectly possible for a consequentialist to accept that rules regarding human rights should always be obeyed, because the consequences of universal obedience to them will be good, even though the rules themselves are not intrinsically "right". Equally, it is possible to accept a set of rules governing behaviour but to judge on the basis of their foreseeable consequences those actions that are not covered by the rules.

In practice, most of us accept this latter position, that is, there are some rules we are not prepared to break but, within those constraints, we consider the potential consequences of our actions before deciding what to do.

To the extent that our behaviour is governed by rules, these rules may have several origins. They may come from our own moral convictions, which may derive from the culture in which we have been raised, or they may derive from the rules promulgated by a religious organization to which we belong; such rules are likely to be the ones that we regard as most important and are the ones we are least likely to break. They will apply to the whole of our lives, not just to our professional activities.

Secondly, there are rules that relate to our professional lives; these may be rules laid down and enforced by our employers or they may be contained in a code of conduct established by a professional body of which we are a member. Our attitude to these will depend partly on how far they correspond to our own moral convictions, partly on how widely respected and observed they are by our peers, and partly on the consequences of breaking them.

Thirdly, there are rules that we accept, more or less willingly, because they make social or professional life easier or because the consequences of breaking them might be unfortunate. "Drive on the left" is an excellent example of such a rule. It is one that we obey, not from any moral conviction or authoritative teaching, but because the consequences of breaking it would be unfortunate. Furthermore, it is clearly relative in that it varies from country to country (and even sometimes from time to time in the same country). While the nature of such rules is not a matter for ethical debate, our attitude to them is; if we ignore them, we may prejudice the well-being of other people and that is an ethical matter.

1.7.2 Sources of moral authority

Some people believe that moral authority lies with the individual, who by reflection and self-analysis develops a set of rules. Others believe that moral authority must be located in larger units – the organization or society, the body politic *or the profession*. If authority lies with a larger unit, it may be collective, in the sense that it reflects a consensus among the members of that unit, or it may be authoritarian, that is, it may lie with a leader or a small group of leaders. All three possibilities have weaknesses. If moral authority lies with the individual's conscience, then what moral basis can the law have. If it is collective, there is a risk that it will never progress; in the absence of strong leadership, democratic bodies are notoriously conservative and the impetus for reform – whether it is the abolition of the slave trade or the legalization of homosexuality – has come more often from the promptings of individual consciences than from the actions of established moral collectives. An authoritarian approach is too dependent on the individual exercising the authority.

The authoritarian approach is typical of totalitarian regimes, both communist and fascist. Within Christianity, the Roman Catholic church takes an authoritarian approach. In other words, the Pope lays down moral teaching and the Church insists that its members accept it. The approach of the Protestant churches has generally been more collectivist in that moral teaching has been the subject of widespread formal and informal debate within a particular denomination (or, sometimes, within an individual church) before being formally adopted. Further, the Protestant churches have commonly, though by no means universally, acknowledged the importance of the individual conscience.

The collectivist approach is implicit in the idea of a professional code of conduct. The profession has decided collectively that its members must abide by certain rules and, by electing to join the profession, members accept this. There is still, of course, some room for individual judgement in interpreting the rules in particular cases.

But the conflict between individual and collective responsibility is at its strongest when individual beliefs clash with an organization's behaviour. This leads to a set of related questions of which the following are typical:

- How far can individuals be held responsible for the behaviour of organizations of which they are part?
- What should individuals do to dissociate themselves from organizations to which they belong but of whose behaviour in some respects they disapprove?

There are no easy answers to these questions. It is clear that a receptionist cannot be held responsible for the fact that the company is collecting medical data ostensibly for research purposes but is selling it to private investigation agencies. Equally, however, it is difficult to hold the chief executive of the company responsible for the fact that the receptionist has a hidden racist streak that reveals itself only in unpleasant behaviour, when unobserved, to low-status visitors. It is tempting to say that individuals should only be held responsible for those aspects of an organization's behaviour over which they have control, but this can easily lead to the situation in which no one appears to be accountable for an organization's misdeeds. Note that we are talking about moral responsibility here. The company itself and its officers may well have a legal responsibility for actions such as those described above but moral responsibility may lie elsewhere[14]. See Section 9.7 for a discussion of some of the legal issues.

The second question is perhaps more widely relevant than the first. Should I resign from my job as manager of the telecommunications division because the chief accountant practises racial discrimination in making appointments in his office? Or should I stay in the hope that pressure from me and from other people like me will change his behaviour or cause the company to fire him? If, to my horror, I find the company I have just joined writes safety-critical avionics software in C, should I resign immediately or should I stay and try to show my new colleagues the error of their ways?

1.7.3 Absolutism v relativism

Absolutists believe that ethics and moral laws are the same at all times, in all places, and in all societies. Relativists believe that they depend on time, place and circumstances.

Relativists are concerned to avoid two evils – or, at least, two attitudes that are now widely accepted as evil – intolerance and chauvinism. In this context, intolerance manifests itself as the desire to impose all aspects of one's own morality on everyone and chauvinism as refusing to accept that any beliefs other than one's own can be valid. Logically, however, there is no difficulty in reconciling absolutism with the avoidance of intolerance and chauvinism. One can tolerate other ethical systems while believing nonetheless that there is only one "right" system. And one can believe that there exists, in the abstract, the perfect ethical system, without believing that one's own or anyone else's system achieves such perfection.

---

14. There is some debate amongst ethical theorists about the extent to which a company can be said to be morally responsible.

As with consequentialism, most of us in practice, adopt a half-and-half position over relativism. We accept the absolute validity of certain rules but recognize that many others depend on the society in which we find ourselves.

Lack of historical and geographical perspective often means that we fail to realize how much morality changes from time to time and from place to place. Attitudes to human rights and to animal welfare illustrate this very clearly.

1.7.4 The doctrine of double effect

One difficulty that arises with rule-based systems is conflict between different rules. It is easy to imagine examples in which the requirement to act in the public interest is in conflict with the duty of fidelity towards an employer or client. Moral theory offers a way of handling this, through the *doctrine of double effect*. According to this doctrine, the foreseeable effects of an action can be divided into those that are intended and those that are merely foreseen but not intended. It is, in certain circumstances, permissible to carry out an action whose intended effects are good even if some of the consequences that are foreseen as possible but that are not intended are bad. Obviously the good effects of the intended consequences of the action must, in some sense, outweigh the possible bad effects that are foreseen.

Notice that the doctrine of double effect is intended to overcome problems in rule-based ethics. Consequentialists have no need of the doctrine because they cannot accept a prohibition against any action.

1.8 Professional codes of conduct

Professional codes of conduct are, by their very nature, collectivist and rule-based. Nevertheless, rule-based ethical systems always seem too rigid and restricted to handle complicated situations on their own and they are incapable of handling situations in which rules conflict or several different actions are possible but all in some way violate the rules. The interpretation of the rules and their application to specific situations may therefore involve individual, consequential reasoning. Although the individual codes themselves have an absolutist tone, the difficulty of establishing international codes has led professional bodies collectively to accept a moral relativism and to decline, for example, to insist that all professional codes demand that members respect human rights.

1.8.1 Codes of ethics and codes of conduct

At the start of this chapter we noted that it is a characteristic of professions that the professional body establishes and enforces a code of conduct on its members. If the professional body is to be effective in regulating the profession, membership must confer some advantages on its members, whether it is a licence to carry out certain activities or simply enhanced prestige. If the body takes seriously its responsibility for the conduct of its members, gross infringements of the code of conduct must lead to disciplinary action, with the possibility of expulsion. The expulsion will deprive the member of the advantages of membership and may thus be open to challenge in the courts. It is important, therefore, that the code of conduct can stand up to such a challenge. In practice, it will probably need to satisfy the following criteria:

1. Its provisions must be in the public interest and not be inconsistent with the law of the land.
2. Its provisions must be generally acceptable to members of the profession.
3. It must be precise, in the sense that it should be possible to establish convincingly whether or not an act violates the code.
4. Its scope should be limited to professional conduct.
5. It should be accurately worded.

It will also need to be demonstrated that the code is applied consistently and that the disciplinary procedures that enforce it are fair.

The terms "code of conduct" and "code of ethics" are both used. It is not altogether clear what distinction is intended. On the whole it appears that a code of ethics is seen as being more aspirational and less regulatory than a code of conduct. The codes that are described as codes of conduct generally come closer to satisfying the rules given above than do those described as codes of ethics. Both codes of conduct and codes of ethics are distinct from *codes of practice*, which are concerned with good practice in doing the job[15]; it is very rare to get expelled from a profession simply for doing the job badly. Codes of practice are discussed in Section 10.2.3.

Professional codes of conduct are particularly valuable in addressing conduct which can be seen as an abuse of the professional status. Doctors can be struck off, that is, deprived of their registration, for entering into sexual relationships with their patients or for drug taking. These clauses are not there because doctors are more sexually active than other members of the population or because they are more inclined to take drugs. Rather, they are there because it would be easy for doctors to take advantage of their professional position to seduce patients or to acquire drugs for non-therapeutic purposes. In the same way, solicitors often find themselves in the position of having custody of clients' money; there is an obvious temptation to use such

---

15. Confusingly, the IEEE-CS/ACM code is entitled *Software engineering code of ethics and professional practice*. It is not in any normal sense a code of practice.

money either to overcome short-term liquidity problems in the practice or to finance speculative investments; they are therefore required to hold clients' money in a separate account. Traditionally, such abuse of professional status has been dealt with severely.

The oldest known example of a code of professional conduct is the Hippocratic Oath. It bears the name of Hippocrates, the Greek student of medicine, who lived from around 460 to 377 BC, although scholarly opinion is unanimous in asserting that he did not write it. It takes the form of an oath, sworn by new doctors, and is still used in a modified form today.

1.8.2 Software engineering codes and their weaknesses

Most codes of conduct affecting software engineers have undergone major revisions during the 1990s. In the United States, the IEEE adopted a revised Code of Ethics in 1990 and the ACM adopted a revised Code of Ethics and Professional Conduct in 1992[16]. As far as software engineering is concerned, these have recently been replaced by a code developed jointly by the ACM and the IEEE Computer Society[17] (referred to as the IEEE-CS/ACM code).

The BCS revised its Code of Conduct completely in 1992. Since this is the code likely to be most relevant to the majority of the readers of this book and is also perhaps the one that best meets the criteria listed in the previous section, it has, with the permission of the Society, been included as an appendix.

The ACM 1992 Code of Ethics is very clearly an aspirational code. It begins with a section entitled "General Moral Imperatives". The first three of these imperatives state that

> *As an ACM member I will . . .*
> 1.1 Contribute to society and human well-being;
> 1.2 Avoid harm to others;
> 1.3 Be honest and trustworthy.

The introduction to the Code makes it clear that these imperatives are intended to apply to conduct as a computing professional. Nevertheless, their scope is both so wide and so imprecise that it is difficult to extract real meaning from them. In comparison, the first rule in the BCS Code:

---

16. Anderson R. *et al.*, "Using the new ACM code of ethics in decision making", *Communications of the ACM*, **36**(2), 98–107, January 1993.

17. The web site http://www.computer.org/tab/seprof contains this code as well as much discussion of it.

> Members shall in their professional practice safeguard public health and safety and have regard to the protection of the environment

is more limited but more precise.

A major weakness of the codes is poor drafting, so that, in the end, they do not mean what they were intended to mean. Because this is so widespread and so insidious in robbing codes of conduct of their usefulness, we shall give three examples of it.

1. Clause 6.05 of the IEEE-CS/ACM code states "[Software engineers shall] not promote their own interest at the expense of the profession, client or employer". This sounds reasonable until you realize that, if you are doing a good job, then changing jobs probably amounts to promoting your own interests at the expense of your employer.

2. As a second example, consider clause 8.01 of the IEEE-CS/ACM code: "[Software engineers shall] not give unfair treatment to anyone because of any irrelevant prejudice." There are two problems here. Surely a software engineer should not treat anyone unfairly, for whatever reason? The second problem is the word *irrelevant*. As the clause is worded, I am allowed to refuse to employ a 50-year-old as a programmer if I believe that only young people make good programmers, because this is clearly a relevant prejudice. However, I must not refuse to employ a member of a religious sect of which I disapprove, because this is an irrelevant prejudice. It is not likely that this was the intention of those who drafted this clause. The wording of clause 8 of the IEEE Code of Ethics (1990) expresses much better what was presumably intended:

    > treat fairly all persons regardless of such factors as race, religion, gender[18], disability, age, or national origin.

3. The Code of Ethics of the American Society of Mechanical Engineers contains, as the second of its "fundamental canons", the statement "Engineers shall perform services only in the area of their competence". On the face of it, this is reasonable but a little thought shows that, if it is interpreted strictly, it will either stifle technological innovation or ensure that technological innovation is carried out only by non-engineers. Clause 20 of the BCS Code of Conduct is better in this respect; it states "Members shall only offer to do work or provide service which is within their professional competence and shall not lay claim to any

---

18. There was apparently some disagreement over the use of this term, doubtless because some members of the working group that produced it shared this author's view that *gender* is a grammatical term and does not have the same meaning as *sex*, which is what is meant here.

level of competence which they do not possess, . . .". The essential point is surely that of not claiming competence that one does not possess.

A second weakness is lack of precision. Clause 4 of the BCS Code of Conduct requires members to "avoid any actions that adversely affect basic human rights." When the clause was written, there was no reference to human rights in the law of the United Kingdom. This did not come until the Human Rights Act 1998 which incorporated the European Convention on Human Rights into British Law[19]. However, the United Nations Charter contains a Universal Declaration of Human Rights, which differs from the European Convention on Human Rights in many ways[20], and there are other declarations on human rights that differ from both. Neither the Universal Declaration, the European Convention, nor the 1998 Act, defines *basic* human rights, which are presumably a subset of the totality.

These are not simply legalistic quibbles. The Universal Declaration on Human Rights declares that everyone has the right to freedom of movement and residence within the borders of each state. The European Convention and the British Human Rights Act say nothing about this. If members of the BCS work on a system for issuing internal passports for a country that restricts internal movement, are they contravening the BCS Code? Clearly their work is adversely affecting a human right defined in the Universal Declaration but is it a *basic* human right? Anyway, they could argue that it is not a human right at all since it is not included in the Human Rights Act nor in the European Convention.

In clause 1.07, the IEEE-CS/ACM Code states that

> [Software engineers shall, as appropriate,] consider issues of physical disabilities, allocation of resources, economic disadvantage and other factors that can diminish access to the benefits of software.

This clause is very widely drawn and is idealistic. It reflects a political view that will not command universal acceptance, even among ACM members. It is difficult to see how it could be effectively enforced.

The 1984 version of the BCS Code of Conduct contained a lengthy section on the code as applied to the consultant. This was removed from the 1992 version in the interests of simplicity. In 1988, the Computer Society of South Africa (CSSA) adopted a code very similar to the BCS (1984) one. However,

---

19. Indeed, although the Act was passed in 1998, at the time of writing (late 1999) it has still not come into effect.
20. The Universal Declaration is very much broader and asserts a much larger set of rights than the European Convention. However, there is no mechanism for enforcing the Universal Declaration while the European Convention establishes the European Court of Human Rights specifically to provide a final enforcement mechanism.

in addition to the section on the code as applied to a consultant, a section was added on the code as applied to salespersons. This contains a number of explicit interpretations of the main code that will seem very relevant to anyone who has experience of selling in the computer industry. To give the flavour, we cite three out of the fifteen:

- Members shall accept only such work as they believe the organization can produce and deliver.
- Members should not denigrate the honesty or competence of a fellow professional in order to gain unfair advantage.
- Members should avoid illegal "informal" price fixing and market sharing arrangements tending to falsify the process of tendering and open competition.

While one may quibble about some of the wording here, it seems a pity that other societies have not chosen to address the conduct of sales people. Selling is perhaps the area of the profession in which the temptations to act unethically are greatest.

1.8.3 International initiatives

The International Federation for Information Processing (IFIP) has made some attempts to develop an international code. The difficulties that this process encountered serve to point up the extent to which ethical approaches differ from culture to culture. To quote Worthington, writing in 1993[21], the IFIP work "was attacked as biased, being written by rich males, with a western European cultural background. It was claimed to not include the issues relevant to females and those with a non-western outlook and with poor third world countries." Without knowing the details of the debate, we can guess that three of the topics that were felt to be influenced by the "western European cultural background" of the writers were human rights, bribery and corruption, and conflict of interest. Most codes coming from professional bodies "with a western European cultural background" refer to these issues; most of those from elsewhere do not. Quite what is meant by "the issues relevant to females" is not clear.

Worthington goes on to say

> It may not be possible to have a detailed code of ethics which [is] standardised across the world. The best might be to require IT professionals to work within the norms of the society they are part of. When working in a different cultural area they must adjust their actions to suit. If they

---

21. Available at URL http://www.peg.apc.org/tomw/virtths.htm on 21 August 1999.

cannot adjust they must decline the work. The alternative is a form of technical cultural imperialism. Imposing alien values in the name of technical advancement.

This is an extreme instance of the relativist position. It would, for example, allow British software engineers to work in other countries on control systems for gas chambers or record systems intended to ensure that all female children were circumcised. They would not be subject to censure by the BCS because they would be working in a different cultural area and so "they adjusted their actions to suit". One does not have to be an ethical absolutist to find this approach distasteful and few would claim that condemning mass killings was cultural imperialism.

Since the members of IFIP are, for the most part, national professional societies, IFIP has now taken the view that it is not appropriate for it to produce a code of conduct. Instead it recommends that national societies should do so and provides a list of issues that they should consider.

Both CEPIS (Council of European Professional Information Societies) and SEARCC (South East Asia Regional Computer Confederation) have produced guidelines to assist member societies in preparation of codes of ethics. The major difference is that the CEPIS guidelines include reference to human rights and to the offering of inducements or bribes, while the SEARCC ones do not.

1.8.4 Contentious issues

Because the social consequences of developments in computing are perceived as being profound, ubiquitous, and long-lasting, several codes of ethics or conduct have tried to make software engineers responsible for the social and economic consequences of their actions. There is a danger here. Predicting the social and economic consequences of any major development may require professional skills in the social sciences that few software engineers possess. If a code of conduct demands that software engineers take responsibility for these matters, it is inviting them to form judgements, and presumably promulgate them, in areas outside their competence, something which is expressly forbidden elsewhere in most codes. Furthermore, their technical competence in software engineering may give their pronouncements an authority they do not merit.

The issue of moral relativism has significant commercial consequences. If country X has a strict code of professional conduct, which is vigorously enforced, there will be some types of work in other countries for which companies from country X cannot bid. This will place companies from country X at a significant competitive disadvantage *vis-à-vis* companies from country Y, which has no such strict code. The arguments here are similar to those concerning arms sales and ethical foreign policy.

The boundary between ethics and politics is a fuzzy one. Some codes of ethics are largely concerned with personal conduct, while others seem to seek to impose political views on members.

Some of these issues relate to a more fundamental conflict. Whom do professional engineers serve? Is it the public, their employer, the profession – or even themselves? In practice, of course, compromises are necessary and most engineers will accept that they have obligations to each of these four groups.

1.9 Applying codes of conduct

The examples that follow are all based on real situations of which the author has direct personal knowledge; in some cases, however, they have been simplified to make the essential point clearer and to prevent the protagonists being identified. Although the examples are discussed largely in the context of the BCS Code of Conduct, none of them led to disciplinary proceedings; indeed, in most cases, the party who might be considered to have breached the Code was not a member of the Society.

1.9.1 Sales proposals

Your company has successfully completed several large high-integrity systems in the field of on-line banking. As a result of these successes, the team responsible for them has left your company to set up on its own. Your company has been asked to bid for another similar system, by an overseas bank that is probably unaware that the team has left. You write a proposal that makes much of your company's experience in the field but fails to say that the team which worked on those contracts has now left. You believe that the company is still fully competent to carry out the work and that this justifies the omission.

Rule 10 is the most relevant to this situation:

> Members shall not misrepresent or withhold information on the capabilities of products, systems or services with which they are concerned or take advantage of the lack of knowledge or inexperience of others.

The example quoted would be a clear case of withholding information on the capabilities of services and (at least if successful) taking advantage of the inexperience of a client who does not think of asking to meet some of the senior staff who worked on the previous projects.

The assumption that the company is still capable of carrying out the work raises another question, addressed by rule 20:

Members shall only offer to do work or provide service which is within their professional competence and shall not lay claim to any level of competence which they do not possess . . .

This situation is not, however, straightforward. It is fairly widely accepted that advertisements, for example, while not containing statements that are false, need not contain information detrimental to the image of the product, unless, as in the case of tobacco, there is a legal obligation to do so.

Rule 20 is concerned with individual members claiming competence. It is generally straightforward although, in practice, there may be a problem of individuals not realizing their own lack of competence. This problem becomes much more serious when it is a company that fails to realize its lack of competence. This seems to have been the case with the London Ambulance System, where the company writing the software had no previous experience of such systems and quoted a totally unrealistic price, which was accepted although it was only a fraction of the price estimated by experienced consultants. It would be unrealistic to assume that all professional members of the BCS are able to judge satisfactorily their or their company's competence to tackle an unfamiliar job. See Chapter 10 for further discussion of this issue.

1.9.2 Integrity and professional status

A consultant employed by a software house is advising a company about a new large-scale hardware procurement. She is recommending a switch from the present multinational supplier to a smaller supplier on the grounds that its prices are substantially lower and it offers better service. She receives a phone call from a senior manager in the multinational supplier saying that, if she persists with the recommendation, he will ensure that her managing director receives reports from several sources of her incompetence and lack of professionalism. Furthermore, he will ensure that her company never again receives any business from his company[22].

Rule 16 covers this situation:

Members shall act with integrity towards fellow members and to members of other professions with whom they are concerned in a professional capacity and shall avoid engaging in any activity that is incompatible with professional status.

---

22. In the real-life scenario on which this example is based, the final threat was a fairly empty one, since the software house had never won any business from the multinational.

The wording is a little strange. One would expect that members should be required to act with integrity towards everyone with whom they are concerned in a professional capacity, not simply fellow members and members of other professions. The manager from the multinational is clearly not behaving with integrity towards the consultant. Even if she is neither a fellow member of the BCS nor considered to be a member of another profession, to threaten someone in this way is surely incompatible with professional status.

1.9.3 Political and social considerations

Suppose that you are asked to work on a system for a country of whose political and social system you disapprove. What should be your attitude in the following cases?

1. The system records inoculations and is intended to improve the protection of the poorest section of society.
2. The system is for government use and clearly implements the country's tradition of sexual or racial discrimination.
3. The system will maintain intelligence for the country's notoriously brutal secret police.
4. The system will control the flow of gas into the gas chambers that are being used to eliminate racial minorities in the country.

While there would seem to be no generally accepted moral objection to the first of these, some software engineers would have refused to work on such a system for South Africa during the period of boycotts aimed at removing the apartheid regime.

The second case poses in perhaps the most acute form the conflict between the absolutist and the relativist positions. It is also one where the influence of the mass media and of single-issue politics is important. There are countries that practise racial and sexual discrimination on an institutional scale that would be abhorrent to very many people in the UK and elsewhere. Because this has not been widely reported and there is no organization pushing to bring the matter to public attention, the situation is not widely known. However, many countries (including our own) have policies of which some of us may disapprove. It is easy to argue oneself into the position where almost no work is morally acceptable.

Only clause 4, with its reference to basic human rights, offers any help in these situations. If the term "basic human rights" is to have any meaning, it must surely include the right not to be murdered or arbitrarily imprisoned. This should prevent a member of the BCS working on systems 3 and 4. The position regarding system 2 is less clear. The apparent weakness of the Code in these areas probably reflects the lack of a consensus among the Society's members.

On the more general question, the concept of proportionality may be of some help. If you are opposed to nuclear weapons and their production is the main part of the business of the company for which you work, you will surely feel that you are unlikely to be able to change the company and that you should not continue to work for it. However, if you disapprove of the policies of the government of Pontevedro and you find that the large telecommunications company for which you work is supplying 5,000 of its latest telephone hand sets to the Pontevedrian Ministry of Health, you may well feel that this is a minor matter and that resignation would be a disproportionate reaction. Furthermore, you might be able to persuade the company not to look for further business in Pontevedro.

1.9.4 Public health and safety

Suppose that you are a database expert and have been asked to write software that maintains records of radiation dosages to which employees at a nuclear installation have been exposed. The input comes from the radiation badges that employees are required by law to wear and the purpose of the software is to flag any employee who is approaching the maximum dosage in a given period. You have been asked to write the software in such a way that the recorded dosage is never shown as reaching the threshold. If you do this, will you be in breach of the BCS Code of Conduct?

The most relevant clauses are clause 1:

Members shall in their professional practice safeguard public health and safety and have regard to the protection of the environment.

and clause 3:

Members shall ensure that within their chosen fields they have the knowledge and understanding of relevant legislation, regulations and standards and that they comply with such requirements.

Unfortunately, neither of these clauses quite fits the case. Although it is in the public interest that employers should not behave in this way, it is not a matter of *public* health and safety but of the health and safety of the employees of one organization; clause 1 is not precisely applicable, therefore. Neither, unfortunately, is clause 3. As a database expert, you may well be complying with all legislation, regulations and standards relevant to your chosen field while breaking the regulations relevant to nuclear installations. This may seem like casuistry but these are arguments that might be put in an attempt to prevent the Society from expelling the member concerned.

In this case, the IEEE-CS/ACM code is much clearer. Clause 6.06 says "obey all laws governing their work, unless, in exceptional circumstances, such compliance is inconsistent with the public interest".

There remains the question of what you should do if you find yourself placed in this situation. Assuming that voicing your concerns to your manager has failed to produce any useful result, you might think of approaching a trade union representative on the organization's Health and Safety Committee. If you do this, you will be in breach of clause 8 of the BCS Code, which requires you to keep information confidential unless your employer gives permission or a court orders you to disclose it. Again the IEEE-CS/ACM Code is more helpful; it requires you to keep the information confidential, "where such confidentiality is in the public interest". The BCS member would have to invoke the doctrine of double effect in order to justify the breach of confidence involved.

Applying the doctrine of double effect to "whistle-blowing" leads to the common sense conclusion that denouncing one's client or employer to a regulatory body is justified if there is a serious breach of the regulatory provisions that threatens the public interest and that cannot be dealt with in another way, because the good effects can be expected to outweigh the bad effects of the foreseen but "unintended" breach of fidelity. If the breach of regulations was merely minor and technical, the good effects intended might well not outweigh bad effects of the breach of fidelity. This again is a matter of proportionality, as mentioned in the previous section.

An appeal to the doctrine of double effect in a case like this would probably be sufficient to convince a professional body that a member should not be disciplined. The legal position has been changed and is now governed by the Public Interest Disclosure Act 1998; a detailed discussion will be found in Section 6.1.5.

1.9.5 Conflicts of interest

Peter is advising a government agency on the introduction of a new and comprehensive computer system to automate many of its operations. He advises the purchase of a package costing several million pounds to handle certain specialized communications requirements. He fails to mention that his wife, Ann, is the sales director of the company that markets the package.

Two of the BCS rules directly address this situation, perhaps because situations like the one described are more common than they should be. Rule 12 says that

> Members shall not purport to exercise independent judgement on behalf of a client on any product or service in which they knowingly have any interest, financial or otherwise

and rule 22 states

> Members shall avoid any situation that may give rise to a conflict of interest between themselves and their client and shall make full and immediate disclosure to the client if any such conflict should occur.

Rule 12 goes much further than rule 22 in that it forbids a consultant from claiming to exercise independent judgement even if he has disclosed his interest. Rule 22, however, covers a wider range of situations, for example, where a management consultant is advising a company on its organizational structure and takes the opportunity to recommend the promotion of her second cousin.

In the scenario described, Peter is clearly in breach of both rule 12 and rule 22 and should have informed his client immediately there was any possibility of his considering software marketed by Ann's company.

The sort of things you should disclose under rule 22 include:

- a directorship or a major financial interest in any business that is in competition with your client;
- a financial interest (except a small share holding in a public company) in any goods or services you are recommending to your client;
- a personal relationship with someone in either of the above categories;
- a personal relationship with any person working for the client who might influence, or be directly affected by, your advice.

It is difficult to be precise about how close the personal relationships have to be. Family relationships can cause a particular problem. In some families second cousins may be ignorant of each other and never have met; in other families, a third cousin once removed is regarded as a close relative who should be helped if at all possible. The essential point is that if an outsider might reasonably think that your advice or recommendations could be influenced by the relationship, you should declare it.

A particular problem may arise when a personal relationship develops during the course of a professional relationship. In one case, such a relationship developed between the contractor's project manager and the client's project manager. In order to be able to maintain the relationship, they prolonged the work far beyond the length of time it should have taken. This is clearly a conflict of interest but the wording of rule 22 is perhaps not clear enough. The contract between the two organizations said that all communication had to pass through the project managers; thus the "client" was well aware of the situation. A requirement to make full and immediate disclosure to "client management and to the member's own management" might perhaps be clearer.

1.10 Further reading

The engineering profession, as opposed to the discipline, is not well served by books. The Finniston Report:

> *Engineering our future*, Report of the Committee of Inquiry into the Engineering Profession, Cmnd 7794 (HMSO, January 1980)

is readily available in academic and other large libraries. It describes the context within which the Engineering Council was founded and the issues that were occupying the profession at the time. Despite its age, it is perhaps the best single document covering the engineering profession in the UK and much of what it has to say is still valid today.

SARTOR:

> *Standards and routes to registration (SARTOR)*, 3rd edn (The Engineering Council, Canberra House, Maltravers Street, London WC2R 3ER, 1997)

describes the current structure of the profession.

The current position regarding licensing of software engineers in the USA is discussed in

> Bagert, D. J. 1999. "Taking the lead in licensing software engineers", *Communications of the ACM*, **42**(4).

The best and most convenient source of up-to-date information on the topics discussed in Sections 1.1 to 1.5 of this chapter is the World-Wide Web. The following is a list of sites used as sources for the material in those sections

> The Engineering Council http://www.engc.org.uk
> (There is a summary of SARTOR available at this site.)
> The British Computer Society http://www.bcs.org.uk
> The Institution of Civil Engineers http://www.ice.org.uk
> The Institution of Electrical Engineers http://www.iee.org.uk
> The General Teaching Council for England http://www.dfee.gov.uk/gtcreg
> (This is a consultation paper. The regulations setting up the Council are contained in Statutory Instrument 1999 No. 1726, which can be accessed through the HMSO site: http://www.hmso.gov.uk.)
> FEANI http://www.feani.org
> Accreditation Board for Engineering and Technology (ABET) http://www.abet.org
> Computing Sciences Accreditation Board (CSAB) http://www.csab.org
> The National Council of Examiners for Engineering and Surveying (NCEES) http://www.ncees.org
> General Statutes of North Carolina http://www.ncbels.org/generalstatues [*sic*]

(Chapter 89C of the statutes contains the provisions relating to engineering and can be taken as fairly typical of the position in most states of the USA.)

Sections 1.6 to 1.9 are better served by books. For a modern and readable introduction to ethics, we can recommend

P. Benn, 1998. *Ethics*. London: UCL Press. (In the series *Fundamentals of Philosophy*.) ISBN 1-85728-453-4.

More extensive discussion of professional codes of conduct, along with discussion of other and wider aspects of professionalism will be found in:

Myers, C., T. Hall & D. Pitt (eds) 1997. *The responsible software engineer: selected readings in IT Professionalism*. London: Springer-Verlag. ISBN 3-540-76041-5.

The following article covers much the same material as this chapter, although from a rather different point of view:

K. C. Laudon, "Ethical concepts and information technology", *Communications of the ACM* **38**(12), 33–39, December 1995.

The work of the IFIP Ethics Task Group was published as

J. Berleur & K. Brunnstein (eds), *Ethics of computing: codes, spaces for discussion and law*. (London: Chapman and Hall, 1996). ISBN 0-412-72620-3.

This book is a valuable source of material for anyone seriously interested in the ethics of the computer profession. It includes a number of discussion papers and the draft international code of ethics that led to the controversy referred to in 1.8.3. It reproduces over 30 codes of ethics or conduct and contains a comparative analysis of them. Unfortunately, this analysis is rather naïve. The book is also beginning to date a little.

Finally, the Web allows many codes of conduct to be consulted. We have already indicated the sites at which the codes of conduct referred to can be found.

Chapter 2

The structure of organizations

It is impossible to live in a civilized society without close contact with many large organizations – schools, universities, public utilities, government and local government departments, the Health Service, commercial and industrial companies, and so on. Despite the huge variety of such organizations, there are many ways in which they resemble each other.

In the first two sections of this chapter, we shall describe the legal forms which such organizations may take and then, in the following sections, we shall discuss the way in which such organizations are structured, with particular emphasis on the things that they have in common. We shall concentrate on *trading organizations*, that is organizations which sell products or services for profit but we shall also indicate how non-commercial organizations fit into similar patterns. Finally, we shall discuss some of the issues which arise in managing such organizations.

2.1 Legal forms of organization

Fundamentally, the law recognizes individuals – human beings who can be regarded as responsible for their actions, in other words, all human beings except those excluded by youth or mental incapacity. Individuals can enter into contracts which can be enforced by the courts; individuals can be tried for crimes; individuals can be sued for damages; individuals can give evidence; Acts of Parliament can impose duties on individuals; and so on.

For all but the smallest business organizations, it is desirable that the organization should be given a legal existence, through a process known as *incorporation*, a word which means literally "making into a body," from the Latin *corpus* – hence the English word "corpse". This can be done in a variety of ways. Bodies such as professional institutions or universities are incorporated by Royal Charter. An organization wishing to become incorporated in this way must persuade the Privy Council that its activities are in the public interest and agree a precise statement of their scope and the organization's powers. Public bodies, such as District Health Authorities or County

Councils, are statutory bodies, that is, they are established by Act of Parliament.

Trading organizations are usually incorporated as *limited companies* but there are two forms of unincorporated trading organization which we should describe briefly. A *sole trader* is an individual who is operating his or her own business. There are no legal formalities attached to becoming a sole trader; one becomes a sole trader simply by starting to operate a business. It may then be necessary to register with Customs and Excise for VAT purposes and to negotiate with the Inland Revenue regarding one's classification for income tax purposes but neither of these is necessary simply in order to become a sole trader. It is possible, and usually wise, for a sole trader to carry on business as a limited company. If this is not done, the trader is personally liable for all the debts of the business so that all the trader's assets, including the family home, are at risk if the business fails. Nevertheless, there is no obligation for the trader to do this.

The Partnership Act 1890 defines a *partnership* as "the relationship which subsists between persons carrying on a business in common with a view to profit". When two or more people are carrying on business together, the law will treat them as a partnership, whether or not they have concluded a formal partnership agreement. The tradition of partnerships has served the public well and they are still the normal vehicle through which, for example, solicitors and general practitioners operate. The framework within which partnerships operate is still basically that established by the 1890 Act, albeit modified in certain respects by subsequent legislation, notably the Insolvency Act 1986. However, for most business purposes, partnership has fallen out of favour. It is risky for the individuals involved because they can be held personally liable for the partnership's debts, including any which may result from one of the partner's exceeding his or her agreed authority in respect of the partnership's business; as with a sole trader, this liability extends to the whole of their personal property, not just their investment in the business. Professional partnerships are usually fairly stable; the arrival of a new partner or the departure of an existing partner are comparatively rare events. In the business world, senior staff come and go much more frequently and, in these circumstances, the partnership mechanisms become clumsy.

Partnerships continue to be important because certain professional bodies require that groups of members wishing to offer their professional services to the public should be organized in this way. The unlimited liability is seen as an advantage in guaranteeing the professional probity of the partners. Within the engineering profession, partnerships were once common among consulting engineers but, since there is no professional or statutory requirement for this form of organization, it survives only in the case of very small partnerships.

2.2 Companies

As we have said, for most business purposes, it is desirable to have an organization which has its own legal existence separate from that of its proprietors. The law governing this is contained in the Companies Acts 1985[1] and 1989.

Companies may be either *public* or *private*. Public companies are companies which are allowed to offer their shares to the public (but need not necessarily do so); their names must end with the words "Public Limited Company" or the abbreviation "PLC"[2] A private company cannot offer its shares to the public; its name must end with the word "Limited" or the abbreviation "Ltd".[3] Public companies must be registered as such; they must have an issued share capital (see below) of nominal value greater than £50,000 and they are subject to greater regulation than private companies.

Companies can be *limited* or *unlimited*. In an unlimited company the shareholders are personally liable for all the company's debts; not surprisingly, this type of company is very rare. A limited company may be limited *by shares* or *by guarantee*. If a company is limited by guarantee, each member, instead of subscribing for shares, undertakes to pay a fixed, usually small, sum towards the company's debts in the event of the company being wound up. This form of organization is commonly used by professional bodies and charities; it is not used by normal commercial organizations.

The essence of a company is that it enjoys an independent existence as a legal person. Ownership of the company is divided into a number of *shares*; an individual or another company may own one or more shares. Individuals who own shares in a company are known as the shareholders or members of the company. Until recently, a company was required to have at least two members. However, the Companies (Single Member Private Limited Companies) Regulations 1992 permit a private limited company to be formed by one person and to have only one member. The Regulations make certain special provisions to enable a separation to be maintained between the member as himself and the company.

Shares can be bought and sold, although, particularly in small companies, there may be restrictions (see below) on who the shares can be sold to; this provides a way of handling changes in membership which is less cumbersome than the mechanisms necessary in partnerships, although the formalities may still be complicated.

---

1. The Companies Act (1985) was a consolidating act, that is an act that, as well as introducing some new provisions, brought together, and therefore superseded, previous legislation in the area.
2. Or, for a Welsh company, their Welsh equivalents, "Cwmni Cyfyngedig Cyhoeddus" or "CCC".
3. Welsh equivalents "Cyfyngedig" or "Cyf".

When a company is set up, its memorandum of association (see below) states what the company's *authorized share capital* is to be and the number and nominal value of its shares; it also states who the initial shareholders (the *subscribers*) are and how many shares each will own. The authorized share capital is the maximum amount up to which the company can issue shares. The company need not, and usually will not, issue all its shares. New companies are often started with an authorized share capital of £100 divided into 100 shares with a nominal value (or *par*) value of £1 each. The nominal value is the value written on the share, which is normally the money paid to the company when the share is first purchased; it bears no necessary relation to any subsequent market value of the share. Companies may issue shares initially at a price lower than the nominal value; such shares are said to be *partly paid* and the owner of such a share must be prepared to pay the balance up to the nominal value to the company when called upon to do so. A company may also issue shares at a *premium*, that is, at a price higher than the nominal value of the shares.

A company is not, in general, permitted to provide any sort of financial assistance to help individuals or other companies to acquire its shares. Indeed, the alleged provision of such assistance is at the heart of accusations of unfair practice in some takeover battles in the late 1980s and early 1990s. There is, however, one important exception to this. A company is allowed to provide financial assistance as part of an employee share ownership plan (ESOP). Such plans are becoming increasingly important as part of the movement to give employees a stake in the companies for which they work. Many small "high-tech" companies operate on the basis that all, or at least a substantial proportion of their shares are to be held by their employees. The shares allotted to employees under such a scheme are normally created by issuing part of the company's hitherto unissued share capital.

Our main concern is with companies limited by shares; this is the normal form for a trading organization. In such companies the liability of each member is limited to the shares he or she owns; in other words the shares may become worthless but the shareholder stands to lose nothing more. The way this works is that, if the company is wound up, all legal claims against the company must be met, so far as is possible given the assets of the company. If all such claims are met in full and there is money left, this is distributed to the shareholders. The shareholders thus stand to lose the money they invested in the company, but there is no claim against any other property they may own[4]. Similarly, the company can only distribute profits to the shareholders

---

4. There are two main exceptions to this. If the shares are only partly paid, the shareholder will be required to pay the unpaid amount. Second, the member may have contracted liabilities in other ways, such as by giving an explicit personal guarantee to secure loans made to the company by third parties.

in the form of a dividend if there are profits to be distributed; furthermore, if the company has made losses in the past, all these losses must be covered by subsequent profits before any distribution is made to shareholders. The shareholders are said to have a *residuary interest* in the company.

In an attempt to reduce the bureaucratic burden on smaller companies, the Companies Act 1989 exempts certain classes of company from certain obligations. To this end, it defines the terms *small* and *medium-sized* companies as ones which satisfy at least two of the three criteria shown in Table 2.1. The terms used in this definition are carefully specified in the Act, as are the provisions for companies moving in and out of these categories from year to year.

Table 2.1 Eligibility criteria for small- and medium-sized company status.

	Small company	Medium-sized company
Turnover	≤ £2,000,000	≤ £8,000,000
Balance sheet total	≤ £975,000	≤ £3,900,000
Average number of employees	≤ 50	≤ 250

2.2.1 The constitution of a company

All companies must have a written constitution, which consists of two documents: the memorandum of association, which controls its external relations, and the articles of association, which state how its internal affairs are to be run. Separate from these documents and not formally part of the company's constitution, there may also be a shareholders' agreement. We shall look at each of these documents in turn.

Professional advice should always be taken when forming a company; the material that follows is intended only to explain the purposes of these documents and some of the important issues which they raise.

The memorandum of association

This document covers the following matters:

- the name of the company. There are several restrictions on the choice of name for a company. The most obvious one is that the name must not already be in use by another company. There is also a long list of words for whose inclusion in a company name prior permission must be sought. This list includes words such as "Parliament" or "Wales", which may give the impression of some official status; words implying a representative role, such as "Association"; and words implying that certain types of service are offered by the company;

- the country in which its registered office will be located – England and Wales, Wales (to the exclusion of England) or Scotland;
- the objects of the company. This is a statement of the type of business in which the company will engage. Up until the Companies Act 1989, it was essential that the objects of the company were stated in terms sufficiently broad to encompass every type of activity in which the company might engage. If the company engaged in business which was not covered by this statement, the activity would have been *ultra vires*, that is, beyond the powers of the company. If the company suffered a loss as a result of such activity, the directors could be required to compensate the company. The Companies Act 1989 effectively abolishes the doctrine of *ultra vires* (although there are some provisions to protect a company from the actions of unscrupulous directors). In particular, the Act allows a company's memorandum of association to state simply that its object is to carry on business as a general commercial company, without being any more specific;
- a liability clause. In the case of a company limited by shares, this clause merely states that the liability of the members is limited;
- the company's authorized share capital and the number and nominal value of its shares.

In addition, the memorandum will conclude with a *declaration of association* along the following lines:

> We, the several persons whose names, addresses and descriptions are written below, are desirous of being formed into a company in pursuance of this Memorandum of Association, and we respectively agree to take the number of shares in the capital of the company set out opposite our respective names.

The articles of association

Many of the issues which must be addressed in the articles of association are very technical. In order to avoid the expense of having to produce a complete set of articles for each company and the consequent risk of errors, a model set of articles is published, known as Table A. Table A was originally a table set out at the end of the Companies Act 1948; it has been amended by subsequent Acts and regulations. If a company does not have its own set of articles, the provisions of Table A apply automatically. In practice, newly formed companies usually adopt the Table A provisions, with modifications to suit their circumstances. The company's articles can be in "long form", in which case all the provisions are written out in full, whether or not they are the same as Table A, or they can be in "short form", in which case only amendments to, and excisions from, Table A are shown. The articles of association of a company usually need to address at least the following topics:

- the rules to be applied in allotting new shares up to the amount of the authorized but unissued share capital of the company;
- the rules governing the transfer of shares. In a small private company it is usually undesirable that members should be allowed to transfer their shareholdings to whomsoever they might wish. One way of avoiding this is to include in the articles of association a provision that a member wishing to dispose of his shareholding must first of all offer it to the existing members; along with this must go some provision for establishing a fair price for the shares if this cannot be done by agreement;
- meetings of members. Meetings of shareholders are called general meetings. Every company is required to hold an annual general meeting (AGM); other meetings are called extraordinary general meetings. The articles must specify how such meetings are to be called, how business at the meetings is to be handled (e.g. how resolutions are to be proposed), arrangements for proxies, how many members constitute a quorum, etc. There is one exception to this requirement to hold AGMs. The Companies Act 1989 allows a private company to pass an elective resolution to dispense with the obligation to hold AGMs;
- appointment and removal of directors. Directors are elected by the shareholders to run the company and they can be removed by a resolution passed at a general meeting. In addition, Table A provides that all directors retire at the first AGM and that one third of the directors retire, in rotation, at successive AGMs; retiring directors are usually eligible for re-election;
- powers of directors. General meetings are too cumbersome to be used for the day to day management of the business; this is the reason for appointing directors. Table A allows the directors to exercise all the powers of the company but in some circumstances it may be desirable to reserve certain powers to the general meeting, for instance the power to borrow beyond certain limits;
- dividends and reserves.

Shareholders' agreements

The articles of association can be changed by resolution at a general meeting by a 75 per cent majority. This may make it difficult to protect the interests of minority shareholders. In order to alleviate possible problems, it is open to the shareholders (or some subset of them) to conclude an agreement amongst themselves governing the way that the company is run and agreeing to use their voting rights to enforce this. Such an agreement can only be varied with the consent of all the signatories.

2.2.2 Directors and the Company Secretary

As we have seen, the directors are elected by the shareholders to run the company on their behalf. They have considerable powers and, in a large company with many shareholders, the effective "democratic control" is very weak. However, this is balanced by a series of obligations.

Directors must act in good faith and for the benefit of the company. Suppose, for example, that a consultancy company is approached to undertake a short assignment. A director who became aware of this and undertook the assignment in a personal capacity, would be breaching this duty. He or she could be required to pay the company compensation for the loss of the contract and might not be allowed to carry it out in a personal capacity.

Directors must exercise the skill and care in carrying out their duties that might be expected from someone of their qualifications and experience. Thus, a director with long experience of managing fixed price, real time projects who signed a contract for such a project without checking, for example, that appropriate design calculations had been carried out, might be held liable for any loss the company sustained as a result of this negligence.

A director who has an interest in a contract made with the company (e.g. owning rights in a piece of software the company is thinking of acquiring) must disclose this interest to the board of directors. Table A further stipulates that the director must not be allowed to vote or be counted in the quorum when the matter is discussed but, in the case of a small company, this may well be varied by the articles.

A company is required to have a company secretary whose statutory duties include the keeping of the various records that the company is obliged to maintain and submitting various statutory returns to Companies House in Cardiff. The company secretary will normally also take responsibility for a variety of related matters. Provided the company has more than one director, the secretary may be, and often is, a director. Because of the technical expertise required, small companies often appoint an outside professional advisor as a company secretary.

If directors allow a company to continue to incur debts when they know or should have known that the company will be unable to repay them, a court can make them personally liable for the company's debts. This means that company directors should keep themselves aware of the company's financial position. There are also certain other, less likely circumstances in which directors can be made responsible for a company's debts, for which more specialist works should be consulted.

Many companies have both *executive* directors and *non-executive* directors. Executive directors are normally also employees of the company, with specific responsibility for certain areas of its activities. Non-executive directors are directors who act in advisory capacity only. Typically, they attend monthly board meetings to offer the benefit of their advice and are paid a fee for their services. It is important to realize that, legally, the duties and responsibilities of non-executive directors are precisely the same as those of the executive directors.

2.2.3 Disclosure requirements

In compensation for the benefits of limited liability, the law imposes on limited companies a requirement to disclose information about their operations. All limited companies must submit an annual return and copies of their accounts to the Registrar of Companies. Over and above this requirement, public companies that wish to have their shares listed on a stock exchange must satisfy the disclosure requirements of that exchange. For the London Stock Exchange, these requirements are listed in a document known as the "Yellow Book".

2.2.4 Corporate governance

In theory, a limited liability company is governed in a simple and democratic way: the shareholders meet annually to receive a report from the directors about the state of the company. If they are unhappy with the way in which things are going, they can elect different directors. Clearly, the job of the directors is to run the company in the best interests of the shareholders and it is the possibility of not being re-elected that encourages the directors to carry out their duties diligently and honestly.

Unfortunately, this simple picture is realistic only for companies with a small number of shareholders. We have already mentioned that, in a large company with many shareholders, the democratic control is very weak. The result is that the directors, together possibly with the senior management, become a self-perpetuating oligarchy. They fix their own remuneration, which in some cases may be felt to be excessive, and they run the company in their own interests rather than that of the shareholders.

It should be emphasized that the type of corporate governance that we have described is largely peculiar to the Anglo-Saxon world – the UK, North America, Canada and New Zealand. Although the concept of a limited liability company is nearly universal, the relationship between ownership, control and management is very different elsewhere in Europe.

Even when the simple picture is realistic, it contains unsatisfactory elements. We have said that the directors run the company in the interests of the shareholders. But there are other people who have a stake in the company, notably its employees, but also those to whom it owes money and, perhaps, the public at large. Who, precisely, should be regarded as the *sta-*

keholders in a company is a question on the answer to which there is little agreement. On the one hand, some writers vigorously maintain that share-holders, as the owners of the company, are free to exercise their rights so as to maximize their income or profits, and that the duty of the directors is to pursue this aim to the best of their ability. Indeed, until the Companies Act 1985, there was no requirement for directors to consider the interests of the employees of the company (and they might have been considered to have acted wrongly had they done so). At the other extreme, it is argued that the activities of many companies, particularly large ones, can affect the public interest and that their direction should be required to take this into account. These issues are not simply a matter for academic debate. There are many circumstances in which the economic interests of the shareholders conflict with the interests of the employees – this is most obviously the case when a takeover bid is made, which may provide shareholders with a handsome profit but will mean many employees losing their jobs.

The relationship between the stakeholders in companies and its most senior management is known as *corporate governance*. The issues are not new; the founder of modern economics, Adam Smith, had some trenchant things to say on the topic in the late eighteenth century and debate has continued intermittently over the two centuries that have elapsed since then. However, a number of *causes célèbres* during the 1980s, together with the debate about harmonization of company law throughout the European Community, have led to extensive discussion in recent years. In 1991, the London Stock Exchange, the Financial Reporting Council and the accoun-tancy profession set up the Committee on the Financial Aspects of Corporate Governance, under the chairmanship of Sir Adrian Cadbury. The report of this committee (known as the Cadbury Report) was published in December 1992. Since the terms of reference of this committee were restricted to the financial aspects of corporate governance, we shall discuss their recommenda-tions further in Chapter 3 (Section 3.9).

2.3 Organizing an organization

However democratic its principles, an organization can only function effec-tively if it has some kind of structure. The tasks that have to be carried out must be identified and agreement must be reached as to who will do what. It is usual to group the tasks together and to assign responsibility for each group of tasks to a specific executive director.

2.3.1 Functional units of an organization

It is common to group the tasks that have to be carried out in an organization into five major functions:

1. production – the activities that directly contribute to creating the products or services that the company sells;
2. quality management – the quality activities necessary to ensure that quality of the products and services produced is maintained at the agreed level;
3. sales and marketing – sales is concerned directly with selling the product, while marketing is concerned with establishing the environment in which the product is sold (e.g. through advertising) and with deciding how the range of products sold by the company should develop;
4. finance and administration – every company needs to pay its bills, to look after its funds, to pay its employees and so on and it is usual to include within this function central services such as data processing and the legal department;
5. research and development – how can the company do better the things that it already does and what other things might it profitably be doing?

It is important to realize that these five groups of functions exist in almost any organization, whether or not the structure of the organization reflects this.

The relevance of this view of an organization is fairly clear when we are considering, say, a car manufacturer. It is much less obvious if we are looking at an institution providing higher education or the Department of Social Security. Nevertheless, it is still a valid and useful classification of the tasks that have to be carried out. As an example of how this structural model applies to a non-commercial organization, we consider the case of a university.

"Production" in the context of a university has two main aspects:

- provision of education in the form of undergraduate and postgraduate courses, research training, short courses provided for industry, etc;
- research, whether carried out for purely scholarly purposes or under contract to government or private industry.

On the educational side internal quality control takes place on at least two levels. The system of using external examiners imposes a control on the quality of the final product, that is, the degree which is awarded. The internal validation process, which is carried out when a degree scheme is first proposed and at regular intervals thereafter, provides a measure of control over the educational process used to produce the final product. Quality control of this sort was well developed in the former polytechnics because their degrees were under the control of the Council for National Academic Awards. It was not until after the former polytechnics became universities, in 1992, that such procedures were imposed on the whole of higher education. This was done by imposing external quality control through the Quality Assurance Agency. This body conducts institutional reviews intended to ensure that each institution of higher education operates appropriate internal quality management procedures across the institution as a whole. It also carries out inspections (teaching quality assessments) of the teaching of individual subjects.

Universities do little direct selling – although a lecturer interviewing an applicant may well be trying "sell" the institution – but marketing, in the form of producing attractive brochures and prospectuses or even direct advertising abroad, is an activity which is now taken very seriously.

The administrative load in a university is surprisingly large. Staff have to be paid and bills have to be paid; student fees have to be collected. The maintenance of student records is an important and substantial task. The preparation of statistics for funding bodies occupies an increasing amount of time.

Research and development which an institution carries out into its own activities (as opposed to research and development carried out, either for specific external clients or for the general public good, as part of the production function) may include the development of new courses and course materials, research into new methods of teaching, new types of courses or the needs of specific classes of students.

The functional units which we have described are frequently used as a basis for the structure of small and medium-sized organizations. This means that a director or senior manager will be responsible for each major group of functions; below them, the major groups of functions will be divided into smaller groups, each under its own manager, and so on. This type of structure is sometimes found in larger organizations but, more typically, at the top level they are structured geographically or on a product line basis, although a functional structure will still be used at the lower levels. It is also usual to handle specialized functions such as legal services centrally even if the rest of the company is structured on a non-functional basis.

2.3.2 Geographical organization

In an organization which operates over a large geographical area, there are inevitably some tasks which are best organized on a geographical basis. If an organization operates in more than one country, for example, it is usually desirable to handle sales and marketing on a country by country basis. Because of cultural differences, an approach to selling a product which may prove very effective in one country can fail completely in another. Indeed, cultural differences may mean that a product which sells well in one country may be almost unsaleable in another. The most obvious examples are in the field of food and drink but there are plenty of examples in the field of professional services.

Even within a single country, the facts of geography may dictate a geographical organization. A large retailing organization will have many branches spread across the country. Geography dictates that the distribution of goods and supervision of the branches is organized geographically.

2.3.3 Organization by product

Where an organization produces several different types of product or services, it may be desirable to use a top-level structure based on this division. This is perhaps the commonest form of structure to be found in really large corporations today. Thus a motor vehicle manufacturer may be organized on the basis of divisions handling cars, vans and light goods vehicles, another handling heavy goods vehicles, and so on; on the whole, the company will be dealing with different customers for each of these types of product and there is comparatively little overlap in design and manufacture between the different divisions.

In software companies this type of structure is often found to be desirable in order to separate fee-based services from the development and sale of products. There is an inherent "culture clash" between these activities. If they are not clearly separated, there is a great risk that staff, particularly the most able, will be moved from product development to fee-based work because the latter brings more immediate and more certain revenue. The result is that the longer term rewards that can come from product development are never realized.

With this sort of organization, each division is likely to be headed by a director; within the division, organization may well be by function. An alternative is that each division is itself a separate company, with its own board of directors. Such companies are known as subsidiaries[5]; they are usually "wholly owned" in the sense that the main company and its nominees own all the shares in the subsidiary. In many cases, the main (or "holding") company does not trade itself; all the trading operations are carried out by the subsidiaries. This form of structure can also be used with a geographical organization, particularly where operations are being carried on in several countries.

2.3.4 Centralization v. decentralization

Whatever the basis of the organizational structure, it is possible for the organization to be centralized or decentralized or a mixture of both. In a centralized organization, many of the detailed operational decisions are taken at the centre; so, for example, details of the expense rates that employees can claim for travel involved with their work or standards for programming in COBOL may be settled at the centre of the organization and apply every-

---

5. The definition of subsidiary is much wider than this. The Companies Act 1989 introduced two definitions, one for accounting purposes and one for other Companies Act purposes.

where within it. Alternatively, in a decentralized organization, as many details as possible are settled at local level.

There are advantages and disadvantages to both approaches. By devolving decisions to the lowest level at which the knowledge and ability to take them exists, it is likely that better decisions will be taken and the performance of the individual units improved. Furthermore, the motivation of the managers of these units is likely to be improved by giving them greater responsibility for the operation of their own units. On the other hand, this can lead to wasteful duplication – it is unlikely to be sensible for six different subsidiaries each to produce its own set of COBOL programming standards. It can also mean that good practice is slow to spread through the organization. There are many organizations in which one can find one division using good modern software design techniques and programming in ADA while another division is still using FORTRAN and flowcharts.

2.3.5 The position of quality management

However an organization may be structured, it is important that ultimate responsibility for quality is kept at the centre. The day-to-day pressures on production and sales create the temptation to skimp on quality procedures in the interests of raising production levels, increasing sales or reducing costs. This can only be avoided by developing a "quality culture" within the organization, that is by creating an environment in which the idea of skipping quality procedures because of other pressures becomes unthinkable. For this to happen, the importance of quality must be seen to be recognized at the highest levels in the organization. The success of Japanese industry, and in particular its car industry, is due in very large measure to its success in establishing a quality culture.

The role of the central quality management function is to establish a quality plan which describes the quality procedures to be followed throughout the organization and how compliance with the plan will be monitored. There are national and international standards such as British Standard 5750, or its international equivalent ISO 9000, which lay down very broadly the requirements which a quality plan must meet; some major purchasers such as the Ministry of Defence and NATO have their own standards. In addition to establishing and maintaining the quality plan, and monitoring compliance, the central quality management function will also have an educational and proselytizing role in creating the quality culture. The detailed, day-to-day activities required to implement the quality procedures must remain the responsibility of the individual units; the job of the central quality function is to ensure that they meet the overall objectives of the organization's quality plan – and that they are carried out.

2.4 Management

The importance of project management will be familiar to all students of software engineering. Failure to manage projects properly has been the root cause of most of the spectacular failures of computer projects. The goal of project managers is to produce systems which meet the users' needs, on time and within budget. Their main concerns are therefore planning, progress monitoring, acquisition and allocation of resources, and quality control. The tools of their trade are bar charts, activity networks, critical path analysis, and so on. The project manager's horizon is the successful completion of the project.

Project management is usually contrasted with *production management* and *corporate management*. Production management is concerned with the management of activities which continue indefinitely and change comparatively slowly; production managers' horizons are both longer and shorter than project managers'. On the one hand, they are concerned with very short term problems, such as the need to restart production as quickly as possible after a breakdown; on the other hand, they are concerned to maintain the productivity and efficiency of their plants over their whole lifetime, perhaps 20 or 30 years. The typical example is management of a production line but there are many examples from widely different fields – operations management in a large computer installation, for instance. Production management is concerned with productivity, efficiency and maintenance of quality. It is an area in which quantitative models have an important part to play.

As a result of efforts to make the development of software less uncertain and more disciplined, it has become fashionable to use analogies such as the "software factory" and to talk about software development in terms of production management. While this trend is desirable, it is easy to be misled by the analogies. Production management is concerned with the replication of a product; software development is concerned with the development of new products. In particular, the lack of effective and usable "software metrics", despite the considerable research activity in this area, makes it very difficult to use quantitative techniques.

General or corporate management deals with the management of the organization as a whole. On the one hand, corporate managers are responsible for the long-term strategy of the organization; on the other hand it is with them that "the buck stops" and so they must monitor the overall performance of the organization and be prepared to handle serious problems which arise anywhere in the organization.

There are, of course, many other characteristics which can be used to classify different management roles. While each has its own peculiar concerns and its own methods for addressing them, there are certain issues and techniques that are common to almost all management roles.

2.4.1 Motivation

How well individuals carry out their jobs depends on several factors:

1. how well they understand what is required of them;
2. their ability;
3. the quality of the facilities provided for doing the job;
4. their motivation, that is how well they want to do the job;
5. the attitude of their colleagues.

While these factors apply generally, they are particularly important in the software industry – and only too often ignored.

Consider the case of a team of 25 people engaged in coding and testing a large real-time system. It is regrettably not uncommon to find a scenario like this:

- Specifications of individual modules are unclear, ambiguous or incomplete. Anyone who asks for clarification is told "Do the best you can with the spec you've got".
- Because of the habit of measuring effort in man months, there is an assumption that people are all the same. The result is that the programmer with a degree in Mathematics is writing the report generation module while the programmer with a degree in Business Studies is struggling with a module to calculate the eigenvalues of a matrix.
- There are five terminals, connected to an overloaded mainframe, shared between the 25 staff; the semicolon key on one of the terminals works only intermittently.
- The staff are housed in a single large room in a converted aircraft hangar. A formal "flexitime" system is in use and employees pay great attention to it, in order to maximize their time off.
- The main subject of conversation at coffee breaks is the appointments pages of *Computer Weekly*.
- Although the company pays competitive salaries, at least once a month there is a leaving party for a member of the team.
- No one shows any interest in what the software is for.
- The company has tried hard to recruit good programmers and, when they first join the project, new recruits seem to perform very well but, after three months, they are indistinguishable from their colleagues.

The inevitable lateness and poor quality of the software coming from this team is primarily a result of management failing to pay attention to the factors (1), (2) and (3) above. This failure results in lack of motivation on the part of individuals and the team as a whole, which, in turn, affects newcomers to the project. There is a gradual decline in the average ability of the team because the most able tend to be the ones who leave first.

We have seen some of the things that demotivate people; what are the things that motivate them? Assuming that the basic necessities of life are taken care of, people are motivated by such things as:

- self-esteem – the feeling that they are doing a worthwhile job and doing it well;
- the esteem of others – their peers, their superiors, their inferiors and their customers;
- satisfaction of social needs – the sense of belonging to a group;
- a sense of security;
- financial rewards.

The relative importance of these will vary from individual to individual and from organization to organization. Surprisingly often, financial reward will be found to be low in the order of priorities. A good manager will try to discover what it is that motivates each of his staff.

It is important that the outcome of good performance in a job should be seen to be an improvement in the factors that motivate the individual. While salary increases are usually welcome, they may not be the most effective way of rewarding good performance. Managers can make clear that they value their staff by consulting them and taking notice of their advice. If working conditions are unsatisfactory they can strive to get them improved. In environments where the salary structure is inflexible and promotion is at the whim of committees that take little notice of performance in the job, this may be the only means the manager has of motivating his staff. Its effectiveness will naturally depend on the respect that the staff have for their manager.

While financial reward may be comparatively ineffective as a motivating factor, it can paradoxically be an effective demotivating agent if it is seen to be grossly inequitable. This happens if salary increases are seen to be given to those who complain loudest rather than to those who perform best. It can also happen through careless recruitment. A particularly bad example was a case where new graduates were being recruited to a company at salaries higher than those then being paid to the graduates recruited in the previous year.

2.4.2 Performance appraisal

The importance of giving staff clear objectives and of measuring their performance against these objectives led, in the 1970s, to the development of a style of management known as management by objectives (MBO). The term has fallen out of favour but the central idea is now widely practised; indeed, it has spread from the business environment, in which it started, to many other areas, such as school teaching, to which its appropriateness is debatable.

The central idea is that of performance appraisal against agreed targets. Managers are required to agree with each of their subordinates what the subordinate's objectives in his or her job should be over the next time period, typically six or twelve months. At the end of the time period, the subordinate's performance is assessed against these objectives and new objectives agreed for the next time period.

In order to make such a scheme work, there are several important points which must be appreciated by all concerned:

- Both manager and subordinate must participate in setting the subordinate's objectives. They should agree that the objectives are both feasible and desirable; this will mean the managers explaining their objectives to their subordinates. They must also identify major obstacles to achieving the objectives.

- It is very desirable that the attainment or otherwise of the objectives should be objectively verifiable. Thus an objective such as "to ensure that the complete sales statistics for the previous month are available by the third working day of the following month" is acceptable whereas "to improve the level of morale in the department" is not. However, this should not be allowed to have the effect of placing undue emphasis on those aspects of the subordinate's job which can be quantified at the expense of equally important but non-quantifiable aspects.

- The subordinate's job must be sufficiently homogeneous to make it probable that the objectives will remain valid throughout the time period. If, for example, the subordinate is a communications expert whose job is to provide advice and assistance as necessary to project teams and proposal writers throughout a software organization, the work is likely to consist of a large number of short tasks which cannot be programmed more than two or three weeks in advance. In these circumstances, it may be difficult to establish any objective more concrete than "keep yourself up-to-date and keep your customers happy". Even this is better than nothing; it does make it clear to the subordinate that time should be spent on keeping knowledge up to date and gives grounds for asking for the time and money to attend conferences and suppliers' briefings.

- Continuing commitment from all levels of management is required. In the software industry, at least, this is perhaps the most difficult thing to achieve. It is not that managers do not appreciate the value of performance appraisal against agreed objectives. More usually, the problem is that appraisal interviews are never as urgent as the next crisis and so get put off indefinitely.

- Staff reviews carried out under the scheme should be diagnostic rather than purely evaluative. In other words, the purpose of the review should be to identify the reasons behind any failure to meet the objectives rather than to take the subordinate to task for failure. Since the review will be the starting point for the objectives for the next period, there is little point in setting the same objectives without some understanding of how performance can be improved.

- It is undesirable that the review procedure should be too closely linked with the salary review procedure. Quite apart from the fact that this may inhibit frankness during the review, there are many factors other than performance over one time period that must be taken into account in a salary review: the state of the market for people with the same skills as the person being reviewed; the need to keep the salaries of employees with similar skills and responsibilities broadly comparable across the company; and the profitability of the company. A subordinate who is perceived as a high-flyer and has succeeded in achieving two out of four very challenging objectives may well merit a larger salary increase than one of lesser potential who has succeeded in achieving more modest objectives completely. On the other hand, trade union pressure has led some universities to introduce schemes that expressly prevent the results of any appraisal being used in promotion procedures.

2.4.3 Sub-optimization

It may happen that, in achieving his agreed objectives, a manager may not act in the best interests of the organization as a whole. More generally and more formally, optimizing the performance of individual units within an organization may not optimize the performance of the whole organization. This problem is known as sub-optimization.

Let us consider two examples:

- A division of a software company is flourishing; it has plenty of business and its services are highly regarded by its customers. Unfortunately, its profitability is very poor, around 1 per cent of turnover. A new manager for the division is appointed and told that his primary objective is to raise profitability to 10 per cent over the next twelve months. He succeeds in doing this by increasing the division's charging rates and holding down salary increases; as a side effect, however, the turnover has decreased by 20 per cent and the number of staff by 30 per cent – and this in a period where most of the division's competitors have increased their turnover by at least 50 per cent. Incensed by the sudden increase in charging rates, two of the division's long-standing customers have transferred their business to a competitor and others are threatening to do so; as a result of the salary policy most of the best staff have left to go to work for competitors and the quality of the work produced by those who are left no longer justifies the division's high reputation. Following his success in achieving such a challenging objective, the manager is promoted and is subsequently heard making disparaging remarks about the problems his successor experiences in running the division.

- The XYZ organization is divided into many autonomous, wholly owned subsidiaries; among them are XYZ Tramways Ltd and XYZ SuperRail Ltd. The managing director of XYZ does not encourage collaboration between the subsidiaries because he believes that a spirit of competition among them leads to better performance. The government of Pontevedro decides that the national rail transport system requires modernizing and that, in such a small country, urban and inter-city transport should be run in an integrated fashion. Invitations to tender are sent to a long list of companies all over the world, including XYZ Tramways and XYZ SuperRail. XYZ Tramways decides to bid, in conjunction with ABC Ferrovie who will handle the inter-city side; XYZ SuperRail decides to bid in conjunction with PQR Strassenbahnen. Because of their high reputations and the quality of the proposals, into which they put a lot of hard work, the short list finally contains only the two XYZ companies, with their partners. The final decision is made on price and goes in favour of XYZ Tramways who in the final submission cut their original price by 20 per cent.

Sub-optimization is inevitable in any but very small organizations. Managers and units within the organization will always seek to optimize their performance in terms of the parameters by which they will be judged. To choose these parameters in such a way that optimizing them will optimize the performance of the whole organization is usually impossible. There is much that can be done, however, to mitigate the effects of sub-optimization.

In the case of the software house, the main difficulty was incompletely specified objectives. If the manager's primary objective had been stated as "to raise the profitability of the division to 10 per cent of turnover, while maintaining and, if possible, improving present sales volumes and staffing levels", the problems would probably not have occurred – although the manager would have been less likely to achieve the objective. The lesson here should be familiar from software requirements specifications: do not assume that your readers will take the same things for granted as you do.

The case of the XYZ group points up the dangers of too much autonomy in a decentralized organization. While for the most part the business of XYZ Tramways and XYZ SuperRail will not overlap, they clearly have interests in common. Group policy should encourage collaboration even if only at an informal level; senior staff of the two companies should meet regularly and it should be natural that something like the Pontevedrian tender should be discussed. On the face of things, it would have been better to submit a tender from XYZ Tramways and XYZ SuperRail jointly; however, there might be good reasons for submitting separate tenders with different partners (the Pontevedrians might be thought to prefer a bid which was not exclusively from one country; or two bids might be thought to increase the chances of success by one or the other). What is clearly contrary to the best interests of the group is to engage in a price cutting war at the final stage.

In both cases, the situation might well have been improved by good personal relations among the managers involved and a willingness to discuss their activities with their colleagues. The culture of some organizations seems to lead naturally to this, while in other organizations it is rare.

2.5 Further reading

There are numerous books on management written for engineers. In general, they emphasize the use of quantitative techniques in manufacturing industry and are not appropriate to the software engineering context. However, the first ten chapters of Chapman et al. (1987) provide a readable and more detailed coverage of the material in this chapter and the next, albeit the emphasis is still on traditional manufacturing industry. It also includes comprehensive bibliographies.

Although it is a more elementary book, Beardshaw & Palfreman (1990) serves to set the material in this chapter (and, to some extent, this book as a whole) in a wider context and is very easy to read.

Among more specialized works, more detailed information concerning company law and the mechanics of running a company will be found in Swinson (1990) and in Stamp & Marshall (1992). Prentice & Holland (1993) gives an excellent overview of the current state of the debate on corporate governance. Handy (1994) gives a more specialized coverage of the later sections of this chapter.

Beardshaw, J. & D. Palfreman 1990. *The organisation in its environment*, 4th edn. London: Pitman.

Chapman, C. B., D. F. Cooper, & M. J. Page 1987. *Management for engineers*. London: John Wiley.

Handy, C. B. 1994. *Understanding organisations*, 4th edn. Harmondsworth: Penguin Books.

Prentice, D. D. & P. R. J. Holland 1993. *Contemporary issues in corporate governance*. Oxford: Oxford University Press.

Stamp, M. & A. Marshall 1992. *Westby-Nunn's company secretarial handbook*, 11th edn. London: Longman.

Swinson, C. 1990. *A guide to the Companies Act 1989*. London: Butterworths.

Chapter 3

Finance and accounting

However good the quality of its products or services, no organization can be successful for any length of time unless its finances are soundly managed. As well as requiring specialist staff possessed of the necessary skills, sound financial management also demands that the whole management of the organization appreciates its importance and understands the ideas on which it is based. The purpose of this chapter is to present those ideas and explain their importance. Inevitably, in the interests of clarity, the material is much simplified and many important provisos and special cases have been ignored or only briefly alluded to; it should not therefore be taken as a complete statement of either law or current practice. In particular, we have largely omitted questions of taxation which, in practice, have a substantial effect on most aspects of a company's financial affairs.

The chapter emphasizes those aspects of finance and accounting with which the newly graduated software engineer is most likely to come into contact. We have thus given prominence to issues such as budgeting, costing and pricing, somewhat at the expense of such topics as annual statements. However, because so many young software engineers are attracted by the idea of starting their own company, we have given some attention to the financial issues involved in doing this.

3.1 The need for capital

It is not uncommon for a group of new or recent graduates in computing to decide to set up their own company to provide software services. Initially at least, their intention is typically to offer contract hire services, that is, to offer their services as programmers charging a daily fee. Not infrequently, however, they also intend to develop packages to meet perceived gaps in the market.

Even if the intention is only to carry out contract hire work, there will be a need to have some money with which to start the venture. Invoices are normally issued at the end of a month to cover the work that has been done during the month. A client is unlikely to pay an invoice within less than one month of receiving it. Two months is more likely with commercial clients and three months is not uncommon; some large companies are notorious for not paying invoices for as much as six or even twelve months. The result is that the group needs enough cash in hand to be able to live for at least three months. Additional money will be needed for the expenses of starting the company.

If the group intends to develop packages, a much larger sum of money is likely to be needed. While the packages are being developed, there will be no revenue coming into the company. For this period cash will be needed for:

- salaries, however small, for the group and for any other staff they may need to employ;
- rent, rates, heating and lighting of the premises used;
- equipment and consumables;
- costs of advertising and marketing the products;
- miscellaneous expenses, ranging from company stationery to travelling expenses for any trips that may be necessary;
- interest on any money borrowed.

However successful the development of the packages, it will take some months before sales reach a level sufficient to cover the company's on-going costs, so, even after development is complete, more cash will be needed.

How does one set about raising this money? The first step is to produce a *business plan*. The purpose of this document is to explain the plans to potential funders and to convince them that the plans are well thought out and that the venture is likely to be successful. It typically contains:

- a description of what the company will be doing, together with information to show that it is technically feasible and that founders of the company have the necessary expertise;
- an assessment of the size of the market and the competition;
- a prediction of the financial performance of the company.

Armed with the business plan, one is in a position to approach potential funders.

3.2 Sources of funds

Government policy in the UK has, over recent years, strongly encouraged the growth of small companies and, as a result, there are many possible sources of funding. However, they can all be grouped under three headings: grants, loans, and sale of equity.

3.2.1 Grants

A *grant* is a sum of money given to the company; while the company is obliged to demonstrate that it has been used for the purposes for which it was intended, it is not intended that the grant should ever be paid back to the organization which gave it. Not surprisingly, grants are only available from government (local or national) and European Commission sources or, very occasionally, from charities. Very often, grants are limited to a certain proportion of the money spent on a particular development and are conditional upon the remainder being raised from other sources.

The availability of grants and other help for new companies depends very much on where the company is located, how many people it expects to employ, and on government policy at the time. Typically, a new company, setting up in an area where maximum assistance is available, might expect to be provided with premises rent free or at half rent for the first 12 months; it might also expect a grant of £15,000 to £20,000, once it is employing five or six people, and a second similar grant when the number of employees reaches ten or a dozen[1]. These grants are intended to assist with capital investment, typically investment in premises and equipment, and are subject to a number of conditions, in particular the raising of capital from other sources, and often the grant is limited to a certain proportion of the capital investment that the company can prove it has made. This means that they are often of limited usefulness to small software companies, whose investment more usually takes the form of employees' time.

A variety of programmes, both national and European, offer grants to assist in the development of high technology products. Examples are the European Community Framework V programme and the SMART programme of the Department of Industry in Britain. Depending on the programme, it may a requirement that the proposed development is collaborative, i.e. involves more than one company, and, in the case of European programmes, that the collaboration involves companies from at least two member states of the European Community. The assistance is almost invariably limited to 50 per cent of the cost of the development and often to less.

3.2.2 Loans

While grants are undoubtedly very helpful, their effect on company finance, for all but the smallest companies, is usually marginal. The major sources of finance are loans and the sale of equity.

---

1. Very much larger grants are, of course, available to large companies building new plants that will create many new jobs.

A loan is a sum of money lent to the company; interest is payable on it, at a rate that may be fixed or variable, and the loan is usually for a fixed period. The company is liable to pay back the loan and, if the company goes into liquidation, the lender is entitled to recover the loan from the sale of the assets of the company. In most cases, security is required for the loan; that is, the loan is associated with assets owned by the company in much the same way that a mortgage is associated with a house. If the borrower defaults, i.e. fails to meet the repayment conditions agreed, the lender can request the courts to make an order that the assets be sold off and the proceeds used to repay the loan. If the company does not have assets sufficient to cover the loan, then the lender may ask for personal guarantees from the directors of the company; this may mean that the directors use their own homes or other property as security for the loan.

It is usual to divide loans into three categories: overdrafts, short-term loans and long-term loans. An overdraft is the most flexible form of loan. Overdrafts are offered by banks; they allow a company (or an individual) to spend more money than is in its account, up to a specified maximum. Interest is only payable on the amount actually owned and the rate is normally comparatively low; it is usually fixed at a certain number of points above the bank base lending rate, the precise figure depending on the bank's view of the credit-worthiness of the borrower. While overdrafts are the most flexible and usually the cheapest way to borrow, there is a price to be paid. A bank can withdraw overdraft facilities without warning, possibly for reasons of general policy that have nothing to do with the borrower. Many small companies have been forced into liquidation unnecessarily as a result of such action by banks.

In contrast, long-term loans are usually made for a fixed period at a fixed rate of interest. The borrower receives the capital (the amount of the loan) at the start of the period of the loan and is committed to paying interest on that amount throughout the period of the loan. Provided the borrower pays the interest on time, the lender cannot call in the loan. The borrower must repay the capital at the end of the period.

As a result of various government initiatives, a 'soft loan' may be available; this is a loan on terms which are less onerous than those that prevail for commercial loans. Soft loans are usually only available to start-up companies; the interest rates may be lower than commercial interest rates and security is not demanded.

3.2.3 Equity capital and gearing

Equity capital is money paid to the company in exchange for a share in the ownership of the company, as described in the previous chapter.

The relationship between loan capital and equity capital in a company is important. It is known as *gearing*[2]. Shareholders are at a much greater risk of getting a poor return on their capital or even losing it completely than are lenders but, in compensation for this, they stand to make a greater profit than lenders if all goes well. To illustrate this, let us take the extreme (and unrealistic) example of a company which has a share capital of £100 and loan capital of £10,000, at 10 per cent. If the company makes an operating profit of £1,000, the interest charges will consume all the profit and the shareholders will receive nothing. If the company's operating profit doubles, to £2,000, the lender will still receive £1,000 but, neglecting taxation and assuming that all the profit is distributed to the shareholders, the shareholders will receive £1,000, a rate of return of 1000 per cent. Furthermore, as the profits increase, the value of the company, and hence the value of the shares, increases. If the company is sold, the shareholders will get much more than their original £100 investment, but the lenders will still only be entitled to their original £10,000, plus interest. If, on the other hand, the company is unsuccessful and goes into liquidation, the lenders will be at the front of the queue of people to whom money is owed, whereas the shareholders will get nothing until everyone else has been paid in full.

Such high levels of gearing are undesirable both from the point of view of the shareholders, because so much of the company's income is committed to interest payments, and from the point of view of the lenders, because shareholders may encourage the company to trade recklessly in the knowledge that they have little to lose and a lot to gain.

3.3 Budgeting and monitoring

A budget is a prediction of the future financial position of an organization covering, usually, the current or the next financial year. In effect, therefore, it is like the financial parts of a business plan and should, indeed, be backed up by the same sort of analysis of the marketing position and the technical feasibility of the company's plans. A complete budget will include predictions for all of the annual financial statements described in Section 3.9. The ordinary manager in a company is, however, much more concerned with budgeting for income and expenditure than with other aspects of budgeting and it is with this type of budget that we shall be concerned in this section.

---

2. The term leverage is used in the USA. This is only one example of some very confusing differences in financial terminology between Britain and North America. In recent years, the globalization of the finance industry has exacerbated this confusion. In Britain the term *stock* is used to mean a loan that can be bought and sold on the stock market, what is otherwise known as a *debenture*; in particular the phrase *Government stocks* refers to fixed interest government loans that can be traded on the stock market. In North America, the word *bond* is used for this and the term *stocks* means what in Britain are usually referred to as shares.

In any large organization, budgets are prepared at several levels. For a medium-sized computer services company, growing rapidly, the top-level expenditure budget, covering the whole organization, might take something like the form shown in Table 3.1.

These budget headings reflect, at least in part, an organization structured along functional lines; for an organization structured geographically some of the budget headings would refer to the costs of the geographical units. The totals under each heading will have been derived from more detailed budgets. Thus the budget for sales and marketing would be broken up into payroll costs for a sales manager and a specified number of salesmen; costs of their cars; travel, subsistence and entertainment costs; costs of mounting stands at exhibitions; and so on.

As well as budgeting for expenditure, it is necessary to predict the value of sales during the year. This again will be broken down into figures for the various areas of activity in which the company expects to engage. For a services company, it is also useful to break down the figures to show the amount which is expected from existing contracts, the amount expected from new contracts with existing clients and the amount expected from new clients. The last of these is inevitably the most uncertain.

Budgeting is an iterative process. The first version of the budget is likely to show expenditure exceeding income, since the operating managers will want to expand their operations while the sales and marketing department will not wish to give hostages to fortune by being over-optimistic about the volume of sales it can generate. Adjustments will have to be made repeatedly until a situation is reached in which budgeted sales exceed budgeted

Table 3.1 Expenditure budget for 1999 with 1998 budget for comparison (£)

	1999	1998
Directors salaries and expenses	504,000	480,000
Sales and marketing	600,000	400,000
Management salaries and expenses	1,125,000	945,000
Accounting and administration	200,000	180,000
Cost of labour	5,550,000	4,890,000
Education and training	165,000	150,000
Support services	41,000	37,000
Premises	600,000	500,000
Postage and telecommunications	90,000	85,000
Equipment maintenance	36,000	33,000
Consumables	22,000	20,000
Secretarial	240,000	190,000
Insurance	38,000	35,000
Professional services	20,000	25,000
Totals	9,231,000	7,170,000

expenditure with a reasonable profit margin; the operational managers are happy that they can service the predicted volume of sales with the budgeted staff levels; and the salesmen are confident that they can produce the predicted sales.

A budget reflects the organization's plans for the coming financial period. Like all plans, it is of limited usefulness in itself but becomes valuable when used as a basis for monitoring the organization's performance. The figures in the budget must be split into monthly (or sometimes weekly) figures; when the actual figures for a month become available they, together with the cumulative figures for the period so far, are compared with the corresponding figures in the budget. If expenditure under a particular heading significantly exceeds the budgeted figure, the reason must be determined quickly and remedial action taken. While in many cases the remedial action will be to reduce expenditure, in other cases – for example, when production costs are over budget because sales are higher than budgeted – the appropriate action may be to update the budget.

3.4 Sales and order intake

As we have seen, a company's costs and therefore, in part, its pricing and the level of overheads which it can afford, depend critically, in the first instance, on the level of sales. Monitoring the level of sales is therefore an important managerial activity and needs to be supported by adequate information. Some products, such as chocolate bars or floppy discs, are comparatively cheap and sell in large quantities. Typically, companies which produce them do so at a steady rate and store them until they are needed to fulfil an order. They expect to be able to despatch an order for a consignment of the product off the shelf, more or less as soon as the order is received. Thus the gap between receiving an order and payment becoming due is very short.

While some companies in the computer industry are of this type – for example, successful producers of desk top computers or very widely used software packages – most companies in the industry produce to order. The most extreme examples are the bespoke software houses, which produce software to meet the specific needs of individual customers or provide the services of staff to support customers who are producing their own software. Although there may be some reuse of software from preceding projects, each order is usually substantially different from any other. In such companies, it becomes important to distinguish between *sales* and *order intake*. The amount of sales in a month is the total value of the invoices issued during the month; the order intake is the total value of the orders received.

A common situation is that a software house will win an order to provide support for a large project which is expected to last for three years; the order might provide for 500 man months of effort at a total cost of £2 million.

Assuming that the basis of the order is contract hire[3], it will generate sales revenue in each of the following 36 months. It is unlikely that the manning pattern will be flat (i.e. the same number of people each month) and, indeed, the pattern agreed initially is likely to be subject to re-negotiation as the project proceeds; furthermore, a contract of this length is likely to include a clause allowing charges to be increased in line with inflation.

In order to monitor the company's sales, it is necessary therefore to calculate, from each order received, the pattern of future sales revenue which it is expected to generate. Furthermore, this calculation will need to be revised from time to time to take into account negotiated changes in the pattern of manning and increases in charges arising from the inflation clause.

3.5 Costing

The price at which an organization decides to sell a product or a service depends on the cost of producing or providing it and on the market conditions – the price and availability of competing products and the elasticity of demand (i.e. how the size of the market for the product will change if the price changes). The notion of cost is a remarkably complicated one and we shall deal with this first.

The cost of producing an item or providing a service is not a well-defined quantity and we need to use different definitions of cost for different purposes. Failure to realize this leads to many lengthy and heated but ultimately pointless arguments. Costs can be grouped into four categories, as follows:

- raw materials and bought-in items;
- costs of equipment;
- direct labour costs;
- overheads.

The relative importance of the four categories will vary considerably from organization to organization and some organizations may place certain costs in different categories; in some, the cost of premises will be treated as a fifth category.

3.5.1 Raw materials and bought-in items

Products are not produced out of thin air. Motor manufacturers buy steel from which they make car bodies; chemical companies buy sulphur from which they manufacture sulphuric acid. Materials such as these, which are

---

3. See Chapter 5 for a description of the various types of contractual arrangement.

bought by a company and processed as part of the company's manufacturing process, are known as *raw materials*.

Companies also buy items that are incorporated, unchanged, into their products – computer manufacturers buy chips from specialist suppliers; motor manufacturers buy door locks. Such items are known as *bought-in items*.

There is usually no difficulty in determining how many of which bought-in items, or how much of each type of raw material, goes into the final product. There is, however, one subtle point concerning the cost of such inputs. A company which uses chips or sulphur will usually carry a stock; it is quite likely that not all the stock was purchased at the same time or at the same price. Since we may not know from which batch the chips or the sulphur used in producing a given unit of output came, how do we decide which price to use in assessing its cost? The usual practice is to adopt a 'first in, first out' policy for costing, regardless of the order in which the items or materials are used. In other words, we use the cost of the oldest batch until we have used a quantity equal to the size of that batch, and then we pass on to the next batch.

In the case of raw materials or bought-in components such as memory chips, whose price may fall dramatically as a result of over-supply, a first in, first out policy for costing may render a company's prices uncompetitive and the current cost then has to be used instead.

3.5.2 Costs of equipment

Let us start with a domestic example: what is the cost of owning and using a car? Suppose that we buy a new car for £10,000, keep it for three years and then sell it for cash; suppose also that we drive 10,000 miles each year. For the moment, we neglect the effects of inflation.

When we come to sell the car for cash at the end of the three years, we may expect to get somewhere in the region of £4,200 – the exact figure will depend on the make and model of car, how well we have looked after it, the time of year and the geographical location, and so on; remember also that, in neglecting the effects of inflation, we are assuming that the price of a new car has remained the same. The difference between what we paid for the car and what we sell it for is the depreciation of the car; it is a real and very important element in the cost of owning the car.

In order to buy the car in the first place, we need to have £10,000 available. We may have to borrow all or part of this sum, in which case we shall have to pay interest on it. This again is part of the cost of owning the car: if we don't buy the car we don't have to pay the interest. Less obviously, even if we do have the £10,000 available from our own resources, there is a cost attached to using the money to buy the car because we must forgo the income that the £10,000 could have brought us. In the simplest case we might have invested the money in a Building Society at, say, 6 per cent per annum.

However, this is not consistent with our assumption of no inflation. Interest rates reflect inflation because lenders expect the interest rate to compensate them for the fall in the value of money as well as providing real earnings; in a time of no inflation, one would not expect the interest rate to be more than 3 per cent. Taking this figure, at the end of the three year period, we would have had £10,927 in our account.

The income of £927 which we have elected to forgo is an example of an *opportunity cost*, that is a cost generated as a result of being unable to take up another opportunity of using the capital. Again we must emphasize that this is a real cost: if we do not choose to buy the car, then we can invest the money in a Building Society and at the end of three years, subject only to possible variations in the interest rate, we will have an extra £927. Of course, there are other opportunities for investing the money – an outsider at 100 to 1 in the 3.30 at Ascot, for example – and therefore other ways in which we might choose to calculate the opportunity cost but such investments are likely to be less certain to produce a predictable return.

The costs that we have dealt with so far are *fixed costs*; that is, they do not vary with the amount that we use the car[4]. Other examples of fixed costs include the Road Fund Licence (£155 per year) and insurance (say £500 per year).

There are other costs which are *variable costs*; these are costs which vary in proportion to the amount the car is used. The most obvious is fuel. If we assume that petrol costs £3.30 per gallon and that, on average, the consumption is 30 miles per gallon, the cost per mile is 11p. Other variable costs vary in a less smooth manner. A set of modern tyres will last for some 40,000 miles if they are properly looked after; a replacement set might cost £200. This gives a cost of 0.5p per mile for wear and tear on tyres. However, since we have only covered 30,000 miles by the time we sell the car, we shall have spent nothing on replacement tyres. Servicing costs are rather similar in nature. We assume that the car needs servicing every 10,000 miles and that a service costs £150; we shall therefore have serviced the car at 10,000 miles and 20,000 miles but not immediately before we sell it.

The costs of owning the car are summarized in Table 3.2.

If we distribute the cost over the 30,000 miles that we have driven, we arrive at a cost of 40.97p per mile. This figure is in line with the costs quoted by, for example, the Automobile Association.

This cost per mile is very dependent on how many miles we drive in the three year period, that is, on the utilization of the car. If we doubled the mileage to 60,000, allowing for additional fuel and servicing plus £200 for a

---

4. Strictly speaking, this is not quite true; the secondhand value of the car may be affected if we do a very high or a very low mileage. However, it is more or less constant over a fairly wide range of use.

Table 3.2 Costs of running a car

Loss of interest on capital	927
Depreciation	5,800
Road fund licence	465
Insurance	1,500
Total fixed costs	8,692
Fuel costs at 11p per mile	3,300
Servicing costs	300
Total variable cost over 30,000 miles	3,600
Total costs	12,292

new set of tyres and £500 for repairs (on the grounds that some repairs other than routine maintenance are likely to be necessary in the second 30,000 miles), the total cost would rise to £16,742 but the cost per mile would fall to 27.90p. This is a dramatic example of the general point that the cost of a unit of output from an asset depends critically on its utilization.

When we come to decide whether to make a journey using the car or whether to make it by some other means, even if our decision is made on purely financial grounds, these are not the cost figures we should use. The fixed costs will not be affected by the extra miles travelled on the journey. The only additional costs will therefore be the variable costs. On the figures given, these amount to 11p per mile for fuel, 0.5p per mile for tyres and 1.5p per mile for servicing, i.e. a total of 13p per mile. This, the cost of obtaining one extra unit of production from a machine, is called the marginal cost.

Opportunity costs have to be treated with care; what we have done above is not in accordance with normal commercial practice. It is appropriate to take into account opportunity costs when we are comparing competing proposals for investment or deciding whether or not to make a given investment (see Section 3.7); once we have decided to make the investment, we have, presumably, decided that it is the best of the available ways in which the company could use the capital and it is no longer appropriate to associate the opportunity cost with the asset. We therefore ignore it in calculating the cost of a unit of production from the asset. The cost of the capital is still real, of course, but it will be treated as an overhead – see below.

Table 3.2 is what economists would call an *ex post* calculation; it is based on a knowledge of what actually happened to our hypothetical car; we can only carry out such a costing after we have finally sold the car. For costing the use of a piece of machinery in industry, we need an *ex ante* estimate of what will happen, that is an estimate that can be made at the start of the life of the machine. This means making assumptions about what happens to the average machine of that type in the same environment. The same type of calculations will be carried out (excluding the cost of capital) but we need to look more carefully at the question of depreciation.

Depreciation can be looked at in (at least) two ways. On the one hand, it reflects the diminishing value of the item, both its market value and its value to the company, as its life passes; on the other hand, it is a way of distributing the cost of owning the item over the work which it produces. There are several ways of calculating depreciation. The two most commonly used are *straight line* depreciation and *reducing balance* depreciation. Suppose the initial cost of the item is C. Using straight line depreciation, we decide the likely life of the item, n years say, and its resale or scrap value at the end of its life, S. We then calculate the annual depreciation as $(C - S)/n$. The notional value of the item at the end of year m ($m \leq n$) is thus

$$C - \frac{m(C - S)}{n} = C\left(1 - \frac{m}{n}\right) + S\frac{m}{n}$$

Straight line depreciation is simple and adequate for many purposes. In particular, it is a reasonable way of distributing the cost of owning the item over its useful lifetime. If, however, we want the depreciated value of the asset to reflect its diminished market value – and, possibly, its diminished value to the company – straight line depreciation is unrealistic; the resale value of an asset normally falls much more in absolute terms during the earlier years of its life than during the later years. The reducing balance method of calculating depreciation reflects this. We choose a factor r ($0 < r < 1$) as the fraction by which the value falls in each year. Thus the notional value of the asset at the end of year m is $C(1 - r)^m$ and the depreciation in year m is

$$C(1 - r)^{m-1} - C(1 - r)^m = Cr(1 - r)^{m-1}$$

We would usually choose r to satisfy the equation

$$C(1 - r)^n = S$$

i.e.

$$r = 1 - (S/C)^{1/n}$$

so that the nominal value at the end of the item's life will still be S, as with straight line depreciation.

Clearly with the reducing balance method, the value of the asset can never fall to zero; if we want to obtain the effect of no resale value we take S to be 1.

Table 3.3 shows for comparison purposes the depreciation and depreciated values, using the two methods, of an item whose initial cost is £10,000. We have taken a life of five years for the asset and a resale value of £2,000 at the end of the period. This implies a rate of 0.3312 for the reducing balance method. It should be clear that, certainly if the item is a car, the reducing

Table 3.3 Different methods of calculating depreciation (£) on an asset which cost £10,000.

Year	Straight line		Reducing balance	
	Depreciation	*Value at end*	*Depreciation*	*Value at end*
I	2,000	8,000	3,312	6,688
2	2,000	6,000	2,215	4,473
3	2,000	4,000	1,482	2,991
4	2,000	2,000	990	2,000

balance method gives a much more realistic picture of the change in its resale value.

For the purposes of internal costing, a company is free to use whatever methods it wishes for calculating depreciation. However, in its published accounts (see Section 3.9) the same method must be used for all assets of the same type and it is therefore common to use the same methods for internal costing as are used in the published accounts.

3.5.3 Cost of labour

Suppose that an employee is paid a salary of £15,000 per year. If that employee works for one hour in order to produce an item, what cost should we attribute to the employee's time?

First, we need to calculate the total cost of employing the employee for one year. In addition to his salary, we are obliged to pay what is known as the Employer's National Insurance Contribution. This depends on the salary in a rather complicated way; for a salary of £15,000, it comes to about £1,500. If the company runs a pension scheme, then it is normal for the employer as well as the employee to make a contribution to this; we assume the employer's contribution is 6 per cent, i.e. £900. In some cases, there may be other allowances payable, such as car allowances or clothing allowances but we shall ignore these. The total cost of employing the employee for the year is thus £17,400.

Next we need to work out how many hours the employee will work in a year. Assuming a five day week, there are 260 possible working days in a year. If there are 20 working days of holiday plus eight days of public holidays, this reduces the total number of working days possible to 232. However, we must make some allowance for days off for sickness. The best we can do is to take the average for the company as a whole, since we cannot predict what will happen to an individual employee; this might be eight days. This brings the total days worked down to 224. (It might be appropriate to reduce this number even further, to allow for time spent in training or time when there is no work to do, for example, but we shall ignore these possibilities here.) If we assume a seven hour day, the total number of hours worked is 1568. The cost per hour is therefore £11.10. A cost calculated in this way is not appropriate for all purposes, as we shall see in the following sections.

3.5.4 Overheads

Some costs (e.g. raw materials, use of specific machinery, some labour costs) can be directly associated with specific products or services. They are therefore taken into account directly in determining prices. Other costs, such as sales and marketing, managers' costs and costs related to the preparation of bids, cannot be directly associated with specific products or services but nevertheless must still be covered by the total revenue. These are called *overheads*. Although they cannot be associated with specific items of production or service, they are nonetheless real costs and, if the company is to be profitable, they must be recovered from revenue.

Some of the overheads can be associated with specific parts of the organization and should therefore be covered by the revenue earned by those parts; these may be called *departmental overheads*. Other overheads can only be associated with the whole organization; these are known as *corporate overheads*.

It is important to realize that what is regarded as an overhead may vary from one organization to another. A software house based at a single site may find it impracticable or not worthwhile to associate the cost of rent, rates, heating and lighting with individual projects or departments; it will therefore treat these as corporate overheads. A computer manufacturer producing peripherals on one site, processors on another and system software on a third, will treat the cost of these premises as a departmental overhead (although the cost of premises for the head office will still be a corporate overhead). A company that runs a number of aluminium smelters at different sites will associate the costs of each site with the aluminium produced there. There is no "right" way of allocating overheads to individual parts of the organization or to individual products. How it is done depends partly on the policy of the organization and partly on the nature of the overhead. There are two basic approaches. Overheads can be added to costs of the inputs (labour, machine time, etc.) or they can be added to the costs of the outputs (products and services). In a bespoke software house, for example, overheads are usually recovered by adding them to the direct labour costs, calculated as in the previous section; this means that if the software house buys in computer equipment which will be delivered to the client along with software which is being developed, no substantial overhead is added to the cost of the equipment (although there may be a small addition to cover the costs of handling and financing it). A manufacturing company is more likely to recover overheads by adding a mark-up to the direct cost of each product. It is usual to make the amount added for overheads a fixed percentage of the cost to which it is being added, whether this is an input or an output, but some organizations use, say, a fixed overhead per man hour, regardless of the direct cost of the man hour.

All these different strategies can sometimes lead to markedly different price structures and it is important to ensure that the resulting price structure does not make the company uncompetitive. In the case of bespoke software houses, mentioned above, an attempt to add overheads to the cost of bought-in computers might make them uncompetitive in comparison with computer manufacturers who offer a software development service and who would, presumably, not expect to add an additional overhead to a product that they have manufactured themselves.

The treatment of overheads can markedly influence the way in which managers behave; in particular, it can alleviate or exacerbate the problems of sub-optimization referred to in the last chapter. We shall quote three examples from our own experience to illustrate the problem.

- An organization treats all the costs of running its fleet of cars, except for petrol, as overheads. As a result, it apparently costs only £25 for an employee to drive from Bristol to London and back, as against £80 return on peak hour trains. Local management therefore encourages employees to drive rather than taking the train.
- A training company had a policy of applying overheads to all its charges. When it expanded its activities into residential courses, it applied this policy to the accommodation costs, with the result that its courses were seen as more highly priced than their (perfectly adequate) quality justi-fied. Eventually it abandoned residential courses because it could not sell places on them at the prices it was charging.
- Department A in a large company is very highly automated and the marginal cost of its production is very low; because of the high capital investment, the departmental overheads are very high and thus are recovered by a very large percentage mark-up on everything the depart-ment produces. In the course of developing the automation, department A produces a novel software package. Department B hears about this package and realizes that it would help solve some of its own problems. It approaches department A asking to be allowed to use the software and expecting to pay a part of the development cost. However, department A's rules require that the very high mark-up is applied to everything it sells and even the 20 per cent discount which it is allowed to offer to internal customers still leaves the package costing more than equivalent packages available commercially. As a result, department B purchases a commercial package, at lower cost to itself but greater cost to the com-pany as a whole.

Within the overall constraint that all overheads must ultimately be recovered from revenue, the following principles should apply to the way that overheads are distributed:

- consistency: similar costs should be treated in similar ways;
- the treatment of overheads should encourage managers to behave in ways which optimize the performance of the company as a whole rather than just the performance of their own department;
- the treatment of overheads should not distort the price structure of the company's products so as to make them uncompetitive.

It should be remarked that it is easier to enunciate these principles in general than it is to implement them in practice.

3.6 Pricing

The prices that a company charges for its products and services are ultimately constrained by the long-term requirement that the revenue from its trading operations must exceed the costs of those operations. Breaking this constraint in one year will mean an overall loss for that year, which may be acceptable if the company's assets and prospects justify it. However, it is clear that the company cannot continue to make losses indefinitely. In the very simple case that a company produces only a single product, this constraint implies a minimum selling price for a given volume of sales.

For a company which provides a range of products or services, the unit price of each item can be adjusted to maximize the company's profits and need not necessarily be related to the cost of providing the item. This is most easily seen by formulating the problem mathematically. Suppose that the company produces n products, numbered 1 to n. The cost of producing unit quantity of product i is c_i. The quantity of product i which can be sold at a unit price of p_i is $q_i(p_i)$, that is q_i depends on p_i. The trading profit is thus

$$\sum_{i=1}^{n} q_i(p_i)(p_i - c_i)$$

We therefore want to choose the p_i in such a way as to maximize this quantity. This choice of the p_i will be constrained by limitations on the q_i resulting from the fact that the company only has limited resources and cannot produce indefinitely large quantities of any of the products.

In certain industries, such as the chemical industry, a more sophisticated version of this model can indeed be used for planning pricing and production strategies. Both the market for the products and the number of producers may well be so large that the amount produced by an individual producer will have little if any effect on the price, which is itself determined by the market. In this case, the p_i are taken as constants and the model can be used to determine the q_i which maximize the trading profit, that is, what mix of products will produce the maximum profit.

For most companies the way in which q_i depends on p_i is much too uncertain for this approach to be useful. Pricing in such circumstances is usually based on the cost of producing the product or providing the service, plus a percentage for profit (and a percentage for overheads if these are not included in the costs used); the result of this calculation may then be modified in the light of perceived market conditions. In some industries, it is normal to discount prices for quantity or for favoured customers so that published prices must be sufficiently high to allow a sale to be profitable even after discounting.

3.6.1 Pricing in software companies

Software companies are typically faced with pricing in three contexts:

1. pricing a bid to provide services, such as consultancy, design or programming, with payment based on the effort supplied;
2. pricing a bid for a contract to supply bespoke software at a fixed price;
3. pricing a software product which they have developed or for which they are agents.

In case (1), the price will depend on the cost of labour, calculated as described in the previous section, plus overheads. However, this price may need to be modified to take into account a number of factors:

• how badly the company needs the business. If there are staff not assigned to useful work who could be employed on the contract being bid for, the company may reduce its price to make its bid more attractive. In extreme cases, a company may bid for the business at little more than marginal cost (i.e. direct labour cost plus expenses) in order to avoid having to lay staff off. Alternatively, if there are no staff likely to be available to do the job or the work could only be done by transferring staff from other projects, to their detriment, the company may decline to bid or bid an unrealistically high price;

• the desirability of the client. Clients may be desirable because the prestige of their name on the company's client list will help the company win other business. Or they may be desirable because they are known to place a lot of business in the general area of the company's activities but it has previously always been placed with competitors. In either case, the company may be prepared to cut its prices in order to win business with the client;

- the general level of the market. If a company's competitors are offering similar services at a lower price, the company may have to lower its price; conversely, if the competitors' prices are known to be higher, the company may raise its prices so that they are closer to those of the competition.

In case (2), the first step is to estimate the resources needed to carry out the project; this is a notoriously difficult task and its results are unreliable. However, software engineering courses usually address this topic at some length and so we shall assume here that the estimating has been carried out. The costs of the labour required and any travel and subsistence expenses can be calculated as before but there will be other costs to be included. If the system as delivered is to include bought-in hardware or software, the costs of these must be included; this may include maintenance costs, operating costs and costs for floor space, insurance and delivery of hardware. On a fixed price contract, it is usually the case that stage payments (i.e. payments made by the client in advance of delivery of the system) lag behind the supplier's costs, so the cost of financing the work must be taken into account (see Section 3.7). Systems of this sort are usually supplied with some sort of guarantee so the cost of servicing this needs to be included. Finally, fixed price projects invariably carry a significant risk; it is normal to increase the total price by a factor of up to 50 per cent, depending on the perceived level of the risk in order, on the one hand, to provide a contingency allowance in case of problems and, on the other hand, to compensate the company for the risk being taken.

Once a price has been determined for a fixed price contract, the same factors as above may cause the company to adjust its price. However, because of the risks involved, the company should be very much more cautious about price cutting; many prestigious software companies have suffered severe financial damage as a result of undertaking fixed price contracts at too low a price and, in some cases, this has resulted in the total collapse of the company.

Pricing software products is very different. The resources used in developing the product should be known and from these the costs of the development can be calculated. The costs of maintaining and supporting the product must also be estimated; these will usually consist of a fairly substantial fixed cost plus a small variable element depending on the number of copies sold (or, perhaps, the number of different clients to whom it is sold). The cost of selling the product must also be taken into account. The pattern of selling and support costs will be very different for a product which is expected to sell a very large number of copies fairly cheaply than for a product which is expected to sell only a few copies but at a high price. A company which already has a number of successful products will already have the necessary sales and support infrastructure and the costs of adding the new product may be quite low; for a company starting from scratch in the products market, the costs can be extremely high.

Since there are substantial fixed costs involved, including the need to recoup the costs of the individual development, the pricing is critically dependent on an estimate of likely sales. Unfortunately, this is always uncertain, particularly since the price may affect sales volumes. Thus, while it is clearly better to sell 1,000 copies at £100 than to sell 100 copies at £500, to pitch the price at £100 and then only sell 100 copies may well be disastrous.

Surprisingly, with most products and services, there is a danger of failing to win orders because the price is too *low*. Nowhere is this more true than in the software industry. This apparent paradox arises because customers usually have an idea of the price they expect to pay and will be suspicious of the quality of the product or the supplier's understanding of their requirements if the price is significantly less than expected.

3.7 Working capital and cash flow

It is perfectly possible for a company to be consistently profitable and yet be unable to pay its bills. This can arise because accounting normally operates on an *accrual* basis. In other words, the proceeds of a sale are treated as revenue from the moment that an invoice is issued, rather than when payment is received; similarly expenditure is treated as incurred at the moment that payment of an invoice is authorized rather than when payment leaves the company's bank account. Profit and loss, assets and liabilities are assessed on this basis.

We have already mentioned the large gap that can occur between issuing an invoice and receiving payment. Some of the delay is a consequence of the procedures which have to be carried out before the invoice is paid – checking that the goods or services have been received and meet their specifications and that their purchase was correctly authorized; some arises because payments to creditors are batched and only take place once or twice a month; and some arises because certain companies have a policy of delaying payment to creditors as long as possible.

A second reason why a profitable company may be unable to pay its bills is the value of its *work in progress*. The development of a large piece of bespoke software may take many months or even years; if the customer is not prepared to pay for it until it is delivered, the company producing it will have to pay the costs of the development before it receives payment and these may include costs of bought-in items. In such circumstances, it is usual to negotiate stage payments rather than leaving all payment until the work is completed. Nevertheless, stage payments rarely cover the full value of the work done up to the point that they are made. Typical arrangements for stage payments are described in Chapter 5. In a manufacturing company, stocks of finished goods and raw materials have to be financed in an analogous way.

Cash has therefore to be found to cover the gap between what a company has to pay out in cash and what it receives in cash. This is known as *working capital*. It is important to understand the difference between working capital, which is money needed to finance the company's day to day operations, and investment capital, which is capital used to enhance the company's productive capacity (e.g. by purchasing new machinery) or to develop new products.

In order to avoid the danger of the company being unable to pay its bills, it is necessary to ensure that sufficient cash will be available. This, in turn, requires the production of a *cash flow prediction*. Typically, such a document shows the amount of cash expected to be received and disbursed in each of the next twelve months, together with the cumulative position. A simple example is given in Table 3.4; note the common accounting convention that figures in parentheses are negative. The variation in cash received will be due to changes in the amount that the company is able to invoice in preceding months – cash received in month 4 depends on the amounts invoiced in months 1 and 2, according to the known payment records of its customers; the irregularity in cash disbursed will reflect such items as rent payable quarterly. From such a table the company's maximum requirement for working capital over the period covered by the prediction can be estimated; in this case it is £34,000. In contracting companies, where the forward cash position can be drastically affected by a single contract, the cash flow prediction will usually be revised monthly.

The commonest source of working capital is a bank overdraft. In contrast to other sorts of loans, the bank specifies the maximum that can be borrowed on an overdraft but interest is only payable on the amount actually owed. Furthermore, the bank can demand repayment of the overdraft at short notice. If a need for more working capital is foreseen, an

Table 3.4 Simple cash flow prediction (£).

Month	Cash in	Cash out	Net monthly cash flow	Cumulative cash flow
1	4,000	15,000	(11,000)	(11,000)
2	5,000	15,000	(10,000)	(21,000)
3	8,000	18,000	(10,000)	(31,000)
4	12,000	15,000	(3,000)	(34,000)
5	16,000	15,000	1,000	(33,000)
6	18,000	19,000	(1,000)	(34,000)
7	20,000	17,000	3,000	(31,000)
8	28,000	17,000	11,000	(20,000)
9	24,000	20,000	4,000	(16,000)
10	16,000	17,000	(1,000)	(17,000)
11	30,000	18,000	12,000	(5,000)
12	23,000	20,000	3,000	(2,000)

increase in the overdraft limit will need to be negotiated. Predicting this need well in advance will serve to convince the bank that the company is well managed and therefore make it more likely that the bank will agree to the request.

3.8 Assessing investment proposals

At any time, there are likely to be several proposals competing for investment resources in a company. They may range from a proposal to invest £100 million in the production of a new supercomputer to a proposal to invest £10,000 in equipping typists with word processors to increase their productivity. The amount of capital which a company can raise for investment purposes is always limited – lenders and investors will only provide capital commensurate with size of the company – and it is usually necessary, therefore, to select from the proposals on the table.

There is no single way of assessing and comparing the different proposals; factors that must be taken into consideration include, for example, the extent to which the proposals are consistent with the company's long-term plans; the risk attached to the proposals; and the availability of the necessary resources even if the money is available. One important criterion, however, is the financial one: which of the proposals will give the best return on the investment? The usual way of determining this is to use the method known as *discounted cash flow*.

Discounted cash flow (DCF) starts from the observation that a sum of money held now is worth more, even in the absence of inflation, than the right to the same sum of money at some time in the future: assuming a 3 per cent interest rate, in the absence of inflation, £100 held now is worth £103 in one year's time, or £100 in a year's time is worth £97.09 now. In general, if the cost of capital is r (expressed as a fraction such as 0.13, not a percentage), then the present value of a cash flow X due in t years' time is

$$\frac{X}{(1+r)^t}$$

The quantity $1/(1+r)^t$ is known as the *discount factor*.

The essence of investment is that money is spent now so as to produce benefits in the future; assuming those benefits can be quantified in monetary terms, we need to ask what is their *present* value. To do this, we calculate the net cash flows that the project will generate over each year of its life and convert these to a present day value. The sum of these gives the *net present value* (NPV) of the project; if the life of the project is n years and the cash flow in year i is X_i the NPV is

$$\sum_{i=0}^{i=n} X_i/(1+r)^i$$

The annual cash flows exclude interest charges on outstanding negative balances or interest receivable from positive balances because these are, in effect, taken into account by the process of calculating the NPV.

Provided that the effects of inflation are taken into account when predicting future cash flows, there is no need to make special provision for handling inflation in a DCF analysis. By using the monetary cost of capital (i.e. the interest rate actually paid), its effects are automatically taken into account. Alternatively, the analysis can be carried out assuming no change in general price levels but in this case the cost of capital should be taken as $(m - i)/(m + i)$ where m is the monetary cost of capital and i is the inflation rate.

As an example of simple DCF analysis, consider a company that is considering the development of a software product. It is estimated that three people will be required for development in the first year and a further person and a half in the second year; suitable staff cost £20,000 per year, including the employer's pension and National Insurance costs. The product will be released in the second year and it is expected that its life will be about four years. Maintenance is expected to require one person, full-time, for three years, dropping to a quarter of a person in the final year. Sales and marketing costs are estimated to be £10,000 in the first year, rising to £20,000 for the next three years and falling to £5,000 in the final year. The product itself is a fairly high value but specialized product. It is expected that about 85 copies will be sold in all, at somewhere between £3,000 and £5,000 a copy. Table 3.5 shows the DCF analysis for the proposal, using 10 per cent as the (monetary) cost of capital, and a selling price of £4,000.

The NPV of the project over its five year life is the cumulative present value shown in the bottom right hand entry, £67,620 but there are other measures of a project's attractiveness which can be deduced from this table.

Table 3.5 DCF analysis for a proposed product development (£).

	Year 0	Year 1	Year 2	Year 3	Year 4
Development cost	60,000	30,000	0	0	0
Maintenance	0	20,000	20,000	20,000	5,000
Sales and marketing	10,000	20,000	20,000	20,000	5,000
Number of sales	0	15	30	30	10
Revenue	0	60,000	120,000	120,000	40,000
Net cash flow	(70,000)	(10,000)	80,000	80,000	30,000
Discount factor	1	0.909	0.826	0.751	0.683
Present value	(70,000)	(9,091)	66,116	60,105	20,490
Cumulative present value	(70,000)	(79,091)	(12,975)	47,130	67,620

One is the *pay-back period*; this is the time required for the project to achieve a positive net cash flow. For the project in the table, this is four years, since the first positive cumulative cash flow is £47,130, at the end of year 3 (remembering that we start from year 0). We can also calculate the *internal rate of return* (IRR) on the project. This is the cost of capital which would lead to the NPV being precisely zero; it is calculated by solving the equation[5]

$$\sum_{i=0}^{i=n} X_i/(1+r)^i = 0$$

for r. The IRR is the maximum cost of capital at which the project would be viable. For the figures in the table it is 40.5 per cent.

A proposal will normally be rejected out of hand if its NPV is not positive, if its pay-back period is greater than some pre-set threshold or if its IRR is less than the current cost of capital. If there still remain projects between which a choice must be made, the organization should probably choose those which have the highest positive NPV. This, however, usually reflects a long term view and other pressures may cause companies to accept the projects with the highest IRRs or the shortest pay-back periods. (Note that a shorter pay-back period generally means less risk, because our assumptions about market conditions are likely to be more reliable over the shorter period.)

Because of its apparently precise nature, there is a tendency to put too much trust in DCF analysis. However precise the calculations, the cash flow predictions are inherently uncertain. An example of the case where uncertainty is comparatively low is the replacement of plant or equipment in the manufacturing or process industries. If the new plant is installed and functioning correctly by the scheduled date and if market conditions do not change dramatically, the cash flow predictions should be reasonably accurate and the major source of uncertainty is the cost of capital; there are, of course, plenty of occasions when the assumptions about installation of the plant and market conditions will prove false but this is likely to be the exception rather than the rule.

If we use DCF analysis to assess a proposal for developing a software product, as we have done above, then the sources of uncertainty are very much greater. Although a net present value of £67,620 and an IRR of 40.5 per cent look attractive, we must take into account that:

- the development may take more resources than estimated;
- the product may not be in a marketable state until later than predicted;

---

5. The solution of this equation involves some non-trivial numerical analysis. Fortunately, most widely used spreadsheets include a facility for carrying out the calculation of the IRR.

- sales may not follow the predicted pattern;
- a competing product may be launched before the product being assessed is available.

It is important, therefore, to carry out a series of DCF analyses with different estimates of the cash flows and the discount rate in order to assess the sensitivity of the results to such changes. If the project remains attractive under the different sets of assumptions, it is comparatively low risk; if it becomes unattractive under small changes, then it is high risk and should probably be rethought. In the given example, if the sales in years 2, 3 and 4 drop to 20, 20 and 5 respectively, the cash flow never becomes positive. Predicting sales this far ahead is very uncertain, so the project should be regarded as high risk. On the other hand, if the sales in years 2 and 3 reach 40, the NPV rises to £130,731. This sensitivity to changes in sales volumes is characteristic of software product developments.

3.9 Annual statements

The Companies Act 1985 requires all limited companies to produce annual accounts and to give a copy of them to the Registrar of Companies for filing; the public has access to these files. The Companies Act further requires that the company accounts should include a balance sheet, a profit and loss account and an auditor's report. It also requires the disclosure of a substantial amount of supplementary information. Companies which fall below certain size thresholds are exempt from some of these provisions. As mentioned in Section 2.2.3, companies whose shares are traded on a stock exchange are also subject to disclosure rules imposed by the stock exchange; these requirements are more stringent than those imposed by the Companies Act.

While the Companies Act places general requirements regarding the disclosure of financial information relating to companies, the details of how this information should be prepared and presented are governed by accounting standards. Until July 1990, these were promulgated by the Accounting Standards Committee (ASC), a joint committee of the six major professional accountancy bodies in the British Isles: the Institutes of Chartered Accountants in England and Wales, of Scotland and in Ireland; the Association of Certified Accountants; the Institute of Cost and Management Accountants; and the Chartered Institute of Public Finance and Accountancy. Its membership also included "user" representatives, drawn from such bodies as the banks, the Stock Exchange and the Confederation of British Industries.

The ASC prepared draft Statements of Standard Accounting Practice (SSAP); these were then adopted by the professional bodies and it became incumbent on their members to adhere to them or to justify any deviation from them. The ASC has now been replaced by a more independent body, the Accounting Standards Board. The SSAPSs are being replaced by Financial Reporting Standards (FRS). These standards often allow a wide variation in practice and leave much scope for individual judgement.

3.9.1 The balance sheet

A balance sheet is a snapshot of the financial state of an organization at single instant – normally the end of an organization's financial year. It shows the value of what the organization owns (the assets) and what it owes (the liabilities). To illustrate this in simple terms, Table 3.6 shows the personal balance sheet for an imaginary student. As is usual, the balance sheet also shows the position twelve months previously, for comparison purposes.

At first sight, the assets part of this balance sheet contains one or two surprising items. The accommodation item refers to the fact that the student has paid a term's fees to the hall of residence in advance; since the balance sheet refers to the position on 31 October, some 60 per cent (six weeks out of ten) of this accommodation has not been used. Depending on the regulations of the hall, if the accommodation is no longer required, the student may be able to get a refund on the unused period or sell it to another student; in other words, the student has paid for the right to live in hall for a further six weeks and this right can be converted into cash and is therefore an asset. In a similar

Table 3.6 Balance sheet for a student (£).

Kenneth Widmerpool Balance Sheet As at 31 October 1999	1999	1998
ASSETS		
Cash in hand	32.50	41.30
Cash at bank	271.15	175.42
CD player and discs	120.00	
Books	40.00	50.00
Bicycle	60.00	65.00
Pre-paid accommodation	300.00	280.00
Debts owed by friends	12.00	
Total assets	835.65	611.72
LIABILITIES		
Credit card bill	124.31	51.22
Student loans	4,200.00	1,300.00
Total liabilities	4,324.31	1,351.22
NET WORTH	(3,488.66)	(739.50)

way, the debt of £12 owed by friends can be turned into cash and is also therefore an asset.

The valuation of assets can be a contentious issue. For the moment we shall simply accept the figures given in the balance sheet but we shall have much more to say on this topic when we come to look at a commercial balance sheet.

As its name suggests, a balance sheet must balance: the total assets and total liabilities should be equal. To achieve this we need to include a *balancing item* on one side or the other; it is often labelled "excess of assets over liabilities" but in this case we have chosen to call it "net worth" because it represents the amount of cash which the student would have if all assets were sold and all debts paid off – in other words, how much the student is "worth". The net worth plus the liabilities together equal the student's total assets.

Commercial balance sheets

Commercial balance sheets are prepared on precisely the same basis as we have just described but the assets and liabilities are grouped into various categories and a single figure is given for each category. There will be several "notes" to the balance sheet describing the basis of the accounts and giving more detail about certain items; such items will cross reference the notes. Table 3.7 is an example of such a balance sheet for an imaginary software services company but no notes have been included.

Assets are classified as current assets and fixed assets. The essential difference between the two is that fixed assets contribute to the company's productive capacity while current assets are items which are bought and sold in the course of its day-to-day trading activities. The fixed assets are further subdivided into investments (e.g. shares in other companies), tangible assets (assets which have some physical existence) and intangible assets (assets such as copyrights in literary works, which have no physical existence).

In most cases the difference between fixed assets and current assets is easily perceived. A new computer bought to provide program development facilities in a software house or a machine tool used to produce printer barrels are clearly examples of fixed assets; a stock of paper for the laser printer is equally clearly a current asset. It should be borne in mind, however, that the treatment of the same item may vary from organization to organization or even within the same organization. Thus, if a company buys a car to enable one of its salesmen to operate more effectively, this is a fixed asset but, if a car dealer buys a car in order to resell it as part of his business, this is a current asset. If the software house buys a computer on which it will implement special software before delivering the whole system to a client, the computer is a current asset, not a fixed one.

Table 3.7 Balance sheet for a services company (£'000)

XYZ Software Ltd *Balance Sheet* *As at 31 October 1999*	*1999*	*1998*
FIXED ASSETS		
Intangible assets	475	–
Tangible assets	960	770
Investments	50	82
Total fixed assets	1,485	852
CURRENT ASSETS		
Work in progress	550	621
Debtors	3,400	2,580
Cash in hand and at bank	2,491	1,770
Total current assets	6,441	4,971
CREDITORS: AMOUNTS FALLING DUE WITHIN ONE YEAR	(3,210)	(2,601)
Net current assets	3,231	2,370
Total assets less current liabilities	4,716	3,222
CREDITORS: AMOUNTS FALLING DUE AFTER ONE YEAR		
Borrowings	(154)	(61)
Provisions for liabilities and charges	(7)	(16)
Net assets	4,555	3,145
CAPITAL AND RESERVES		
Called up share capital	318	308
Share premium reserve	350	145
Profit and loss account	3,887	2,692
Shareholders' funds – equity	4,555	3,145

Fixed assets

Fixed assets will be shown as such on the balance sheet and will be depreciated over the years according to the company's normal practice. They will be recorded in the company's fixed asset register and, from time to time, their presence will be physically checked. If a fixed asset is sold for a sum higher than its depreciated value then the company must show the difference as profit. Because of these complicated procedures, it is usual to treat all purchases of less than, say, £1,000 as expenses in the year in which they are incurred.

There are some items which are difficult to classify. Bought-in software is one such example. If a company commissions the development of bespoke software, at a cost which can easily run into hundreds of thousands, if not millions, of pounds, it usually expects that this will increase its productive capacity, in one way or another. In other words, it should be treated as a fixed asset and its cost written off over its expected useful life. However, it is not uncommon to see such purchases written off in the year of purchase, unless the software has been bought as part of a complete system including hardware. The rationale for this would seem to be that the staff costs of a company's DP department are usually treated as part of the costs of its day-to-day operations, since much of its activity is indeed part and parcel of these operations; the result is that software developed in the DP department is not treated as a fixed asset. Software commissioned from an external contractor is usually procured in this way as an alternative to developing it "in-house" and it is therefore treated in the same way. However, the Finance (No. 2) Act 1992 explicitly provides for bought-in software to be treated on a par with plant and machinery for the purpose of claiming capital allowances[6] and, since the end of 1998, both bought-in software and software developed in-house are included in the national accounts; with such official encouragement, it is likely that the capitalization of expenditure on software will become more common.

A particular problem is presented by the capitalization (i.e. treatment as a fixed asset) of research and development (R & D). On the one hand, expenditure on R & D is usually intended to improve the company's productive capacity; its results should therefore be treated as a fixed asset. On the other hand, the level of uncertainty in R & D is so high that any valuation is potentially misleading. The formal position is that R & D expenditure should be written off in the year in which the costs are incurred with the exception of development expenditure associated with specific marketing plans for a commercially viable product, which may be capitalized. In the USA, there are strict rules regarding the capitalization of software that is developed for sale; these rules are based on a rather unrealistic model of the product life cycle. In the UK, a variety of different treatments are acceptable, including the US one.

Intangible fixed assets are the source of much discussion in the accounting profession. Software is generally regarded as an intangible asset but it is more tangible than many items, brand names, for example, which are often shown as intangible assets. An item that frequently appears under intangible assets on the balance sheets of software product companies is goodwill. This might arise, for example, if XYZ Ltd purchased another company, PQR Ltd, that owned the rights in a profitable package. If, as is likely, the package was not

6. Special tax allowances for capital expenditure, intended to encourage investment.

shown as an asset on PQR's balance sheet, XYZ would probably have paid much more to buy PQR than the value of its net assets. The difference between the price paid for PQR and the value of its net assets represents XYZ's estimate of the value of the rights in that package (and, possibly, other things such as the value of PQR's name). This needs to be shown on XYZ's balance sheet. While it would be preferable for the value of the package to be shown explicitly, this is not normal practice and the whole of the difference between the purchase price and the value of PQR's net assets is normally shown under the heading of goodwill. It will then, of course, need to be amortized over a fixed period. The notes to a company's accounts will normally itemize any acquisitions and give details of the goodwill arising from each one. When Internet companies change hands a similar situation occurs but, in this case, the intangible assets may be much more difficult to identify; they are certainly less tangible than the rights to a package.

In contrast to current assets, fixed assets are part of the company's productive capacity; they are not therefore expected to be sold in normal trading operations and resale value is irrelevant; what is needed is a measure of their value to the company. In practice, this is done by reducing their value each year in accordance with the company's depreciation policy. The value of certain types of fixed assets, in particular property, may increase rather than decrease. Public companies therefore usually arrange to have their property revalued at regular intervals (typically every five years or so) and include this valuation in the balance sheet.

Current assets

The rules for valuing current assets are very different from those for valuing fixed assets. Current assets must be valued at the lower of cost and net realizable value (the money that would be obtained by selling them, less any expenses of the sale). This is appropriate because current assets are part of the company's day-to-day trading operations and are expected to be sold. In the case of bespoke software acquired by a company and treated as a current asset, its resale value is probably nil – bespoke software is usually of use only to the company that commissioned it and the scrap value of used software is zero; it will not therefore appear in the balance sheet.

Manufacturing companies will usually have items in their list of current assets covering stocks of finished products, i.e. stocks of whatever it is they produce that have not yet been sold to customers, and stocks of raw materials. Contracting companies will usually have an item for "amounts recoverable on contracts" or "work in progress", that is work being carried out under contract to clients that has not yet been billed. The valuation of any of these items is subject to a degree of uncertainty. The finished goods have not yet been sold; it might prove impossible to sell them. The work in progress value on a software contract may be based on the assumption that the software is 90 per cent complete but software projects have been known to remain 90 per cent complete for a very long time.

Over-optimistic valuation of stock or of work in progress was followed by two spectacular company collapses in the 1970s. In the case of Pergamon Press, large stocks of expensive scientific books, translated from the Russian, were valued at their selling price, despite the fact that there was little likelihood of selling them. In the case of Rolls Royce, a new generation of aero-engines was being produced under a fixed price contract; the work in progress was valued on the basis of the resources so far expended, rather than on the basis of the resources required to complete the work; the difference between the two valuations was substantial. In both cases, the companies ran out of cash and their bankers refused to provide further loans once the true situation became apparent. In the case of Pergamon, the incorrect valuation appeared to have been deliberate, and hence fraudulent[7]; in the case of Rolls Royce it was simple incompetence.

Liabilities

The liabilities section of a commercial balance sheet effectively distinguishes between current liabilities, which are those which fall due within twelve months of the date of the balance sheet and long-term liabilities. (Note that the difference is also apparent in the student's balance sheet, where there is a clear difference between the debt to the credit card company, which has to be repaid quickly, and the student loan, which does not.) The current liabilities will usually be those that have been incurred in the company's normal trading operations while the long-term liabilities will arise from funds borrowed for investment in fixed assets. However, even a long-term loan eventually comes to its final year and will then appear under current liabilities. It is usual to arrange current liabilities next to current assets in the balance sheet so that they can be deducted to give a figure for "net current assets".

The phrase "provisions for liabilities and charges" refers to items which the company knows it will have to pay but whose precise amount may be uncertain; this may include tax on previous years' earnings which has still to be assessed or work which may have to be carried out by the company under warranty.

After deducting the short- and long-term liabilities, we are left with a figure that shows the company's net assets, what we called the net worth in the case

---

7. It was the collapse of the Pergamon group that led Department if Industry inspectors to describe the late Captain Robert Maxwell as "unfit to be a director of a public company", despite which condemnation he was subsequently permitted to become chairman of Mirror Group, with the now well known consequences.

of our student. In the case of a company, it is customary to show how these net assets have come about. In the example shown, there are three items. Called-up share capital is simply the face value of the shares that have been issued; the figure from the profit and loss account is simply the total value of the profits and losses made by the company since it was established; and the share premium reserve is the extra money raised when shares have been sold at above their face value.

3.9.2 Profit and loss account

A *profit and loss account* (usually called an *income and expenditure* account in the case of non-profit making organizations) shows what has happened to an organization's financial position over a period of time – usually, again, the organization's financial year; it records the money received and the money spent. Table 3.8 shows such an account for our imaginary student. It is important to observe that the excess of expenditure over income, that is, the amount that the student has overspent, is the same as the difference in his net worth between 1998 and 1999. This will usually be the case in simple situations where there has been no capital investment. In more complicated cases, particularly with commercial organizations, other items enter into the relationship.

Table 3.8 Income and expenditure account for a student (£).

Kenneth Widmerpool Income and Expenditure Account Year ended 31 October 1999	1999	1998
INCOME		
Contribution from parents	1,000.00	1,000.00
Income from summer job (net)	1,851.35	1,467.43
Total income	2,851.35	2,467.43
EXPENDITURE		
Course fees	1,025.00	1,000.00
Hall fees	1,980.00	1,850.00
Transport	125.78	101.32
Food	1,203.40	990.38
Entertainment	1,261.33	840.25
Depreciation	30.00	30.00
Total expenditure	5,600.51	4,811.95
EXCESS OF INCOME OVER EXPENDITURE	(2,749.16)	(2,344.52)

Just as in the balance sheet, there is a certain arbitrariness about the way in which items have been aggregated. We could, for example, have lumped together "Food" and "Entertainment" under the heading "Living Expenses" or have split "Transport" into "Road" and "Rail". We have chosen to show the income from the summer job net (i.e. the take home pay) rather than show it gross with tax and national insurance on the expenditure side.

Some explanation of the depreciation item is required. The net figure at the bottom of the profit and loss account should reflect the extent to which the organization – or, in this case, the individual – is better or worse off at the end of the year than at the beginning. Clearly, a fall in the value of the assets tends to make it worse off. Depreciation, although it is not an expenditure in the sense that cash is paid out, reflects this decline and is therefore shown as an expenditure.

Commercial profit and loss accounts

Although the same basic idea underlies a commercial profit and loss account, its appearance is very different from the one above. Table 3.9 shows an example for our fictitious computer services company. Just as with the balance sheet, we see that items have been aggregated into very broad categories; the notes to the accounts will usually provide more detail. A package

Table 3.9. Profit and loss account for a services company (£'000).

XYZ Software Ltd Profit and Loss Account Year ending 31 October 1999	1999	1998
TURNOVER		
Continuing operations	14,311	11,001
Acquisitions	407	
Total turnover	14,718	11,001
Cost of sales	(11,604)	(8,699)
Gross profit	3,114	2,302
Other operating expenses	(1,177)	(805)
OPERATING PROFIT	1,937	1,497
Interest payable	(23)	(27)
Profit on ordinary activities before taxation	1,914	1,470
Tax on profit on ordinary activities	719	480
Retained profit for the year	1,195	990

company, for example, might show in the notes how much of its income came from sales of packages, how much from training and consultancy, and how much from maintenance contracts.

A number of points about this statement need to be explained. First, the turnover for a company acquired during the year is shown separately from the turnover from continuing operations, that is, operations that were carried on in 1998 and 1999. This is to facilitate the comparison between the two years. In the same way, if part of XYZ Ltd had been disposed of in 1998, its turnover would have been shown under the heading 'discontinued operations'.

A second point is the distinction between 'cost of sales' and 'other operating expenses'. This distinction is an uncertain one and some companies do not show the items separately. However, for a package software company, there is a real difference between, on the one hand, expenditure on selling, printing documentation, installing software, and so on, all of which are the costs of sales, and expenditure on the development of new versions of existing packages or on new products, which would come under the heading of other operational expenses.

The bottom line of the profit and loss account shows the retained profit for the year, that is the profit not paid out in tax or dividends to shareholders; this is added to the cumulative retained profit in the previous year's balance sheet to give the value of the retained profit shown in the new balance sheet.

The profit and loss account gives very little information about where the company's revenue during the year has come from or how it has spent its money. Such information is normally given in the notes to the accounts. The 1997 Annual Report and Accounts of Logica plc, for example, gives a breakdown of turnover and profit by geographic area – UK, continental Europe, North America, and Asia Pacific/Middle East. It shows numbers of staff and expenditure on wages and salaries, on social security costs, and pension costs and other costs are also broken down into a number of categories. Package companies will often also show a breakdown of revenue into licence fees, maintenance charges, and consultancy fees – see, for example, the 1998 Accounts of London Bridge Software Holdings plc. On the whole, software companies are fairly open in revealing information in the notes to their accounts but the level of detail provided in other sectors varies enormously from company to company.

3.9.3 Other statements

The perceived need for greater openness and more extensive disclosure of companies activities has led to the inclusion of further statements and more extensive notes in companies' annual reports. Some are required by stock markets and some have simply become regarded as good practice. On the whole, but by no means universally, software companies set good examples in this regard.

The most important of the new statements is the cash flow statement. As we have already pointed out, the income and expenditure account does not show expenditure on capital items, only their depreciation; capital expenditure affects the balance sheet but the balance sheet does not give sufficient information to deduce how much this expenditure amounts to and how it was funded. The link which ties the balance sheet and the profit and loss account to the capital expenditure is the cash flow statement. A moment's examination of our student's financial statements will reveal that, because there is no cash flow statement, there is no explanation of where the money to purchase his CD player came from.

The cash flow statement (Table 3.10) explains the change in "cash" between the dates of two successive balance sheets. Cash is defined[8] as "cash at bank and in hand and cash equivalents less bank overdrafts and other borrowings repayable within one year of the accounting date".

The first source of cash is the operating profit before tax generated during the year. This needs to be adjusted for certain items which may appear in

Table 3.10 Cash flow statement for a services company (£'000).

XYZ Software Ltd Cash Flow Statement Year ending 31 October 1999	1999	1998
NET CASH INFLOW FROM OPERATING ACTIVITIES	2,105	1,620
Returns on investments and servicing of finance	(23)	(27)
Capital expenditure and financial investment	(320)	(265)
Taxation	(719)	(480)
Acquisitions and disposals	(380)	
Equity dividends paid		
Cash outflow before financing	(1,342)	(772)
NET CASH INFLOW BEFORE FINANCING	763	848
FINANCING		
Issue of share capital	215	100
Repayment of long term loan	(50)	
Net cash inflow from financing	165	100
INCREASE IN CASH IN THE YEAR	928	948

8. In SSAP 10.

the profit and loss account but do not involve the movement of money in or out of the company. The most obvious of these is depreciation. This was entered in the profit and loss account to reflect the extent to which the life of the fixed assets was consumed during the year; in no way did it reflect the movement of money out of the company and so it must be added to the profit.

Following the adjusted figure for the operating profit, there are a number of items that may lead to cash flowing out of the company for reasons that are nothing directly to do with its operations. Taxation, interest payable and dividends paid are obvious examples. Capital investment in equipment or premises is another reason for which cash may flow out of the company, as is the purchase of another company. In some circumstances, e.g., the disposal of a subsidiary company, these items can give rise to an inflow of cash. When all these items are added together and subtracted from the operating profit, we arrive at a total figure for the inflow or outflow of cash into or out of the company before taking into account any changes in the financing of the company. The final section of the cash flow statement shows the effect on the cash position of changes in the financing of the company. The company has issued new shares and raised £215,000 through this; it has also paid off £50,000 of long term debt. Both of these, of course, affect its cash position and the bottom line of the cash flow statement reflects this; it gives the overall change in the company's cash position over the year.

The alert reader will recall that XYZ's balance sheet shows that, despite the fact that a loan of £50,000 has been paid off, the long-term debt has increased from £61,000 to £154,000 and that there is nothing in the cash flow statement to account for this. It almost certainly arises from the acquisition of another company. The statement shows that £380,000 was spent on acquisitions; the likelihood is that the company bought substantial debts, which were taken over by XYZ as part of the deal.

At this point we should make clear that the financial statements for XYZ Software Ltd show a vigorous company growing very rapidly in an expanding market; they are typical of many IT services companies in the 1990s but not typical of many other industries.

3.9.4 Historical cost and current cost

So far, in our description of annual statements we have ignored the fact that prices change over time. In saying that current assets are valued at cost or net realizable value, whichever is the lower, we implicitly assumed that the word "cost" meant the amount of money paid for the asset, what is known as the *historical cost*. This assumption was built into accounting practice from the start but, in periods of high inflation, it can lead to annual statements giving a very distorted view of a company's financial affairs. Concern over this led to extensive discussions and consultations and eventually to the issue of SSAP 16[9] laying down guidelines for *current cost* accounting and requiring that certain categories of "large" companies include accounts prepared on this basis in their annual statements.

To illustrate the problems caused by historical cost accounting, consider the simple case of a retailer who buys refrigerators from a wholesaler and sells them to the public. Suppose that, on 1 January 1998, he has £4,000 and no refrigerators in stock. On 2 January, he buys 20 refrigerators for £200 each, which he sells during the year for £300 each; on 31 December, he has £6,000 and no refrigerators. Since he is in the same position on 1 January 1999 as he was on 1 January 1998, except that he now has £6,000 instead of £4,000, it is reasonable to conclude that he has made a profit of £2,000 over the period 1 January to 31 December 1998. Delighted with his business acumen, he goes out on 2 January 1999 to buy another 20 refrigerators.

Suppose now the price of refrigerators to the retailer has increased to £300 during 1998. The 20 refrigerators he buys on 2 January 1999 will cost him all of his £6,000. If we take the results of his trading from 3 January 1998 to 2 January 1999, we see that his position is unchanged; in both cases he has 20 refrigerators and no money. In other words, it would appear that he has made no profit over the period.

The solution to this apparent paradox is, of course, that the £6,000 that he has on 31 December 1998 is only "worth" the same as the £4,000 that he had on 1 January 1998 – at least, in terms of its power to buy refrigerators. However, it illustrates graphically the distortion that can be introduced by the historical cost basis.

The problems of taking inflation into account in financial statements are many and subtle; they are beyond the scope of this chapter but the interested reader is referred to the Further Reading section for books which cover the topic in more detail.

3.10 Capital and its maintenance

The concept of *capital maintenance* is subtle but it has important practical consequences. The capital subscribed by members of the company is to be seen as a (rather ineffective) guarantee that the company will be able to meet its obligations. Certainly, a lender is likely to take the size of the issued share capital of the company into account when deciding whether or not to make a loan. For this reason, a company is not allowed to issue shares at a discount, i.e. for less than their nominal value, because this would lead to the actual capital received by the company being less than the issued share

---

9. Now withdrawn!

capital[10]. Similarly, a company cannot pay back to the shareholders any of their original contribution. The practical consequence of this is that a dividend must not be paid to shareholders unless the company has "profits available for the purpose", that is, the algebraic sum of the realized and retained profits and losses over the lifetime of the company is positive. "Retained" means not previously paid out in the form of dividends or tax. The term "realized" is relevant because, in the case of profits and losses made on the disposal of fixed assets, a realized profit or loss occurs only when the asset is actually disposed of, not when its value in the company's books changes. The effect of these rules is that the company's capital can only be eroded by the losses it makes, not by any payment to shareholders.

If the accounting is done on the basis of historical cost, capital is maintained only in terms of money values. A profit is recorded when the money value of the net assets at the end of the year exceeds the money value of the net assets at the start of the year. Alternative approaches might be to say that the productive capacity of the company must be maintained or that the purchasing power of the net assets must be maintained; either of these approaches seems more realistic than simply maintaining the money value of the capital. Nevertheless, the practical difficulties of such approaches are considerable.

3.11 Auditing[11]

The Companies Act 1989 requires that company accounts should be accompanied by an auditors' report. The purpose of the report is to provide members of the company and the public at large with an assurance that, in the opinion of the auditors, the accounts give a "true and fair view" of the state of the affairs of the company. With one or two minor exceptions, only members of the three Institutes of Chartered Accountants (in England and Wales, of Scotland and in Ireland) and of the Association of Certified Accountants are eligible for appointment as auditors and they must satisfy certain criteria of independence of the company.

It is not practicable for auditors to check every financial transaction that has taken place during the year. Instead they work by examining the ade-

---

10. As was mentioned in Chapter 2, a company can issue shares partly paid but in this case the shareholder is obliged to pay the unpaid amount when called on to do so, which will certainly happen if the company goes into liquidation.

11. In recent years the meaning of the term "audit" has been extended and it is widely used to cover the external checking of any type of company procedure; thus a "quality audit" of a project may be carried out to ensure that the project is operating in accordance with the company's quality control procedures.

quacy of the company's financial procedures and controls and by making detailed checks on a small sample of transactions, to see that they have been carried out in accordance with the procedures, and on a sample of the assets, to ensure that they exist. The latter may involve, for example, contacting some of the company's debtors to confirm that they agree that they owe money to the company or checking that what is claimed to be a ton of tungsten is indeed tungsten and not some much cheaper metal. In addition, analytical review procedures are used to confirm the reasonableness of the total figures shown in the annual statement.

It is important to understand the limits of auditors' responsibilities, a topic addressed at some length in the Cadbury Report (see Section 2.2.4). First of all, accounting standards permit the figures in the annual statements to be presented in a variety of different ways. The auditors' responsibility is limited to certifying that the accounts have been prepared in accordance with these standards; auditors have no authority to question whether the particular choices are the most appropriate for the company, provided that they are used consistently. While it may be hoped that the Accounting Standards Board will impose tighter standards, it can only do this if it can obtain a reasonable consensus in favour of changes; the many special interests involved make this difficult.

Secondly, there is the issue of whether the company is a "going concern". In other words, is the company likely to survive its next financial year? It is perfectly possible to imagine the circumstances in which the balance sheet and the profit and loss account present a picture of a healthy bespoke software house, which the auditors can certify is true and fair, and yet the company has little chance of surviving the next twelve months – consider, for example, a company which has been totally dependent on a single, large and lucrative contract that is just ending, with no further business on the horizon. If auditors have reason to suspect that the company is not a going concern, they are expected to carry out procedures to test the position, typically by examining cash flow predictions and seeking assurances that suitable credit facilities will be available over the next twelve months. But if they have no such suspicions, they are not required to take such action. Both the Cadbury Report and Auditing Practices Board have made recommendations that would mean more positive statements, properly justified, would have to be produced.

The primary responsibility for preventing and detecting fraud lies with the directors of the company, not with the auditors. Auditors, however, do have a responsibility to do their work in such a way as to have a reasonable expectation of finding anything seriously misleading in the financial statements and, of course, if they find evidence of fraud, they have a duty to report it to the directors. Larger organizations employ internal auditors who have the responsibility of ensuring that company financial procedures are properly followed and of preventing fraud.

In addition to the question of the duties and responsibilities of auditors, a second area of concern addressed by the Cadbury Report is the independence of auditors. Although the auditors are formally appointed by the shareholders and report to them, the nature of their work inevitably means that they will develop a continuing relationship with the management of the company rather than with the shareholders. It may well be that the firm carrying out the audit will also be undertaking other types of work for the company. Suggestions have been made that an auditing firm should be prohibited from undertaking non-audit work for its audit clients and that companies should be required to change their auditors every few years. The Cadbury Report rejected these suggestions but recommended that fees paid to auditors for both audit and non-audit work should be shown separately in the accounts and that audit *partners* (i.e. the partner in the auditing firm who takes responsibility for the audit) should rotate.

3.12 Further reading

A much more extensive treatment of the material in this chapter will be found in

Blackstaff, M. 1999. *Finance for IT decision makers: a practical handbook for buyers, sellers, and managers*. London: Springer Verlag.

It is, however, aimed more at IT managers in large user organizations than at entrepreneurs in small high technology companies.

The annual reports and accounts of software companies are well worth reading in order to get an overall view of the industry and its finances. They are readily available either in hard copy, through services offered by, amongst others, the *Financial Times* and various stockbrokers with a presence on the Internet, or they can be accessed directly at the companies' web sites. (Hard copy is often more reliable; the notes to the accounts are often omitted on the web site.) As a starting point we suggest looking at Logica, Cedardata, Admiral, Kalamazoo, London Bridge, and Sage.

The accounting practices in the US software industry are dealt with very fully in:

Morris, J. M. 1992. *Software industry accounting*. Wiley. Somerset, NJ: Wiley.

It addresses the important question of software revenue recognition, i.e. the point at which software revenue can safely be recognized in a company's accounts but it does not, unfortunately, address the question of software developed in house, for internal use.

There are innumerable books on accounting that will take the reader beyond what is covered in this chapter. The material in Sections 3.1, 3.2, 3.9, 3.10, and 3.11 is usually described as financial accounting; a good treatment for non-specialists will be found in:

Atrill, P. & E. McLaney 1999. *Financial accounting for non-specialists*. 2nd Edn. Prentice Hall.

Two good books on management accounting, which is the subject of Sections 3.3 to 3.8, are:

Upchurch, A. 1998. *Management accounting: principles and practice*. London: Financial Times/Pitman
Williamson, D. 1996. *Cost and management accounting*. Prentice Hall.

Chapter 4

Anatomy of a software house

The purpose of this chapter is to study in detail a hypothetical company in order to understand the application, in practice, of some of the ideas described in the two previous chapters. Although the company is hypothetical, it is based on the author's experiences in the software industry.

4.1 The company

Syniad Software Ltd was founded some ten years ago by four friends and colleagues who still own most of the shares in the company; all four are members of the Board of Directors, along with two others who were recruited later.

The company specializes in the production of bespoke software for clients who demand work of high quality; much of this work is advanced, in the sense that it demands the use of techniques that have only recently been developed or, in some cases, demands the development of completely new techniques. Along with this development work, there is a significant amount of consultancy work in similar areas.

Syniad's head office is some 40 miles west of London. An office south of Manchester was opened in 1993 and some 40 staff are based there. An office was opened in Delft in the Netherlands in 1996; the only staff based there are its manager, a salesman and a secretary but a number of contracts have been won and carried out using UK-based staff.

4.2 Company structure

The top level structure of the company is shown in Figure 4.1.

The Operations Director is responsible for all the revenue earning operations of the company. It is his job to ensure that all projects are completed satisfactorily and that resources are available to carry out the projects that the company wins; he is also responsible for ensuring that the utilization of

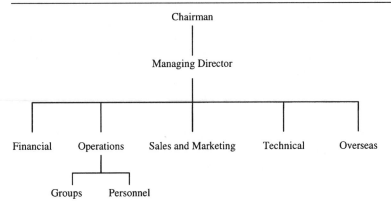

Figure 4.1 Syniad's top management structure.

revenue earning staff is kept at a satisfactory level. As is natural, given these responsibilities, the personnel function reports to him.

The Technical Director is responsible for:

- quality management;
- research and development;
- marketing at a technical level (e.g. arranging for staff to give papers at conferences);
- technical training (as opposed to training in, say, project management or presentational skills, which are the responsibility of the personnel function).

Some aspects of this structure deserve comment.

The separation of responsibility for quality management from responsibility for day-to-day operations is much to be commended; as we have said in Chapter 2, such separation is essential for effective quality control. The division of responsibility for training could potentially lead to conflict, as could the division of responsibility for marketing. In practice, there are few problems because the individuals in question have good personal relationships with each other and take care to discuss all areas of possible conflict.

More problems arise from the position of the personnel function. There is, inevitably, a tension between the Operations Director's desire to maximize staff utilization and revenue, on the one hand, and the individual employee's career aspirations on the other. A specialist in IBM mainframe software may feel, for example, that career opportunities in that field are limited and wish to gain experience of other types of hardware; however, so long as the company has projects which involve IBM mainframes, such a specialist can command a higher charging rate when used on such work and it will therefore be in the interests of the Operations Director not to provide the opportunity to move to other work. Similar problems arise when the Operations Director wants an individual to work abroad but the individual's personal circumstances make this inconvenient or undesirable. The personnel function should be able to act as an intermediary in these circumstances but it is difficult for it to do so while it reports directly to the Operations Director.

A similar tension may also exist between the Operations Director's short-term objectives and the longer term goals of the company. It is sometimes said that the art of running a software house is the art of matching people to projects in an optimal way; what is optimal depends, of course, on individuals' aspirations and the organization's strategic plans, as well as short-term needs.

The groups are each managed by a group manager; a group consists of somewhere between 15 and 50 staff working in a reasonably homogeneous area. Some groups serve specific market sectors, such as banking, while others (usually the smaller ones) cover specific technical specialities such as databases. When potential new business is identified, it is assigned to a specific group. This group will then be responsible for providing the sales staff with the support necessary to win the business and for carrying out the contract when it is won. In theory at least, staff have a sense of belonging to a group and regard their group manager as the manager who is permanently responsible for their career in the company. In practice, because projects often require expertise from more than one group, staff often find themselves working on projects for groups other than the one to which they belong and the sense of group identity is diluted.

This points up what is perhaps the most serious problem of organizational structure which Syniad faces, what we may term "clashing structures". Consider what happens if the company is asked to bid for installing a communications system for a bank in the Netherlands. The manager of the Dutch office will have made the initial contact and has local knowledge which will be essential if the contract is to be won. However, in order to put together a credible bid, he will need assistance from specialists in the market sector (banking) and in the technology (communications); he may well need assistance also, perhaps in the form of copies of proposals from similar bids in the past, from the sales and marketing staff at Head Office. He himself reports principally to the Overseas Director but has to keep the Operations Director satisfied about the running of projects and the staff utilization, the Sales and Marketing Director happy about sales and the Finance Director content with the way in which the Dutch company's finances are handled. Inevitably, this gives rise to conflicts over priorities.

It is worth remarking that Syniad's organizational structure shows elements of all three of the types of organizational structure described in Section 2.3. At board level, there is a basically a functional division of responsibilities but with a geographical element represented by the director responsible for overseas operations. Within the operations division, the group structure is analogous to a product line organization in a manufacturing company. In a company of the size of Syniad, the distinction between centralization and decentralization has little meaning. Centralized policies and procedures are widely used but they have usually been developed within one part of the company and have been adopted by general consent.

4.3 Management of staff

Management of staff has been critical to Syniad's success so far and will remain so in the future. The company's ability to expand depends on its ability to recruit and retain staff; its reputation in the market place depends on the quality of its staff. The directors and senior management are well aware of this and much time and effort is devoted to it.

When the company was small, with less than about 50 staff, there were few problems. The directors knew all the staff personally and most had been recruited through personal contacts. Staff were loyal to the company and this loyalty showed itself in a willingness to work unpaid overtime when necessary and to maintain high technical standards regardless of the extent of supervision. For their part, the directors put a lot of effort into keeping all employees informed about the company's activities and were able to take a sympathetic attitude to any personal problems that arose. Although the company was not able to organize much training itself, it encouraged and was willing to pay for staff to go on training courses provided by other organizations. Almost no one left the company during this period.

As the company grew, problems became apparent. Although the general quality of the staff remained high, it was inevitable that some recruits proved to be less able and less industrious than expected. The directors were not able to build up the same level of personal relationships with the new staff and loyalty to the company diminished. Because of the high quality of the original staff, many of them were now in senior positions; this, together with their long-standing personal ties with the directors, led newer staff to feel that the company was run by a clique and that they would always remain outsiders. Although this feeling was patently contrary to the facts – many senior staff were recent recruits – it was not conducive to building up company loyalty. The rate at which staff were leaving the company became a cause for concern.

Management reacted swiftly to these problems. Staff appraisal procedures were set up with the object of ensuring that:

- employees' achievements and contributions to the company were properly recorded;
- staff knew what was expected of them and what they needed to achieve in order to gain promotion;

- proper plans for training and career development were made and regularly reviewed;
- employees were aware of the company's opinion of their performance.

Employees are appraised and their salary reviewed every six months. Appraisals are normally carried out by the manager to whom the employee is directly responsible; they are then reviewed by the employee's group manager. At the same time as the staff appraisal scheme was introduced, the group structure was created and group managers were specifically charged with building up good personal relationships with their staff and with keeping staff fully informed about Syniad's activities. The result of these changes was that morale increased again and the rate of loss of staff decreased, although the atmosphere of the company when it was small was never recaptured.

Despite the overall success of Syniad's staff management, there are still perceived to be a number of difficult problems to be overcome:

- how to provide continuity of management as staff move from project to project;
- how to exploit and foster group expertise (e.g. the collective expertise of the company's six database experts) in an environment in which the members of the group are usually working on different projects;
- how to maintain standards and company loyalty as the company continues to grow.

The biggest difficulty, however, in developing and pursuing a consistent and satisfactory personnel policy, is the unstable nature of the business. Syniad lurches from the position in which it is desperate to recruit staff to service the contracts which it has, to the position in which it is desperate to get business in order to keep its staff on revenue earning work. In either of these situations it is difficult to ensure that staff work on projects which are appropriate to their skills, their desires and their planned career development. This is ultimately a consequence of the company's under-capitalization, a point that we shall develop further in Section 4.6.

4.4 Producing the budget

Staff in the company are broadly divided into technical or *revenue earning* staff and *non-revenue earning* staff; the latter include management, secretarial, accounting and so on. The crux of the problem in producing the budget is to estimate the costs of the revenue earning staff and the revenue which they can be expected to earn. Overhead costs, including the costs of non-revenue earning staff must then be contained within the sums likely to be available.

Revenue earning staff are divided into seven grades, numbered 1 to 7, with grade 7 as the most senior. For each grade, the average direct cost (i.e. salary

+ National Insurance + employer's pension contribution + perks) in 1999 was calculated, using the July 1999 payroll. The average number of revenue earning days per employee in each grade was calculated for the period 1 August 1998 to 31 July 1999; this number varies from grade to grade because:

- different grades have different training needs;
- senior grades tend to spend more time on non-revenue earning activities such as sales support;
- senior technical staff are usually more specialized and it therefore takes longer to redeploy them once they have completed a project.

The figures estimated for 1999 are shown in Table 4.1.

The 2000 figures have been prepared using the 1999 figures as a base, adjusting them in the light of the following inputs:

- the sales staff's estimates of how much more business they could sell, and at what rates, if the staff to handle the business were available;
- the personnel department's estimates of the company's ability to recruit new staff of a suitable calibre and to retain existing staff;
- the personnel department's estimate of salary trends in the industry;
- the operations director's view of the staff utilization rates achievable;
- specific expansion plans, e.g. plans to open an office in a new location;
- the financial director's estimate of the company's ability to raise funds for expansion.

The 2000 figures are shown in Table 4.2.

The work of preparing a budget needs to be started well in advance of the period to which it refers and so estimates have to be made on the basis of the best information available. The figures for the first half of 1999 have therefore been used to estimate the figures for the whole of 2000. If the second half of 1999 shows a marked difference from the estimates, it may prove necessary to revise this table, and hence the whole budget, at a very late stage. While this may be unavoidable, it is certainly undesirable. If the revenue is lower than estimated, it will upset plans and commitments already entered into. Nothing is worse for the morale of the staff than to be forced to withdraw from plans that have already been announced. Even if the position is better than predicted, the result may be a scramble to implement ill prepared and badly thought out plans for expansion.

The uncertainty about the direct costs and revenues for 2000 is inherent in the budgeting process. More avoidable is the excessively optimistic character of the predictions. What is being predicted is an increase in staff of about 16 per cent; an increase in the already high level of staff utilization; and a substantial increase in charging rates. The author's experience suggests that this combination of performance improvements will only be possible in a very

Table 4.1 1999 staff costs and revenue figures (£).

Grade	Number	Annual cost	Days worked	Utilization (per cent)	Daily cost	Charge rate	Total cost	Total revenue
1	20	18,500	195	87	94.87	195	370,000	760,500
2	25	23,000	205	92	112.20	220	575,000	1,127,500
3	42	27,000	206	92	131.07	255	1,134,000	2,206,260
4	41	30,500	204	91	149.51	305	1,250,500	2,551,020
5	27	36,600	198	88	184.85	370	988,200	1,978,020
6	20	39,800	185	83	215.14	440	796,000	1,628,000
7	15	44,000	160	71	275.00	560	660,000	1,344,000
Totals	190			88 (avg)			5,773,700	11,595,300

Table 4.2 Predicted staff costs and revenue figures for 2000 (£).

Grade	Number	Annual cost	Days worked	Utilization (per cent)	Daily cost	Charge rate	Total cost	Total revenue
1	25	19,500	198	88	98.48	215	487,500	1,064,250
2	30	24,150	208	93	116.11	245	724,500	1,528,800
3	50	28,350	210	94	135.00	290	1,417,500	3,045,000
4	50	32,025	207	92	154.71	350	1,601,250	3,622,500
5	32	38,430	200	89	192.15	410	1,229,760	2,624,000
6	24	41,780	190	85	219.89	500	1,002,720	2,280,000
7	19	46,200	165	74	280.00	630	877,800	1,975,050
Totals	230			90 (avg)			7,341,030	16,139,600

well run company, blessed with excellent sales staff, in the most favourable of market conditions. The 2000 figures might be acceptable as performance targets but should not be used as a basis for planning.

The other side of the budgeting process concerns overhead costs, that is costs which are not directly related to the company's ability to generate revenue[1]. Table 4.3 shows the 1999 estimates and the predicted figures for 2000. The general principle used in arriving at these figure has been to increase all the 1999 figures by 5 per cent to allow for inflation and then to increase by a further 21 per cent those overheads that are expected to increase proportionately to the planned increase in staff. The two main exceptions are rent and rates, and interest. In the case of rent and rates, the company's rents are fixed and not due for review in 2000; the only increase is therefore that predicted for the business rate.

Interest is more complicated. A separate cash flow prediction is produced from which the cash needs of the company in 2000 can be established. Once it is decided how to finance these, the interest payments can be calculated. As a rule of thumb, a company such as Syniad needs working capital of about 25 per cent of its annual turnover, i.e. about £3 million for 1999. Depending on

Table 4.3 Overheads for 1999 and 2000 (£).

	1999	2000
Rent and rates	700,000	720,000
Building maintenance	84,000	88,200
Heating and lighting etc.	40,000	42,000
Cleaning	20,000	21,000
Telephone and postage	85,000	108,039
Equipment depreciation	20,000	25,421
Equipment maintenance	12,000	15,253
Directors' salaries and expenses	480,000	504,000
Management salaries and expenses	945,000	1,201,145
Sales and marketing salaries and expenses	900,000	1,143,947
Secretarial	190,000	241,500
Library and information services	32,000	40,674
Training courses	180,000	228,789
Insurance	25,000	31,776
Legal expenses	20,000	25,421
Interest	400,000	600,000
Total	4,133,000	5,037,166

---

1. A separate, and comparatively small, budget is produced for capital expenditure and it is from this that the figure for depreciation is obtained. Company cars are leased and do not therefore give rise to any depreciation.

interest rates, this can lead to an interest charge of anything from £350,000 to £750,000; we have assumed figures of £400,000 for 1999 and £600,000 for 2000.

The budgeted figures for 1999 and 2000 look very healthy for this type of company. The predicted profit for 1999 is £1,688,600 which is 15 per cent of turnover; for 2000 it is £3,761,404, 23 per cent. However, a 10 per cent drop in turnover – perhaps caused by failure to maintain the level of the charging rates or by a drop in staff utilization – would reduce the 1999 profit to £532,070, only 4.6 per cent. Moreover, a worst case scenario is the one in which the costs, both direct and indirect, for 2000 attain their budgeted level, £12,378,196, while revenue remains at the 1999 figure of £11,595,300, to give a loss of £782,896.

This demonstrates very clearly that the company's expenditure plans for 2000 cannot be allowed to go ahead in full, all at once, but must be conditional on the revenue and forward sales figures showing the right trend. In other words, the company's financial performance must be carefully monitored.

4.5 Monitoring financial performance

Monitoring Syniad's performance against the budget should, in principle, be straightforward. Each month, the income and expenditure under the various heads are compared and, if significant deviations are observed, corrective action is taken. In practice, this simple procedure presents many difficulties.

4.5.1 Costs and revenue

A major problem is caused by random fluctuations, themselves the product of many individual factors, for example:

- The budget assumes that, over the twelve month period, staff will increase by a total of 30; in other words the excess of joiners over leavers will be 30. In the absence of any reason for believing otherwise, this will have been shown as a net monthly increase of 2.5 staff. However, while the budgeted figure of 30 may well prove to be correct, it is unlikely to follow this neat pattern; in some months there may be a net increase of seven or eight, while in other months there may be a net decrease.

- Large projects will cause significant deviations from the budget in various ways. The call for proposals for a large project will take several senior technical staff away from revenue earning work on to the preparation of the proposal; this may last for as much as a couple of months, or even longer. On average over the year, the utilization of that grade of staff may accord with the budget but it will be much lower for the period of proposal preparation. During a big project, the overall level of staff utilization may increase, because so many staff are continuously and fully employed on the project but the end of the project often sees staff becoming available at a rate greater than that at which they can be deployed on to other projects, thus adversely affecting utilization.

- In fixed price projects, revenue is accrued on the basis of the increase in the value of work in progress. Even the most conscientious of project managers will not normally re-estimate the whole project every month; rather, the increase in work in progress will be calculated monthly by applying a formula mechanically and, once every few months, the project will be re-estimated. The result of this is likely to be a hiccough (one way or the other) in the monthly revenue – it may even turn out to be negative.

4.5.2 Project costing

Because of these difficulties in monitoring the overall performance of the company, Syniad also tries to monitor the financial performance of individual projects, through a project costing system. The costs and revenue of each project are calculated each month and the cumulative gross margin (i.e. the difference between total costs and total revenue to date on the project) calculated as a percentage of the total revenue. Project managers are set a target of 60 per cent for the gross margin on their projects.

In practice, this system does not work well. Project managers complain that there is usually little they can do about the costs, since these are dominated by the payroll costs of the staff, and nothing they can do about the rates, since these were determined by the sales staff who carried out the initial negotiations. In addition, they usually have difficulty reconciling their records of the non-staff costs with those used by the accounts department, because of uncertainty about which month a charge will be allocated to.

4.5.3 Sales

The budgeted increase in revenue derives partly from increased charge rates, partly from better staff utilization and partly from an increased number of staff. All these factors are influenced by the forward sales position, that is by the staff required and the rates earned on the work to which the company is committed in the coming months. Two reports are used for assessing and monitoring the sales position.

The *confirmed sales report* shows, for each grade, the number of staff in that grade who are committed to contracts in each of the following twelve months and the total expected revenue from that grade in each month.

The *sales prospects report* shows, for each sales prospect, the potential value of the sale, its likelihood and the likely start date. The likelihood is reported on the following scale:

- 0.1 indicates that the client has an identified requirement which is expected to be met by commissioning a software house, but that Syniad has not yet been asked to quote for the business and there is no certainty of being asked;
- 0.3 indicates that Syniad has been asked to quote for the business or will be asked in the near future;
- 0.5 means that Syniad has quoted for the business and is short listed or, for other reasons, is in competition with no more than two other companies;
- 0.7 means that Syniad has been offered the business, subject to negotiation (possibly on price, possibly on contractual conditions, possibly on technical content);
- 0.9 means that negotiations are concluded but no signed contract has yet been received.

Prospects that merit a likelihood of less than 0.1 are not included in the sales prospects report. These likelihoods are based on experience which suggests, for example, that Syniad will win, on average, about three out of ten contracts for which it has been asked to bid. Obviously, much of the information in this report is very subjective but the report still provides a useful and disciplined way of assessing the fruits of the salesmen's activities.

Taken together, the confirmed sales report and the sales prospects report enable a reasonably accurate assessment of future staff needs and revenue to be made. In particular, they allow recruitment tactics for the next two or three months to be determined. Note, however, that this is at a very coarse level; a need for an increased number of grade 4 staff may be apparent but the reports do not indicate, for example, whether they should have experience in air traffic control systems or payroll.

A particular difficulty arises with large projects at a likelihood of 0.5. Such a project, if the company is successful in winning it, may suddenly require a fairly substantial number of staff. There is a considerable risk in recruiting the staff before the project is won but it may be impossible to recruit them quickly enough if the company waits until it knows whether it has won the contract. Moreover, it seems to be in the nature of such projects that the decision date is frequently deferred but, the moment the decision is taken, the client expects an immediate start.

4.6 Long-term planning

As well as short-term, i.e. year-by-year plans, a successful company needs to have strategic plans covering, say, the next five years. The day-to-day hassle of running the company makes it very difficult to produce strategic plans and, even more, to monitor the progress of the company towards their achievement. Nevertheless, the ability to plan strategically and to achieve strategic objectives is the hallmark of well run, successful companies.

Strategic planning in Syniad has two related aspects. The first is to identify appropriate long-term goals and the second is to identify and formulate plans to overcome those problems which are inhibiting it from attaining these goals. We are talking here, of course, of what may be called "structural" problems rather than day-to-day problems.

4.6.1 Expansion plans

The directors of Syniad want to see the company become one of the leading companies in its field in Europe. Although it is difficult to estimate the size of the market for the type of services which it provides (because publicly available figures aggregate its market with many markets in which it has no interest), it is clear from the size of the companies which it sees as competitors that, at present, its UK market share is less than 5 per cent and its market share elsewhere in Europe is minuscule. The directors wish to see the company ultimately attain a market share of 15 per cent in the UK and 10 per cent across the rest of Europe. As a step towards this, they are formulating a plan to raise the UK market share to 10 per cent and to attain a market share of 5 per cent in Holland, Germany, Denmark and Italy, within the next five years. It is estimated that this means increasing the staff from the present 200 to around 1200.

Expansion on the scale desired depends on the ability to recruit and retain suitable staff and on the ability to raise the necessary funding. It will also require the ability to run a much larger and multinational organization.

A major strategic decision concerns the staffing of the foreign operations. The model used so far in Holland has been to employ a nucleus of sales and management locally and to staff the projects from the UK. There are considerable advantages in continuing with this model:

- it retains the idea of a single pool of technical staff available for any project, and thus makes it easier to find appropriate staff for each project and easier to maintain a satisfactory level of utilization;
- the company knows how to manage UK staff but managing foreign staff is bound to be different – employment legislation, for example, varies very widely amongst the countries of the European Community – and it is difficult to find managers with suitable expertise;
- UK based staff cost less than staff employed in most other European countries, even allowing for the need to pay subsistence expenses when they are abroad.

However, despite the success of this model on the comparatively small scale of the Dutch operation, it might very well not work elsewhere. In particular, the Dutch are both able and willing to carry out technical work in English; this will be much less true of Germany and Italy. The proposed expansion would mean that, instead of the present 10 per cent of Syniad's business being carried out on this basis, something like two thirds of the business would be done in this way. This would mean recruiting a very large number of staff prepared to spend a lot of time abroad and many of them would need language skills. This does not seem possible.

The decision has therefore being taken that Holland will continue to operate on the present basis and that the Danish company, when it is established, will operate on the same basis, since Denmark is a comparatively small market in which English is always likely to be acceptable as the working language. The German and Italian companies, however, will operate primarily with local nationals from the start, although specialized technical expertise will be brought in from the UK when necessary.

In the case of Germany and Italy, there remains the question of whether to recruit local managers to start the companies from scratch or whether to try to buy existing companies. Buying an existing company has the advantage that the risks are lower; the company will already have contracts which are generating revenue and will have the contacts to win further contracts in the future. On the other hand, the initial investment will be large and Syniad will have to raise a lot of capital; there may be difficulties in integrating the company with Syniad; and there is the risk that the staff in the company will be unhappy about the change of ownership and leave rapidly, thus destroying the value of the investment. Building a company from scratch involves much less investment and there will be fewer problems of integration but the risks are high; success depends crucially on being able to recruit the right person as local manager. Initially it has been decided to pursue both avenues. A search will be made both for suitable local managers and for suitable companies; the position will be reviewed when more is known about the availability of candidates in either category.

4.6.2 Company image

Syniad already has an image as a software house producing high-quality, state-of-the art software for demanding and prestigious clients; such clients are usually prepared to pay a slight premium for using Syniad's services on projects which demand high quality. The directors are happy with this image.

There is one respect, however, in which the image of Syniad – and, indeed, the image of all comparable companies – is deficient. Firms of management consultants have succeeded in building an image of providing high value services at a high price; their charging rates are typically some 50 per cent higher than Syniad's, for comparable staff. A significant amount of their work is comparable to that carried out by Syniad. It is particularly galling to see a member of staff, often not one of the most competent, leave Syniad to join a firm of management consultants who then charge for the ex-employee's services at a much higher rate.

It is a long-term aim of the company to bring its charging rates up to the level of management consultants. Apart from exhorting the sales force to negotiate the highest possible rates, however, there is no strategy for bringing this about. If it were achieved, it would enable much more money to be spent on training and information services; it would enable target staff utilization levels to be reduced, thus making it easier to assign staff to projects in accordance with their career development plans; and it would enable the company to invest more in technology for improving the software development process. All these, in turn, would improve still further the company's quality image and assist it in recruiting and retaining staff, so ultimately furthering its expansion plans.

4.6.3 Product mix

At present, Syniad relies for its income entirely on *fee-based revenue*, that is revenue that is tied to fees charged for the services of individual employees. As a result, competition means that its income is limited to some multiple of the payroll cost of the revenue-earning employees; what this multiple is depends upon the company's image and its success in persuading clients of the high quality of its staff, but it is unlikely to rise much higher than about 2.5. Profit, as a percentage of turnover, will depend on the efficiency of the operation, in particular on maintaining high utilization while keeping overheads low. Such efficiency will, however, tend to militate against the high quality that the company is pursuing – maintaining high-quality staff requires significant expenditure on staff training and development, for example.

The directors of Syniad look enviously at the producers of packaged software. Once a company has made the initial investment in developing a package, large numbers of copies may be sold at very little extra cost and without employing large numbers of extra staff. This frees the company from the limitations of fee-based revenue. However, product development is expensive and risky; only a small proportion of the software products developed achieve a level of sales that really justifies the initial investment. Syniad does not have the money to develop new products. Even if it did, it is doubtful whether the directors would be prepared to risk investing it in speculative development. They realize that the company does not have the expertise or the infrastructure to enter the very crowded market for high-volume packaged software. Instead, the policy is to look for opportunities to develop specialized products that build on experience gained in bespoke projects or to seek licensing agreements from overseas suppliers of such products. To date the policy has shown few signs of success.

4.6.4 Finance

Many of the problems that have been noted are a consequence of the under-capitalization of Syniad, that is, there is not enough money invested in the company; this is a problem common to many similar companies. One difficulty is that the result of increased investment would be too ephemeral to appear on the balance sheet or be used as security for a loan. Some of the capital raised might be spent on hardware, which certainly would appear on the balance sheet. But most of it would be spent on new or improved procedures, standards and methods; on increased training and improved career development for staff (including financing a lower utilisation rate); on improved library and information services; and on product development. While such expenditure would certainly help the company to win more business and charge higher rates, its results are intangible and are valueless outside the context of the company. This means that it must be funded from profits, from loans secured against the personal property of the directors, or from new equity capital; profits and secured loans simply cannot generate the investment required so the company must look for new equity.

The desire to expand into Europe, with the concomitant acquisition plans, also makes it necessary to raise further funding. Again it is doubtful whether this could be done completely from loan capital; the risks involved are such that potential lenders will require a say in the running of the company which only a shareholding will give them.

The company is handicapped by the large interest charges that it is paying for its overdraft, essentially the working capital it needs to cover the gap between invoicing and receiving payment. If this could be funded internally, the company's profit would look much healthier.

If Syniad were to be sold, the purchaser would probably be prepared to pay somewhere between £15 and £20 million. Since the shares are almost all held by the original four founders, they are, on paper, very rich people. However, they have no access to this wealth; they can only live on the salaries they are paid as directors. Inevitably, there will come a time when they wish to turn some, at least, of this wealth into cash. This means selling some of their shares.

All of these factors lead inexorably to one conclusion. Fresh equity capital is needed. It can be obtained only by selling a part or the whole of the company. This may be done by selling the company to another company, or by turning the company into a public company with a stock exchange flotation, or in various other ways. (There are many recent examples of real companies similar to Syniad following one or other of these paths.) However it is done, such a change will affect the character of the company and the working lives of its staff.

4.7 Conclusions

Syniad, despite its problems, is a successful and well-managed company. However, the directors' grandiose expansion plans, if they were to come to pass, would change the company from a comparatively small, largely uk company into a large (by software house standards) multinational. Although there are examples of similar companies following a somewhat similar track in the past, there is no real evidence to suggest that the directors have the expertise to manage this transition or to run the resulting company. Nor is it obvious that the resulting company is one in which the directors or the present employees would wish to work; certainly its character will be very different. In any case, their plans are only likely to be achieved if Syniad either seeks a stock exchange flotation or sells out to another company or other investors. The directors might possibly reconsider their plans and aim for a much more modest expansion, perhaps through agreements for collaboration with comparable companies elsewhere in Europe. However, it seems probable that Syniad has now reached a point where it can no longer thrive as a private company and its future must, inevitably, be very different from its past.

Chapter 5

Computer contracts

Computing has presented far fewer problems for the law of contract than it has in other areas of the law such as intellectual property, discussed in Chapter 6, and in the criminal law, which forms the subject matter of Chapter 11. There are a number of reasons for this. Contracts set out the agreement between the parties: they set out the aims of the parties; provide for matters arising while the contract is running, ways of terminating the contract and the consequences of termination. Where there are gaps in the agreement because the parties have failed to contemplate a particular issue, it is a function of contract law to fill them, for example by implying terms; also contract law provides rules for the termination of the contract if performance becomes impossible; and sometimes, although fairly rarely, it sets aside contracts which are too harsh or unconscionable.

There are almost never disputes over contracts which run perfectly. An analogy can be made with a good marriage, where there is no need for the law to intervene. But, if things go wrong, in a contract or in a marriage, the law provides a framework for the settlement of points of disagreement, and for the termination of the relationship.

Contract law since its inception has handled disputes. An example can be given of a ship chartered to carry a cargo, where, for instance, the cargo rots before reaching port, or the ship sinks, or the ship and its cargo are impounded in the course of a war. What are the rights and remedies of the parties to the charter agreement? Is there a contract of insurance covering the loss of the goods or the ship, and is liability for any matter excluded under the insurance contract, such as loss caused through warfare? Agreements for the provision of goods and services etc. connected with computing present no insuperable problems for a set of laws which has been regulating commercial dealings and handling disputes for many hundreds of years.

One noticeable growth area is e-commerce. However, again the law is able to cope; sometimes with minor modifications, e.g. relating to electronic signatures to documents exchanged over the Net. Since the advent of the Internet, the market has globalized to a far greater extent than ever before, and there is greater need for international harmonization of laws. The EU has therefore been very active in line with its policy of removing distortions of trade within the internal market and also in facilitating trade by EU businesses. There are therefore directives and proposals for directives on:

1. legal protection for encrypted services in the internal market;
2. electronic signatures;
3. electronic commerce;
4. distance contracts;
5. distance selling of financial services.

One of the problems with computing contracts is that many lawyers are still not familiar with the technology. But, on the other hand, even fewer computer scientists are familiar with the law; and as both lawyers and computer scientists use jargon known almost only to themselves, the difficulties are compounded. These difficulties are however receding, for more lawyers are becoming familiar with computing through use of computers at home and in work; there are more lawyers specializing in this area of the law; and many books have been written describing the framework of computer contracts, and providing model contracts or precedents, which lawyers can adapt to the needs of their clients. Let us hope that more computer scientists will become familiar with the law.

Hilary Pearson[1] made a very telling statement when she said that, while optimists make the best deal makers, pessimists make the best contract writers. When it comes to drafting a contract, lawyers in particular are born pessimists. This often gives rise to frustration on the part of a business client who is excited by the possibilities of a deal which may have taken considerable time and effort to negotiate. Resolving potential and hypothetical points of difficulty may just be seen as time-wasting by the client.

It is possible to avoid formal written contracts for the supply of goods or services, and to work on a basis of oral discussions only, or on the basis of a set of loosely drafted heads of agreement, but for the security of all parties to the deal, it is much better to set out clearly the terms on which each is to work, and to provide for such matters as the method of payment; what happens if there is a defect in the goods, software or services provided. It is also advisable to settle the appropriate methods of terminating the agreement – for instance, the length of notice required to terminate the agreement; and whether the length of notice should vary at different times in the course of the agreement, or on the occurrence of certain events. Drafting a document which sets out all of these matters takes time, but in many cases it is better to pause and think it

1. Pearson, *Computer contracts* (London: Financial Training), 1984.

out in advance, than it is to face difficulties later, when commercial and other factors may change and when all may not appear to be as clear-cut or financially beneficial as was originally thought.

It is important that a contract is set out in a clear and logical manner and that it is complete and consistent. There should be no ambiguity and the parties to the agreement should be left in no doubt as to their rights and duties. Ambiguity and doubts can lead to performance which is viewed as unsatisfactory. This can lead to disagreement and the expenditure of time, effort and therefore money, in resolving the matter. This is the last thing that the parties to a commercial agreement need and want. As stated earlier, it is much better to avoid the problems initially by careful preparation and drafting. However, if there is a dispute, and often these are unavoidable because they are caused by circumstances beyond the control of the contracting parties, it is again important that the contract is properly drawn up, for at this stage it will be interpreted by outsiders, for example by lawyers and judges, or maybe by accountants or a trustee in bankruptcy if one of the parties has become insolvent; and outsiders, even more than the contracting parties themselves, will need to be able to envisage and understand the intricacies of the deal, and will require clarity and consistency in the documentation.

In the course of their work, software engineers are likely to come across many different types of contract – insurance contracts, contracts of employment, contracts with hardware suppliers, consultancy contracts and so on. In this chapter we shall concentrate on contracts which are relevant to the development and supply of software; in particular, we shall describe in some detail the elements which go to make up contracts for the supply of software which is to be custom-built for a client for a fixed price, for this illustrates most of the issues which are likely to arise in contracts regarding the provision of software and related services. Other specialist works should be consulted by those interested in the other types of contracts. A number of these specialist works are listed in the section on Further Reading at the end of this chapter.

5.1 Contracts for the supply of custom-built software at a fixed price

5.1.1 Structure of the contract

Producing a good contract costs a lot of money; good commercial lawyers are not cheap. For this reason, software suppliers try to use what are known as standard form contracts, which are used or intended to be used many times over. Such a contract might consist of:

- a short introductory section, which specifies, among other things, the names of the parties to the contract;

- a set of standard terms and conditions;
- a set of appendices or annexes.

The standard terms and conditions do not change from one project to another; they contain references to the annexes, which contain all the project specific material.

5.1.2 The introductory section

The first part of the contract is brief; it states that it is an agreement between the parties whose names and registered addresses are given. It is dated and signed by authorized representatives of the parties. It often begins with a set of definitions of terms used in the course of the agreement, set out either in alphabetical order, like a dictionary, or in the order in which they appear in the rest of the contract. These definitions explain precisely what the parties mean by certain words or phrases. Once the term is defined, its use elsewhere in the contract should conform only to that definition, thereby ensuring consistency and avoiding ambiguity. Definitions are also useful in cutting down descriptions elsewhere and avoiding the need to change the standard terms and conditions. For example, the definitions section will tell us that Company X Ltd, the software house, is to be referred to throughout the contract as "The Company", and Company Y Ltd, which has commissioned the work, is to be known throughout as "The Client".

It is also important that the introductory section states that the contract consists of the introductory section itself, the standard terms and conditions, the annexes (which should be listed), together with any documents listed in the annexes, such as the requirements specification (discussed in the paragraph below) and nothing else. This is to avoid, for example, the situation in which statements made by an over-enthusiastic salesman while trying to win the business are claimed by the client to constitute part of the contract.

The following subsections discuss the issues which must be addressed by the standard terms and conditions.

5.1.3 What is to be produced

It is clearly necessary that the contract states what is to be produced. There are usually two levels of reference here: the standard terms and conditions refer to an annex and the annex then refers to a separate document which constitutes the requirements specification. It is important that the reference to the requirements specification identifies that document uniquely; normally this will mean quoting a date and issue number.

Software engineers will be familiar with the problems of producing requirements specifications. A specification sets out the detailed requirements of the client. Ideally, the specification should be complete, consistent and accurate and set out all that the client wants to be done in the performance of the contract. Unfortunately, we know that it is very difficult to achieve this ideal standard and, even if we succeed, the requirements of the client may evolve as the contract proceeds, and sometimes the changes may be substantial. How are these changes to be accommodated by a contract which, in a sense, freezes the requirements of the parties to those at one particular time by incorporating the original specification into the contract? The answer is that the contract should provide a procedure for making variations to the specification or job description, then follow this through by providing a method of calculating payment for work done to facilitate the changes, and also perhaps provide for a variation of the level of anticipated performance, and maybe also vary the method of acceptance testing. In other words, once again, the contract should anticipate events and provide an agreed formula for modification.

5.1.4 What is to be delivered

Producing software for a client is not, usually, a matter of simply handing over the text of a program which does what is required. It is important, therefore, that the contract states (usually in an annex) what precisely is to be provided. The following is a non-exhaustive list of possibilities:

- source code;
- command files for building the executable code from the source and for installing it;
- documentation of the design and of the code;
- reference manuals, training manuals and operations manuals;
- software tools to help maintain the code;
- user training;
- training for the client's maintenance staff;
- test data and test results.

5.1.5 Ownership of rights

It is important that the contract should also state just what legal rights are being passed by the software house to the client under the contract. Ownership in physical items such as books, documents or discs will usually pass from the software house to the client, but other intangible rights, known as intellectual property rights, present more problems. Intellectual property law forms the subject matter of Chapter 6. As we shall see there, software is potentially protectable by a number of intellectual property rights, such as copyright, design rights, confidentiality and trade marks. It is important for the contract to state precisely who is to own these rights. Do they pass to the client or are they retained by the software house?

Let us take copyright as an example. Copyright is owned by the author of a work, which in the case of a literary work, or a computer program which is not computer generated, is the person who creates it. All of these technical terms are explained in Chapter 6 to which reference should be made. But if the person who creates the program is an employee acting in the course of employment, then under Section 11 of the Copyright, Patents and Designs Act 1988, the copyright belongs to the employer. Therefore, if a software house employs a programmer, copyright in the programs belongs to the software house. On the other hand, if a program is written for a software house by an outside consultant or independent contractor, who is not one of their employees, Section 11 will not apply, and, as is explained in Chapter 6, the consultant owns the copyright. Ownership in copyright passes only by written assignment or transfer. If the consultant owns the copyright, the software house should consider whether it wants ownership of the copyright either in order to retain it itself, or in order to pass it on to the client. If ownership of the copyright is to pass from the consultant to the software house, a term to that effect should be inserted into a written contract between the consultant and the software house. An oral agreement to transfer the property right is insufficient.

The next decision to be taken is whether the copyright in the program should pass from the software house to the commissioning client; or whether it should remain with the software house. If ownership of copyright passes to the client it is known as a sale or assignment and again a written agreement is necessary. Furthermore, the agreement will usually provide that copyright is only to pass to the client when the final payment has been made in full. If copyright is to remain with the software house and the client is merely given permission to use the software, this is known as a licence.

If a commercial firm commissions a software house to write a program especially for it, the client will often want exclusivity. This can be achieved in a variety of ways. Normally the client will want to be the outright owner of the copyright, so that others can be prevented from using it. Another way to achieve exclusivity is to ask for an exclusive licence to use the copyright, ownership of which remains in the software house. If the client has an exclusive licence to use the software, it is the only organization entitled to use it. If the client takes ownership of the software or has an exclusive right to use it, the software house cannot make money from the software by licensing others to use it. The software house must therefore make its entire profit on the work from that particular deal. The cost to the client is therefore at its highest. If, however, the software house retains the right to allow others to use it, the costs are spread more widely and the cost to the commissioning client may be diminished. In these cases, ownership in the copyright in the software remains with the software house and the commissioning client is given a non-exclusive licence. The commissioning client may still retain some control over the extent to which the software is distributed to others by retaining a right to veto the grant of licences to others. Care must, however, be taken as the veto could be used to stifle competition and may fall foul of competition laws.

Where the client is granted a licence, the following matters should be dealt with in the contract:

1. duration of the licence – a licence should be for a fixed period; or there should be some provision for termination, for example by giving notice, or on the happening of certain events, common terminating events being death, or insolvency;
2. the licence agreement should state whether the licensee can assign or transfer the licence to another. If there is no provision giving the licensee the power to transfer the licence to another, then the licence is probably not assignable;
3. scope of the licence: does the licence cover use on one particular computer, or can the software be run on other machines. If so, is the licence limited to one site? If the client is one of a group of companies, can others in the group also benefit from the licence?
4. confidentiality: the licence will often seek to restrain the licensee from allowing anyone other than company employees to become familiar with the use of the software. This can be an embarrassment for educational establishments who wish to purchase the software for use by their students.

If the supplier retains the copyright, major problems can arise for the client if the supplier goes into liquidation or otherwise ceases to trade. The supplier is then no longer able to maintain the software but the client may be unable to obtain copies of the up-to-date source listings of the programs and any tools used to construct them, in order to commission maintenance from a third party. One way around this difficulty is for the contract to specify that, after acceptance, a copy of the listings and documentation is placed in escrow; this means that the copy is placed in the hands of a third party (usually a lawyer) to be released to the client if and when certain defined circumstances arise. The escrow copy is replaced whenever the software is updated.

5.1.6 Confidentiality

A second area of intellectual property law which should be considered in a software contract is confidentiality. The commissioning client may well have to pass confidential information about its business operations to the software house. On the other side of the coin, the software house may not want the client to divulge to others details of the program content or other information gleaned about its operations by the client. It is usual in these circumstances for each party to promise to maintain the confidentiality of the other's secrets, and for express terms to that effect to be included in the contract.

Confidentiality is discussed in the chapter on intellectual property rights (Chapter 6), to which reference should be made.

5.1.7 Payment terms

The standard terms and conditions will specify the payment conditions, that is something along the lines that:

> Payment shall become due within thirty days of the date of issue of an invoice. If payment is delayed by more than thirty days from the due date, the Company shall have the right, at its discretion, to terminate the contract, or to apply a surcharge at an interest rate of 2 per cent above the bank base lending rate.

In practice, such clauses are only brought into effect in extreme cases, since using them is likely to destroy the goodwill between supplier and client on which the success of the project depends.

It would be unusual, in a project of any significant length, for all payment to be delayed until the work is complete and accepted. An annex will usually specify a pattern of payments like the following:

1. an initial payment of, say, 15 per cent of the contract value becomes due on signature of the contract;
2. further stage payments become due at various points during the development, bringing the total up to, say, 65 per cent;
3. a further 25 per cent becomes due on acceptance of the software;
4. the final 10 per cent becomes due at the end of the warranty period.

Such a pattern has advantages for the supplier in that it reduces the financial risk arising from possible insolvency of the client or from default for other reasons and it reduces possible cash flow difficulties. If the client is not prepared to accept a payment pattern of this type, the supplier is likely to demand a premium to cover the increased risk and the costs of financing the development. In negotiating the payment pattern, the supplier will usually seek to have the stage payments becoming due on fixed calendar dates while the client will try to have them tied to the achievement of specific project milestones, e.g. approval of the design specification.

5.1.8 Calculating payments for delays and changes

It happens not infrequently that progress on the development of a piece of software is delayed by the failure of the client to meet obligations on time. While the supplier will be expected to use its best endeavours to rearrange activities so as to avoid wasting effort, this is not always possible. The contract should therefore make provision for payments to compensate for the wasted effort, incurred, for example, when the client fails to provide information on a due date or when changes are requested which result in extra work.

The contract must specify the process by which these extra payments are to be calculated. Typically, an annex will include daily charging rates for each grade of staff employed on the contract and the amount of extra effort to be paid for will be agreed at progress meetings.

Delay payments and payments for variations to the original requirements are, perhaps, the commonest cause of contractual disputes, not only in software engineering but in most other contracting industries – the construction industry is a notorious example. One reason for this is that competitive bidding for fixed price contracts often means that the profit margin on the original contract is very low so that companies seek to make their profit on these additional payments.

5.1.9 Penalty clauses

The previous subsection dealt with compensation for delays caused by the client; delays caused by the supplier are handled differently.

The normal mechanism used is to include a penalty clause which provides that the sum payable to the supplier is reduced by a specified amount for each week that acceptance of the product is delayed, up to a certain maximum. Thus, on a contract of value £1 million, the penalty might be specified as £5,000 per week up to a maximum of £100,000.

Delays in delivering working software are notoriously common; it might therefore be expected that contracts for the supply of software would normally include such a penalty clause. Paradoxically, such provision is comparatively rare. There are three reasons for this:

- Suppliers are very reluctant to accept penalty clauses and anything stronger than the example quoted above is likely to lead to reputable suppliers refusing to bid.
- If the contract is to include penalty clauses, the bid price is likely to be increased by at least half the maximum value of the penalty.
- If the software is seriously late and penalties approach their maximum, there is little incentive for the supplier to complete the work since he will already have received in stage payments as much as he is going to get.

It should be realized that the cost of delays on fixed price contracts is very high, regardless of penalty payments. Every delay eats into the supplier's profit margin. As a result, suppliers are strongly motivated to produce the software on time and delay is usually the result of genuine technical difficulties (or incompetence!) rather than lack of motivation.

5.1.10 Obligations of the client

In almost all cases where work is being carried out for a specific client, the client will have to fulfil certain obligations if the contract is to be completed successfully. The following is a (non-exhaustive) list of possibilities:

- provide documentation on aspects of the client's activities or the environment in which the system will run;
- provide access to appropriate members of staff;
- provide machine facilities for development and testing;
- provide accommodation, telephone and secretarial facilities for the company's staff when working on the client's premises;
- provide data communications facilities to the site.

The general terms and conditions will normally state that a list of specific obligations and the dates at which they will be required is given in an annex. It will also state that failure to meet these obligations may render the client liable for delay payments.

5.1.11 Standards and methods of working

The supplier is likely to have company standards, methods of working, quality assurance procedures, etc. and will normally prefer to use these. More sophisticated clients will have their own procedures and may require that these be adhered to. In some cases, the supplier may be required to allow the client to apply quality control procedures to the project. The contract must specify which is to apply.

5.1.12 Progress meetings

Regular progress meetings are essential to the successful completion of a fixed price contract and it is advisable that standard terms and conditions require them to be held. The minutes of progress meetings, duly approved and signed, should have contractual significance in that they constitute evidence that milestones have been reached (so that stage payments become due) and that delay payments have been agreed.

5.1.13 Project Managers

Each party needs to know who, of the other party's staff, has day-to-day responsibility for the work and what the limits of that person's authority are. The standard terms and conditions should therefore require each party to nominate, in writing, a Project Manager. The Project Managers must have at least the authority necessary to fulfil the obligations which the contract places on them. It is particularly important that the limits of their financial authority are explicitly stated, i.e. the extent to which they can authorize changes to the cost of the contract.

5.1.14 Acceptance procedure

Acceptance procedures are a critical part of any fixed price contract for they provide the criteria by which successful completion of the contract is judged. The essence of the acceptance procedure is that the client should provide a fixed set of acceptance tests and expected results and that successful performance of these tests shall constitute acceptance of the system. The tests must be provided at or before the start of the acceptance procedure; within reason, there may be as many tests as the client wishes but extra tests cannot be added once the test set has been handed over. The purpose of this restriction is to ensure that the acceptance procedure can be completed in reasonable time.

Other points to be addressed under this heading include who shall be present when the tests are carried out and what happens if the tests are not completed successfully.

5.1.15 Warranty and maintenance

Once the product has been accepted, it is common practice to offer a warranty period of, typically, 90 days. Any errors found in the software and reported within this period will be corrected free of charge. This clause is, of course, subject to negotiation; reducing or eliminating the warranty period will reduce the overall cost of the contract and prolonging the period will increase it.

Once the warranty period is over, the supplier may offer, or the client demand, that maintenance will continue to be available on request. Since such maintenance is likely to involve enhancement of the software rather than simply correction of faults, the resources required are unpredictable – the client almost certainly does not know what enhancements will be required in two years' time. For this reason, a fixed price for the maintenance will not be appropriate. Maintenance will therefore usually be charged on a time and materials basis; the client may possibly be required to commit to taking a fixed number of days of effort each year in order to compensate the supplier for the need to retain knowledge of the system.

5.1.16 Indemnity

It could happen that, as a result of the client's instructions, the supplier is led unwittingly to infringe the intellectual property rights of a third party or that, through carelessness or dishonesty, the supplier provides a system which infringes such rights – perhaps through using proprietary software as a component of the system delivered. For this reason, it is advisable to include a clause under which each party indemnifies the other for liability arising from its own faults in this respect.

5.1.17 Termination of the contract

There are many reasons why it may become necessary to terminate a contract before it has been completed. It is not uncommon, for example, for the client to be taken over by another company which already has a system of the type being developed, or for a change in policy on the part of the client to mean that the system is no longer relevant to its needs. It is essential, therefore, that the contract make provision for terminating the work in an amicable manner. This usually means that the supplier is to be paid for all the work carried out up to the point where the contract is terminated, together with some compensation for the time needed to redeploy staff on other revenue-earning work. The question of ownership of the work so far carried out must also be addressed.

5.1.18 Arbitration

Court action to resolve a contractual dispute is likely to be expensive. For this reason, it is common practice for contracts to include a statement that, in the event of a dispute that cannot be resolved by the parties themselves, they agree to accept the decision of an independent arbitrator. Provision is usually made for the arbitrator to be appointed either by the President of the British Computer Society or by the President of the Institution of Electrical Engineers. Both bodies maintain lists of qualified arbitrators who have the necessary technical understanding.

An arbitration clause will usually state that, if arbitration is required, it will take place in accordance with the Arbitration Act 1996. This Act of Parliament lays down a set of rules for arbitration that cover many eventualities and reference to it avoids the need to spell these out in detail; most of the provisions of the Act are optional, in the sense that they come into effect only if the contract contains no alternative provision.

Some organizations may be unwilling to accept an arbitration clause because they feel that they are signing away some of their legal rights.

5.1.19 Inflation

In lengthy projects or projects where there is a commitment to long term maintenance, the supplier will wish to ensure protection against the effects of unpredictable inflation. To handle this problem, it is customary to include a clause which allows charges to be increased in accordance with the rise in costs. The Government publishes several different financial indices; the Retail Price Index is the most widely known but the most appropriate one for the purposes of this type of contract is the Business Costs Index.

The clause should state how often (once a year, twice a year) charges can be increased and how the effect on the overall price is to be calculated.

5.1.20 Applicable law

Where the supplier and the client have their registered offices in different legal jurisdictions or performance of the contract involves more than one jurisdiction, it is necessary to state under which laws the contract is to be interpreted.

5.2 Other types of software services contract

There are four types of contractual arrangement which are widely used in connection with the provision of software services:

- contract hire;
- time and materials;
- consultancy;
- fixed price, as described in the previous section.

5.2.1 Contract hire

Under a contract hire agreement, the supplier agrees to provide the services of one or more staff to work for the client; the staff work under the direction of the client and the supplier's responsibility is limited to providing suitably competent people and replacing them if they become unavailable or are adjudged unsuitable by the client. Payment is on the basis of a fixed rate for each man day worked; the rate depends on the experience and qualifications of the staff. Contract hire is sometimes referred to disparagingly as "body shopping". Closely related are the freelance agreements under which individuals sell their own services to clients on a basis similar to contract hire.

Contract hire agreements are very much simpler than fixed price contracts because the supplier's involvement and responsibility are so much less. Issues such as delay payments, acceptance tests and many others simply do not arise; however, as mentioned earlier, ownership of intellectual property rights generated in the course of the work must be addressed.

5.2.2 Time and materials

A time and materials contract (often referred to as a "cost plus" contract) is somewhere between a contract hire agreement and a fixed price contract. The supplier agrees to undertake the development of the software in much the same way as in a fixed price contract but payment is made on the basis of the costs incurred, with labour charged in the same way as for contract hire. The supplier is not committed to completing the work for a fixed price, although a maximum payment may be fixed beyond which the project may be reviewed. Many of the complications of fixed price contracts still occur with time and materials contracts – ownership of rights, facilities to be provided by the client, progress monitoring arrangements, for instance – but others, such as delay payments and acceptance testing do not; this is not to say that no acceptance testing is done, only that it has no contractual significance since nothing contractual depends on its outcome.

It may be wondered why any client should prefer a time and materials contract to a fixed price contract – surely it is better to have a contract which guarantees performance for a fixed price rather than one in which the price is indeterminate and there is no guarantee of completion? In the first place, it often happens that the work to be carried out is not sufficiently well specified for any supplier to be prepared to offer a fixed price; part of the supplier's task will be to discover what is required and to specify it in detail. Secondly, a supplier always loads a fixed price contract with a contingency allowance, to allow for the risk that unexpected factors will cause the project to require more resources than originally estimated. If all goes well, the supplier makes an extra profit; this is the reward for risk taken. By accepting a time and materials contract, this risk and the possibility of extra profit (in the form of a lower cost) are effectively transferred to the client, who also avoids the dangers of having to pay excessive sums to have minor changes incorporated into the specification. All this having been said, it remains the case that there is a strong movement away from time and materials towards fixed price, noticeably in the defence field.

5.2.3 Consultancy contracts

The use of consultants is now widespread both in private industry and in public bodies. Consultants are typically used to assess some aspect of an organization and to make proposals for improvements. The end product of a consultancy project is therefore usually a report or other document. Consultancy projects are usually undertaken for a fixed price but the form of contract is very much simpler than the fixed price contracts so far described.

There are two reasons for the comparative simplicity of consultancy contracts. First, the sums of money are comparatively small and neither side stands to lose a great deal. Second, while it is possible to demonstrate beyond doubt that a piece of software does not work correctly and, thus, that the supplier has failed to fulfil the contract, it is not usually possible to demonstrate unequivocally that a report fails to fulfil a contract. The client has to rely on the desire of the supplier to maintain a professional reputation and in practice this usually proves sufficient to ensure that the work is of an acceptable standard.

It should be obvious that confidentiality is of particular importance in consultancy contracts. It is also important that the contract refers explicitly to the terms of reference of the consultancy team and, in practice, these are perhaps the commonest source of disagreements in consultancy projects. As a result of their initial investigations, the consultants may discover that they need to consider matters which were outside their original terms of reference but the client may be unwilling to let this happen for any one of a number of possible reasons.

5.3 Liability for defective software

The law in this area is complex. It is dealt with only briefly here. A fuller discussion is to be found in Reed (ed.): *Computer Law* (4th edn.); and in Rowland and Macdonald: *Information Technology Law*, both of which are noted in the Further Reading section at the end of this chapter; and you should refer also to Chapter 10 of this book.

Firstly we should look at terms implied into a contract by the law. Just which terms are implied will depend on the type of contract under consideration. If it is a contract for the sale of goods, the Sale and Supply of Goods Act 1994 implies that the goods shall be of satisfactory quality and fit for their purpose. Section 1(2) of the 1994 Act, which amends Section 14 of the Sale of Goods Act 1979, provides that goods are of satisfactory quality if they meet the standard that a reasonable person would regard as satisfactory, taking into account any description of the goods, the price (if relevant) and all other relevant circumstances. The quality of goods includes their state and condition and the following (among others) are in appropriate cases aspects of the quality of the goods:

(a) fitness for all the purposes for which goods of the kind in question are commonly supplied;
(b) appearance and finish;
(c) freedom from minor defects;
(d) safety;
(e) durability.

There is no breach of the implied term if a matter which might make the goods unsatisfactory is specifically drawn to the buyer's attention before the contract is made.

A major difficulty is whether software constitutes goods for the purposes of the Sale of Goods Act 1979 and the 1994 Act. Goods are defined in Section 61 of the 1979 Act in a way which covers physical (tangible) items such as books, discs and hardware but may well exclude intangible items such as software[2]. However, it is arguable that software on a disc, particularly mass-produced software, where the value of the software in itself is not too great per individual disc, might come within the definition of "goods" in much the same way as does music on a cassette, the images on a video tape, or the words in a book. It has long been recognized that a book, which has some unprinted pages or contains pages from another book instead of the one requested, is a defective item of goods. By analogy, a defective piece of software might also be caught by the legislation. But while this argument might apply to mass-produced software such as computer games and common word-processing packages the position of bespoke software is probably quite different.

A contract for the supply of bespoke software is more appropriately classified as a contract for work and materials. The work, which has gone into producing the software, in the form of research and development, is the most important component of the contract. Goods (or materials) supplied, such as tapes, discs or manuals are subsidiary items. The distinction between a contract for the sale of goods and one for work and materials is essentially one of emphasis. The classification of customized software might well be quite difficult. However, the legal consequences of the classification are important, for if the contract is one for work and materials, the Sale of Goods Act will not apply. Instead the contract falls under the Supply of Goods and Services Act 1982, and this Act implies into the contract a term that the software must have been written with reasonable skill and care. This is a notoriously vague notion. Only a moment's thought will show that it does not accord a great deal of protection for the commissioning client. It in no way guarantees that the software is "bug-free"; only perhaps that the number of bugs, or the problems caused by the bugs, is no more than could reasonably be expected from the reasonable software house producing bespoke software to those specifications at that time. Because of the difficulty in applying this standard, a contract will often contain an express guarantee, for example to cure defects for a certain length of time after delivery. Guarantee clauses should be carefully drafted for the software house and carefully construed by the commissioning client, for obviously much will depend on the precise wording used.

The foregoing account has considered the liability of a software house in contract law. There are of course other ways in which a software house can be rendered liable for defective software which causes loss or damage[3], for example, the tort of negligence, or the law relating to negligent misstatement might

2. See also Chapter 10.
3. For damage which causes physical injury see Chapter 10.

apply. These might cover either physical damage or financial loss, although it is generally more difficult to recover for financial loss in negligence than it is to recover for physical damage to the person or to property. Also, it is difficult to prove negligence. For this reason, and to conform to an EC Directive, a strict liability regime for property damage and personal injury was introduced by the Consumer Protection Act 1987 under which it is not necessary to prove fault in order to establish liability. There are, however, difficulties in applying this Act[4]. These matters are outside the scope of this chapter, the aim of which is to introduce computer contracts.

5.3.1 Exclusion of liability

The aim of a party drafting a contract will be to minimize liability under the contract, or to exclude it altogether. The law is governed by the Unfair Contract Terms Act 1977. Briefly, the 1997 Act provides that liability for death or personal injury can never be excluded. Liability for other forms of damage (such as property damage) can be excluded, but only in so far as it is reasonable to do so. Liability under the terms implied under the Sale of Goods Act 1979 (merchantability or fitness for purpose) or under the Supply of Goods and Services Act 1982 (to use reasonable skill and care) to which we referred earlier cannot be excluded in a consumer sale, but in a non-consumer sale they can be excluded if the exclusion is reasonable. In order for the sale to be a consumer sale, the requirements of Section 12 must be satisfied. This means that the buyer must be a private person; the buyer must buy from a seller who is acting in the course of a business; and the goods must be of a type ordinarily supplied for private use or consumption. If I buy a computer game from W. H. Smith to play at home on my microcomputer, Section 12 is satisfied, and under the 1977 Act the implied terms cannot be excluded. However, where the client commissions bespoke software from a software house in order to use it in the course of business, this is not a consumer sale, and the implied terms can be excluded if it is reasonable to do so. Reasonableness is ascertained by reference to guidelines laid down in Schedule 2 to the Unfair Contract Terms Act. Matters to which the court would have regard in assessing whether it is reasonable for a supplier to exclude liability include:

- the relative bargaining powers of the parties;
- opportunities to contract with others who do not use the same exclusionary terms;
- whether the customer knew or ought reasonably to have known of the existence and extent of the term (note here that in practice contracting parties should always read all contracts before entering into them and

---

4. See further Chapter 10.

should seek advice on matters such as the extent of any exclusion clause or clause seeking to limit liability);

● whether the goods were manufactured, processed or adapted to the special order of the customer.

5.3.2 Standard form contracts and limitation of liability

It was stated at the start of this chapter that a software house will often try to use a standard form contract in its dealings with its commissioning clients. Section 3 of the Unfair Contract Terms Act contains special provisions for standard form contracts. In the present context it provides that a software house using a standard form contract cannot, again unless it is reasonable to do so,

(i) exclude or restrict liability for its own breaches of contract; or

(ii) claim to be entitled

(a) to render a contractual performance substantially different from that which was reasonably expected of it; or

(b) in respect of the whole or any part of its contractual obligation, to render no performance at all.

If a standard form contract limits liability in damages to a fixed or determinable sum, Section 11(4) applies. This provides that:

Where by reference to a contract term ... a person seeks to restrict liability to a specified sum of money, and the question arises (under this or under any other Act) whether the term or notice satisfies the requirement of reasonableness, regard shall be had in particular ... to (a) the resources which he could expect to have available to him for the purpose of meeting the liability should it arise; and (b) how far it was open to him to cover himself by insurance.

Standard form contracts do therefore have their drawbacks. Unfortunately the Act gives no guidance about when a contract, which is used several times, becomes "standard form". It is, however, at least arguable that standard terms offered by one party to another for purchases over the Internet are standard form[5].

---

5. One further piece of legislation which should be noted is the Unfair Terms in Consumer Contracts Regulations 1994 and 1999, which implement EC Directive (93/13/EEC) on Unfair Terms in Consumer Contracts. This relates to terms in general and not just to exclusion clauses; but it applies only to contracts between consumers and sellers or suppliers who deal on terms which have not been individually negotiated. It is therefore relevant to Internet shopping by individuals, but not to the acquisition of bespoke software by a business and thus is not dealt with in this chapter. See further Koffman and MacDonald: *The law of contract*, 3rd edn (Tolly Publishing, 1998), Chapter 11.

There are a number of cases on the Unfair Contract Terms Act and on the requirement of reasonableness. The cases must, however, be treated with caution for the decision in each turns on its facts and just because one case is decided one way it does not mean that all others will follow. One example is *St Albans City and District Council v International Computers Ltd* [1996] 4 All ER 481. The facts were that the council had ordered a computer system from ICL to enable them to compute the Community Charge for the forthcoming year. ICL insisted on using its standard terms and conditions which stated that its liability "will not exceed the price or charge payable for the item of Equipment, Program or Service in respect of which liability arises or £100,000 (whichever is the lesser). . .". Errors in the software and incorrect advice from ICL's project manager resulted in an overestimate of the population of the area, an undercharge of residents and a loss to the council of £1.3 million.

The judge at the initial hearing, Scott Baker J. found that the software was not fit for the purpose for which it was provided and that ICL's project manager had been negligent. ICL were therefore in breach of contract. As ICL had dealt on the basis of their standard terms and conditions, Section 3 of the Unfair Contract Terms Act 1977 applied and the clause limiting liability had to be measured against the requirement of reasonableness. Applying the factors listed in Section 11(4) and Schedule 2 (above), the judge noted that ICL were a substantial organization with world wide product liability insurance of £50 million; that all potential suppliers of the system dealt on similar standard terms; that the council was under pressure to install the system before the Community Charge was introduced; that although the council was a business and not a consumer, that it did not usually operate in the same commercial field as a normal business and that it would be impractical for it to insure against commercial risks. On balance, the judge found that the clause limiting liability to £100,000 was not reasonable and was therefore ineffective. ICL appealed, but the Court of Appeal agreed with the decision of Mr Justice Scott Baker. However, as stated above, whatever the final outcome in this case, its value as a precedent will be limited, for each case turns on its facts. It cannot be concluded that henceforth no limitation of liability clause in a contract for the supply of a computer system will be valid. It does, however, show the pitfalls surrounding contract negotiation and a need to tailor such clauses to the circumstances. Dogged reliance on standard terms and conditions can prove expensive.

5.4 Further reading

There are a large number of books on computer contracts, most of which are written mainly for lawyers. The following is a list of books which are easier to read and understand, and yet give insight into the difficulties and practicalities.

Bainbridge, 1996. *Introduction to computer law*, 4th edn. Chapters 14–22. London: Pitman.

Reed (ed.), 2000. *Computer law*, 4th edn. Blackstone Press (especially the chapters on hardware contracts, software contracts and liability).

Rowland and Macdonald, 1997. *Information technology law*. Cavendish Publishing, Chapters 3 and 4.

Chapter 6

Intellectual property rights

Intellectual property rights are often the most valuable assets owned, used and developed by a software house. One has only to contemplate the earnings of a company such as Microsoft and its owner, Bill Gates, to appreciate their significance. Intellectual property rights include confidential information, patents, trade marks, designs and most importantly the copyrights protecting computer programs. They protect information stored by electronic means and all of the paperwork which accompanies a program, such as the user manual, plus any multimedia packages and most items on the Web. Great care should be taken to protect, exploit and enforce intellectual property; and all contracts between a software house and its employees, consultants, suppliers and customers should address the issue.

Intellectual property rights should be seen as a package. Different rights protect different products, but just as the components of software combine to form a package, so too do intellectual property rights. The name under which a product is sold may be registered as a trade mark or protected as an unregistered business name; the hardware or a process used in its manufacture may be protected by a patent and patents are increasingly available for software too; semi-conductor chips may be protected by the topography right, a variant of the unregistered design right; the look of the product may be registered in the Designs Registry; software can be protected by copyright, as can accompanying documentation; the know-how which goes into the development of the product may be protected as confidential information, as may information about a client's business gleaned in the course of work.

Unauthorized use of intellectual property can be stopped by injunction and damages may be sought for infringement of these rights. Raids can be made to seize infringing materials. The law is constantly changing with technological advance; and the changing market and the growth of the Internet has raised questions about the relevance and enforceability of copyright and the ownership of domain names. The impact of the EC is considerable and much of the debate surrounding reform of the General Agreement on Tariffs and

Trade (GATT) concerned the protection of intellectual property rights in the face of widespread piracy of software products. It is vital that industry be aware of its rights and obligations and that every step be taken to enforce them.

6.1 Confidential information

The first aspect of intellectual property law we shall consider is the legal protection of confidential information. This can protect programs, data and ideas. It is especially important that information should be kept confidential if a patent application is to be made[1].

Confidentiality clauses can be incorporated into contracts or they may be implied by law. Every software house should consider inserting confidentiality clauses into contracts with employees, consultants and clients. All too often employees leave to set up their own businesses or to work for rivals. The information carried away in their heads or in the documents in their briefcases can represent a significant leakage of commercial advantage. On the other hand, it is unfair to tie employees and others too tightly. Preventing them from using any knowledge acquired in the course of their work is not in the public interest and mobility of labour is desirable. The law has to find a balance.

Three conditions must be satisfied before an action for breach of confidence can succeed:

1. the information must be confidential;
2. the information must have been disclosed in circumstances which give rise to an obligation of confidence;
3. there must be an actual or anticipated unauthorized use or disclosure of the information.

The action to prevent unauthorized use or disclosure of confidential information is a civil one. The criminal law is rarely involved. However, the Law Commission have proposed that there should be a new offence covering the misuse of a trade secret and this will be discussed in Chapter 11.

6.1.1 What is confidential information?

Information will be protected only if it is confidential. Non-confidential information, unless protected, e.g. by copyright or a patent (see further below), is

---

1. See Section 6.12.

deemed to be in the public domain and can be used by anyone. Confidential information was defined in a wide and general way by Lord Greene in the case of *Saltman Engineering v Campbell* [1948] 65 RPC 215, as information "which is not public property and public knowledge". This is useful in that it encompasses potentially any category of information, from personal confidences, to trade secrets and sensitive government information, any or all of which a computer scientist might handle in the course of his or her work, or all or any of which a firm may want to protect against unauthorized use or disclosure by others.

6.1.2 When will an obligation of confidence be imposed?

There is also no limit to the range of circumstances in which an obligation of confidence can arise: it is a question of fact to be decided in each case, but useful guidelines for commercial situations were given by Mr Justice Megarry in *Coco v Clark* [1969] RPC 41. He said that, as a general rule, an obligation of confidence would lie whenever a reasonable man standing in the shoes of the recipient of the information would realize on reasonable grounds that the information was being given to him in confidence. He said that where information of commercial or industrial value is given on a business-like basis or with a common object in mind, such as a joint venture or the manufacture of articles by one party for another, the recipient is under a heavy burden if he seeks to refute the contention that he is bound by an obligation of confidence.

Generally, an obligation of confidence will be imposed whenever confidential information is disclosed for a limited purpose. The recipient of the information will then be under a duty to use the information for the limited purpose only, and if he discloses or uses the information for any other purpose, he will be in breach of his obligation, and is liable to be restrained by injunction or subject to other appropriate remedies. For example, in *Saltman Engineering v Campbell* [1948] 65 RPC 203, the plaintiffs gave to the defendants confidential designs for tools, which the defendants were to manufacture solely for the plaintiffs. When the defendants manufactured the tools on their own account, they were held to be in breach of an obligation of confidence. The court held that the designs had been handed over for a limited purpose only and the defendants were not entitled to use them, or the information contained in them, for any other purpose. Thus, by analogy, if a software house is given information concerning a client's secret manufacturing processes in order for it to program robots to perform certain tasks in the course of the process, the software house, and by extension its employees, would not be able to use that information for any other purpose.

6.1.3 Sources of an obligation of confidence

Express contract

A common source of an obligation of confidence is an express contract. The contract may deal solely with confidentiality, or the term imposing the obligation may just be one term among many dealing with other matters. Parties who are aware that information is confidential, and that its unauthorized use or disclosure would be disadvantageous to them, would be well advised to enter into express contracts of confidentiality with their confidants before making a disclosure. Confidentiality clauses are to be found in almost any form of contract under which confidential information is likely to be disclosed, for example contracts for the supply or maintenance of hardware or software, consultancy and employment contracts, and agreements for the provision of data services. As well as setting out the terms on which the information is disclosed, putting express terms in a contract will emphasize confidentiality and warn of the seriousness of the discloser's desire to protect the secrets.

An express contract dealing with confidentiality may be oral or in writing, although writing is clearly advantageous for evidential reasons. No particular form is necessary, so long as the intent is clear, and it is common for the obligation of confidence to be set out in a letter which, in practice, follows a fairly standard pattern. In return for the release of the information, the confidant agrees to treat it as confidential and to use it only for the limited purpose intended. However, it is normal to qualify the agreement by providing that in three cases the obligation shall cease, namely:

- if the information subsequently becomes publicly available other than by breach of confidence on the part of the confidant;
- if it was lawfully in the confidant's possession before the agreement;
- it was acquired by the confidant after the agreement, from a third party who was not also bound by an obligation of confidence to the discloser.

Another useful device for protecting confidential information is what can be described as a "black box" agreement. In *Paul (Printing Machinery) Ltd v Southern Instruments (Communications) Ltd* [1965] 1 WLR 1, the plaintiffs supplied a telephone answering machine to one of the defendants under a contract for hire, which specified that the defendant was not to remove the machine from the address and position at which it was installed, nor could he interfere in any way with the machine or with any of its electrical connections. In breach of this agreement, one of the defendants allowed another defendant to remove it, to take it apart and to examine it. Damages would obviously not have been an appropriate remedy, as the plaintiff clearly wanted to preserve the "secrets in the box". As a result, the court granted an injunction restraining the defendants from using or disclosing confidential information gleaned from the unlawful inspection. This type of contract is obviously useful in the supply of computers, or other technologically advanced equipment, where the secret parts can be shielded from view.

Implied contractual obligations

An obligation of confidence may also be implied into a contract. An implied term can provide the entire obligation of confidence, or it may supplement an express term. An example of its supplementary role is *Thomas Marshall v Guinle* [1978] 3 All ER 193, where an employee was subject to an express clause prohibiting the *disclosure* of confidential information belonging to his employers. However, on the facts of the case, the employee had been *using* the information for his own purposes, and not disclosing it to others. The court held that the express term against disclosing confidential information could be supplemented by an implied term prohibiting its use.

Obligations of confidence owed by employees

Employees are in a rather special position. The case of *Thomas Marshall* referred to above shows that a contract of employment may contain both express and implied obligations to respect the confidentiality of information acquired by an employee in the course of his employment. While the employee continues to be employed by the employer, the obligation of confidence is quite strict. But what happens after that contract comes to an end, for example when the employee goes to work for someone else, or sets up in business on his or her own account? Can he or she use all or any of the information learned in the course of the previous employment?

After the termination of a contract of employment an ex-employee continues to be bound to respect the confidentiality of information imparted in the course of the former employment. This obligation may be found in an express contractual term, called a covenant in restraint of trade, or in an implied contractual obligation, called the obligation of good faith and fidelity. However, both of these obligations are subject to the qualification that a former employer can only restrain the use of confidential information acquired by employees in the course of their employment; the employer cannot restrain them from using information which has become part of their general knowledge and skill. However, pinpointing the dividing line between protectable confidential information and unprotectable general knowledge and skill is one of the most difficult issues in this area of the law, but obviously it is of fundamental importance. If the information is classified as being confidential, the ex-employee cannot use it; whereas if it is part of general knowledge and skill he or she can, and there is nothing that the former employer can do to prevent the ex-employee from using it, or disclosing it to another, unless for example the information is protected by some other law, such as the Official Secrets Act 1989.

Guidelines which can be used in classifying information as either confidential, or as part of the employee's general knowledge and skill, were given in *Faccenda Chicken v Fowler* [1987] Ch.117, a case decided by the Court of Appeal. Here, Lord Justice Neill said that all of the circumstances of the case should be considered, but the following matters are among those to which attention must be paid:

- *the nature of the employment*: employment in a capacity where confidential information is habitually handled may impose a high obligation of confidentiality, because the employee could be expected to realize its sensitive nature to a greater extent than if he were employed in a capacity where such material reached him only occasionally;
- *the nature of the information itself*: information would only be protected if it could properly be classed as a trade secret, i.e. if it was of a highly confidential nature such as a secret process; but the fact that circulation of the information was restricted to a limited number of individuals might throw a light on the status of the information and its degree of confidentiality;
- *whether the employer impressed upon the employee the confidentiality of the information*;
- *whether the relevant information could be easily isolated* from other information which the employee is free to use or disclose.

Rather surprisingly, Lord Justice Neill in *Faccenda Chicken* also said that additional protection should be afforded to an employer where the former employee is not seeking to earn a living by making use of the body of skill, knowledge and experience acquired in the course of his or her career, but is merely selling to a third party information acquired in confidence in the course of the former employment. This is new and we shall have to wait for subsequent cases to see if this proposition is followed. It may just be a reflection of a feeling that employment cases have been too generous to employees and have laid too little emphasis on the protection of the confidential information.

As we saw earlier, confidential information may be protected by either an express term of the contract of employment, or an implied term. Generally, from the point of view of the employer, an express term is preferable. Firstly, it acts as an explicit warning to the employee that the employer is serious about maintaining confidentiality and is likely to take action if the obligation is breached. Secondly, an express term protecting confidential information can be coupled with, and strengthened by, a covenant in restraint of trade, which states that after termination of the contract of employment, the employee shall not work in a given geographical area, or in a specified area of work, for a certain length of time (such as two years).

The problem with covenants in restraint of trade is that the courts are likely to declare them void and unenforceable if they are unreasonable and go beyond what is necessary to protect the employer's business. A well-drafted clause will not restrict the employee for too long a period of time, and will not cover too wide an area of work or too wide a geographical area. This last criterion of not covering too wide a geographical area may, however, have to be ignored in the case of a computer programmer working in a global market with Internet communications.

Garden leave and long notice periods

A variant on the covenant in restraint of trade is the newer option of "garden leave" plus a prolonged period of notice which must be served before the employee can leave and work for others. The aim of this combination is again to delay the employee taking up work elsewhere in the hope that by the time the employee does so, his or her knowledge of the former employer's trade secrets will be out of date. Terms to this effect must be inserted into the contract of employment. They will not be implied.

The terms could be useful if a key programmer were to announce that he or she wishes to leave to work for a rival concern. The employer could require the employee to give, say twelve months notice, during which time he or she could be switched to other interesting[2], but non-confidential or non-strategic work, or be offered the opportunity to take paid leave without loss of benefits (garden leave) for the same period. This type of clause is as yet relatively untested in the courts, but is likely to be measured by similar criteria to a covenant in restraint of trade. The clause should not therefore be too restrictive, this again being gauged by the extent to which it is necessary to protect the employer's trade secrets.

Obligations of confidence owed by independent contractors

There is an increasing trend in high-technology areas, particularly computing, for people to be brought in to solve problems or to do particular jobs, not in the capacity of employees, but to act as consultants, or independent contractors. The obligation of confidence owed by independent contractors may well be different from that owed by employees, although here again the law is uncertain.

---

2. To prevent dissatisfaction and consultation of solicitors.

Initially the law is much the same as for employees. Thus, while a consultant is working for another, he or she is under an obligation to respect confidentiality; and after the contract has been performed, the former consultant can be bound to continue to respect confidentiality either under the express or the implied terms of the contract. And, like an ex-employee, he or she cannot be bound to respect the confidentiality of information which has become part of his or her general knowledge and skill. But it is at this point that the law relating to employees and independent contractors may well diverge.

As we saw earlier, *Faccenda Chicken* lays down guidelines for the classes of information which can be protected from use or disclosure by employees, but arguably that case does not apply to independent contractors. Other cases dealing solely with independent contractors show that they can be bound to respect a much wider range of confidential information than can employees, i.e. less knowledge might be held to form part of an independent contractor's general knowledge and skill; more might be protected as confidential information; and hence an independent contractor may be able personally to use less knowledge about the job than may a former employee.

It might follow from this that a firm might be much safer in contracting for work to be done by independent contractors than by employees. This could have a considerable effect on employment policy. However, it is probable that the law would draw a distinction between independent contractors hired for a short time to do a specific job, and those hired on a long- or longer-term basis. In the case of long-term independent contractors, they are much more likely to be treated in the same way as employees, and the guidelines in *Faccenda* are more likely to be followed. This is again an area of uncertainty and it does not take much ingenuity to think up examples for which there are no answers. This is one of the joys of the study of law!

Equity

If there is no contract imposing an obligation of confidence, all is not lost. A third source of an obligation of confidence is another area of law called Equity. We met the test for imposing an equitable obligation of confidence earlier. In *Coco v Clark* [1969] RPC 41, Mr Justice Megarry said that an obligation would lie when a reasonable man standing in the shoes of the recipient of the information would realize on reasonable grounds that the information was being given to him in confidence. In that case there was no contractual obligation of confidence, as the parties were negotiating for the entry into a contract, but had not yet agreed terms when the disclosure was made. Negotiations foundered and no contract was ever entered into. The defendants did, however, make use of the information disclosed to them. The court decided that although the information given in the case of *Coco v Clark* was not confidential, had it been so, the recipients could have been restrained from using it under an obligation of confidence.

The importance of the case also lies in the general discussion of the circumstances in which an equitable obligation of confidence will be imposed. As we saw earlier, Mr Justice Megarry said that where information of commercial or industrial value is given on a business-like basis or with a common object in mind, such as a joint venture or the manufacture of articles by one party for another, the recipient is under a heavy burden if he seeks to refute the contention that he is bound by an obligation to respect confidentiality. In the absence of a contract between the parties, this obligation will be equitable.

A person who wishes to make a disclosure of confidential information can rely on the equitable obligation of confidence. But in practice, it is better to protect the information by express contract, as was discussed above, if only for the reasons which we stated earlier, namely that the recipient of the information is given an express warning about confidentiality, and this emphasizes to a much greater extent the serious intent of the discloser to enforce confidentiality.

6.1.4 The position of third party recipients of confidential information

We have discussed the position of one who receives confidential information directly from the person who is entitled to that information, e.g. an employee who, in the course of employment, is told the employer's trade secrets. Here generally the employee is bound to respect the confidentiality of that information. But what happens if the employee passes the secret to another, e.g. to a rival concern? The rival is not in a contractual relationship to the employer and hence there can be no contractual obligation to respect confidentiality, but here again Equity may step in and hold that the rival is under an equitable obligation to respect confidentiality, particularly if the rival has what is known as "unclean hands", that is has been less than honourable in his or her dealings; this phrase covers a wide spectrum of abuse. Furthermore, if the rival had deliberately induced the employee to breach an obligation of confidence to the employer, the rival could also be liable in tort for inducing a breach of contract.

By way of contrast, an innocent third party recipient may be excused liability for use of confidential information before being told that information has been passed in breach of an obligation of confidence, but thereafter may have to pay for its use. Equitable remedies are discretionary, and much will depend on the facts of the case.

6.1.5 Public interest

Finally, the obligation to respect confidentiality is not absolute. If it is in the public interest that information should be disclosed, then it can be disclosed. For example, in *Lion Laboratories v Evans* [1985] QB 526, the plaintiff company manufactured computerized electronic equipment known as the Lion Intoximeter, which was used by the police to measure the level of alcohol in the breath of people suspected of drunk driving. Readings from the machine were used as a basis for prosecution. Confidential internal memoranda produced by the company indicated that readings from the machines were often inaccurate. Two of the plaintiffs' employees gave copies of the memoranda to a national newspaper, the *Daily Express*, which at that time was conducting a campaign against the use of the Intoximeter by the police.

The plaintiffs sought an injunction to restrain publication of the information by the newspaper on the grounds of breach of confidence and breach of copyright. The actions failed, as the Court of Appeal held that there was a public interest in the disclosure of the information, as it might lead to the reappraisal of a device which had the potential for causing wrongful conviction for a serious offence. The Court said that in these circumstances there was a "just cause or excuse" for disclosure. But this does not mean that henceforth obligations of confidence will be set aside lightly. For example, Lord Griffiths was careful to emphasize that the decision should not be treated as a "mole's charter". The court made it clear that there was a difference between matters which, on the one hand, it was in the commercial interest of newspapers to publish and which might merely be of public interest to read, and, on the other hand, matters which it was in the public interest to disclose. Only in the latter cases would the public interest permit disclosure of confidential information. Furthermore, the press might not always be the appropriate medium for a disclosure. In other cases it might be more appropriate to disclose the information to the police or other authorities. That was not however the case here, where disclosure through the press was allowed.

We do not know what happened to the employees in *Lion Laboratories*, but Yvonne Cripps, in her book, *The legal implications of disclosure in the public interest* (see Further Reading), chronicles a number of cases where the employees have lost their jobs as a result of the disclosure and effectively have been prevented from working for anyone else ever again. While Equity may refuse an injunction to prevent the disclosure of information in the public interest, the common law has generally taken the approach that disclosure of confidential information is a breach of the implied duty of good faith in the contract of employment, which may justify dismissal or other disciplinary action. The position of the employee has, however, recently been improved by the Public Interest Disclosure Act 1998.

The Public Interest Disclosure Act 1998 amends the Employment Rights Act 1996. The 1998 Act protects a "worker" from being victimized by the employer when the worker makes what the Act calls a "protected disclosure". A "worker" is an individual who works under a contract of employment, or who contracts "to perform personally services for another party to the contract whose status is not by virtue of the contract that of a client or customer of any business undertaking carried on by the individual". Self-employed computing consultants are therefore not covered by the Act, but they have no need of its protection, as they cannot of course be dismissed or otherwise victimized by their employer. Programmers seconded from other firms are, however, covered, for the 1998 Act extends protection to, among others, agency and seconded employees; and also to many homeworkers and teleworkers, provided they do not ordinarily work outside Great Britain.

A worker will be protected against victimization for disclosure if he makes (a) a qualifying disclosure, (b) in certain prescribed circumstances. A "qualifying disclosure" means any disclosure of information which, in the reasonable belief of the worker making the disclosure tends to show one or more of the following: a criminal offence; failure to comply with a legal obligation; a miscarriage of justice; danger to health and safety; environmental damage; or information showing concealment of any the these. This is narrower than the range of disclosures allowed under *Lion Laboratories v Evans* (above). As a result, some disclosures in the public interest which are allowed under that case, will not fall within the 1998 Act and the disclosing employee will not be protected from victimization by the Act.

A qualifying disclosure made in appropriate circumstances to an appropriate person becomes a protected disclosure, entitling the worker to protection against victimization. The PIDA lists six cases where a disclosure by a worker is a protected disclosure. Basically, the Act encourages private or semi-private disclosures, either to the employer, or to the person committing the wrongful act, and many employers have produced Codes of Practice on Public Interest Disclosure, which also specify other persons to whom disclosures may be made and the way the matter is to be handled. Only if it is of a more serious nature, or if the private or semi-private route has failed, may the employee be justified in disclosing to a wider audience, such as the press, but in this case close attention needs to be paid to the minutiae of the Act, for there are many pitfalls for the public spirited, but poorly advised employee. Dismissal of an unprotected employee may not be an unfair dismissal and compensation may not be payable by the employer; also, any other disciplinary action may not be in breach of contract. The 1998 Act therefore remedies many of the abuses highlighted by Cripps (see Further Reading, below) and furthers the policy of permitting, and even encouraging, disclosure of otherwise confidential information in the public interest; but it is a cautious piece of legislation and it is to be hoped that the courts will not further restrict its scope when interpreting its provisions, for although the judges have defined public interest widely in the past, they have not also championed the rights of the victimized employee and have been unwilling to curtail the powers of the employer to control the activities of the workforce.

6.1.6 Confidential information and the criminal law

When a spy obtains secret information without consent and by nefarious means, is he or she committing a criminal offence? When a former employee leaves one job and goes to work for another and tells the new employer the trade secrets of the former employer should the employee be taken to court and fined or imprisoned? These are issues which have long been debated and which raise very important practical issues, not least for the software engineer who proposes to work for a firm for a few years in order to gain experience, then to move on to employment elsewhere. The discussion above concerned the civil law, and questions of suing for damages or seeking injunctions to prevent use or disclosure of confidential information. It is a wholly different matter to brand as a criminal someone who leaks or misuses information and to fine or imprison them. These issues are covered in Chapter 11.

6.2 Copyright

Copyright protects more items generated by businesses or by individuals than any other aspect of intellectual property law. It protects the form in which various things such as words, numbers and drawings are laid out. It can therefore protect, among other things, business letters, manuals, diagrams, computer programs, and lists, e.g. of customers or suppliers. The copyright system has recently come under great pressure with the growth of the Internet and moves towards digitization. The problems lie not so much with the laws themselves, but with the difficulty in enforcing them. On the one hand, Internet communication and digitization open up vast new markets for copyright works, but on the other hand, copyright owners face the spectre of unlimited piracy through uncontrolled copying. What we will probably see over the next few years are stronger laws, more rights for copyright owners, widespread licensing schemes and greater use of technical anti-piracy or copy-monitoring devices and electronic rights management systems.

Copyright law gives six exclusive rights to the owner of copyright. These are the rights to:

- copy the work (and copying includes reproducing the work in any material form; storing the work in any medium by electronic means; and making copies which are transient or incidental to some other use of the work, i.e. it also covers the use of a computer program);
- issue copies to the public;
- rent or lend the work to the public;
- perform, play or show the work in public;

- broadcast the work or include it in a cable programme service;
- make an adaptation of the work or to do any of the above with an adaptation.

These rights are exclusive, in that a copyright owner can prevent another from doing any of these things without permission. Permission is usually granted by contract, normally in the form of a licence to use a work in a particular way. The six exclusive rights apply equally to published and to unpublished works. Copyright arises automatically on creation. Thus, unlike a patent, there is no need to register a copyright (see further below).

The law is now to be found in the Copyright, Patents and Designs Act 1988, as amended by various statutory instruments, such as the Copyright (Computer Programs) Regulations 1992 and the Copyright and Rights in Databases Regulations 1997. The 1988 Act replaced an earlier Copyright Act of 1956. Many of the amendments in that Act were necessary because of technological developments in the preceding 30 years. For example, in 1956 computing was in its infancy; and videos, photocopying machines, compact discs and many other modern methods of storing, transmitting, manipulating and copying data were unknown. The 1992 regulations were an attempt to implement the EC Directive on the legal protection of computer programs[3]. This sought to harmonize copyright protection for computer programs throughout the European Union and thus prevent distortions in trade between member states which might otherwise be caused by varying legal protection. The latest reforms from Europe take the form of a Proposal for a Directive on harmonization of copyright in the Information Society[4], which focuses on copyright in the digital world, the explosion of Internet communication and the opportunities that this presents for European business.

The 1988 Act applies to works created after 1 August 1989. The Copyright Act 1956 applies to works created between 1 June 1957 and 1 August 1989; and the Copyright Act 1911 to works created between 1 July 1912 and 1 June 1957. Such matters are however beyond the scope of this chapter, which concentrates on the 1988 Act and its subsequent amendment. Copyright laws also differ as between different countries and if protection is to be sought abroad, different rules might apply. In particular it should be noted that laws in the United States of America are often quite different. This should be borne in mind when marketing software in the US.

---

3. 91/250/EEC, 14 May 1991.
4. COM(1999) 250(final).

6.2.1 Copyright works

Only certain things are protected by copyright law, and these are known as works. Under the 1988 Act there are nine types of works, divided into three categories. If a work does not fall within any of these categories it is not protected by copyright law. The three categories are:

1. original literary, dramatic, musical and artistic works;
2. sound recordings, films, broadcasts and cable programmes; and
3. the typographical arrangement of published editions.

Literary works

Many of the items listed in the preceding paragraph are further defined in the Act, so as to widen the list of protected subject matter. Section 3 of the 1988 Act states that the phrase "literary work" includes a table or compilation, a computer program, preparatory design material for a computer program and certain databases.

Databases

The law on databases changed in 1998 following implementation of the EC Directive on the legal protection of databases[5]. The Directive was brought into force by the Copyright and Rights in Databases Regulations 1997, which amend the Copyright, Designs and Patents Act 1988.

Some databases are protected by copyright as literary works. The Act defines a database as a collection of independent works, data, or other material, which (a) are arranged in a systematic or methodical way, and (b) are individually accessible by electronic or other means. This covers both electronic databases and e.g. a traditional paper-based card indexing system. But, a database will only constitute a literary work and attract copyright protection as such if the database is original; and for these purposes "original" is given a special meaning. Under Section 3A(2) of the 1988 Act "a database is original if, and only if, by reason of the selection or arrangement of the contents of the database the database constitutes the author's own intellectual creation." Protection is unlikely to be given to an alphabetical listing of telephone numbers in a geographical area[6]; or to a comprehensive or complete database of historical records; but is given to a database of poetry

---

5. EC Directive 96/6EC.
6. As in the US Supreme Court decision in *Feist Publications Inc v Rural Telephone Service Inc* 113 L Ed 2d 358 (1991).

selected thematically, because thematic selection is likely to satisfy the requirement of "intellectual creation".

Is this fair to the producers of telephone directories and comprehensive databases and the like? These fulfil valuable social and economic needs and take time and cost money. To get around this and to reward and encourage the producers of the databases which fall outside the range of copyright protection, we now have a new property right, called the database right, which subsists in a database "if there has been substantial investment in obtaining, verifying or presenting the contents of the database". This right is also given to owners of databases protected by copyright, but as copyright is more comprehensive and lasts longer, few copyright owners are likely to rely on it[7].

The database right (which is also called a *sui generis* right, because it is a specially invented right, outside the normal categories of intellectual property law) is a stand-alone right covering databases only, which is given to the maker of the database, or if made by an employee, to the employer; and the right is infringed by anyone who, without the consent of the owner of the right, extracts or re-utilizes all or a substantial part of the contents of the database. The right lasts for 15 years, which is usually much longer than the commercial shelf-life of many of these products. If a database is substantially revised, time may start running afresh. Copyright, by way of contrast, lasts for the life of the author or creator, plus 70 years (see further below).

Databases may of course contain other copyright works, e.g. full texts (literary works); drawings and photographs (artistic works); video (films); and sound clips (literary works, musical works and sound recordings). These underlying works may also be protected by copyright and care should be taken in identifying the owners of copyright in them when reproducing them either in paper form, or in multimedia packages, or on Web pages (see further below). It is unusual for the owner of copyright in the database, or the owner of the database right, also to be the owner of the copyright in each of the underlying works.

Computer programs

Computer programs and compilations of computer programs are protected as literary works. *IBCOS Computers Ltd v Barclays Bank Highland Finance Ltd* [1994] FSR 275, 289 (see further below), concerned an ADS program which was made up of a composite of interrelated programs, routines and subroutines. There were 335 programs, 171 record layout files and 46 screen layout files. Each of these was protected by copyright, but so too was the overall package

---

7. See Copyright and Rights in Databases Regulations 1997.

as a compilation; and a compilation is itself a literary work for the purposes of copyright.

There is no definition of a computer program in the 1988 Act, it being thought inappropriate to fix a definition to today's technology which might become obsolete in a very short time. The definition of a literary work was changed by the 1992 Regulations to include preparatory design material for a computer program. This was probably unnecessary, as most preparatory material would have been protected anyway. However, the 1992 amendment takes the issue beyond doubt and ensures that the program is protected from the earliest possible moment. There is no definition of preparatory material, but it should cover flow charts expressing the algorithm or other schematic representation of the logic of the program[8].

Other copyright works can be found in a computing product. There might be artwork on the packaging, drawings in the preparatory materials, graphics and photographs used to produce screen images. These are artistic works. The layout of the printed page in the manual could be a typographical arrangement. There might also be music (a musical work), lyrics (a literary work), a sound recording and a film (or video); and all or any of these works can be expected in a multimedia package.

Fixation

Section 3 of the 1988 Act states that there is no copyright in a literary, dramatic or musical work unless and until it is recorded, in writing or otherwise. For example, if a composer writes a piece of music, there is musical copyright in the written score; but if jazz musicians are improvising, no copyright will arise, unless the music is, for example, recorded on tape. If it is recorded, the jazz musicians have copyright in the work, even if the recording is made without their permission. They can therefore prevent copies of the tape being distributed to the public without their consent.

As stated above, a literary work (and thus also a computer program) must be recorded "in writing or otherwise" before it is protected by copyright. Writing is defined to include "any form of notation or code, whether by hand or otherwise and regardless of the method by which, or medium in or on which, it is recorded". There should therefore be few problems with the question of the fixation of computer programs, except perhaps with a program which is stored only in a volatile computer memory, where it might be difficult to argue that it has been "recorded". However, if such a "volatile" work is copied by another, which is of course the abuse towards which these laws are directed, the copier will probably put the work onto a storage

---

8. *Encyclopaedia of Information Technology Law*, para 2.112.

medium, and here an analogy with the recording of the jazz improvisation might be appropriate, with the result that the unauthorized fixation would give rise to a copyright in the creator of the work, as before.

Mere ideas which are not recorded, but perhaps only remembered by persons who heard them being expressed, are not protected by copyright. This can have important practical implications. If an idea is not embodied in a patented invention, and is not recorded for the purposes of copyright law, the only way in which it can be protected from exploitation by others is as confidential information. But if it was not disclosed in circumstances which impose an obligation of confidence, then it will not be protected by intellectual property laws.

6.2.2 Who owns copyright?

The first owner of copyright is the author of a work. The author is the person who creates a work. The term author is most appropriately used to describe the writer of a literary work, but thereafter language is stretched beyond its normal usage so that for the purposes of the 1988 Act:

- the author of a sound recording is the producer;
- the author of a film is the producer or principal director;
- in the case of a broadcast the author is the person making the broadcast;
- the author of a cable programme is the person providing the cable programme service in which the programme is included;
- if the work is the typographical arrangement of a published edition, the author is the publisher.

Computer-generated works and computer-aided design

If a literary, dramatic, musical or artistic work is computer generated, the author is the "person by whom the arrangements necessary for the creation of the work are undertaken".

"Computer-generated" is defined in Section 178 of the Act as a work "generated by a computer in circumstances such that there is no human author of the work". Computer-generated works should be contrasted with works which are computer-aided, for example the computer-aided design of a boat or a car. If a work is computer-aided, the author of the work is the person who designs the boat with the aid of the computer. But under Section 178, if the work is computer-generated, the author may well be the person who loads the program and enables the computer to function, rather than, say the programmer, although the Act is loosely drafted and somewhat ambiguous. It will undoubtedly be the subject of litigation. Furthermore, it may not always be easy to say whether a work is computer-aided or computer-generated, and this may also cause problems.

Employees

An important exception to the general rule that the author of a work is the first owner of copyright in it arises if the author is an employee. Section 11 provides that where a literary, dramatic, musical, artistic work or film is made by an employee in the course of employment, the employer is the first owner of any copyright in the work, subject to any agreement to the contrary.

Section 11 does not apply to independent contractors, who retain copyright in works created by them and all the exploitation rights of a copyright owner. If a firm contracts with a consultant, for example for the design of computer programs, or for the production of a report, it should therefore consider inserting a clause in the commissioning contract dealing with copyright ownership, for the commissioning company may want to own copyright itself. Assignment (or transfer) of copyright will be considered later.

6.2.3 Duration of copyright

Copyright does not last for ever, but its duration varies as between different categories of works. Thus in the case of:

- literary, dramatic musical or artistic works, copyright expires at the end of the period of 70 years from the end of the calendar year in which the author dies, i.e. copyright lasts for life plus 70 years; but if the work is computer-generated, the ordinary rule does not apply, and copyright expires at the end of the period of 50 years from the end of the calendar year in which the work was made;
- sound recordings: here copyright lasts for 50 years from the end of the calendar year in which it is made or released;
- copyright in a film lasts for 70 years from the end of the calendar year in which the death occurs of the last to die of the following persons: the principal director, the author of the screen play, the author of the dialogue, or the composer of music especially created for and used in the film;
- broadcast or cable programme: copyright continues for 50 years from the end of the calendar year in which the broadcast was made, or the programme was included in a cable programme service;
- where the work is the typographic arrangement of a published edition, copyright lasts for the shorter period of 25 years from the end of the calendar year in which the edition was first published.

Reference to the end of the year means that copyrights always expire on 31 December.

The length of copyright protection was extended in many cases by the EC Duration Directive[9]. As computer programs and original databases fall within the definition of a literary work they will be protected for the entire life of the author, plus 70 years, which in practical and commercial terms is often ridiculous. Also, as a result of the Directive, many works which fell out of copyright after mid-1975 have had their copyright revived, e.g. the musical works of Sir Edward Elgar. But, the extended term of copyright does not apply to all foreign (non-EU) works and to all works of foreign authors, where reference has to be made to the laws of another country. This form of discrimination did not operate before 1996. The law is now unduly complex and is very difficult to apply in practice, as there are many exceptions and anomalies.

6.3 Infringement of copyright

There are two categories of infringement of copyright: primary infringement and secondary infringement. Each of these will be considered in turn.

6.3.1 Primary infringement

As we saw earlier, the owner of the copyright has the exclusive right to do any of the following six acts:

- copy the work;
- issue copies to the public;
- rent or lend the work to the public;
- perform, play or show the work in public;
- broadcast the work or include it in a cable programme service;
- make an adaptation of the work, or to do any of the above with an adaptation.

Anyone else who does any of these acts without the consent of the copyright owner is liable for primary infringement of copyright, *even if they did not know that the work was protected by copyright.* Primary infringement of copyright infringes only the civil rights of the copyright owner. It can be committed entirely innocently and is not regulated by the criminal law[10].

---

9. EC Council Directive 93/98/EEC of 29 October 1993, harmonizing the term of copyright and certain related rights, and repealing Article 8 of the Directive on the legal protection of computer programs. Directive 93/98/EEC was given effect in English law by the Duration of Copyright and Rights in Performance Regulations 1995, which amended the Copyright, Designs and Patents Act 1988 from 1 January 1996.
10. Cf. secondary infringement, discussed below (Section 6.3.7).

6.3.2 Copying

It is an infringement of copyright in a literary work, including a computer program and a sufficiently original database (see above), to copy it without the consent of the owner. Copying is governed by Section 17 of the 1988 Act and means reproducing the work in any material form; and the Proposed EU Directive on Copyright in the Information Society[11] refers to this as the reproduction right. In English law, copying includes storing the work in any medium by electronic means. It covers downloading from a disc to the RAM of a computer; storing the work in the memory of a computer; digitization; making back-up copies (see Section 6.4.2); or otherwise storing the work in a machine-readable medium independent of the computer including floppy disc, hard disc, compact disc, ROM, EPROM or magnetic tape.

Copying also includes making copies which are transient or incidental to some other use of the work and covers storing the work in RAM and the display of a work on a VDU or in scratch pad memory or other temporary buffer store. Thus, the use of any work which is in digital form, existing only in a computer memory, on the Internet, or on a carrier such as a CD-ROM, inevitably involves an act of copying and will infringe copyright unless the use is a licensed one. Whilst it is normally possible to read a non-digitized book or to listen in private to a sound recording without the consent of the copyright owner, consent (express or implied) is needed for any use of digitized information, even a private use. This is a matter for concern for all users of the digital environment.

If someone produces an identical product there will be a presumption of copying and hence of breach of copyright, for the chances of a second person devising a product completely without copying the first, either consciously or unconsciously, are small. At civil law the plaintiff has to prove on the balance of probability that copying took place; and does not have to reach the criminal standard of proof, namely, beyond reasonable doubt. However, it is for the defence to argue that despite similarity, there was no copying. For example, the defendant may not have had access to the plaintiff's program and thus could not copy; or the similarities may be due to the use of standard routines organized in the usual way; or both parties may have derived items from a third party or used material in the public domain, e.g. from a toolkit or shareware.

In practice, proving copying is much easier if, for example, a deliberate error has been written into the work, or an unnecessary line of programming ("a smoking gun") has been introduced into a computer program, which could not have been included in the look-alike, except by copying. It is also useful to deposit a copy of a program with a responsible person in

---

11. COM (1999) 250 final.

order to prove that the work was in existence in that form on a particular date.

The person liable for infringement is the person who does the copying. If a library provides a photocopying machine for users, the users make the copies, not the library. If an Internet service provider merely provides the computing facilities for the customers, without any vetting of material passing through its computer, it is arguably the customer who requests material who does the copying, not the service provider, but each case will depend on its facts.

Copying a substantial part

It is not necessary to copy the whole of a work in order to infringe copyright, for Section 16 provides that there is infringement if either the whole of the work or a substantial part is copied. The difficulty is to establish just what is a "substantial part" and each case will depend on its facts. For example the test is not just quantitative, but is also qualitative; thus if the work is a book of detective fiction which is 500 pages long, reproducing only the last page or even the last paragraph which reveals the name of the murderer, may well amount to reproducing a "substantial part". It is therefore no defence to argue that only a small part was copied if that part was a key element. A key element of a sound recording by James Brown may be one his famous grunts. Digitally sampling this without consent, then releasing it as part of another recording may well amount to copying a substantial part and to breach of copyright.

Non-literal copying

Problems arise when an employee, who has written a program for his or her employer, goes to work for someone else and is then set to design a similar product. The programmer may start from scratch on the new program, but is familiar with the structure and routines of the old program and may follow the same course. Is the program which results a copy of the first? Does the adoption of the same structure, sequence and organization amount to copying a substantial part of the work and so constitute an infringement of copyright? This is known as non-literal copying and is discussed in 6.3.3 below.

6.3.3 Idea v expression

In the United States a distinction is drawn between the idea behind a copyright work and its expression. The idea is not protected by copyright, but the expression is. If the structure, sequence and organization of the program is the idea behind the program it is unprotected, but if it forms part of the expression, then its use will infringe the copyright and sale of imitative products may be restrained by an injunction and damages sought.

It is sometimes difficult to distinguish between the idea and the expression of a computer program and there is little agreement on the most appropriate test. One of America's most eminent judges, Judge Learned Hand, said in 1930 that "Nobody has ever been able to fix that boundary and nobody ever can"[12]. This shows that the problem is not new.

The two most important US cases on idea/expression and non-literal copying of computer programs are *Whelan Associates v Jaslow* [1987] FSR 1 and *Computer Associates v Altai* 23 USPQ 2d 1241 (1992). These are important in a European context for Article 1 of the Software Directive provides that:

> Protection in accordance with this Directive shall apply to the expression in any form of a computer program. Ideas and principles which underlie any element of a computer program, including those which underlie its interfaces, are not protected by copyright under this Directive.

However, the Copyright (Computer Software) Regulations 1992, which purport to implement the Directive, do not contain a statement to the same effect. The English definition of copying therefore remains as in Sections 16 and 17 of the 1988 Act (above), the test being whether what has been taken amounts to a substantial part. The idea/expression dichotomy has, however, been referred to in the cases and thus may be entering English law via this route rather than via legislation. The main case is *John Richardson v Flanders* [1993] FSR 497, but this was criticized in *IBCOS Computers Ltd v Barclays Mercantile Highland Finance Ltd* [1994] FSR 275.

Copyright laws aim to strike a balance between the protection of the rights of the owners of copyright and the rights of the users of the system. The issue is to what extent the law should prevent competitors from developing further the innovations of others. *Whelan v Jaslow* (above) held that the structure of a program was part of its expression and was therefore protectable; and copyright had been infringed by a second program which showed structural similarities. *Whelan* thus favoured the copyright owner and could have the effect of stifling the development of rival products. Is this a good thing?

In *Altai* the balance was shifted. *Whelan* was thought to have given too much protection to the owners of copyright and too little incremental development was allowed. The court in *Altai* suggested a three-stage procedure for determining substantial similarity. First, the court should break down the allegedly infringed program into its constituent structural parts. Secondly, it should examine each of these parts for such things as incorporated ideas, expression that is necessarily incidental to those ideas, and elements that are taken from the public domain, thus sifting out all non-protectable material. Thirdly, what is left after this process of elimination should be compared with

---

12. *Nichols v Universal Pictures* (1930) 45 F (2d) 119 (US).

the structure of the allegedly infringing program. The court said that in constructing this test,

> ... we seek to ensure two things: (i) that programmers may receive appropriate copyright protection for innovative utilitarian works containing expression; and (ii) that non-protectable technical expression remains in the public domain for others to use freely as building blocks in their own work.

In the English case of *John Richardson v Flanders* [1993] FSR 497, Ferris J adopted a variant of the US *Altai* test. He said the court should first decide whether the plaintiff's program as a whole is entitled to copyright protection. Secondly, it should decide whether there are any similarities between the plaintiff's program and the defendant's. Thirdly it should decide whether any similarity was attributable to copying; and fourthly, it should decide whether any copy amounts to a substantial part of the plaintiff's program, assessing this by application of the abstraction, filtration and comparison test of the US case of *Computer Associates v Altai*.

However, the *Richardson* test was criticized as being unhelpful in the later English case of *IBCOS Computers Ltd v Barclays Mercantile Highland Finance Ltd* [1994] FSR 275. There, Jacob J said that US copyright law is not the same as ours, particularly in the area of copyright works concerned with functionality and with compilations (and here the plaintiff's program was protectable as a compilation: see below). A claim for infringement of copyright in English law should be dealt with in the following order:

1. What are the work or works in which the plaintiff claims copyright?
2. Is each work "original"?
3. Was there copying from that work?
4. If there was copying, has a substantial part of the work been reproduced?[13]

In *IBCOS*, the plaintiff's program comprised 335 program files, 171 record layout files and 46 screen layout files and attracted copyright as a compilation of programs[14]. The compilation was original in that a very substantial amount of skill, labour and judgement had gone into its formation. When assessing copying, Jacob J said that the court should consider the text of the code, the program structure and design features. Whether there was copying of a substantial part was essentially a value judgement for the court, which

---

13. This was confirmed as the correct test by Pumfrey J in *Cantor Fitzgerald International v Tradition (UK) Ltd* (1999) (unreported).
14. Compilations are protected as literary works: see above under the heading Literary Works.

would be aided in reaching its decision by expert evidence. A large part of Jacob J's judgement was given over to analysing the similarities and differences.

In *IBCOS* the imitative program was an enhanced version of the program it was alleged to have copied. It was obvious that there had been disc-to-disc copying and that what had been taken was a substantial part of the original. However, even if copying had been non-literal, the meticulous approach of Jacob J could equally have been applied to analyse the two programs. There is no need for the court to be tied down by the abstraction, filtration and comparison methodology of *Altai* and *John Richardson*.

The status of idea v expression is more difficult. As stated earlier, it is embodied in the Directive, but not incorporated into the 1992 Regulations, which were supposed to have implemented the Directive. The distinction between idea and expression is criticized in *IBCOS* and found difficult to define and to apply in all of those legal systems of which it forms part. The law is bound to change, but in which direction?

Readers might consider the following:

1. The difficulty of advising either a software house or a programmer as to precisely what is protectable now and might be protectable at some unspecified time in the future should the programmer want to work for someone else or as a self-employed person in the design of computer programs.
2. A software house has assigned copyright in an accounts package to a client. The software house is approached by a second client for another accounts package. What can the software house do without copying the first? What effect does this have on costs?

6.3.4 Home taping

One other issue connected with copying, which has aroused considerable interest, is home taping, for this has turned large sectors of the community into potential law breakers. Section 70 of the 1988 Act legalizes home taping but only for limited purposes. It states that:

> The making for private and domestic use of a recording of a broadcast or cable programme solely for the purpose of enabling it to be viewed or listened to at a more convenient time does not infringe any copyright in the broadcast or cable programme or in any work included in it.

Thus, what is known as time-shifting is legalized, i.e., recording a programme or film broadcast on television in order to watch it at another, more convenient time. However, the exemption does not cover for example:

- building a library of films shown on TV, where the motive is other than viewing at a more convenient time;
- copying a compact disc onto cassette in order to play it in the car or on a personal stereo;
- taping a selection of music in order to play it at a party, except in the case of the radio broadcast when this constitutes private and domestic use, which may be a question of scale and venue.

It would have been much better if all home taping for private and domestic purposes had been legalized. The law in its present form is unenforceable, it leaves copyright owners uncompensated, and may even bring copyright laws into disrepute.

6.3.5 Adaptation

It is an infringement of copyright to make an adaptation of a copyright work; to copy an adaptation; to issue copies of the adaptation to the public; to perform, play or show the adaptation in public; or to broadcast it or include it in a cable programme service. These can be done only with the consent of the copyright owner. Making an adaptation includes translating a work, e.g. from English to French; converting a computer program from one language or code into another; or making an arrangement or altered version of a program[15].

6.3.6 Rental right

As we have seen, one of the rights of a copyright owner is to prevent the issue to the public of copies of a copyright work (the distribution right). However, under the old law, once a purchaser had bought a copyright work, the copyright owner had no statutory rights to prevent its further distribution, so long as the work was not copied. For example, a video rental shop could buy a copy of a film and rent it to the public, and the copyright owner would receive no further royalties, even though the video shop was making a profit from the commercial exploitation of the work. This was felt to be unfair.

The law was changed, firstly by the 1988 Act, to give a right to the owners of copyright in sound recordings, films or computer programs to prevent rental or lending of those works by others without permission. The

---

15. But note that an adaptation which amounts to a distortion and to a derogatory treatment cannot breach the moral right to object to derogatory treatment (section 80 of the 1988 Act), for this right does not apply to a computer program or to any computer-generated work (section 81) (see further below).

right did not apply to other copyright works, such as books, where some authors were already compensated by a Public Lending Right[16] when their books were borrowed from a public library. However, implementation of the EC Directive on rental and lending[17] extended the rental and lending right to authors of most copyright works, not just to the authors of computer programs, films and sound recordings. The right does not, however, apply to lending between friends; nor to books loaned by public libraries.

6.3.7 Secondary infringement

This is covered by Sections 22 to 26 of the 1988 Act, but in order to fall within these sections, the person infringing must know or have reason to believe that his or her actions involve infringement of copyright. Like primary infringement, secondary infringement breaches the civil rights of a copyright owner, but most importantly, secondary infringement may also amount to a criminal offence, punishable by a fine and/or imprisonment. Secondary infringement is therefore a much more serious matter and is designed to catch those who trade in, and who therefore make a profit from, pirated goods; or who provide the apparatus or premises for infringing performances of copyright works.

Secondary infringement occurs, for example, where a person:

- imports an infringing copy other than for private and domestic use;
- possesses an infringing copy in the course of a business;
- sells or lets for hire an infringing copy;
- exhibits in public or distributes an infringing copy in the course of a business;
- distributes infringing copies otherwise than in the course of a business to such an extent as to affect prejudicially the owner of the copyright;
- makes, imports, sells, hires or possesses in the course of a business an article specifically designed or adapted for making copies of a copyright work;
- transmits the work by means of a telecommunications system (other than by broadcasting or inclusion in a cable programme service) knowing or having reason to believe that infringing copies of the work will be made by means of the reception of the transmission in the United Kingdom or elsewhere;

---

16. See the Public Lending Right Act 1979, as implemented by the Public Lending Right Scheme 1982.
17. Directive 92/100, OJ L346/61. The Directive was brought into force on 1 December 1996 by the Copyright and Related Rights Regulations 1996.

or, with certain other qualifications,

- permits a place of public entertainment to be used for a performance which infringes copyright in a work;
- provides apparatus, or premises where apparatus is going to be used for an infringing performance of a copyright work;
- supplies a copy of a sound recording or film where it is known that or there is reason to believe that it, or a copy of it, is likely to be used in order to infringe copyright.

6.3.8 Copy protection

Many works in electronic form are now copy-protected, that is, some means has been introduced to prevent the work from being copied; or to reduce the quality of any copies made; or to identify works, performances and rights owners through electronic rights management systems. And, given the difficulty of enforcing copyright in the digital environment, many copyright owners see these copy protection devices as of greater practical utility than their civil rights under the law.

Section 296 of the 1988 Act provides that anyone who (a) makes, imports, sells, or lets for hire etc any device or means specifically designed or adapted to circumvent copy-protection, or (b) publishes information intended to enable or assist persons to circumvent copy protection is to be treated in the same way as if he was infringing copyright in the copy protected work; and is subject to the same remedies as a copyright infringer (see further below) including, for example, seizure of any devices used to circumvent copyright, or equipment used to make such devices. However, in both cases the person making (etc) the device or publishing the information will be liable only if he or she knew or had reason to believe that the device or information would be used to make infringing copies.

Use of the Internet has focused international attention on the need to harmonize the rules on technical devices and electronic rights management systems. Provisions were included in the WIPO Copyright Treaty and the WIPO Performances and Phonograms Treaty (1996). Both of these have been signed by the European Community, and are to be implemented through the Proposed Directive on Copyright in the Information Society[18]. This will necessitate changes to English law, although the principles will remain the same.

---

18. (1998) O.J. C108/6.

6.4 Acts permitted in relation to copyright works

Some acts are permitted under the 1988 Act, even though they would other-wise amount to breach of copyright. The range of these has been extended by the EC Directive on the Legal Protection of Computer Programs and by the Copyright (Computer Software) Regulations 1992 which have amended the 1988 Act. It is not proposed to discuss all of the acts permitted by the 1988 Act, but rather to select those of greatest importance for software engineers.

6.4.1 Fair dealing

To fall within the fair dealing provisions and thus not to infringe copyright, copying must be for one of the following purposes:

- private study, or research;
- criticism or review;
- reporting current events.

Any type of copyright work may be used for the purposes of criticism or review, therefore an extract from a computer game may be broadcast in a television programme reviewing software; and part of a poem may be included in a critique of a poet's work, so long as in both cases, sufficient acknowledgement of copyright ownership is given.

Only literary, musical and artistic works may be copied for the purpose of private study and research, not, e.g. sound recordings or films. Home taping of these was discussed earlier. However computer programs fall under the heading of literary works and thus at first sight students of computing may copy paper manuals and computer programs for private study or research, so long as not too much is copied. However, Section 29 of the 1988 Act (as amended by the 1992 Regulations) now provides that it is not fair dealing

(a) to convert a computer program expressed in a low level language into a version expressed in a high level language, or
(b) incidentally in the course of so converting the program, to copy it.

These acts are permitted *only* if done in the course of decompilation for the purpose of interoperability, on which see further below.

How much may be copied?

A difficult issue is how much may be copied under the fair dealing exceptions. The only generalized answer that can be given is that "it all depends", but the overriding consideration is that the use must be fair, i.e. it must not unfairly exploit the rights of copyright owners. Views on the matter differ, according to the interests at stake. For example, publishers have tended to state that only a certain proportion of a work may be copied without payment of a royalty, and further they have said that copying outside these bounds will be treated by them as copyright infringement. Statements to this effect are often displayed beside photocopiers.

In certain circumstances, copying the whole of a work may be fair dealing, but not if copying is just more convenient than going to a shop and buying or ordering the work, or if it is just cheaper to copy than to buy. In many instances, there are licensing schemes and the safest, although certainly not always the cheapest approach, is to pay the licence fee, and to copy only in accordance with the terms of the licence. If a notice beside a photocopier or other documentation states that copying may be done only within the terms of a licensing agreement, copying outside those terms will be in breach of contract. In an educational establishment, such as a university, copying in breach of the licence may be a disciplinary matter. The university has to protect itself against action by copyright owners.

6.4.2 Making back-up copies of computer programs

Section 50A of the 1988 Act provides that:

> It is not an infringement of copyright for a lawful user of a copy of a computer program to make a back-up copy of it which is necessary for him to have for the purpose of lawful use.

A licensee is an example of a lawful user. Any clause in a licence or other agreement which prohibits or restricts the right to make a legitimate back-up copy is void. However, Section 50A only authorizes copies "necessary ... for the purpose of lawful use". If a program is supplied on floppy disc, then copied onto the hard disc, no further back up copies are necessary and no further copies are allowed.

6.4.3 Transfers of works in electronic form

If the original purchaser, A, sells the program to another person, B, B's position is governed by Section 56 of the 1988 Act. This deals exclusively with works in electronic form. It therefore will not cover the transfer of paper manuals.

Section 56 provides that if A had express or implied permission to use, copy or adapt an electronic work (e.g. to translate it into another computer language), or to make copies of an adaptation, then unless there are express terms to the contrary in the original licence, B is entitled to do the same. However, if A sells to B, he transfers all of his rights to B. Thus if A retains and uses any copies himself, his original licence no longer operates, and his use of the program or of any copies of it will be in breach of copyright. Section 56 therefore gives permission to use the work to one person at a time; it does not allow an increase in the number of authorized users.

6.4.4 Decompilation for the purpose of interoperability

The European Commission has been very concerned that Europe develop a strong software industry. This requires the protection of intellectual property rights, but not to the extent that further development of software products is prohibited or unduly inhibited, e.g. by copyright laws. One type of advance which steers a course between protection and development is the production of programs which are interoperable. The original program is protected, yet new ones can be spawned. The difficulty is to decompile and study the old program in order to engineer the new without infringing copyright. This could be done under the 1988 Act in its unamended form only under the fair dealing provisions (above), arguing that this was private study or research and that the use was fair. These arguments may have succeeded in some cases, but by no means in all and each case would depend on its facts. Heavy expenditure by the industry thus rested on an uncertain legal foundation.

Now, Section 29 of the 1988 Act provides that it is not fair dealing:

(a) to convert a computer program expressed in a low level language into a version expressed in a high level language; or
(b) incidentally in the course of so converting the program, to copy it.

However, if the decompilation is for the purpose of interoperability, a lawful user may do either of these acts provided:

(a) it is *necessary* to decompile the program to obtain the information *necessary* to create an independent program which can be operated with the program decompiled or with another program (the permitted objective); and
(b) the information so obtained is *not used for any other purpose* than the permitted objective

However, decompilation will not be permitted if the lawful user:

- has readily available the information necessary to decompile the program – software houses can prevent decompilation of their programs by providing this in printed or other form;
- does not confine the decompiling to such acts as are necessary to achieve interoperability – a wider sweep is not permitted;
- supplies the information obtained by decompiling to any person to whom it is not necessary to supply it in order to achieve the permitted objective

– displaying this on an electronic notice board or publishing it in a computer magazine is not permitted;
- uses the information to create a program which is substantially similar in its expression to the program decompiled or to do any act restricted by copyright – decompilation should be for interoperability, not for imitation.

The right to decompile cannot be excluded or limited by a clause in a licence agreement.

6.4.5 Error correction

Under Section 50C of the 1988 Act, the lawful user of a program (e.g. a licensee) may copy and adapt a computer program provided this is necessary for his lawful use and this is not prohibited by any contract term.

Section 50C is widely drafted, but it is stated that in particular it allows a lawful user to copy or adapt a program in order to correct errors. This is rather like the general right to repair property, e.g. a car. No agreement for the purchase of a car ever contains a clause limiting the right to repair it. This would be contrary to public policy and consumer expectations. However a specific provision is necessary for a copyright work, for alteration does infringe the right of a copyright owner, whereas repairing a car body panel does not affect any residual right of the manufacturer of a car.

6.4.6 Databases

The Database Regulations 1997 introduced a new Section 50D into the 1988 Act. This provides that it is not an infringement of copyright in a database for a person who has a right to use the database to do anything which is necessary for the purposes of access to or use of the contents of the database or any part of it. This means that it will not infringe copyright if a licensee downloads, i.e. copies the database or part of it in order to access or use it.

One other recent addition to the 1988 Act is Section 29(5) which provides that "The doing of anything in relation to a database for the purposes of research for a commercial purpose is not fair dealing with the database". This is interesting in that the other provisions of the Act do not draw a distinction between commercial and non-commercial research.

6.5 Remedies for breach of copyright

In general, a copyright owner has, in an action for infringement of copyright, all the usual civil remedies of search and seizure, injunction, damages and an action for an account of profits made in breach of copyright. However, if it is shown that at the time of the infringement of copyright the defendant did not know and had no reason to believe that copyright subsisted in the work, then the plaintiff is not entitled to damages against the defendant, but may still seek any of the other civil remedies.

At the other end of the scale, if the infringement is flagrant and the justice of the case requires it, the court is given a discretion to award additional damages, i.e. a sum over and above that necessary to compensate the plaintiff for any loss that may have been incurred as a result of the defendant's breach.

A copyright owner is also given an important power to enter premises without using force in order to seize infringing copies, or articles specifically designed or adapted for making copies, thus allowing seizure and confiscation of, for example, a computer used to make illegitimate copies of computer programs; or of photocopiers; or of equipment used to copy video tapes etc. There are also special provisions to permit seizure from street traders.

6.6 Licensing and assignment of copyright

Copyrights can be licensed to others, called licensees. When a work is licensed, the copyright owner retains ownership of the right, but allows others to use it for all, or for a limited number of purposes. A licence may be exclusive, i.e. it may give one person only the right to use the copyright; or it may be non-exclusive, where any number of persons may be licensed to use it, e.g. licences used on software, such as computer games or for word-processing, which are sold through retail outlets. A licence need not be in writing, although it usually is.

An assignment is different. Here a copyright owner, called an assignor, transfers rights of ownership to another person, called an assignee. The assignee therefore acquires more than a licensee, in that the licensee merely has the right to use the work in accordance with the licence, and does not acquire ownership. To give full legal title an assignment must be in writing, and it must be signed by or on behalf of the assignor, that is the person transferring the copyright.

When a copyright owner dies, copyrights do not also die, for it will be remembered that copyright, for example in a literary work, lasts for life plus 70 years[19]. Copyrights can be transferred in a will, or if there is no provision in a will dealing with them, they will be dealt with under other rules of succession. They will also pass on bankruptcy to a trustee in bankruptcy.

An assignment need not be for the entire copyright period, e.g. it may be for the first ten years only; and it may not deal with all facets of the copyright. For example, a novelist may assign the hardback rights to one publisher for five years; the paperback rights to another publisher for six years; the film

---

19. See Section 6.2.3.

rights to a motion picture house for the full copyright period; and the rights in a computer game which he has written and based on the book, to a software house.

Copyright in works not yet created (future copyrights) may also be assigned. This has been quite common in the music business, where a record company may contract with a promising singer-songwriter to support him or her in the early years of his or her career in return for ownership of all copyrights in music yet to be written. This happened to Elton John[20] and Gilbert O'Sullivan[21]. In their cases, the agreements were unfairly biased in favour of the companies, and the artists were able to have them set aside by the courts; but the circumstances have to be extreme before the courts will interfere with contracts freely entered into. Thus, George Michael was unable to get out of his recording contract and copyright assignment, as he knew precisely what he was doing at the time he signed the agreement and he has been advised by some of the best lawyers in the field[22]. As a result of the George Michael case, it is now more common in the music industry to find assignment of copyright over one work, or works created over a fairly short period, rather than over the entire career of the singer–songwriter.

6.7 Moral rights

For the first time in English law, the 1988 Act gives to an author the right to be named as the author of a work (known by the sexist term "paternity right") and the right to object to any modification which is prejudicial to the author's honour or reputation (the integrity right). These are called moral rights. They are not copyrights as such, but many copyright principles are applied to them. The paternity and integrity rights are highly circum-scribed, and in particular they cannot be claimed by the author of a compu-ter program or of a computer-generated work, although they can be claimed by the authors of other relevant works, e.g. a computer manual in paper form. Because of their limited relevance for software engineers, they will not be considered in any greater detail here.

One further moral right is the right to object to false attribution of a work. This right is available to any person who is falsely stated to be the author of a computer program or any other literary, dramatic, musical or artistic work.

---

20. *Elton John v Richard James* (1985) (unreported).
21. *Gilbert O'Sullivan v Management Agency and Music Ltd* [1985] 3 All ER 351.
22. *Panayiotou v Sony Music Entertainment (UK) Ltd,* Times, 30 June 1994.

6.8 Designs

It was stated earlier that there can be copyright in an artistic work, for example a drawing, and that this normally lasts for the lifetime of the artist, plus 70 years. This statement must now be qualified. Drawing and designs, whether on paper, or on any other tangible medium, or in the form of data stored in a computer, are frequently used to manufacture industrial items, such as crockery, furniture, cars, aeroplanes, ships etc. One aim of copyright law is to prevent persons other than the copyright owner from copying either the drawing or any three-dimensional model produced from the drawing. Copyright can exist for an awfully long time. For example, a designer may design a boat when 25. He or she may live until 75. Copyright will last for a further 70 years, with the result that it may last for around 120 years. This has been criticized as too long a period to protect industrial items. Progress is made through imitation, to a greater or a lesser degree. While the owner of copyright deserves some protection at law for research, development and effort, the full copyright term is too long. The law has therefore been changed, but unfortunately not simplified. It is to be found in the Copyright, Designs and Patents Act 1988, the Registered Designs Act 1949 (as amended and supplemented by the Registered Designs Rules), and the Design Right (Semi-Conductor Topographies) Regulations 1989, 1992 and 1993 (for semi-conductor chips). Also, we now have the Designs Directive[23] and a proposal for a Council Regulation on Community Design[24]. As this is a book primarily intended for software engineers and the design laws apply to hardware, they will be considered only briefly here.

How do design laws work? Let us use the example of a drawing of a machine tool which is to be manufactured industrially. The drawing itself will be protected by copyright as an artistic work. Thus if anyone copies this drawing directly and without permission, they will be in breach of copyright. Under the pre-1988 laws, if anyone copied the tool made from the design drawings, they would be indirectly copying the drawings and also be liable for breach of copyright. Now, however, the law relating to indirect copying of designs used industrially has been changed. Instead of the tool being protected by copyright law, it is excluded from copyright (unless the tool is itself an artistic work, which is unlikely) and is protected instead by a new unregistered design right, which also is governed by the Copyright, Designs and Patents Act 1988. The design could also be registered in the Designs Registry at the Patent Office before the tool is manufactured industrially (i.e. before 50

---

23. Directive 98/71/EC of the European Parliament and of the Council of 13 October 1998 on the legal protection of designs.
24. Amended proposal for a Council Regulation (EC) on Community Design.

copies are made). It will then also be protected under the Registered Designs Act 1949 (as amended).

So far as the computing industry is concerned, the new unregistered design right is likely to be the most important method of protecting designs, for it potentially covers such things as the layout of circuit boards and component designs. It will also have considerable impact on the design and manufacture of semi-conductor chips. Semi-conductor chip protection is governed by the Design Right (Semi-Conductor Topographies) Regulations which adapt the design right of the 1988 Act to protect the topography of semi-conductor chips.

6.8.1 Unregistered design right

The new design right lasts for up to 15 years. Certain conditions have to be satisfied before the right can attach. Firstly the design must have been embodied in a design document. This is defined in Section 51 of the 1988 Act as "... any record of a design, whether in the form of a drawing, a written description, a photograph, data stored on a computer or otherwise." Thus if the machine tool was designed with the aid of a computer, and the design is stored in the memory of the computer, this can be a design document.

The definition of a design document is also crucial in ascertaining the extent of the new right, for a document cannot be a design document unless it embodies a design. Design is defined in section 51(3) as follows:

> design means the design of any aspect of the shape or configuration (whether internal or external) of the whole or part of an article other than surface decoration.

Surface decoration, for example, intertwined flowers or a picture of an apple, is not caught within in the definition of design for these purposes. It therefore falls outside the new design right and would be protectable by copyright in the usual way (i.e., as a work of artistic copyright), or it may be protected under the Registered Designs Act 1949.

To be protected under the new design right the design must also be original. Originality is a requirement of both copyright and patent law, but in both those sets of laws it means different things. In designs law we meet a third meaning. Firstly the design must not have been copied; and secondly, under Section 213(4) of the 1988 Act, the design must not be "commonplace in the design field in question at the time of its creation".

Even if all of the above criteria are satisfied, not all designs are protectable by the new right. Section 213(3) provides that there can be no design right in:

(a) a method or principle of construction; or
(b) features of shape or configuration of an article which:

(i) enable the article to be connected to, or placed in, around or against another article so that either article may perform its function; or

(ii) are dependent upon the appearance of another article of which the article is intended by the designer to form an integral part; or

(c) surface decoration.

Category (b) above covers what are known as the must-fit and must-match exceptions. It is not an infringement to copy aspects of the design which are essential to ensure that another article will connect with or fit against the original article[25] or which are dependent on the appearance of the original article where the new article is intended to form an integral part of it. Spare parts are a good example of items falling within this description. Indeed the exemption was designed to prevent manufacturers (e.g. of cars) claiming a monopoly in the right to manufacture (or to licence the manufacture) of spare parts (such as exhaust pipes) to fit their cars. In *British Leyland v Armstrong* [1986] AC 577, this practice was held to be anti-competitive in that it was stifling competition in the spare parts market and keeping prices artificially high.

Under the new law, copyright will not protect spare parts manufactured from design drawings and neither will the new design right. As we shall see later[26], spare parts which are purely functional and lacking in eye-appeal (i.e. not aesthetically pleasing) are not protected by the Registered Designs Act 1949, nor are designs of items which "must fit". This lack of protection is designed to stimulate competition. However, not all protection is denied. If a product is truly innovative, it may be patentable, but most of the items falling within the "must-fit" and "must-match" exemptions will be spare parts and will not be sufficiently novel to qualify for a patent.

While the Designs Directive will change the law relating to registered designs, unregistered designs law will not be affected.

6.8.2 Registered designs

The Registered Designs Act 1949 provides a special regime of protection for designs of products which are aesthetically pleasing. Purely functional items which do not satisfy these criteria are not registrable, nor are the must-fit items excluded from the unregistered design right by the 1988 Act (see above). Items which "must match" are registrable, e.g. crockery in a tea set. The 1949 Act can be of relevance to computer scientists, for the design

---

25. This is reminiscent of decompilation for the purposes of interoperability: see above.
26. See Section 6.8.2.

of such external features as keyboards and VDUs may fall within the Act, but internal components cannot.

Designs falling within the Act must be registered (hence the name, Registered Designs Act). They can be protected for 25 years. Changes will have to be made when the Designs Directive[27] is implemented, but these changes will not be major. The EU Designs Regulation[28] will create a new European registered design right conferring protection across the whole of the European Union. There will then be a choice of registering design rights in each country separately (the national route) or registering at one central office for the whole EU (the European route).

6.9 Trade marks

Trade marks, trade names and distinctive get-up (such as the appearance of a McDonald's restaurant and the characteristic golden "M" or double arches) can be very valuable commercial assets, diverting sales from equally meritorious but less well-known or less attractively named merchandize. They should be chosen with care and nurtured through marketing. The "Marlboro" mark has been valued at $40 billion world-wide and appears on one in every four cigarettes sold in the United States. But, if they are successful, marks and get-up may be copied by others, either blatantly by pirating, or perhaps more subtly, but just as effectively, by other forms of imitation which siphon off custom. This section looks at the legal protection of marks and names.

There are two ways of protecting trade marks: firstly, under the Trade Marks Act 1994; and secondly, protection at common law, under the tort of passing off. It is not essential to register a trade mark at the Trade Marks Registry, but a registered mark will be protected under the Act and at common law, whereas an unregistered mark has only common law protection.

When deciding whether to register, the following points should be borne in mind, in addition to those discussed in more detail below. Firstly, if a mark is registered, a rival trader is more likely to discover it through searching standard sources for marks already in use, and is therefore more likely to avoid using that same mark or a confusingly similar one. Secondly, a registered mark is protected from the date of its registration, whereas protection at common law is dependent on acquiring goodwill after use in the market. Thirdly, registered trade marks are protected throughout the country, whereas common law protection may be strictly local. A firm providing computing services in Worcester may not be able to prevent a firm in

---

27. See note 23 above. The Directive must be implemented by 28 October 2001.
28. See note 24 above.

Brighton from using the same unregistered trade mark if the services provided by the Worcester firm are merely local, rather than national or international.

Protection at common law is cheaper, as no fees are paid for registration, but litigation at common law can be more complex, and protection under the statutory scheme is stronger. A trader who does not initially register, and thus has only common law protection, can subsequently decide to register a mark if it is commercially successful. This is sometimes the wisest course, as then money is spent only on those marks worth protecting. Furthermore, in contrast to most other intellectual property rights, the monopoly in a trade mark can be perpetual, provided in the case of a registered mark, the appropriate fees are paid for renewal of registration.

Care should be taken in choosing a mark which will be used in other countries and all translations should be checked carefully for ambiguity or inaccuracy. When Pepsi entered the Chinese market for the first time, sales were fantastic, but company officials were perplexed to learn that most of the product was being poured onto the ground. They were horrified to discover that the slogan "Come alive with Pepsi" had been translated as "Pepsi makes your ancestors come alive"! Other examples of inappropriate marks registered for use in the United Kingdom following literal translation from other languages are "Skin a Baby" for baby cream and "My Pee" for a soft drink. Careful market research is clearly needed for all foreign markets.

Private individuals can handle their own trade mark registrations, but the law is complex and the procedure can be time-consuming. It is therefore advisable to seek professional assistance. The easiest way to discover the names of local trade mark agents, or patent agents who also take on this kind of work, is through Yellow Pages in the telephone directory. The UK Trade Marks Registry is at the Patent Office, near Cardiff. The European Trade Marks Registry is in Spain. This handles the registration of trade marks for the whole territory of the European Community. They are called Community Trade Marks. This chapter concentrates on English law and the Trade Marks Act of 1994. However similar laws are to be found in other EU states following harmonization by Council Directive No. 89/104.

We consider first the statutory scheme for the protection of trade marks in the UK (registered marks), then the common law (unregistered marks).

6.9.1 Registered trade marks

What is a trade mark?
Section 1 of the Trade Marks Act 1994 states that a trade mark means

> any sign capable of being represented graphically which is capable of distinguishing goods or services of one undertaking from those of other undertakings. A trade mark may, in particular, consist of words (includ-

ing personal names), designs, letters, numerals or the shape of goods or their packaging.

Marks like Microsoft, Pierre Cardin, the Shell logo, IBM and Lotus 1-2-3 are all registrable under the 1994 Act, but so too is the distinctive shape of goods and their packaging, reversing an earlier decision by the House of Lords under the Trade Marks Act 1938 that it was not possible to register the distinctive shape of the Coca Cola bottle[29].

6.9.2 Grounds for refusal of registration

The 1994 Act is market-orientated. It begins with the principle that trade mark should be registered unless specifically excluded. The emphasis on registrability represents a shift in policy from the provisions of previous UK statutes; and the exceptions are designed to reflect the interests of industry and to prevent confusion in the market place.

The grounds for refusal to register a trade mark are divided into two categories: absolute (section 3) and relative (section 5). Firstly, Section 3(1) provides that a sign which does not satisfy the definition of a trade mark in Section 1 (above) shall not be registered. One of the elements of the definition was that the sign must be capable of being represented graphically, which includes being described in writing. Smells (e.g. of perfume or after shave) may be difficult to register because of this requirement.

Secondly, trade marks which are devoid of any distinctive character will not be registered, unless they have acquired a distinctive character through use. Trade marks which have been used for some time may not therefore have to be as distinctive in themselves as marks which have not yet been used or have only just been launched. The name International Business Machines Inc. is not distinctive and would not be registrable in itself, but if not already registered it would be registrable because it has become distinctive through use.

Thirdly, trade marks will not be registered if they consist exclusively of signs or indications which serve to designate the kind, quality, quantity, intended purpose, value, geographical origin, the time of production of goods or of rendering services, or other characteristics of goods or services. This paragraph can prevent a trader from acquiring a monopoly over the use of common descriptive words, phrases or indications of the geographical origin. York Trailers had problems with the equivalent provision under the 1938 Act. Anyone who tried to register the name "Floppy Discs" would be refused. However, if the trader has been using a mark which potentially falls foul of this provision, but can prove that it has become distinctive of the goods

---

29. *Coca Cola* [1986] RPC 421.

or services through use, then once again there will be no objection to its registration. Similar reasoning underlies Section 3(1)(d) which prevents the registration of a mark which has become "customary in the current language or in the *bona fide* and established practices of the trade". In addition, a trade mark cannot be registered if it is contrary to public policy or to accepted principles of morality; or if it is deceptive; or if its use is prohibited by law.

Section 5 sets out the relative grounds for refusal to register a trade mark. Basically, these prevent registration of a mark which is the same or similar to the mark already used by another trader. The onus is on the opponent to registration to demonstrate a likelihood of confusion.

6.9.3 Infringement of a registered trade mark

Registration of a trade mark gives an exclusive right to use the mark and the right to sue others if they make improper use of it. The acts amounting to infringement are set out in Section 10 of the Act. They cover use of the same or a confusingly similar mark in circumstances which would cause confusion on the part of the public, or cause the public to assume an association between the marks; or if it would take unfair advantage of the trade mark owner's reputation, or be detrimental to the distinctive character or reputation of the mark. Use of names such IBN, National Business Machines Inc., M&S Trading, St Mitchell, Zerocks and Antimonopoly (for a board game) would doubtless invite litigation.

6.9.4 Comparative advertising

Comparative advertising was severely restricted by the previous Trade Marks Act of 1938, which provided that it was an infringement to "import a reference" to a registered mark. Thus if Ford advertised their cars as being cheaper than Volvo cars, if Volvo was a registered mark, Volvo cars could bring an action against Ford for infringing their trade mark. This was anomalous and an undue restriction on an advertising practice which could provide useful information to consumers and was not necessarily harmful to trade. Use of the trade mark in this illustration serves only to identify the goods of the rival producer. Any deception, e.g. as to the price comparison, should be regulated by other laws.

Under the 1994 Act, "importing a reference" no longer constitutes an infringing act. Greater liberty in comparative advertising is allowed. A trade mark owner will be able to restrain use of a trade mark for the purpose of identifying goods or services only if it is contrary to honest practices in industrial or commercial matters and would take unfair advantage of or be detrimental to the distinctive character or repute of the mark (Section 10).

6.9.5 Other non-infringing acts

A trade mark is not infringed by the use by someone of his own name or address; or of indications describing amongst other things, the kind, quality, quantity, intended purpose or geographical origin of his or her goods or services; or from using a trade mark to describe the intended purpose of accessories or spare parts, providing in each of these cases the use is in accordance with honest practice and is not such as to take unfair advantage of, or be detrimental to, the distinctive character or repute of the trade mark (Section 10).

6.9.6 Pirated goods and criminal offences

Piracy of software is a serious problem. Pirated goods generally account for around 5 per cent of world trade and were the main reason for the emphasis in the GATT talks on the protection and enforcement of intellectual property rights. Piracy is endemic in countries such as Malaysia and Thailand. This harms software houses from other countries and thus other economies, but it also harms the local economy for it inhibits the development in those states of industries such as publishing, film making, the sound recording industry and the writing of computer software. Under the GATT agreement, countries where piracy is rife have to amend their laws to protect intellectual property rights and demonstrate effective law enforcement, or face trade sanctions.

In order to combat piracy, Section 92 of the 1994 Act states that it is an offence for a person with a view to gain, or with intent to cause loss, to do any of the following without the consent of a trade mark owner:

- apply a unauthorized trade mark to goods;
- sell or let for hire, or offer or expose for sale or hire, goods or packaging which bear an unauthorized trade mark;
- have in his possession, custody or control in the course of business, for sale or hire goods (or packaging) which bear an unauthorized trade mark.

Goods which have been placed on the market in the EC with the consent of the trade mark owner and are then resold without alteration do not fall within the ambit of Section 92, nor can the trade mark owner take civil action to prevent their resale.

6.10 The tort of passing off

The second method of protecting trade marks and trade names is under the common law tort of passing off. Passing off is an action used by one trader against another who imitates the former's trade mark, trade name, product get-up or trading style in a way which causes actual or potential loss, and which causes confusion amongst the consuming public as to the source of goods or services.

The action for passing off overlaps with the action for infringement of a trade mark based on the use of another's mark, but it also operates in a wider range of circumstances and can be used to protect any sort of mark, registered or unregistered. In *Erven Warnink v Townend* [1979] AC 731, Lord Diplock said there were five common elements in an action for passing off:

- a misrepresentation
- made by a trader in the course of trade
- to prospective customers or ultimate consumers
- which is calculated to injure the goodwill or business of another, and
- which causes actual damage to that other.

The tort is best illustrated through the cases. In *Reddaway v Banham* [1896] AC 199, the plaintiffs, who sold their product under the unregistered mark "Camel Hair Belting", succeeded in an action for passing off against the defendants who had begun to use that same name on their goods. Evidence showed that the plaintiffs had built up a substantial reputation in that name, and that the phrase "Camel Hair Belting" had acquired not only a primary meaning of goods made of camel hair, but also, a secondary meaning of goods sold by them. Imitation of the name thus amounted to a misrepresentation as to the origin of the goods.

The reasoning in *Reddaway* was taken much further in a line of cases called the "drinks" cases[30]. Here it was held that groups of traders correctly using a particular appellation for their products (here champagne, sherry and Scotch whisky, or those making their product to a particular recipe, such as advocaat), could prevent other traders from using those names when their products did not conform to the standard description of goods of that type. Thus egg flip could not be described as advocaat, and whisky made in Japan could not be called Scotch. These cases are regarded as extending the action much further than previously, in that for the first time the actions were commenced by groups of traders to protect a trading reputation owned by them collectively.

The action for passing off can also protect the get-up or general appearance of goods, or the trading style of a business. For example in *Reckitt and Colman v Borden* [1990] 1 All ER 873, the defendants were prevented from marketing their lemon juice in lemon-shaped containers which closely resembled the Jif lemons produced by the plaintiffs. The court held that the plaintiffs had built

---

30. *Bollinger v Costa Brava Wine Co.* [1980] Ch 262 (champagne); *Vine Products v Mackenzie* [1969] RPC 1 (sherry); *John Walker v Henry Ost* [1970] RPC 489 (scotch whisky); *Bulmer v Bollinger* [1974] FSR 334 (champagne perry); *Warnick v Townend* [1979] AC 731 (advocaat).

up a substantial reputation in the sale of juice in that type of container, and allowing someone else to use a similar one would cause confusion amongst consumers as to the origin of the product.

A major change in the law since the *Borden* case was decided is that the shape of a product is now registrable as a trade mark under the Trade Marks Act 1994 (see above). However, this does not render the tort of passing off redundant, for the actions for infringement of a registered mark and for passing off now merely overlap. In the event of one action failing on a technicality, the other might well succeed. Also, not all shapes will be registered, for registration is costly. Passing off is the only cause of action for the trader with an unregistered right.

6.11 Domain names

If someone wishes to purchase goods from, say, Marks and Spencer, they may well search on the Internet to see if M&S have an on-line catalogue. They are quite likely to guess that the company is registered with the domain name of Marksandspencer.com or Marksandspencer.co.uk., i.e., that its domain name is the same as the name under which it trades, or is the same as its trade mark. Also, they may assume that the company using Marksandspencer.com is the same as the company using Marksandspencer.co.uk; and that both addresses are used by the High Street store with which everyone in the UK is familiar and not by another firm "cybersquatting" on its trade name and reputation. This may not, however, be the case. Another person may be using that domain name and this may well cause confusion to customers and harm to Marks and Spencer; or another person may have registered that domain name speculatively and with no intention of using it themselves, but solely with a view to selling the address to Marks and Spencer[31].

There is an inherent conflict between domain names and intellectual property in the form of registered and unregistered trade marks; and the rapid development of e-commerce caught many companies with well-known trade marks completely unawares. These conflicts stretch the capacity of the judicial system to prevent unfair competition because:

- trade mark laws are generally territorial, covering one country or, as in the case of the European trade mark, a group of countries, whereas domain names operate in the global market;
- litigation can be slow and expensive;

---

31. As in the first UK case. *Harrods Ltd v UK Network Services Ltd*, 9 December 1996 (unreported), where the defendants had registered the name harrods.com. They were not using it themselves, but had registered it solely with a view to selling the address to Harrods Ltd. Marks and Spencer and Burger King have also sued cybersquatters successfully in the British courts.

● there are problems in enforcing judgements in cases with an international dimension and where the infringers operate in a virtual world.

These problems have not however deterred the courts from granting injunctions to restrain infringement of a registered trade mark or to prevent passing off at common law (see above). It is then for the successful plaintiff to try to pin down the defendant in whichever state he or she operates, using international conventions for the enforcement of judgements.

It was, however, recognized early in the development of the Net that there was a need to regulate domain name disputes in some other way. In 1998, the US government called upon the World Intellectual Property Organization (WIPO) to look into the matter and to recommend to the Internet Corporation for Assigned Names and Numbers (ICANN), the corporation established to manage the domain name system, an international system of registration of domain names which would take into account pre-existing intellectual property rights and provide a straightforward method of dispute resolution.

WIPO has now reported[32], recommending improved standard practices for registrars charged with allocating domain names, including the requirement that domain name holders file accurate personal names and contact details, so that, if there is any dispute, the domain name holder is easily traceable by the holder of any conflicting intellectual property right. Furthermore, there is a new on-line dispute resolution procedure in cases of cybersquatting, which could lead to cancellation of registrations in appropriate cases; and, where a case is brought before the courts in a given country, the holder of domain names should submit to the jurisdiction of that court, thus alleviating problems of jurisdiction jumping and the enforcement of judgements. Also, they recognize that famous and well-known marks have been the special target of "predatory and parasitical practices on the part of a small, but active, minority of domain name registrants" (the Marks and Spencer problem discussed above), thus, WIPO recommend that famous and well-known marks should get special protection. This is to be a cyberspace application of the rights given to owners of famous and well-known marks under the Paris Convention for the Protection of Industrial Property and the TRIPS Agreement[33].

6.12 Patents

Until very recently, patents have been of limited use to software engineers. This is because the law provided that they were not, in themselves, patentable. However, the courts have got around this limitation and statute law and

---

32. Final Report of the WIPO Internet Domain Name Process, 30 April 1999, see http://wipo2.wipo.int/process/eng/final-report.html.
33. Agreement on Trade-Related Aspects of Intellectual Property Rights 1994.

international treaties are to follow suit in the very near future. This is thus an area of great potential for computer scientists.

A patent gives to an inventor a monopoly in an invention. This means that the inventor is given the exclusive right to use or exploit the invention for a defined period. In the United Kingdom, a patent lasts for twenty years, provided all of the appropriate fees are paid. The person who takes out a patent is known as a patentee, and this monopoly entitles the patentee to use or exploit the invention personally, share it with others in a co-operative venture, or sell it.

The monopoly granted by patent law is so strong, that the owner of a patent may even exclude independent inventors from the market. When several people are working towards the same goal, there is therefore often a race to patent, in order to secure monopoly rights. This sometimes happens when drug companies are searching for a cure for a particular disease, such as Aids. This is in marked contrast to the monopoly given by copyright law, which as we have seen does not prevent another from independently (i.e. without copying) creating and exploiting the same thing.

Despite the strength of the patent monopoly, it is not necessarily a licence to print money. For example, if a patent confers a substantial market advantage, the owner of the patent should anticipate potential competitors using every means possible to break the patent. The better the patent and the more commercially desirable the breakthrough, the more likely it is to be challenged. For example, if competitors can produce a similar product or process, which is not covered by the patent, they will be free to market it and to erode the commercial advantage of the patentee. If they can prove that the subject matter of the patent has been used or disclosed before, as will be explained below, they can invalidate the patent. Competitors may just decide to infringe the patent in the knowledge that the patentee does not have the psychological or financial resources to fight a court case. Patent litigation can last for years and is extremely expensive and patent actions, being civil matters, must be fought by the parties themselves, not by the state. Patent litigation is not for the faint-hearted. But, inventors should not be discouraged too much. They should just be realistic and not anticipate an entirely trouble-free ride to the bank. The worst may not happen and patents do confer such a strong commercial advantage that all inventors would be well advised seriously to consider taking out patent protection. Patents do deter most competitors, at least from direct imitation, and if the inventor does not want to enter the market place alone, he could always try to join forces with others more willing to take the risk, e.g. through a joint venture, or by licensing or assigning the patent to another.

There is no obligation to patent an invention. If an inventor decides not to patent, he can rely on other intellectual property rights, such as trade secrecy, copyrights or the designs laws. However, intellectual property rights act together to form a package of rights protecting innovations, and it is as well to use as many of these as possible, as the more weapons there are in the armoury, the greater the chances of success.

6.12.1 What can be patented

Strangely enough, the Patents Act does not define an invention. It merely sets out a number of criteria which must be satisfied before an invention can be patented. The law is very careful not to create too many monopolies. It therefore set up a number of hurdles to patentability. Section 1 of the Patents Act 1977 provides that a patent may only be granted if:

- the invention is new;
- it involves an inventive step;
- it is capable of industrial application;
- the subject matter of the invention does not fall within an excluded class.

This equates with Article 52 of the European Patent Convention (see Section 6.12.10 below). The same criteria are therefore applicable in most European countries. We shall now consider each of these requirements in turn.

6.12.2 The invention must be new

This means that the invention must not have been disclosed or used publicly before the date of filing the patent application. This is an absolute requirement and means that all inventors must be very careful not to disclose their invention unless the person to whom the disclosure is made is bound to keep the information confidential. Care should be taken when giving conference papers, discussing matters at the bar, writing articles for publication, submitting grant applications or preparing general business documentation.

In practice many inventors will discuss their invention with others before filing. At the very least they will discuss it with a patent agent, but they may also need finance for the project and thus also discuss it with bankers, lawyers, accountants etc., as well as component manufacturers. In each case the confidentiality of the information should be stressed. The extent to which the law protects confidential information was discussed earlier in this chapter. In each of the circumstances referred to in this paragraph an obligation to respect confidentiality may be implied, but it might be wiser to obtain express undertakings not to use or disclose information without the consent of the inventor.

In order to assess the novelty of an invention, officials at the Patent Office will search the world-wide literature in that field, and even publication years before, e.g. in an obscure journal available only in one library, will destroy novelty. But the information must be available to the public, hence, if it is known somewhere, but kept secret, this will not destroy its novelty. If the

Patent Office searches discover prior use or disclosure, the patent will not be granted. But all is not safe even after the patent is granted, because competitors can use lack of novelty at the time of filing to challenge the patent. Competitors therefore frequently employ researchers to search the literature in the hope of finding something which they can use to attack the patentee's monopoly. If the invention is not new, no-one can patent it, and a patent already granted will be revoked.

6.12.3 The invention must involve an inventive step

An inventive step is rather more difficult to describe. It means that the advance claimed in the patent specification must not be obvious. It would be contrary to public policy to grant monopolies to things which are obvious, and anything which is obvious is arguably already in the public domain and not novel. The standard against which obviousness is judged varies from country to country, but in English law, we use the views of hypothetical persons who are skilled in that particular field, but who do not seem to be terribly original in thought, merely well-read and able to search the literature for information which exists, but which is not already known to them.

The test is fairly artificial and it is very difficult to assess with hindsight whether a solution to a particular problem was obvious or not. Some solutions seem startlingly obvious once they have been put forward, it is just that no-one thought of doing it that way before. A good analogy would be the answer to a crossword puzzle that someone has been struggling over for hours. When told the answer, it seems obvious, but it was certainly not that before. Perhaps the most straightforward question to ask in order to assess whether there has been an inventive step, is: would the solution be very plain to the hypothetical person skilled in the art, who had not read this particular patent specification?

6.12.4 The invention must be capable of industrial application

The third requirement of patentability is that the invention must be capable of industrial application. This simply means that the invention must have a practical application. Another way of expressing this is to say that the invention must have a technical effect.

6.12.5 What is not patentable?

A further list of matters which are not patentable is contained in Sections 1(2) and 1(3) of the Patents Act. Some of these are excluded for public policy reasons; others because they are more appropriately protected by copyright; and others because they are no more than disembodied ideas, schemes or formulae, which have no practical, physical dimension in which they can be commercially exploited. The most important for present purposes are:

- a scientific theory, e.g. a law of physics, cannot be patented, but if a machine is invented which is a practical application of the law, this may be patentable;
- a mathematical method, e.g. a method of calculating a square root: this may be a very useful idea, but again, unless it is embodied into, for example, a new machine, it is not patentable, in much the same way as a scientific theory is not protected;
- a literary, dramatic, musical or artistic work or any other aesthetic creation: these are protected by copyright if reduced to a material form, e.g. written down or put onto film[34].

This, together with the following exclusion means that databases will not be patentable;

- the presentation of information: again this is covered by the law of copyright;

and most importantly,

- a scheme, rule or method for performing a mental act, playing a game or doing business, or a *program for a computer*.

At first sight, the exclusion of a computer program from the list of items which can be patented looks tremendously important. However, as we shall see, the exclusion has been eroded almost out of existence by the courts. And in the year 2000, there is to be an Intergovernmental Diplomatic Conference to make changes to the European Patent Convention, one of which is likely to be the removal of the express ban on the patenting of computer programs. Thus patenting is likely to be an area of great activity for software houses in the next few years.

The move away from patenting computer programs was led by the United States, where the government, and following their lead, the United States Patent and Trade Mark Office (USPTO), felt that an outright and strictly interpreted ban on patenting computer programs was not in the interest of US software industry, nor therefore in the national interest, given the importance of software products for the US economy. Where the US leads, so Europe follows and little by little, the ban has been softened until now it is but a shadow of its former self and is soon about to disappear.

---

34. See Section 6.2.

The critical case, which goes further along the line of software patents than any other previous decision of the courts in Europe, is *IBM/Computer programs* (No.96305851.6) (1999)[35]. Here the EPO decided that a computer program was not excluded from patentability if it produced, or was capable of producing, a further technical effect beyond the normal physical interaction between software and hardware, i.e. it is potentially patentable if it makes something else do something. This follows from Article 52(2) and (3) of the European Patent Convention, which says, in effect, that while it is not possible to patent a computer program as such, it is possible to patent something which is more than just a program – something which can be called, for simplicity, a "program plus". This line of reasoning had been followed in courts across Europe for some years, with decisions becoming ever more liberal. But in the IBM case, the EPO Technical Board of Appeal went so far as to say that,

> a patent may be granted not only in the case of an invention where a piece of software manages, by means of a computer, an industrial process or the working of a piece of machinery, but in every case where a program for a computer is the only means, or one of the necessary means, of obtaining a technical effect ... where, for instance a technical effect of that kind is achieved by the internal functioning of a computer itself under the influence of the said program. In other words, on condition that they are able to produce a technical effect in the above sense, all computer programs must be considered as inventions within the meaning of Article 52(1) [... of the European Patent Convention ...], and may be subject matter of a patent if the other requirements provided for by the EPC are satisfied.

Following this decision, the UK Patent Office has issued new guidelines on patents for computer programs[36].

6.12.6 Who may apply for a patent?

In English law, anyone can apply for a patent, but it will only be granted to the inventor, or subsequent assignees, i.e. the persons to whom the inventor has transferred patent rights. This may have happened if, for example, the inventor has sold the rights over the patent.

Inventorship is a complex notion. It causes no problems in the rare instance where the inventor can genuinely say that the invention was all the inventor's own work, but nowadays, most new products and processes are created as a result of team work. In this case, the inventor is the person

---

35. Available on the European Patent Office (EPO) web site, www.european-patent-office.org.
36. These can be found on the UK patent office web site, www.patent.gov.uk.

who conceived the inventive idea, so, for example, if a research worker thinks of a new product, and instructs a technician to prepare it, even though the technician actually produces the first product of this type, the inventor is the person under whose instructions the technician has been working. But, if the invention comes as a result of two or more people bouncing ideas off each other, there may be joint inventorship. There are however many grey areas in between, where professional advice should be sought. Particular care is needed if a patent is to be taken out in the United States.

6.12.7 Employee inventors

Prior to 1977, it had become the practice of employers to require employees to assign to their employers, all inventions made by the employee during the currency of the contract of employment, and in some cases, even to assign rights to inventions made after the contract had terminated. This was obviously unfair and sometimes contrary to the doctrines of the common law. As a result, the law was reformed by the 1977 Act. Section 39 of the Patents Act now provides that inventions belong to the employee, except in only two situations, where they belong to the employer, and any contract which purports to diminish the rights of an employee is unenforceable. Under the Act, an invention will belong to the employer only if:

- the invention was made in the course of the normal duties of the employee, or in the course of duties falling outside normal duties, but specifically assigned to the employee, and the circumstances in either case were such that an invention might reasonably be expected to result from the carrying out of the duties; or
- the invention was made in the course of the duties of the employee and at the time of making the invention, the employee had a special obligation to further the interests of the employer's undertaking. This will cover inventions made, for example, by senior management.

If an invention belongs to the employee, the employee is free to exploit it, e.g. by selling it or by setting up in business on the employee's own account (so long as the employer's trade secrets are respected). If the invention belongs to the employer, Section 40 of the 1977 Act gives the employee a right to compensation, but only if the patent is "of outstanding benefit" to the employers. This will obviously negate the right of an employee to compensation under the Patents Act in most cases. However, many employers have entered into more favourable agreements with their workforce concerning employee inventions, in the hope of encouraging employees to invent, and also to prevent bad feeling in cases where an employee has produced a patentable invention which benefits the employer, but maybe not to the extent that statutory compensation is payable.

6.12.8 Professional advice

The owner of the patent can apply for a patent, draft the specification and prosecute the application through all of its stages in the Patent Office. This is not, however, desirable, except for large firms which have their own patent departments. Patenting is a highly specialized business and is best dealt with by a patent agent. The names and addresses of local patent agents can be obtained from the Yellow Pages of a telephone directory.

6.12.9 The patent application and foreign filings

The timing of a patent application is of crucial importance. It is not necessary to perfect the invention before an application is made and too much delay may mean that someone else will patent first. As a general rule, if an invention appears to be patentable and of commercial interest, an application should be filed. If in doubt, apply. At this early stage, all that need be filed at the British Patent Office is an indication that a patent will be sought, a description of the invention and the filing fee.

The date of the application is important. It gives what is known as a priority date. Under international conventions, filing in one convention state gives to the applicant, the right to claim a monopoly in the invention in any other convention country from the date of the first application, so long as the applicant files his other foreign applications within twelve months of the first application. Hence, a British applicant, who files in the UK, will have a year in which to file for a patent in the United States, and the application there, or anywhere else in the world, will be unaffected by patent applications by other inventors, or other publication during that year. That is, novelty will not be destroyed by publication, or use, anywhere else, in the year after the first application.

Within twelve months of the initial application, a full patent specification should be sent to the British Patent Office and to Patent Offices in other countries where patents are required. This work will normally be done by a patent agent, who will use contacts abroad and will arrange for all of the necessary translations to be made. It is important to brief the patent agent several months before the expiry of the twelve month period, as there is a considerable amount of preparatory work to be done.

If a patent is going to be commercially important, patents should be taken out in most, if not all, of the likely countries in which it will sell, or where other persons will make the invention, or carry out the process, if they are not otherwise prevented by patent laws. If the patentee does not envisage carrying on business in those countries, then the idea can always be licensed to others, in return for, for example, an up-front payment and/or royalties. Patent agents will advise their clients on licensing deals. There is also a society, called the Licensing Executives Society, whose members specialize in this kind of business.

Once a patent application has been made, the literature is searched by staff at the Patent Office to ascertain the novelty of the invention, the patent application is published and it is examined to see that it meets all the criteria of patentability. These can be complex procedures and may involve regular correspondence with, and visits to, the Patent Office. This will normally be handled by the patent agent. Patenting is a lengthy process. It often takes four years before a patent is granted.

In this section we have concentrated on the principles of patenting in English law. It should again be noted that the laws of other countries are not necessarily the same, and that some inventions may be patentable in some countries, but not in others.

6.12.10 Patenting in Europe

Patenting in a large number of countries involves a great deal of duplication of effort and is expensive. As a result, a number of European countries have combined together to simplify procedure and to cut costs. The European patenting system is separate from the European Union, although there is an inevitable overlap of membership. All members of the European Union have signed the European Patent Convention, plus Switzerland and Norway.

As a general rule, if an applicant wants to patent an invention in more than three of these countries, it is cheaper to use the European route than to apply for separate national patents. Let us suppose that a British applicant wants to obtain patents in Britain, France, West Germany and Switzerland. The procedure is to apply to the British Patent Office specifying the European route to patents in those four countries. The patent application is forwarded by the British Office to The Hague for a formal examination to see that the documents are in order. There then follows a search to ascertain novelty. About eighteen months after filing, the application is published, together with the search report. The documents are sent to European Patent Office in Munich, where the application is examined to make sure that the invention is patentable in accordance with the criteria of the European Patent Convention. The British Patents Act is based on the European Patent Convention and hence the law applied is generally as has been described above.

Once the centralized procedure of search and examination has been completed, it might be expected that there would be a single European patent granted. In fact, countries have been unable to agree on this although there may eventually be a single patent, called the Community Patent for all EU member states. At present, an applicant whose application succeeds is granted a bundle of national patents for those countries requested. In our example, the applicant would be granted by the European Patent Office, British, French, German and Swiss patents. Hence, it is possible for a

British patent to be granted in two ways, either by a national application processed solely by the British Patent Office, or by applying for a British patent through the European system. For an inventor, for example in the United States, who wishes to acquire patents throughout Europe, the European system is easier and cheaper. Hence, more and more British patents are being granted in this way and there has been a substantial decline in the amount of patent work being handled by the British Patent Office in recent years.

There is one major disadvantage of using the European patent procedure. If a patent application is not particularly strong, it may be safer to apply separately to national offices, as then if a patent is denied, for example in Germany, it will not affect an application for a French patent; whereas, if a European application fails, patents cannot be granted in any of the designated countries. However, this means that a patent granted by the European route tends to be stronger, as potential competitors who suspect that the national route has been used rather than the European route because the patents are not strong, might feel more confident in challenging those patents in the courts. The tactics of patenting require very careful consideration.

6.12.11 Patent co-operation treaty

If a British applicant additionally wishes to obtain patents in countries outside Europe, another international convention, the Patent Co-operation Treaty (PCT), can be used to further simplify procedures and reduce costs. The PCT is administered by the World Intellectual Property Organisation (WIPO), a United Nations agency, situated in Geneva. It enables an inventor to file an International Patent Application for a centralized search and preliminary examination, thus minimizing work which has to be done in each country. Reports produced by the searching and examining divisions are then sent to the national patent offices of those countries in which patents are requested for them to take the final decision on whether to grant a national patent. If patents are sought by this route in countries which are members of the European Patent Convention, the files may be passed to the European Patent Office, in which case the application is known as a Euro-PCT application.

Inventions concerning computers are marketable world-wide and thus patents should be sought in all major developed countries using the international patent conventions. Any firm which is unable to market on a world-wide basis should consider licensing all of its intellectual property rights for use by others. They may be the firm's most valuable assets.

6.13 Further reading

Coleman, A. 1994. *Intellectual property law*. Longman Law, Tax and Finance.

Cornish W. R. 1999. *Intellectual property law*, 4th edn. Sweet and Maxwell.

Cripps, Y 1994. *The legal implications of disclosure in the public interest: an analysis of prohibitions and protections with particular reference to employers and employees*, 2nd edn. Sweet and Maxwell.

Dworkin, G. and R. Taylor 1989. *Blackstone's guide to the Copyright, Designs and Patents Act 1988*. Blackstone Press.

Encyclopaedia of information technology law. Sweet and Maxwell (loose-leaf).

Firth, A. with J. Phillips (eds) 1998. *Introduction to intellectual property law*, 4th edn. Butterworths.

Reed C. (ed.) 2000. *Computer law*, 4th edn. Blackstone Press.

Chapter 7

The framework of employee relations law and changing management practices

7.1 Employee relations

Employee relations is about the rules governing employment. Since people are employed to produce goods or services and such production entails a process, we may further say that employee relations is about the rules governing the work process.

What sort of rules are we talking about? Little can be inferred from the individual contract of employment. It is a contract of service entailing a duty to perform that service in return for payment of wages or salary. However, because the precise form of work performance or service (including the degree of effort) cannot be specified in advance, the employment contract is inescapably open-ended. On the other hand, there is a statutory obligation for the employer to provide a written statement of the main terms and conditions of employment – a duty extended by the Trade Union Reform and Employment Relations Act of 1993, as a result of the Proof of Employment Relationship Directive of 1991. Because the contract of employment is, rightly or wrongly, so central in British employment law, in the event of disputes, the courts may deem certain terms to be implied by the contract.

The normal state of affairs, then, is for the employer, and, by extension, the management acting as agent for the employing organization, to decide the terms and conditions – or rules – of employment. These rules include anything from pay and normal hours of work to health and safety rules. Establishing rules and procedures remains one of the main ways that management exercises responsibility for the control of the work process. Management is about control. Control necessitates effective organization of the work process by the use of established procedures but also the ability to improvise by gaining the co-operation of employees.

In most industrial countries such unilateral regulation of employment by management is not the only way of deciding and administering the rules governing employment. In many industries and services, employers have recognized trade unions for collective bargaining purposes. Collective bargaining is a peculiar phrase to describe regulation of aspects of the work process by management jointly with unions representing collectivities or groups of employees. Managers, on behalf of companies or organizations, negotiate with full time trade union officials or employee representatives of the union at the workplace, in order to reach collective agreements about pay and other conditions of employment.

7.1.1 Importance of procedures

The basic sort of collective agreement establishes a negotiating procedure by way of standing committee and procedural rules, such as, what to do in the event of a failure to agree (for example, provision for arbitration). The procedural rules are utilized to arrive at substantive rules relating to pay and conditions, such as hours of work, holiday entitlement, shiftwork arrangements, overtime, bonuses and fringe benefits. Other procedures, including importantly, disciplinary procedures (to be followed in dealing with misconduct at work and infringement of work rules) and appeals or grievance procedures (that might, for example, be used to appeal against appraisal or grading decisions), are a normal part of a collective bargaining relationship between an employer and a trade union.

In the event of a failure to agree, disputes procedures often have recourse to conciliation and arbitration by third parties. In Britain, among its many other advisory services, the Advisory Conciliation and Arbitration Service offers such a facility. Finally, if all else fails and the dispute cannot be resolved, it is generally considered legitimate to impose sanctions, such as a strike or overtime ban. Strikes are rare in Britain these days but thirty years ago many managers believed that British industry was strike-prone. Actually, even then, 90 per cent of workplaces were strike-free but its association with strikes gave the detractors of the collective bargaining model of employee relations plenty of propaganda.

The applicability of the collective bargaining model of employee relations to software workers is very limited. Trade unions have made little impact among software workers, so terms and conditions of employment are largely unilaterally set by employers and managers. However, it must be emphasized that employee relations issues are part of day-to-day management because they involve control of the work process, whether or not unions play any part. Limited forms of co-management, such as joint consultation with employee representatives, can to some extent, though never entirely satisfactorily, substitute for unions. It is important, however, for software workers to know about the collective bargaining/union model of employee relations because few industries or companies are now untouched by computers and in many the introduction of computerized work processes may be a union–management issue. It is valuable to visualize the user environment where a software program might affect employee relations, as they frequently do.

7.2 The framework of collective labour law

Apart from unilateral management decisions and collective bargaining, the other way that rules governing employment can be made is by the law. Labour law is that part of the law that deals with individuals and legal persons in their capacity as employees or employers, it is concerned with work and relationships arising from it. Labour law is concerned with both the collective and the individual aspects of the employment relationship. Collective labour law deals with collective industrial behaviour and institutions for regulation of employee relations, such as trade unions and collective bargaining.

Apart from brief interruptions (including the short-lived 1971 Industrial Relations Act), the British industrial relations system between 1906 and 1980 was arguably the least legally regulated in the world. So much so, that some observers characterized it as a voluntary system, in that the law abstained from intervention in collective bargaining and collective conflict between employers and trade unions. A peculiarity of this system was that trade unions were granted immunity from being sued for damages resulting from industrial action such as strikes, so long as they were in contemplation or furtherance of a trade dispute. To some labour lawyers this was a "golden formula" but to others it was always rather suspect, because it laid down no positive and definite rights to strike and concomitant obligations. Britain's mediocre strike record in the 1970s, culminating in the public sector and road haulage strikes of the "winter of discontent" in 1979, left it tarnished. The main strategic aim behind government policy on industrial relations since then has been to shift the balance of power from trade unions to employers. Conservative governments were relentless in seeking to limit the role of trade unions, to such effect that by 1993 the British industrial relations system was among the most strictly legally regulated, with at least six acts regulating the conduct of strikes. Their main method was to narrow the scope of the immunities from tort actions, increasingly confining union activity to the actual place of work and stipulating numerous procedures before a lawful strike could be undertaken.

7.2.1 Restraining the unions

The process of reining in the trade unions was begun with the 1980 Employment Act. The then Secretary of State for Employment believed that modest restraints on unions and the "right" to strike would suffice. Secondary action – that is action not directly against the employer but against a supplier or customer firm by "blacking" or boycotting its products or services – was outlawed except in limited circumstances. Pickets were permitted to picket only their own place of work. Trade unions were encouraged to use ballots of their members by entitlement to reimbursement from public funds for ballot costs, though this was withdrawn in later legislation.

The process of narrowing trade union immunities against tort actions continued with the 1982 Employment Act which redefined the term "trade dispute" to restrict the scope of immunity. Instead of being merely "concerned with" matter such as terms of employment, a "trade dispute" now had to "relate wholly or mainly to" such matters; to be lawful a dispute must be limited to one between workers and their own employer. The blanket immunity from legal action previously enjoyed by the unions was repealed. There were limits on the damages that could be awarded, but several unions found themselves liable to punitive damages and costs.

The 1984 Trade Union Act required trade unions to ballot their members before industrial action. If no ballot was held or if the ballot did not comply with stipulated rules then the immunity from legal action was removed, though it was up to the employers to initiate action. The rationale of this act appeared to be to encourage responsible trade unionism by placing unions under control of majority membership opinion, though the evidence was slight that strikes had been instigated by the militant few.

The Employment Act of 1988 gave union members a right to challenge industrial action in the courts if it was not legitimized by a properly conducted ballot. Further rules were stipulated regarding the conduct of ballots. Controversially, the Act also gave members a right to compensation from their union if they were disciplined for disobeying a strike call, even if it was supported by a ballot. This seemed potentially to contradict the encouragement given to majority rule contained in the 1984 Act, in that majority rule presumably presupposes abiding by the will of the majority, as long as it is not tyrannous.

The 1990 Act reflects government annoyance about unofficial strikes on London Underground that had reportedly been organized clandestinely. A union would now be legally responsible for such actions by its members and must repudiate unofficial industrial action in order to escape liability; a formula designed to drive a wedge between unions and disgruntled members, but that would also have the effect of dissolving negotiated control over industrial conflict.

Unofficial strikes among electrician members of the AEEU employed by sub-contractors on the Jubilee Line extension in November 1998 showed that such legislative restrictions are far from certain to halt unofficial action and conflict. Despite allegations of sabotage, managers made no obvious attempt to invoke the law, realizing perhaps that this may have further weakened the tenuous authority of union officials who were saying: "If our people are responsible for sabotage there will be hell to pay. We will take a very dim view indeed"[1].

---

1. Clement, "Jubilee Line hit by sabotage".

7.2.2 The legislation consolidated

In 1992 the Trade Union and Labour Relations (Consolidation) Act entirely replaced seven statutes and brought together many provisions of the Employment Acts of 1980, 1982, 1988 and 1990. However, it could hardly be said to simplify matters for those engaged in industrial relations since it contains 303 sections and three Schedules comprising 192 pages. The Act has been very well summarized by Aileen McColgan[2] who commented that it:

> does not change the law but it does serve to highlight the legislative changes. Trade unions are no longer immune from liability in tort for actions taken in the context of secondary and unofficial action and their freedom to indemnify members against fines imposed for offences or for contempt of court has been removed, as has their power to discipline members for refusing to take industrial action regardless of the fact that action has been called in compliance with the myriad balloting requirements imposed since 1979. Trade union members on the other hand have been granted a wealth of ammunition against unions. This ammunition includes the right to sue in respect of "unjustifiable" discipline or the unreasonable refusal of a trade union to grant them membership; the right to complain to the Certification Officer about their union's failure to keep "so far as is reasonably practicable" up-to-date registers of membership or to comply properly with the legislative restrictions on the application of funds for political objects; and the right to apply for a court order to prevent their union inducing members to take or continue industrial action which has not been properly balloted upon.

The Trade Union Reform and Employment Relations (TURER) Act of 1993 imposed further restrictions on strikes. These include the appointment of an independent scrutineer to oversee ballots on industrial action; the phasing out of financial assistance for ballots; making postal ballots compulsory; requiring the union to give to employers notice of intention to ballot, names of those employees taking part and to notify the ballot result, with at least seven days notice of industrial action. Any individual is now allowed to seek an injunction against a union where there is unlawful industrial action where the action will, or is likely to, prevent or delay the supply of goods or services or reduce their quality. Under a late amendment, the TURER Act allowed employers to deny pay rises or other benefits to employees who refuse to sign personal contracts. In practice, consequently, employers can bribe staff not to be union members, for there is less point in being in a trade union if one is no longer part of a collective bargaining process. The

---

2. McColgan, "The Trade Union and Labour Relations (Consolidation) Act 1992", p. 32.

TURER terminated the Bridlington arrangements against inter-union poaching of members, allowing employees to join any appropriate union of their choice, even if the employer does not recognize that union. Check-off arrangements, whereby unions have membership dues deducted at source by the employer must be re-authorized every three years, which is bound to have a negative impact on union membership and finances.

The main theme of this legislation was an attack on the institutions of industrial relations, especially collective bargaining. Not only have statutory supports been removed but it has been decentralized and mainly confined to the enterprise or establishment. In addition, unions have been faced with financial and accountability requirements that impose bureaucratic procedures on them. The overall effect of government policy in industrial relations seems to have been, step-by-step, to reduce union power. The interaction of labour law and deflationary economic policies has achieved this objective, although the effect of structural decline in industries on union strength is difficult to separate from the cautionary effect of the threat of fines and sequestration. Since 1997 the position of the unions has improved somewhat with the election of a Labour government and relatively favourable EU legislation. In 1998, for the first time for many years, union membership rose slightly.

7.2.3 The European Union and British labour law

In one respect the British system has retained some of its "voluntary" character. Collective agreements between unions and employers are not legally binding. An alternative route might have been taken to a more closely regulated system, one that might have been perceived as more even-handed. This would have been to clearly set down and codify rights to unionize, strike and peacefully picket and to clearly define peace obligations for the duration of collective agreements, whilst defining unfair industrial relations practices. The British state does offer a system of conciliation and arbitration through the Advisory Conciliation and Arbitration Service (ACAS) but there is no scope for the European distinction between disputes of interest (about economic and substantive bargaining to renegotiate agreements) and disputes of right (about interpretation of existing agreements and contracts). To model the system further on European lines would also encompass co-determination rights that confer on workers a managerial role in the enterprise in the form of workers directors on a supervisory (second tier) board and participation through works councils. In 1994, after many false starts, a directive on the establishment of European Works Councils was finally adopted unanimously by the Labour and Social Affairs Council of the EU. Companies with more than 1,000 employees and at least 150 in two or more member states must set up European Works councils to inform and consult worker representatives on issues of transnational significance. Over 200 British registered companies with interests in the EU are affected.

It is easy to dismiss these councils as gimmicks. Renault management closed an assembly plant in Belgium without consulting its European works council. However, some human resource managers believe that the councils could become useful tools for unions. "For the first time, workers now have statutory backing for giving key information on a company's performance and investments. They have a right to meet and question senior boardroom executives. The councils also provide unprecedented opportunity for employees to come together, network and adopt a common position. This will feed down to collective bargaining machinery"[3].

Changes to the law on consultation and redundancy contained in the Trade Union Reform and Employment Relations Act 1993 originate in European legislation – the 1992 revision of the European Collective Redundancies Directive of 1975 on which the previous UK law was based. Redundancy consultation must now also include ways of avoiding the dismissals; reducing the numbers to be dismissed, and, mitigating the consequences of the dismissals with, significantly, a view to reaching agreement with trade union representatives. The law on consultation is now extended to any dismissal where there are reasons not related to the individual concerned. For example, there will need to be consultation on any proposed dismissal where an employee refuses to accept a new contract on revised terms and conditions. As Wyatt[4] has noted, in the UK the principles of direct effect and the supremacy of European Community (European Union) law are secured by sections 2 and 3 of the European Communities Act.

7.3 Examples of the new labour laws in action

As a result of the legislative changes, certain unions that, by accident or design, challenged the law, were repulsed or penalized. The first controversial case was when Mercury sought an injunction against the National Communications Union. The union had refused to connect Mercury to the main British Telecom network as the first shot in its campaign against the privatization of BT. The High Court ruled that the dispute was a trade dispute and therefore lawful. However, the Court of Appeal ruled that the dispute was primarily aimed at preventing privatization. Sir John Donaldson, MR, thought that if the dispute was mainly about terms and conditions of employment, it was inconceivable that the union would not seek negotiations to protect its job security agreement. There was no

---

3. A Barnett, "Pow-wow but does it mean Power?".
4. Wyatt, "Enforcing EEC social rights in the UK".

evidence that the union had sought such negotiation. *(Mercury Communications Ltd v Scott Garner*[5]*)*.

In 1986, News International, having transferred its operations to Wapping, secured High Court injunctions against the print unions, SOGAT '82 and the National Graphical Association, to restrict picketing at the Wapping site where the unions were now not represented. The court order banned picketing outside that plant and at the depots of the road haulage firm, TNT, which distributed News International's titles. SOGAT '82 was subsequently fined £25,000 and then incurred sequestration of its assets. *(News Group v SOGAT*[6]*)*. The NGA was fined £25,000 as a result of secondary picketing at Wapping.

In 1988 legal action against the seafarers' union further demonstrated how much the legislation had achieved in enforcing the "right to manage". The union, whose main dispute was with the P&O management's aim to impose more exacting working conditions, tried to extend the dispute nationally by striking against other ferry companies. First fined £7,500 and then £150,000 for secondary action against Sealink, the union soon incurred sequestration of its head office and paltry assets. The P&O management was therefore able to localize the dispute and ultimately crush the strike as a result of the 1982 Act that narrowed the definition of a trade dispute.

In 1989 dockers registered in the National Dock Labour Scheme pressed their union, the Transport and General Workers' Union, to oppose the repeal of legislation governing the dock labour scheme. Authorized by ballot to organize strike action, the union was hindered and delayed by running up against the narrowed trade dispute definition, among other stipulations in the courts *(Associated British Ports and others v Transport and General Workers' Union*[7]*)*.

In March 1994, NATFHE, the union of teachers employed in colleges of further education, had to cancel a planned strike against changed employment contracts: probable increased weekly hours, no limit on weekly teaching hours and reduced holiday entitlement. The colleges employers' forum was able to obtain an injunction because NATFHE had not provided a list of members, as required by the 1993 Act. Subsequently, this legal test case was upheld in the Court of Appeal *(Blackpool and Fylde College v National Association of Teachers in Further and Higher Education*[8]*)*.

According to one jurist, "the decision of the UK Employment Appeals Tribunal in *Lewis and Britton v E. Mason*[9] is an indication of the depths to

5. [1983] IRLR 494; [1984] 1 All ER 179.
6. [1986] IRLR 227.
7. [1989] IRLR 291, 305.
8. [1994] IRLR 227.
9. [1994] IRLR 4 (EAT).

which British labour law has sunk in recent years"[10]. Britton was employed as a driver with the firm of E. Mason. A manager told him to drive one of the firm's lorries to Edinburgh. Discovering that the vehicle did not have a heater and not willing to spend the night in an unheated lorry cab in the middle of winter, he agreed to go provided he was given an extra £5 for bed and breakfast. The manager rejected this request and when Britton refused to go, he was immediately dismissed. Another driver was asked to go but as he also stipulated conditions that were unacceptable to the manager, he too was dismissed. After a discussion among the workforce, including the two sacked drivers, it was agreed that Lewis, another driver employed by the firm, should negotiate on their behalf. He telephoned the manager and told him that if the dismissed drivers were not reinstated, the others would not come into work the next day. The manager replied that he would not be held to ransom and promptly dismissed Lewis and the others. Lewis and Britton took their complaint of unfair dismissal to an industrial tribunal. However, the tribunal found that they had been taking part in industrial action and therefore the dismissals were fair. "That an employee who takes industrial action should thereby be in breach of contract and also lose protection against unfair dismissal is not immediately obvious to the student of labour law"[11]. Perhaps not – internationally; nationally, it is only too obvious.

7.4 The framework of individual employment law

Basically, individual employment law regulates the individual employment relationship as it arises from the contract of employment. However, the employment contract has arguably been vapid for most practical purposes. Since it leaves so much unsaid, the courts have, over the years, reached verdicts by inferring terms implied in the contract but this has not necessarily improved matters. In the British tradition, the notion of subordination has been a key criterion for determining whether or not an employment relationship exists. This is particularly pertinent for the computer and software industry and occupations. Although the normal situation remains one where permanent employees predominate, various forms of sub-contracted and free-lance work are growing in importance. The contractual position is likely to be of most significance in relation to telework:

> The relationship of teleworker to employer can be ambivalent. Certain conditions are similar to those of self-employed contractors because the workplace is located away from the company and work is performed

---

10. Dolding, "Unfair dismissal and industrial action".
11. *Ibid.*

more or less autonomously. On the other hand, teleworkers are dependent on the work given to them by the employer and they are also subject to the employer's authority in areas such as output. If the relationship between an employer and a teleworker is clearly recognized on both sides as one of subordination, then the teleworker is clearly entitled to the same working conditions and social security coverage as other workers in the enterprise. He or she is entitled to the same dismissal procedure, sick pay, unemployment benefits, paid leave, minimum wage etc. However, if the relationship is formally one of self-employment, but in fact involved substantial elements of subordination, the teleworker runs the risk of being deprived, without justification, of employment rights and social protection[12].

Mass teleworking will not take-off into self-sustained growth until houses, towns and villages are designed and constructed with teleworking in mind. So the benefits of teleworking are likely to be felt only by future generations. However, some foundations are in place, such as televillages. One development near the Brecon National Park at Crickhowell offers employment opportunities through provision of a telecentre, serviced office space, studios and workshops.

It is vital therefore for managers considering teleworking to decide whether teleworkers should be retained as self-employed sub-contractors or as stand-alone freelances. For the generality of workers, what used to be called the statutory floor of individual employment rights was severely weakened in Britain during the 1980s. Employment security was curtailed by extension of the minimum period for eligibility to claim unfair dismissal to two years. Earnings-related supplement to unemployment benefit was abolished and, later, entitlement to unemployment benefit severely reduced. The Wages Councils that administered statutory minimum rates of pay for certain industries were abolished by the TURER Act of 1993.

Until 1994, the rights of part-time workers were much worse. Arguably, the widening gap between employment rights and protection in Britain, compared with other European Union countries, and, ideological differences about free market economics, lay behind the British government's rejection of the Social Chapter of the Maastricht treaty. However, by 1994 it was becoming clear that the opt-out was outweighed by the force of European Union law and the European Communities Act of 1972. In a landmark ruling, the House of Lords declared that part-time workers must have the same redundancy and unfair dismissal rights as full-timers. The decision also confirmed the right of the Equal Opportunities Commission to challenge British legisla-

---

12. Di Martino & Wirth, "Telework: a new way of working and living", p 545.

tion as incompatible with European Union law by judicial review. In Britain some 90 per cent of part-time workers are women.

The European Commission has proposed three directives to regulate the employment of part-time and temporary employees. These include giving part-time workers a *pro rata* right to holiday, seniority and dismissal allowances. They would also have the right to *pro rata* treatment in respect of pensions and sick pay, as well as access to any social services and training provided by the employer. It also proposed that part-time employees who work at least eight hours per week should come within the National Insurance scheme, regardless of how little they earn.

7.4.1 The social dimension of the European Union

The European Community Charter of fundamental social rights of workers was approved by the eleven member states other than the UK in 1989. It was effectively a direction to the Commission to develop initiatives for the implementation of the rights listed in the Charter – using the legal instruments available under the Treaty of Rome. It is primarily intended to set a floor of minimum standards in order to contain "social dumping", which is to say, unfair competition for investible funds by cutting wages and working conditions. For example, the maternity leave directive sets modest minimum provisions, rather than requiring every state to adopt Denmark's generous standards. Similarly, the working time directive does not require every state to adopt Germany's tough restrictions on night and weekend working for a working week lower than the 48 hours required by the directive.

On the evidence, the Social Chapter is needed more urgently in Britain than in most other European countries. The UK has one sixth of the total European Union population but a far higher proportion of the EU's poor and unemployed. Britain has the worst child care facilities and poorest parental leave provisions and the biggest but least protected part-time workforce in the EU.

Since the EU regulation on business transfers (The Acquired Rights Directive) was transposed into UK law by the Transfer of Undertakings Protection of Employment regulations, it has been automatically unfair to dismiss an employee when a business changes hands or when a public corporation is privatized unless it can be shown that the dismissal is for economic, technical or organizational reasons. Hence it would not be lawful for a new owner of a firm to dismiss the existing manager simply to bring in someone else with whom the new owner is more familiar. The same rules apply to hospitals that change to NHS trusts, and to local authority services that are transferred following Compulsory Competitive Tendering. The case law on The Acquired Rights Directive has become quite extensive and given rise to some anomalies, particularly as it overlaps with other legislation, such as the Employment Rights Act 1996. Essentially, however, the position is governed by the European Court authority of *Daddy's Dance Hall*[13], i.e. an employee cannot waive rights given to him under the Directive. Therefore an employer cannot validly agree with an employee to amend the employment contract where the transfer is the reason for this, even if the employee is overall no worse off. Cases appealed to the House of Lords in 1998 (*Wilson*[14] and *Meade and Baxendale*[15]) confirmed this. An employer may agree a change in terms and conditions of employment after a TUPE transfer but if the reason for that change is the transfer itself, the change will be invalid. It is hard to disagree with the comment of McMullen[16] that such cases are justifiable in terms that an employee, "whilst able in many cases freely to consent to a change in terms and conditions, consents often reluctantly in the face of the harsh reality of the need to stay in employment".

Some sections of the Trade Union and Employment Rights Act 1993 directly reflected the influence of EU lawmaking. For instance, it included improvements to women's employment rights. It made dismissal for any reason connected with pregnancy unlawful; it removed the service qualification for bringing an unfair dismissal claim on grounds of pregnancy; it provided for suspension from work on pregnancy grounds for health and safety reasons; it provided for a minimum of 14 weeks maternity leave and stipulated that all terms and conditions, except for actual remuneration, must be maintained. The Act also permitted measures to restrict publicity of sexual harassment cases and new rights to challenge collective agreements on grounds that they are discriminatory.

The Working Time Directive, passed by majority vote because it was deemed a health and safety measure, is likely to have a significant impact in the UK. Without such restrictions, it had been predicted that UK working hours – the longest in Europe – would continue to lengthen. Not that the directive prevents voluntary decisions to work in excess of the 48 hour limit. Moreover, it was thought, at one stage, that there would be little impact on hours actually worked due to the vast array of exemptions. In fact, the directive has more bite than at first appeared. It guarantees set breaks and a minimum three weeks paid holiday. Furthermore, after the first litigation to settle exactly what the regulations mean, it is apparent that employees have considerable protection. The case[17] was brought by five members of the colliery supervisors' union (NACODS) who had been working more than an average of 48 hours per week. They refused to sign opt-out agreements issued by the employer and applied for a declaration from the court clarifying

---

13. Case 324/86 *Foreningen af Arbejdsledere i Danmark v Daddy's Dance Hall A/S* [1988] ECR 739.
14. *Wilson v St Helens Borough Council.*
15. *Meade and Baxendale v British Fuels Ltd* [1998] IRLR 706.
16. McMullen, "TUPE: waiver of employment rights and contract changes after *Wilson*".
17. *Barber and others v R. J. B. Mining* [1999] IRLR 417.

their legal position. It was held that they were entitled to a declaration to clarify their position under their contracts of employment. The implication is that employers can ask employees to work in excess of 48 hours but employees can refuse and this gives them a considerable negotiating lever.

Several industries were exempted from the original directive, including air, rail road and sea transport but there are EU Commission proposals to extend the provision of the Directive to previously excluded areas. A report of April 1999 by Raphael Chantene MEP suggested that any review of the directive should end such exclusions.

7.5 Equal pay and sex discrimination

It was under European Community law that the UK was obliged to amend equal pay legislation to equal pay for work of equal value and then to legislate on effective means of enforcement. Nevertheless, the gender wage gap for all occupations remains one of the widest in the European Union. How much of this is due to discrimination and consequent segregation of women into a limited range of low-paying occupations and industries is hotly debated by economists. In 1987, Miller[18] estimated that if women's occupational distribution exactly replicated that of men, the wage gap would be reduced by only 5 per cent. Segregation has increased with the big rise in part-time and temporary working, most evident in low skill jobs taken up almost entirely by married women. "The much trumpeted rise in women's employment in Britain is found to have consisted entirely of the substitution of part-time for full time jobs in the post World War Two period up to 1988"[19]. Research has indicated that employers do not in general discriminate directly against female part-time workers in respect of basic rates of pay[20]. In fact, in manufacturing and retailing there are instances of female part-timers benefiting from the implementation of equal pay by increased hourly wages. However, the same study found fairly widespread segregation that would make it practically difficult for equal pay law to have any effect. The procedure to bring an equal pay claim is long-winded and it is doubtful whether part-time workers would have the access or resources required. However, two directives under the former Social Charter have indicated an emergent model of regulation of individual employment relationships by European Union law. One of the four categories was about atypical hours and employment relationships. In every member state of the EU, the majority of part-time workers is female. As a consequence, any treatment of part-time workers that is less favourable than that accorded to full-time workers constitutes indirect

---

18. "The wage effect of the occupational segregation of women in Britain".
19. Hakim, "The myth of rising female employment".
20. Robinson & Wallace, *Part-time employment and sex discrimination legislation in Great Britain*.

discrimination and is prima facie unlawful under EU law, unless it can be otherwise justified. The European Court has upheld claims to equal treatment by part-time workers with respect to occupational pensions, sickness benefits, pay adjustments and severance pay.

Female entrants to information technology courses in the UK have not tended to rise:

> Somehow it has got itself an image that it is not useful to society, as well as male-dominated. People are not having contact with IT in a positive way. The big-scale automation processes in many industries have been a precursor to job losses which, in this climate, is negative. We have to make IT something that people find exciting and challenging[21].

On the contrary, technology industries lend themselves to the sort of flexible career that many women want – in particular part-time working and career breaks. First, IT achievement is not a nine-to-five job. Tasks are project-based and each project can be split up into a series of discrete parcels of work that can be done in the office or outside it. Secondly, IT-related jobs have the technical infrastructure to enable people to work from home.

7.6 The decline of the collective bargaining model of industrial relations

Reform of industrial relations had been a preoccupation of successive British governments for over thirty years before the 1980 Employment Act. It is arguable that the relentless anti-trade union legislation, deflationary economic policies and removal of public support for collective bargaining in the next thirteen years had a much greater impact than all the reform efforts. The main cause of the reconstitution of management-labour practices during the 1980s were the deep recession and mass unemployment of 1979–81, the acceleration of technical change and increased emphasis on inward investment. Under the impact of intensified international competition, these factors led to a reassertion of managerial prerogatives.

7.6.1 The flexible firm

There was postulated an apparently rather stylised theory or model of the "flexible firm" – with a core of flexibility deployed, multi-skilled permanent employees and a periphery of part-time, temporary and sub-contracted workers. It was criticized as not reflecting a more uneven reality in which core

---

21. Jean Irvine, quoted in Bradshaw, "Opportunity is knocking".

functions of certain businesses (for example, retailing) were themselves part-time and precarious. Nevertheless, flexibility, in the sense of adaptability and willingness to change work practices, became one of the most over-used words in the industrial relations lexicon. Much of the expansion of insecure and irregular work can be explained by sectoral shifts in the structure of employment, by cost-cutting measures and by rationalization; other changes reflect a plethora of managerial practices and not simply a strategy of flexibility. Flexibility, in general, tended to be an assertion of management prerogative in a recessionary and volatile industrial relations climate.

Examples of the variegated effect of flexibility and changing work practices have been extensively reported in the research journals and in textbooks of industrial relations and human resource management. A representative selection is provided under *Further reading* at the end of this chapter. For the software engineer, the main interest in this lies in; (i) the use of software in increasing managerial control of employees; (ii) the general effects on the wider system of industrial relations; (iii) how software workers are themselves affected by changing work practices and casualization. Closer discussion of (iii) will form part of the following chapter. All industries and occupations are now affected by (i) the use of computerized information systems, such as CAD/CAM, computer integrated manufacturing systems and flexible manufacturing systems; computerized reservation systems, electronic point of sale and automatic debit systems. Although beneficial savings in time and resources may result, this also depends on the increased control and surveillance over employees that such systems afford. For clerical work, the word processor can feed back the amount of typing done. Computerized reservation systems help to fill aeroplane capacity but also intensify the work of flight attendants. In the supermarket, software tells the manager the speed at which the checkout worker is pushing shopping past the till – the "item rate". In manufacturing, software is used to enhance Total Quality Management programs by recording defects and to press for just-in-time production. The ultimate is for products to be only worth making if they are consumed almost immediately they are produced and for the service (for example, arrival by aircraft) to exactly reflect demand but this tends to result in intensification of labour.

7.6.2 Just-in-time production

An example was the just-in-time customer assembly production plan installed by ISTEL Limited for Rover's Cowley plant. Rover aimed to select orders for build in a given period some five days ahead. From this could be developed a detailed "Time Delivery Schedule" requirement on a supplier, to provide pallets of given components, at a given time, directly to the factory, as part of an agreed load. ISTEL also introduced a technique of labour allocation, TARDIS (Time and Recording Direct Input System). To use the system, each employee is issued with an identity badge bearing her photograph and signature. This badge is used to "clock in" at the specific terminals. At each transaction, the intelligent clock immediately passes the employee's details to a central computer. Information is then available for management to redeploy labour from one department to another. Any absentees can have reasons for the absence recorded and notified to a separate computerized personnel record system. At the end of the week, the computer analyses clockings against shift patterns and calculates hours to be paid. A press release claimed that ISTEL's TARDIS package "has been successful in giving Rover the required monitoring of its Rover 800 series workforce".

The findings of Sewell & Wilkinson[22] in their study of a Japanese-owned electronics factory are similar:

> The day at the panel section begins with the production manager and team leaders looking at their schedules and "customer" (final assembly) requirements for the day. The labour they have available is determined by a Labour Hours Analysis which, based on production schedules and standard times, gives the number of labour hours required in each area on a month-by-month basis. A shopfloor PC will tell team leaders and the production manager their precise labour needs for a given level of efficiency in the light of the day's schedule.
>
> The Labour Hours Analysis, carried out on a PC with internally developed software, takes account of operator efficiency, attendance ratios, non-productive work ratios, learning curves on new models, etc., based on retrospective information. Production managers and team leaders are then expected, on a monthly basis, to agree to targets with a specified amount of labour.

On (ii), the wider effects of changing employment practices, Sheila Rothwell[23] reported that research examining evidence for the core-periphery model found that part-time working and flexi-hours continued to increase, though not usually for strategic reasons. IBM set up its own consultancy firm, Skillbase, and was moving towards greater use of human resource consultancy by, for example, developing other forms of labour-only sub-contracting. The office services agency, Manpower provided, employed and managed all the staff on one IBM site. This form of "partnership sourcing" in conjunction with an office staff agency was also adopted by Hewlett Packard at one site. A renewed interest in teleworking in 1992 reflected a new business interest in linking developments in technology, various forms of de-layered business network structures and new work practices. British Telecom gave managerial and professional staff the right to work from home on agreed conditions.

---

22. "Human resource management", p. 144.
23. "Annual review article".

7.6.3 Precarious types of employment

However, while it is true that, for middle class professionals accustomed to self-employment, this new commercial world is an opportunity to carve out new careers, for those less well educated and remunerated it means power-lessness and reduced living standards.

> The growth in labour market flexibility has become another way of describing the erosion of trade union power and deregulation of employ-ment conditions that has characterized the last 14 years, and, with it, a growing proportion of the population is finding that making a living is rough, tough and poorly-paid[24].

7.6.4 The effect on collective bargaining

According to the 1992 Workplace Industrial Relations Survey[25], it was quite clear that collective bargaining has declined. By 1990, key elements of the system of collective representation had faded and the reality of declining union presence was undeniable. The proportion of employees covered by collective bargaining agreements fell from over 70 per cent in 1984 to 54 per cent in 1990. The workplace survey provided hardly any evidence con-trary to the view that unions and collective bargaining have ceased to be fundamental features of the British system of industrial relations. Another survey – of 98 companies – by Industrial Relations Services, reported that the goal of linking pay more closely to performance was the main reason for de-recognizing unions and switching to personal contracts. Over 25 per cent replied that they had abandoned collective bargaining in one or more areas of the company, with 15 citing performance pay as the main reason for its abandonment[26].

The findings of the 1998 Workplace Employee Relations Survey[27] con-firmed the continuing decline of union and collective bargaining-based indus-trial relations. There are no unions at all in 47 per cent of workplaces, compared with 36 per cent in 1990. Union recognition is even more strongly associated with establishments employing large numbers than in 1990. The survey reported a very strong link between union membership and manage-rial attitudes towards unionism. Management hostility towards unionism is closely associated with low trade union membership: nearly two thirds of employees are union members in the 29 per cent of workplaces where man-agement is in favour of union membership; in the 17 per cent where manage-

24. Hutton, "A country of casuals".
25. Milward, Stevens, Smart, Hawes, *Workplace industrial relations in transition*.
26. Industrial Relation Services, Industrial relations review and report 553.
27. Cully and others, *The 1998 Workplace Industrial Relations Survey: first findings*.

ment is not in favour, union membership is very low indeed. The implication is that – on the reasonable assumption that at least some of the employees in these workplaces would be willing to join unions – the statutory recognition procedure introduced by the Labour government in 1999 might have considerable impact.

However, this is unlikely to be so among software employees. One reason is their relatively high earnings due to their scarce skills. Consequently, even less pertinent for such workers is the national minimum wage (1998). However, it is worth emphasizing that this piece of legislation is "rather a reflection of the industrial weakness of trade unions"[28] and nothing to do with the EU social dimension, despite the fact that several EU countries already had a national minimum wage. Furthermore, "the complexity of the legislation has been increased both by the extension of the excluded categories of worker and especially in the more elaborate, and in parts near incomprehensible drafting of the provisions on identifying the working time in respect of which the NMW has to be paid"[29].

In the business schools and in management books and journals, there has been considerable discussion, of a mainly prescriptive kind, in favour of human resource management. Opinions vary about how far this represents an actual change in personnel management practice[30], but its impetus came from the pervasive view that traditional personnel management had failed to promote the potential benefits of effective management of people[31]. Human resource management appears to derive from theories and beliefs about motivation and other ideas connected to the subject of organizational behaviour, though these ideas have now been around for nearly fifty years. Actually, the reconstitution of management–employee relations in the human resource format is linked to the acceleration of technical change, creating the need for more flexible use of labour, and, to transnational capital movements and inward investment with more amenable labour practices as one of its price tags. Critics of human resource management allege that its fine words are mainly a cover for intensification of labour and cost-cutting[32], and that there is little evidence of a strategic approach[33].

On the whole, so far, perhaps it is not unfair to say that human resource management has been most noticeable in its "resource" aspect, rather than in its "human" aspect. It may be that its strategic, proactive and integrative

---

28. Simpson, "A milestone in the legal regulation of pay: the National Minimum Wage Act 1998".
29. Simpson, "Implementing the NMW – the 1999 Regulations."
30. Guest, "Human resource management and industrial relations".
31. Skinner, "Big hat, no cattle: managing human resources".
32. Delbridge, Turnbull, Wilkinson, "Work intensification under JIT/TQM, new technology".
33. Storey & Sisson, "Limits to transformation: human resource management in the British context".

aims are particularly appropriate in newer occupations, such as software development. Consequently, this is the main theme of the following chapter.

7.7 Summary and conclusions

The industrial relations environment facing the software professional has changed as dramatically as technology in engineering. Whereas before 1980 the British industrial relations system would have been adequately character-ized as voluntary, it is now one of the most tightly legally regulated in the world. The successive Conservative governments after 1979 enmeshed trade unions in a web of legal restrictions and were largely successful in their strategic aim of shifting the balance of power in industrial relations strongly towards employers. However, the aim to deregulate has been partly fru-strated by directives deriving from the social charter of employee rights of the European Union. Structural and technological changes have encouraged economic growth in areas where unions are not strong. There has been a concerted effort among managers to develop practices that are more cost effective in their use of human resources, with emphasis on employment planning, simpler management structures, performance appraisal and perfor-mance-related pay, and non-unionism or restricted unionism. As a result, collective bargaining has become much less important. However, research findings on employee job satisfaction, particularly those from the 1998 Workplace Employee Relations Survey, show a clear association with effec-tive employee consultation. So, although there has been only a slight revival in collective industrial relations institutions and procedures, union recogni-tion and joint consultation remain relevant to good management practice.

7.8 References

Barnett, A. 1997. "Pow-wow but does it mean power?" *The Observer*, 24 May.

Bradshaw, D. 1991. "Opportunity is knocking", *Financial Times I*, 16 August.

Clement, B. 1998. "Jubilee Line hit by sabotage", *The Independent*, 20 November.

Cully, M. and others 1998. *The 1998 Workplace Employee Relations Survey: first findings.* Department of Trade and Industry.

Delbridge, R., P. Turnbull and B. Wilkinson 1992. "Work intensification under JIT/ TQM", *New Technology, Work and Employment*, **7**(3).

Di Martino, V. and L. Wirth 1990. "Telework: a new way of working and living", *International Labour Review*, **129**(5).

Dolding, L. 1994. "Unfair dismissal and industrial action," *Industrial Law Journal*, 23(3).

Guest, D. 1992. "Human resource management and industrial relations", *Journal of Management Studies*, **24**(5).

Hakim, C. 1993. "The myth of rising female employment", *Work, Employment and Society*, **7**(1).

Hutton, W. 1993. "A country of casuals", *The Guardian*, 30 March.

McColgan, A. 1993. "The Trade Union and Labour Relations (Consolidation) Act 1992", *Industrial Law Journal*, **22**(1).

McMullen, J. 1999. "TUPE: waiver of employment rights and contract changes after '*Wilson*'." *Industrial Law Journal*, March.

Miller, P. W. 1987. "The wage effect of the occupational segregation of women in Britain", *Economic Journal*, **97**.

Milward, N. 1994. *The new industrial relations?* Policy Studies Institute.

Milward, N., M. Stevens, D. Smart and W. R. Hawes 1992. *Workplace industrial relations in transition.* Aldershot: Dartmouth.

Robinson, O. and J. Wallace 1983. *Part-time employment and sex discrimination legislation in Great Britain.* London: Department of Employment.

Rothwell, S. 1993. "Annual review article", *British Journal of Industrial Relations*, **31**(1).

Sewell, G. and B. Wilkinson 1993. "Human resource management in: "surveillance" companies", in Clark, J. (ed.), *Human Resource Management and Technical Change.* London: Sage.

Simpson, R. 1999. "A Milestone in the legal regulation of pay: the National Minimum Wage Act 1998", *Industrial Law Journal*, **28**(1).

Simpson, R. 1999. "Implementing the NMW – the 1999 Regulations", *Industrial Law Journal*, **28**(2).

Skinner, W. 1981. "Big hat, no cattle: managing human resources", *Harvard Business Review*, **59**.

Storey, J. and K. Sisson, 1990. "Limits to transformation: human resource management in the British context", *Industrial Relations Journal*, **21**(2).

Wyatt, D. 1989. "Enforcing EEC social rights in the UK", *Industrial Law Journal*, **18**.

7.9 Further reading

Mabey, C., G. Salaman and J. Storey, 1999. *Human resource management: a strategic introduction.* Blackwell.

Salamon, M. 1998. *Industrial relations: theory and practice.* Prentice Hall.

Chapter 8

Human resource management and software engineering

Whereas the previous chapter was intended to give the software engineer some knowledge of employee relations in the wider economy, attention will now be directed at software workers and their management. The theme is the importance of human resource management in software development and production. Criticism that the term does not accurately reflect prevailing reality has already been noted. For present purposes, this is beside the point. We might as well accept that, in the broadest sense, human resource management is a managerial crusade that, with difficulty, might be challenged on the grounds that it equates profitability or value for money with social desirability. The prescriptive and procedural elements of human resource management do, nevertheless, provide a model framework for the development of sound management practices. That is to say, whatever might be the reality of management practices in industries that are competing by redundancy and rationalization, its ostensible emphasis on the management of people, staff training and development, a strategic approach and the notion of the "learning organization" do suggest that human resource management is particularly appropriate for software work. To what extent this is so is the main theme of this chapter.

It is considered in four parts. First, a stylized, ideal type or stereotypical model of human resource management is sketched, emphasizing features salient for management of software work. Since it is recognized that such stereotypical models give an impression of stability, uniformity and tidiness that just does not exist, the second section refers to more fragmented, discontinuous aspects of software work. It is so heterogeneous that it is not an industry as such and there are growing numbers of contract and teleworkers. Nevertheless, the very phrase "software engineering" does imply a standardized approach and the considerable evidence about its costs and benefits is discussed in the third section. By way of conclusion, it is recognized that human resource management is necessarily about control and adaptability but not at the cost of proper procedures for the management of personnel.

8.1 A model of human resource management – salient features for software engineering

There is broad agreement about what constitutes the stereotypical features of a model human resource management framework. Above all, it appears to denote a strategic, proactive stance. A corresponding commitment to the organization is expected from employees. They are therefore autonomous in the sense of, to some degree, managing themselves. So a united or unitary perspective is apt because everybody can be relied upon to pull in the same direction[1], even though individualized for performance appraisal and pay. Nevertheless, job roles are flexible, adaptable and empowered, not rigidly and formally defined from the top. Rather than being a specialist and somewhat Cinderella function of management, human resource management is the responsibility of all managers and integrated into line management. Its final generalized feature rather begs the question. That is the maximum utilization of human resources available to the enterprise. The question is how. It is not clear that it is best achieved by meticulous human asset accounting. This is such a key issue that it is discussed in the final section of this chapter. The other features of the human resource management model and their salience for software work are now expanded in turn.

8.1.1 Long-term, strategic and proactive in style

According to Piganiol[2]

> in this new approach, the human factor is explicitly included from the very start; job analysis in the broadest sense is one of the bases for scenario-building. The scenario evaluation stage takes account of what the workers will be likely to accept, proposals they might oppose, required periods of notice and the expected training arrangements.

Human resource planning or what used to be called manpower planning is of great significance for managers responsible for locating and developing resources for the information technology environment. As Westerman & Donoghue[3] point out, the problems associated with personnel in an information technology environment require a disciplined approach to establishing numbers of staff; the utilization of personnel; the development and education of employees, together with the construction of comprehensive human resource management policies that are not only responsive to immediate

---

1. Fox, Man mismanagement, p. 135.
2. "Industrial relations and enterprise restructuring in France", p. 625.
3. Westerman & Donoghue, *Managing the human resource*, p. 13.

needs but also are building blocks for the medium- and long-term corporate requirements. Managers may want to make a projection of future staff needs based on expected demand and output and the necessary inputs of capital and labour. The future is irremediably unforeseeable but even a crude projection, taking into account retirements, promotions and average levels of job quits, is better than simply reacting to events. Computerized personnel management systems, including databases of employee characteristics, are a valuable tool for managers in assessing present and future staffing requirements. Such information systems go hand-in-hand with rigorous and meticulous procedures for recruitment, reward and promotion. A key issue for human resource management is skills retention and development. Although it is a fallacy that planning is impossible when change is rapid and unpredictable, we do need to take seriously the objection to excessive presumed rationality and top-down strategy:

> Arguments for the efficacy of formal planning and strategy as a method of ensuring organizational survival and growth rest upon some dubious assumptions about people's abilities to process information and, in general, to learn from experience[4].

There has also been a growing realization that high-powered software engineering technology is next to useless unless there is a certain level of sophistication in the development environment. Thinking about software maturity assessment, some of the issues under relevant criteria are not to do with technology at all but ergonomics, such as investment in work stations or terminals; individual or open plan offices.

In any case, the integration with corporate strategy that is held to be a key feature of human resource management needs to be much broader in scope in software work. It needs, for example, to face the human resource problems encountered in trying to integrate software engineering with custom-built data-processing applications. Because users are unable to visualize the detail of a transformed working environment, it is impossible to define data processing requirements in advance. The main problem is to define the application, rather than produce well-engineered software. "Software engineering has a role to play in data processing. CASE tools produce robust applications quickly. Formal methods ensure programs consistent with applications specifications"[5]. Factory methods – further discussed in Section 8.3 – may be appropriate but "correct specification of a new application has to be founded on the quaking bog of previous applications if old applications are not to become barriers to new business opportunities. The nearer software engineer-

---

4. Staber & Aldrich, "Human resource strategies: some ecological cracks?", p. 112.

5. Cornes, "The siren song of software".

ing moves to the business definition, the more likely it is to contribute to solving the major problems of data processing"[6].

There is no automatic linkage between advanced technology and flexibility. Some forms of software can be complex and rigid, so flexibility is a matter of design choices in the software. This, in turn, has implications for human resource strategy in software development. In short, human resource planning faces particularly severe commercial pressures in the information technology environment. It is not therefore a panacea but it can make a contribution. Westerman & Donoghue (1989) suggested several problems in software development that are more likely to occur in the absence of human resource planning: the members of a prestigious project team who have no idea of their long-term future and who are forced to leave if they are to avoid stagnation and a long-term maintenance role; the highly prized experts on one piece of software who, in a short space of time, become experts on an antique software package; the valued and loyal programmers condemned to support old undocumented systems while contractors work on new glamour applications because nobody planned the manning aspects for the total life cycle of the product; the end users who see the system as an electronic version of their previous operation who cannot appreciate the fundamental conceptual difference between processes and the power of information technology because nobody planned their education.

8.1.2 Commitment to the organization

Originally, Walton[7] tried to define human resource management by making a distinction between control through reliance on the rules governing employment (such as in the collective bargaining model of industrial relations discussed in the previous chapter) and commitment that would come from empowering employees with status and responsibility for quality production. However, Anthony[8] was surely correct to argue that control is an ever-present requirement for management. Consequently, the real challenge is to shift employee attitudes from mere compliance with rules at work to commitment and self-motivation. Broadly defined, this signifies a commitment to staff development as part of the "learning organization" and firm-specific skills that are less transferable between firms. The new notion of skill is at once less definite and yet more vital, referring "not so much to the technical qualifications of employees but to their qualities in terms of attendance, flexibility, responsibility, discipline, identification with the company and, crucially, work-rate"[9].

---

6. *Ibid.*
7. Walton, "From control to commitment in the workplace".
8. Anthony, *The foundations of management.*
9. Morgan & Sayer, *Microcircuits of capital*, p. 167.

8.1.3 Self-management

Advocates of human resource management often talk of empowering the employees with responsibility for production quality. Workers are called upon actively to exercise joint "proprietorship" of that small business denoted by their project teams and to participate in the full range of tasks involved in building a perfect product on time. This is far from total self-management, rather a kind of bounded or quasi-autonomy. Team working is a vital element. Bill Gates, among others, has made the point that software is much better done in very small teams. Some products like OS/2 break down to smaller parts that different teams can make but many products cannot be so divided. For example, Microsoft had 15 people working on the Excel product, trying to crack the original Lotus spreadsheet program. A huge amount of effort may be devoted to directly communicating with employees, whatever their grade. Since many professional jobs are decidedly autonomous, authority relations between management and worker are somewhat blurred. Direct and regular face-to-face contact between managers and workers is emphasized. As well as improving supervision, this builds trust and helps maintain motivation. The trick is to reconcile motivating individuals with team-building because it is teams, not individuals, who complete projects. This is far from straightforward because performance appraisal, assumed to be central in most human resource management strategies, can have a disastrous effect on team-building. One answer is to build it into performance management. In a case study of self-managed teams in the Digital Equipment Corporation at Colorado Springs, USA, it was found that team-based appraisal seemed to improve participation, commitment and productivity[10].

8.1.4 Unitary perspective

In the unitary perspective, the entire enterprise is regarded as analogous to a team with one focus of loyalty and one focus of authority. This is distinct from actual teamwork among small groups of workers. It draws a sharp contrast with the pluralistic perspective of the collective bargaining model wherein the enterprise is seen as a coalition of different interest groups[11]. Human resource management generally disparages collective bargaining of pay with groups of workers as monolithic and demotivating, unsuited to the individualistic emphasis on flexibility and commitment – but individualized pay systems can themselves be demotivating. Managements in general do not like the trade union predilection of the "rate for the job". However, when it comes

---

10. Norman & Zwachi, "Team appraisals – team approach".
11. Fox, *Man mismanagement*, p. 135.

to motivation, individualized performance-related pay is very much a double-edged weapon. In fact nearly all studies of motivation, whilst acknowledging that pay is important, controvert the notion that it is an effective motivator. Research by Bevan & Thompson[12] of the Institute of Manpower Studies found no link between improved company performance and performance-related pay. From their survey of Inland Revenue staff, Marsden & Richardson[13] concluded that "the positive motivational effects of performance pay had been, at most, very modest". Research conducted on behalf of the Institute of Personnel Management and the National Economic Development Office[14] cast doubt on performance-related pay as a motivator. In short, performance-related pay rarely achieves completely what it is meant to do. Despite its widespread popularity, there are often far more effective systems of motivation and reward for managements to introduce if they want to improve their organization's performance[15].

In software development particularly, a crucial part of keeping effective workers content is a system where they can be promoted without having to become managers. At Microsoft a talented software developer can stay just that and yet rise to the top tier of elite "architects". These architects are not company directors despite their seniority, but report to the chief executive on an informal basis.

8.1.5 Flexible work roles

The human resource management approach tends to criticize bureaucracy; frankly, this is a bit of an Aunt Sally as all organizations are bureaucratic to some degree. All the same, the idea is that rather than the organization being mechanistic and centralized, with job roles formally defined, the roles are flexible with devolution of decision-making and an organic or fluid organizational structure. According to the American management consultant, Rosabeth Kanter[16], high-tech firms in particular exhibit four main characteristics affecting their management structure: the aforementioned need to motivate and retain technical talent; decentralization; looser authority structures and matrix organization. Conventionally, the management at a particular site or establishment is grouped according to staff function (horizontal grouping into production, marketing, accounting etc.) with delegation via line management down to first-line supervision. The matrix concept attempts to reconcile the advantages of specialization with those of co-operation across

---

12. Bevan & Thompson, "Performance management at the cross-roads".
13. Marsden & Richardson, *Does performance pay motivate? A study of Inland Revenue staff.*
14. Cannell & Wood, *Incentive pay: impact and evolution.*
15. Ridley, *Motivating and rewarding employees: some aspects of theory and practice.*
16. Kanter, "Variations in managerial career structures in high technology firms".

the functions and "refers to a situation where a manager or professional has reporting relationships in two directions, or, in effect, along two dimensions of a matrix"[17]. So it is also an attempt to decentralize decision-making while still maintaining the advantages of coherent central direction. For example, an engineering manager might report to both a director of engineering and a program manager for a current program or activity assignment. Matrix organization is complicated and may cause confusion, so companies that don't need it are well advised to steer clear of it.

Kanter[18] extended her argument, claiming that "the power to shape the parameters of the product and to interpret the customer's demands can be devolved extensively through corporate hierarchies. To accommodate this shift in the locus of responsibility, hierarchies may have to splinter into loose federations of product- and customer-focused units". Although change is all-pervasive and the shift to new fluid structures fairly obvious, organization theorists have struggled to conceptualize it. Paradoxically, so fissiparous are the tendencies that generalization is difficult. One attempt is the *adhocracy*, claimed to be the only structure "generally responsive to the turbulent, information intensive complexity of our changing industrial environments. It has an informal, organic structure in which people are co-ordinated by mutual adjustment and the need to create collaboratively. Authority shifts between persons whose knowledge is the most relevant at the moment and management has more to do with the integration and co-ordination of expertise than with supervision or control"[19].

8.1.6 Integrated into line management

Rather than the personnel function being specialist and apart, human resource management is envisaged as largely integrated into line management, such that all managers are responsible for it. Writing about the "new corporate identity" and appointment of a human resource director at BA, Hopfle remarked that "this heralded a fundamental change in what had previously been the personnel department. Administrative procedures formerly attached to the personnel role were handed over to line management"[20]. It has been suggested that such developments are bad news for the future of the personnel management function. Beaumont reckoned that "perhaps the worst case scenario is that personnel will remain responsible for collective employment issues (i.e. collective bargaining) and that line man-

---

17. *Ibid*, p. 113.
18. Kanter, *When giants learn to dance: mastering the challenges of strategy, management and careers in the 1990s*, p. 280.
19. Hampden Turner, "Henry Mintzberg: a profile".
20. Hopfle, "Culture and commitment: British Airways", p. 118.

agers, together with external consultants, will concentrate on the growing package of measures for the individual employee"[21]. Whilst this does not appear to have happened, the degree of integration of any genuinely strategic human resource management into line management has surely been limited in most industries.

8.1.7 Maximum utilization of human resources

Of course, improving the utilization and cost effectiveness of human resources is important but measuring information technology productivity is far from straightforward. The work processes are complex and just what ought to be the definable unit of output against which an input of human resource can be compared is controversial. Some approaches to measurement may potentially mislead managers so that they fall into the trap of concentrating on the detailed activities, rather than value-added. The following example is from hardware but also applies to software:

> ICL's Ashton-under-Lyne factory invested heavily in training and developing its workforce in order to improve flexibility and in raising standards through empowerment and quality initiatives. This shifted the emphasis from how much an hour workers are paid to how value can be added in each hour that people are employed.
>
> The approach has resulted in sharp improvements in quality, cycle time and productivity. From start to finish, a standard PC is built in ten minutes.
>
> Employee relations have also improved; labour turnover is only 1 per cent. Building on this, each member of the workforce receives a mandatory eight days of training a year[22].

It would be misleading to suggest that such approaches are widespread.

> Typically, British managers do not see their role as being crucial in the training and development of the employees with whom they work. The prime signal managers receive from the top (for example, in the form of appraisal criteria, reward systems and promotion patterns) is that what really counts is delivering short-term results in physical and (especially) financial terms[23].

The under-side of human resource management, for which decentralization and empowerment may provide a façade, is its potential, particularly

21. Beaumont, *Human resource management*, p. 13.
22. Wheatley, "Revival begins at home for computer makers".
23. Storey & Sisson, *Managing human resources and industrial relations*, p. 176.

when combined with information technology, for intrusive surveillance of employees. According to Winfield effective use of human resources now means exactly what it says:

It is the possibility of computer surveillance of work rate that allows decision makers to look more critically now than ever before at work output in offices. Simply attending – selling your time – may have been tolerated in the past; what is now possible and indeed demanded by monitoring and control systems is nothing less than effective work. It is nothing short of people's attention and total dedication to the task in hand that is now being asked for[24].

At a London conference on electronics and privacy in June 1999 it was reported that all staff using computers should now assume that they are being monitored. Research by Infosecurity, a computer security concern, found that office workers spend an average of 30 minutes a day using on-line facilities, such as buying and selling shares, rather than working for their employers. In June 1999 a woman lost an unfair dismissal case after being fired for booking a holiday on the Internet from her workplace after 150 web searches[25]. Since it pertains to the contract of employment, this seems to be an issue that will give rise to great legal creativity with various defences available. A secretary who was sacked because of her "Internet addiction" claimed unfair dismissal in the first case of its kind to go before an employment tribunal in August 1999. If the tribunal had found that she had an addiction, her lawyers would have been able to make a claim under the Disability and Discrimination Act 1995 that provides for unlimited compensation[26]. In October 1999 a senior female executive was dismissed after she sent an e-mail to her firm's personnel department expressing disgust at the homosexual practices of another employee.

Human resource management is therefore Janus-faced. It promises participation but may deliver continuous monitoring and surveillance. This is some way from the high trust, commitment model that some advocates of human resource management as something completely different try to portray. However, the human resource management commitment model is optimal for software work. This is because programmers must keep drawing attention to their failures and be rewarded for doing so. "This is a tough proposition for commercial companies and almost unthinkable in adversarial (them or us) or fear-based cultures. Management gets the impression that the

24. Winfield, Organisations and information technology, p. 30.
25. Sabbagh, " 'Staid' Britons share the online profits".
26. Verraik, "Woman fired for internet over-use".

project is going well and has no idea what's actually happening at the grass roots level. By the time they find out, it's too late"[27].

8.2 The structure of software development and production

Software development and production in the sense of manufacturing can be distinguished. The main business is software development, with mass production of software packages sometimes integrated, sometimes sub-contracted. While full-time employees form the majority of workers in software development and production, the business is so heterogeneous and fragmented that to speak of an industry is potentially misleading. Many software workers are employed by companies whose software development is definitely ancillary to their main business. They may not be interested in commercializing their own software in case this distracts from delivering systems for the main business.

Witham[28] provided a summary of the various categories of non-permanently employed workers. A freelance worker is one to whom work normally done by a permanent employee is sub-contracted. The freelance contacts the end-user, arranges the work content and duration, scale of charges and schedule directly, signs a contract directly with the end-user and performs the work either on-site or at base. Freelancing also signifies that the sub-contractor is an individual without partners or employees.

Body-shopping is not as such a method of working but, more accurately, refers to the relationship between the worker and employer. The individual is selected to perform a piece of work by virtue of relevant experience and availability. The immediate employer – agency, consultancy or software house – will have no say in the content of the job which is determined by the end-user of the contract services. Agency probably means freelance agency where the agency is responsible for finding the work and arranging contractual details with the client. A variant is employment by agency where the contract between freelancer and agency is an employment contract, usually for only the duration of the work stipulated by the client. When an agency deploys complete project teams, it is known as a contract house. A contract house is different from a software house in that self-employed people are used and in not itself specifying the nature of the work or its technical content, just recruiting and paying the workers. Software houses may use some self-employed workers and also supply their own body-shopped workers. The human resource plan of a good software house may be to do as much work as possible either in-house or, if on-site, under their own human resource management. Even so, the software house may be obliged to body-shop its

---

27. Schofield, "Counting the cost of failure.
28. Witham. "*Computer guide to the contract industry*".

own workers. Workers earning fees are better than idle hands. The software house gains a contact and possible future client. Sometimes work for which the software house originally tendered has been taken over by the client but the original software project team stays on-site. Witham commented that the better software houses do not like this practice but more rapacious outfits that purport to be software houses but are really glorified body-shops, are less fastidious.

While the self-employed are a fundamental resource in information technology contract labour, Witham reckoned that there are relatively few on account of financial obstacles presented by current legislation. Whether or not that is the case – and it is debatable – software is especially suited for entrepreneurial, sub-contracted networks. Norman Macrae, formerly of the *Economist* was among the first to predict such globalized entrepreneurial commerce, with most work accomplished by free agents using computer networks. The prototype version of this is teleworking by homeworkers or employees of a business or government agency who work part-time or full-time at home rather than at the employer's premises. The production technology involves some mix of office computer system, home PC and telephone line.

Teleworking is simply work by remote control. Usually the worker is working from home and maintaining contact with the employer or, if self-employed, other business, through communications networks. It reduces commuting by making the work flow to and from the worker. It could have a significant impact on public transport systems in London and other big cities. Partly for this reason the UK government published a guide to teleworking and supports this method of flexible employment.

Because teleworking means different things to different people, it is hard to quantify how many people are involved. The expression can be used to mean anything from keying in data at a remote telecentre factory – such as centres used by the major commercial banks – to travelling sales staff with laptop computers and the idyllic life of the well-paid professional working from a country cottage, yet maintaining employee status and a desk at head office with the individual bargaining power of scarce skills.

In fact, for many, the reality of working at least part of the time from home, linked to the office with a computer and a modem, is rather less idyllic. Teleworking is often little more than a hi-tech version of traditional industrial homeworking – with the employer saving overhead and child care costs. Not surprisingly, telecommunications and IT companies, such as BT, IBM and Digital, have led this change in working practices. While BT have offered employees home-based telework as a union-negotiated option, others, including sections of the Civil Service, British Gas and Scottish Power, have introduced telework to cut costs and increase the commercial advantages of flexible working. Ideally, employer and employee gain: for example, when the Co-operative Bank gave employees in its bad debt collection department the chance to work from home, productivity went up to 40 per cent – an example, perhaps, of the commitment model of human resource management.

Trade unions tend to be suspicious of all kinds of homeworking. It is a form of employment that makes collective organization and representation very difficult. At least the Communication Workers' Union is in a good position to wire up local union offices. However, BIFU, the Banking Insurance and Finance Union, has found cases of members compelled to work from home on a lower grade.

Inevitable as the growth of teleworking will be, it must be acknowledged that it is not suitable for everyone. Furthermore, whilst it has been associated with a shorter working week, this is slow in coming. The greatest challenge is for managers to manage people whom they rarely see. All the talk of corporate culture is difficult to reconcile with a widely dispersed workforce less able to feel genuinely part of the company.

There are many examples of "off-shore"-telework. American firms use local workers for electronically linked data processing and administrative work in countries such as Barbados, China, India, Ireland, Jamaica, Korea and Mexico. This is only one aspect of the globalization affecting software production. Some consider that programming is too lowly a task to be done in the UK or Singapore and is more efficiently sub-contracted to India or China where intelligent and experienced graduate programmers will do it for a lower price. Ed Yourdon[29] predicted massive unemployment among the ranks of American programmers, systems analysts and software engineers, warning that international competition will put American programmers out of work, just as Japanese competition put American automobile workers out of work. Yourdon's solution was building world class software development teams. In fact, the US software industry was well ahead of the Japanese. Japan had constructed literal software factories and it was argued[30] that these posed a challenge to Western management. The failure of the challenge is discussed next.

8.3 The software factory

The analogy of software production with industrial scientific management principles goes back to the research of Kraft & Dubnoff[31]. It is a rather different issue to posit that standardized techniques can be applied to software development, as though it were a type of manufacturing. In general, it is inaccurate to conflate the term software engineering with rigid division of labour. It is more to do with structured programming, i.e. a logical, struc-

29. Yourdon, *Decline and fall of the American programmer.*
30. Cusumano, *Japan's software factories: a challenge to US management.*
31. Kraft & Dubnoff, "Job content, fragmentation and control in computer software work"

tured approach to programming and with software tools to assist productivity. An early definition of software engineering was "the establishment and use of sound engineering principles in order to obtain software that is reliable and works efficiently on real machines"[32]. By setting out the three key elements of methods, tools and procedures, it enabled the manager to control the process of software development. The methods refer to the wide range of tasks in building software – project planning and estimation; system and software requirements analysis; design of data structure; program architecture and algorithm procedure; coding; testing and maintenance. The methods often introduce language-oriented notation and criteria for software quality. Tools provide automated support for methods. They may be integrated so that the information created by one tool can be used by another, thereby establishing a system for the support of software development (CASE). The procedures hold the methods and tools together and control timing by defining a sequence in which the methods will be applied.

However, creating the software that actually does the work is not completely an engineering discipline, even though some software professionals aspire to that. Computer programs are mostly still written the same way they have been for 40 years – by hand – and individual programmers are much more like creative writers than brickies. This is why large-scale government computerization projects are much more likely to go wrong[33].

Clearly, the aim of an industrial approach is more effective management to maintain and enhance quality and productivity. The question is whether increased structuring will achieve that or run the risk of "over-engineering" and detachment from end-user environment that may emanate from the "siren song of software"[34]. Since, although Cusumano's book[30] is not a prescription for management, it examines this issue in detail, it is worthy of further comments. At the beginning of the 1990s, Toshiba operated the Fuchu software factory employing 2,300; Hitachi had two software establishments employing 4,000 programmers and systems engineers and 7,000 employees in subsidiaries and sub-contractors. Fujitsu had two software factories employing 3,500 engineers with 14,000 employees among subsidiaries and sub-contractors. NEC operated five software factories with just under 10,000 employees. According to Cusumano, these large scale operations had solved the classical problem in software engineering – how to replace craft control and design autonomy with factory discipline, reliable planning and systematic quality control.

The companies gained from labour in two ways: "The prospect of lifetime employment and long term careers within these large firms guaranteed that

32. Bauer, *Software engineering*.
33. Schofield, "Counting cost of failure".
34. Cornes, "The siren song of software".

programme engineers did not quit, as many would probably have done in the US"[35]. Furthermore, they could hire young workers unskilled in software but train them to use a standardized methodology and tool set as reusable designs. However, as the down-sizing and flexibilities of the 1990s accelerated, the software factories proved out-moded. Software was no longer seen – as in the Japanese *keiretsu* model – as an addition to hardware. Rather, "the *keiretsu* structure had inhibited the development of general standards and strong software vendors and, with standards now emerging, they are coming from external players, that is US firms"[36].

Rather than pointing to a solution to the management problems that occur in software development and production, as in other business activities, Cusumano may have inadvertently encouraged readers to make a typical management mistake by seeking a process to solve a problem involving people. In that context, the challenge for human resource management is to replace compliance with rules with trust and support, to replace the idea that employees serve the manager with the idea that managers enable the employees to do their work – and to empower the employees to use their energy and creativity on behalf of the business. Reviewing Cusumano's book, Crocca suggested that "just as the Japanese adopted the scientific method, we have to adopt the emotional method: be sensitive when dealing with people and analytical when dealing with process. Management must resist looking to science for "silver bullet" solutions to people problems"[37].

8.4 Training and human resource management

In the first edition of *Professional Issues in Software Engineering*, the software gap – or skills gap – was discussed. This has not been filled. Despite universities establishing more IT and computing courses and applications rising strongly, the industry continues to generate more vacancies than capable recruits. Research for Microsoft predicted 1.6 million job vacancies in IT by 2002 when the industry and universities increase training places. The perception of IT careers does not help in recruitment. Mark East, education group manager at Microsoft UK was reported in June 1999 as believing that "the view is that most techies are nerds with beards who program all day"[38].

It is true that university computer science degrees tend to be pseudo-scientific and rather theoretical. More traditional courses do emphasize programming and the theory of software engineering. Consequently, students

---

35. Berggren, "Japan as number two".
36. *Ibid.*
37. Crocca, "Review of M. Cusumano, Japan's software factories".
38. Pritchard, "Great jobs, good money, few takers".

associate computing degrees with science and maths – both areas where applications have fallen over the last decade.

By contrast, there are innovative courses aimed at multimedia. Furthermore, from an industry point of view, the mathematically-based computing degree is not always necessary. Business management needs graduates who can work with IT without the theory of computer science. "Research carried out by NOP for Microsoft found that 20 per cent of people entering the IT industry did so without formal IT skills"[39]. Computing companies find that IT graduates often lack transferable or "people-handling" skills, such as communications and a broader knowledge of how businesses work. Dr Neil Barrett, senior fellow at Bull, reckoned that "from an industry point of view, we are often better placed to take people with good generalist degrees and turn them into engineers". Although computer scientists have learned to use elegant, compact languages and pure programming techniques, they can stumble in creating real applications in a real workplace. "They are people who understand the finer details of software programming but cannot program. We have to start again and teach them the methods and tricks we work with"[40]. The answer may be degree schemes that combine computer science with business studies. However, a more radical solution may be for the industry to create some sort of mechanism that can compensate for job insecurity, perhaps by creating the equivalent of a Dock Labour Board of permanently paid employees on whom the various software companies can draw when necessary.

8.5 Conclusion: human resource management in software – commitment and control

The tensions and contradictions between a factory approach and human resource management can be demonstrated by reference to a software package using the programming technique of object-oriented software. An object-view presumes that any transaction or business operation starts with an object and gives a choice of related activities. An object can be any item used by anyone in her everyday work. Activities to do with that object – information, an invoice, even a diary date for a customer – are all options attached to that object and a user simply picks the relevant activity.

Accessibility to information was the feature that convinced a multinational health care group's management to spend an initial $500,000 on a revamped personnel package of this type. The company had been reorganized to emphasize European, rather than local, control of operations in the region. Managers in its five business lines became responsible for profit and loss,

---

39. *Ibid.*
40. *Ibid.*

making information about salaries and other employment costs a vital part of the European picture. As the director of human resources put it, "we call it a human resources system but it is really a business system because line managers will have access to it"[41]. He advocated a devolution of personnel responsibilities to line managers. The application of the package was aimed at giving a thousand managers easy access to the Europe-wide information that they need to assess and react to the ever-changing deployment of staff.

The case hints at the dichotomy in human resource management. This is to say, control by rules or control by influencing the organizational culture to emphasize loyalty, seriousness, commitment and responsibility. Walton[42] tried to extract the essence of human resource management by saying that it necessitated a move "from control to commitment". But this will not really do because, as Anthony put it, "if management is not accepting responsibility for the control of labour, then it is not managing"[43].

Rather, the contrast that human resource management displays is between compliance and commitment as different forms of managerial control. The main expression so far of human resource management is in the trend to integrate personnel management with senior and middle line management. The idea is to move away from compliance-based and rules-based systems of control that often involved collective bargaining about pay and conditions in a centralized, mechanistic organization structure. Instead, Kanter[44] has advocated forms of control that instil personal commitment because the rules and procedures "stifle initiative and creativity" in an atmosphere that is "emotionally repressive". Therefore human resource management purports to aim at "responsible autonomy"[45], empowering employees with responsibility for production and product quality. Unfortunately, however, the main approach to this so far is a kind of smothering dogma. For example, a mission statement is introduced, there are strategic plans and constant talk of changing the culture that implies a monolithic unitary perspective for the organization. "Commitment" seems to involve "the internalization of management-derived and sanctioned beliefs, norms and values, in the sense that they become part of the core of the individual's perceptual world; thereby they develop into moral obligations"[46]. Moreover, for all the talk of culture management and empowerment, there seem to be even more layers of bureaucratic control than under explicitly rule-based systems. Much of this

41. Gooding. "New objective for software".
42. Walton, "From control to commitment in the workplace".
43. Anthony, *The foundations of management*, p. 1.
44. Kanter, *When giants learn to dance: mastering the challenge of strategy, management and careers in the 1990s*, p. 20.
45. Friedman, *Industry and labour*, p. 84.
46. Johnson & Gill, *Management control and organizational behaviour*, p. 36.

"re-bureaucratization" is concerned with measuring outputs and performance and there is a great growth industry in inspection and monitoring.

Management may attempt to dispense with responsibility for control of some employees by use of sub-contracting. Many companies have done this for cleaning and catering services. But this is hardly a move to commitment as sub-contracted workers cannot be expected to have loyalty to anyone. So commitment can be expected only among core, permanent workers. Even here, commitment may be one-sided. Vicki Smith[47] observed that a commitment to paternalistic lifetime employment patterns by a banking company concealed a covert plan for cutting personnel – charging middle managers with "managing up" (raising individual productivity) or "managing out". The device used was the performance appraisal in order to penalize or push employees. Here, moving from compliance to commitment meant that managers should "'reorient their thinking away from bureaucratically constricting standardized job descriptions based on position and focus instead on increasing results in order to contribute to improved corporate performance". This they would do by setting "stretch" objectives: upgrading people by pushing them to achieve ever higher levels of output.

The sort of software discussed at the beginning of this section and the TARDIS example in the previous chapter show that human resource management can be a subterfuge for intensification of the bureaucratic approach and its actual centralization. "Assessing and reacting to the ever-changing deployment of staff" is facilitated by labour hours analysis, carried out on a PC and taking account of operator efficiency, attendance ratios, "non-productive work" ratios, learning curves etc. Human resource management may therefore mean an intrusive surveillance of employee performance.

Even if this dark side of human resource management is acceptable on grounds of efficiency, "business need", flexibility and commitment do not justify the manipulation and favouritism that can be unleashed by passing personnel management to line management. If moving to commitment entails extinction of necessarily bureaucratic rules of procedure and consistency, human resource management is humbug. Fair treatment of all employees, due process (for disciplinary cases etc.) and consistency must be the foundation of any human resource management that aims to secure the trust and commitment of employees.

This is obviously the opposite of "management's right to manage irrespective of whether this is fair and reasonable"[48] of concealing information from subordinates, feigning ignorance, side-stepping of official procedures to gain one's own way and resort to expediency. Properly carried out and fairly

---

47. Smith, *Managing in the corporate interest*, p. 47.
48. Clark, "Procedures and consistency versus flexibility and commitment in employee relations", p. 80.

implemented, the human resource management model is about procedures in employment relations. Systematic recruitment and selection techniques, training needs analysis and performance review are fundamental features of the model. Consequently, although human resource management must recognize that managers operate within markets, if it means anything, it also means that they do so by "assembling and maintaining human associations in sustainable organizational forms"[49]. Essentially, the challenge for managers of software development is that high-trust, knowledge-based organizations need managers who can cope with complex, social, political and moral environments. Over-emphasis on the "bottom-line" and resource facet "ignores the institution-building and nurturing role of management so clearly recognized by our competitors"[50]. The importance of procedures for consistency should be apparent to software engineering managers more than most. So even if we accept that world-class software organizations will move aggressively towards specification-level reuse because the specification models are contained in CASE repositories – the people who constitute the project team cannot be stored in a repository. Nevertheless, their experience and co-partnership ought to be maintained – by human resource management approaches to software productivity which often result in bigger gains than technical approaches.

8.6 References

Anthony, P. 1986. *The foundations of management.* London: Tavistock.

Bauer, F. L. 1972. *Software engineering.* Amsterdam: North Holland.

Beaumont, P. 1993. *Human resource management.* London: Sage.

Berggren, C. 1995. "Japan as number two", *Work, Employment and Society,* **9**(1).

Bevan, S. and Thompson, M. 1991. "Performance management at the cross-roads", *Personnel Management,* November.

Cannell, M. and Wood, S. 1992. *Incentive pay: impact and evolution,* Institute of Personnel Management and National Economic Development Office.

Clark, J. 1993. "Procedures and consistency versus flexibility and commitment in employee relations", *Human Resource Management Journal,* **4**(1).

Cornes, R. 1990. "The siren song of software", *The Guardian,* 19 July.

Crocca, E. T. 1993. "Review of M. Cusumano, Japan's software factories", *Administrative Science Quarterly,* **37**(4).

Cusumano, M. 1991. *Japan's software factories: a challenge to US management.* New York: Oxford University Press.

Fox, A. 1974. *Man mismanagement.* London: Hutchinson.

Friedman, A. 1977. *Industry and labour.* London: Macmillan.

Gooding, C. 1993. "New objective for software", *Financial Times,* 10 November.

---

49. Reed & Anthony, "The barbarian elite".
50. *Ibid.*

Hampden Turner, C. 1990. "Henry Mintzberg: a profile", *Business Strategy Review*, **1**(1).

Hopfle, H. J. 1993. "Culture and commitment: British Airways", in D. Gowler, K. Legge and C. Clegg (eds), *Case studies in organizational behaviour and human resource management*. London: Paul Chapman.

Johnson, P. and J. Gill, 1993. *Management control and organizational behaviour*. London: Paul Chapman.

Kanter, R. M. 1985. "Variations in managerial career structures in high technology firms", in P. Osterman (ed.), in *Internal labour markets*. Cambridge, MA: MIT Press.

Kanter, R. M. 1989. *When giants learn to dance: mastering the challenges of strategy, management and careers in the 1990s*. London: Unwin Hyman.

Kraft, P. and S. Dubnoff 1986. "Job content, fragmentation and control in computer software work", *Industrial Relations*, **25**(2).

MacLeod, D. 1994. "Hi-tech dream life becomes work-at-home nightmare", *The Guardian*, 22 March.

Marsden, D. and R. Richardson, 1991. *Does performance pay motivate? A study of inland revenue staff*. London School of Economics.

Morgan, K. and A. Sayer, 1988. *Microcircuits of capital*. Boulder, Colorado: Westview Press.

Norman, C. A. and R. A. Zwachi, 1991. "Team appraisals – team approach", *Personne Journal*, September.

Piganiol, C. 1989. "Industrial relations and enterprise restructuring in France", *International Labour Review*, **36**(2).

Pritchard, S. 1999. "Great jobs, good money, few takers", *The Independent*, 3 June.

Reed, M. and P. Anthony 1993. "The barbarian elite", *The Observer*, 7 November.

Ridley, T. 1992. *Motivating and rewarding employees: some aspects of theory and practice*. Work Research Unit, Advisory Conciliation and Arbitration Service.

Sabbagh, U. 1999. " 'Staid' Britons share the online profits", *The Independent*, 30 June.

Schofield, J. 1999. "Counting the cost of failure", *The Guardian*, 2 July.

Smith, V. 1990. *Managing in the corporate interest*. Berkeley, CA: University of California Press.

Staber, U. and H. Aldrich, 1989. "Human resource strategies: some ecological cracks?" *Industrial Relations Journal*, **20**(2).

Storey, J. and K. Sisson, 1993. *Managing Human Resources and Industrial Relations*. Milton Keynes: Open University Press.

Trapp, R. 1999. IT Transforms the world of work. *The Independent*, 13 May.

Verraik, R. 1999. "Woman fired for Internet over-use", *The Independent*, 23 August.

Walton, R. E. 1985. "From control to commitment in the workplace", *Harvard Business Review*, **53**, March–April.

Westerman, J. and P. Donoghue, 1989. *Managing the human resource*. Englewood Cliffs, NJ: Prentice Hall.

Wheatley, M. 1993. "Revival begins at home for computermakers", *Independent on Sunday*, 21 March.

Winfield, M. 1991. *Organisations and information technology*. Oxford: Blackwell Scientific Publications.

Witham, I. 1987. *Complete guide to the contract industry*. Thames Ditton, Surrey: Redmore Publishing.

Yourdon, E. 1993. *Decline and fall of the American programmer*. Englewood Cliffs, NJ: Prentice-Hall.

8.7 Further reading

Dutton, W. H. 1999. *Information politics in the digital age*. Oxford University Press.

Chapter 9

Health and safety at work

9.1 The problem

Health and safety at work usually only hits the headlines when there is a major disaster. Unfortunately, in recent years there has been an unprecedented number of these and we can still recall with horror the Zeebrugge ferry disaster, the Kings Cross fire, the Piper Alpha explosion, and, most recently the Paddington rail crash. Although all of these involved the activities of people at work, one circumstance that made them particularly newsworthy was that, with the exception of Piper Alpha, the majority of people who suffered as a consequence of the incidents were members of the public. It is a sad fact that, although society reacts keenly to disaster, by immediately establishing public inquiries and instigating extra safety measures, there is much less interest in the steady toll of individual deaths, injuries, and cases of disease which occur due to activities at work.

The number of fatal accidents at work has fallen sharply since the beginning of the 1970s but around 200 employees each year still die as a result of accidents at work and a significant number of members of the public lose their lives as a result of work activities. More significantly, perhaps, although the number of fatalities at work declined during the 1970s and 1980s, a plateau seems to have been reached during the 1990s and there appears to be no sign of any continuing downward trend. The most recent statistics also show an apparent increase in the number of injuries sustained as a result of work activities, although comparison with previous years is not straightforward because of changes in definition contained in the Reporting of Accident, Disease and Dangerous Occurrences Regulations 1995[1]. Injuries, disease and accident are by no means confined to a few industries, but are spread throughout the spectrum of work activity[2]. Although some industries are

---

1. SI 1995/3163.
2. For details see, e.g. *HSE Safety Statistics Bulletin 1997/8* available at http://www.open.gov.uk/ hse/hsestats/ssb9798.pdf

inherently more dangerous than others, the average worker does not expect to be at increased risk by the simple act of going to work, until, of course, an accident occurs.

There is nothing like an accident for motivating people to adopt safe working practices. The problem lies in changing attitudes *before* catastrophe occurs and in creating a safe working environment, or at least one that is as safe as is possible. The best way of achieving this is by building in safety from the start in plant design, factory layout, training, supervision, job descriptions and so on, but so often this is compromised by other considerations which may seem to be more important in the short-term, such as pressure of time or financial concerns. This has obvious implications for the design of the control software that is now ubiquitous. Increased automation has brought great benefits to manufacturing industry in terms of increased efficiency and product quality, as well as in improved control and monitoring. Because of the success of this technology we have to ensure that increasing complexity in the pursuit of enhanced productivity does not introduce additional hazards. In many high-risk areas, such as the oil, chemical and nuclear industries, the safety systems themselves are often computer controlled; the software must be of the highest integrity and must handle safely all foreseeable eventualities. Similar considerations apply to other applications, such as "fly-by-wire" aircraft, where proper control is wholly dependent on the correct and safe operation of the aircraft's computer systems. There is clearly an enormous responsibility on those who design and implement software for all potentially hazardous applications, and particularly for safety-critical applications such as those mentioned here.

This chapter will consider the law relating to health and safety at work, discuss possible methods of achieving safety in practice and highlight some of the problems in doing so. Measures which might be taken to ensure the integrity of software destined for use in safety-critical software and the way in which this area of activity might be regulated are discussed in more detail in the next chapter. However the factors which have influenced the development and approach of the modern legislation relating to health and safety at work may also provide lessons which are of value in creating rules to promote safety in more diverse areas and so the general principles which can be identified in the legislation relating to health and safety at work should be kept in mind when reading the chapter following.

9.2 Historical background

Following the industrial revolution, it soon became apparent that safe working conditions in the new mills and factories, which were the response to the increased technological development in that era, would not be established without a suitable legal framework to ensure compliance. The first Act was passed in 1802 particularly to safeguard young people in textile mills[3]. Thus commenced the production of vast amounts of legislation designed to protect people at work. The majority of the statutes were very specific and were usually enacted in response to particular patterns of industrial diseases and accidents. It was soon recognized that this rather piecemeal approach was not entirely satisfactory and, at intervals in the nineteenth and twentieth centuries, Factories Acts were passed in an attempt to provide a comprehensive code applicable to all types of industry. The final statute of this type was the Factories Act 1961. However, technology was advancing at such a rate that frequently many of the enactments were out of date or in need of amendment as soon as they were on the statute book. It had become clear by the late 1960s that the mass of legislation was both cumbersome and ineffective. The number of industrial accidents was not decreasing, and large numbers of workers were not covered by *any* health and safety legislation as they were employed in establishments to which the Factories Act or other similar enactments[4] did not apply.

It was time for a new approach which would be capable of more flexibility to cope with the constantly changing requirements of industry, would include those not yet protected by legislation, and would also protect the public who, as we have already seen, may find themselves affected by the work activities of others. Consequently, in 1970, a committee on Safety and Health at Work was set up under the chairmanship of Lord Robens. Amongst other things, it had as its terms of reference:

> To review the provision made for the safety and health of persons in the course of their employment ... to consider whether any further steps are required to safeguard members of the public from hazards, other than general environmental pollution, arising in connection with activities in industrial and commercial premises and construction sites and to make recommendations.

9.3 Report of the Robens Committee 1972

The Robens Committee reported comprehensively and in detail[5], but the following is a particularly succinct comment:

---

3. An act for the Preservation of the Health and Morals of Apprentices and others employed in cotton and other mills and cotton and other factories (42 Geo. 3, c. 73).
4. Examples include the Agriculture (Safety, Health and Welfare Provisions) Act 1956, The Mines and Quarries Act 1954, The Offices Shops and Railway Premises Act 1963 and The Nuclear Installations Act 1965.
5. 1972 Cmnd 5034.

> Apathy is the greatest single contributing factor to accidents at work. This attitude will not be cured so long as people are encouraged to think that health and safety at work can be ensured by an ever-expanding body of legal regulations enforced by an ever-increasing army of inspectors.

This statement summarizes accurately the change in emphasis brought about by the Robens Report. Consider the opening sentence quoted above. Here is the first suggestion that people at work may themselves be a factor in producing a safe environment, and the statement further mentions changing attitudes. Clearly this is a rather more intransigent problem than machinery guarding or the control of toxic fumes, for instance. The attitudes of people, and their actions, depend on a large number of external and internal stimuli; modification of attitudes and motivation to a particular course of action requires a much more subtle approach. The Robens Committee was of the opinion that the primary responsibility for safety at work lies with the people who create and work with the hazards, i.e. it should be the concern of *all*, whether the managing director or the floor sweeper, although obviously the levels of responsibility will vary considerably. Safety should not have to rely on a rigid regime of rules superimposed from outside.

The "ever-expanding body of legal regulations" has already been mentioned, what of the "ever-increasing army of inspectors"? The first factory inspectors had been appointed in 1833 to enforce the legislation, and had proliferated with the increasing number of statutes. In particular, different and autonomous inspectorates were responsible for the workers covered by the various enactments already referred to, viz.: Factory Inspectorate, Mines and Quarries Inspectorate and so on. However, to speak of an "army" is perhaps a misnomer as at the time of the Robens Report there were approximately 700 in the Factory Inspectorate. The report itself envisaged this rising to about 1000 with the recommended new legislation which would create responsibilities for workplaces previously not covered. One of the main problems with the "ever-increasing army of inspectors" arose out of demarcation between the areas policed by the various inspectorates and the inspectors appointed by the local authorities (to inspect offices, shops etc.), especially in premises where more than one of the Acts applied. To summarize, the main recommendations of the Robens Committee were:

- Safety and health objectives should be clearly defined at all levels within firms.
- Workers should be more involved in safety and health at their workplace.
- There should be a legal duty on employers to consult their employees on safety and health matters necessary at their workplace.
- A National Authority for safety and health should be established.
- Existing statutory provisions should be replaced by provisions under a new enabling Act.

- Voluntary codes of practice should be introduced.
- The scope of the legislation should be extended to include all employees (with minor exceptions) and the self-employed.
- The existing safety and health inspectorates should be amalgamated.
- New administrative sanctions should be adopted.
- Local authority work should be co-ordinated with that of the new authority.
- The interests of the public should be taken into account in the new legislation.
- General fire precautions should be dealt with under a Fire Precautions Act.
- The Employment Medical Advisory Service should function as part of the new authority.

It was therefore proposed that the traditional approach based on detailed statutory regulation should be reformed. It should be replaced with a legal framework within which effective self-regulation of working conditions could be created by employers and employees working together. To assist in this process, it was suggested that greater use should be made of voluntary standards and codes of practice produced by the industries themselves to promote better conditions. It was expected that this would free the statutory inspection services to increase their advisory role, but would also enable them to concentrate more effectively on serious problems where more stringent control might be necessary. This philosophy and reasoning lay behind the passing of the Health and Safety at Work etc. Act 1974 which occurred as a direct result of the Robens Report.

9.4 The Health and Safety at Work etc. Act 1974

The Health and Safety at Work Act was intended to herald a new approach to health and safety legislation in the UK. The intention was, and is, that this Act together with ancillary regulations made under it would replace all existing health and safety legislation. However, because of the mass of pre-existing legislation and the complexity of industry, it was expected that this would take some time to accomplish and at the present time it is still not complete. The situation has been made more complex by a variety of EC law on health and safety matters (see Section 9.4.11). Consequently the Health and Safety at Work Act and associated regulations coexist with any pre-1974 legislation still in force and also with regulations implementing EC directives. This body of law is referred to as the *relevant statutory provisions* within the Health and Safety at Work Act. A detailed study of the Act is beyond the scope of this book but it is instructive to study the areas where the new and old legislation differ and the way in which the recommendations of the

Table 9.1 Comparison of pre- and post-1974 legislation.

	"Old" legislation (pre-1974)	"New" legislation (1974 onwards)
1.	Premises, i.e. factory, office etc.	Employment is the only necessary criterion.
2.	Specific requirements, e.g. Factories Act 1961 s14(1):- Every dangerous part of any machinery . . . shall be securely fenced. . . and s22(2):- Every hoist or lift shall be thoroughly examined by a competent person at least once in every period of six months . . .	General (and far-reaching) requirements, e.g. Health and Safety at Work Act 1974 s2(1):- It shall be the duty of every employer to ensure so far as is reasonably practicable the health, safety and welfare at work of all his employees. The Act also covers others such as the self-employed, and the public if they are affected by the activities of those at work.
3.	No requirements on manufacturers or suppliers. In certain instances, the owner or hirer of a machine may be liable, rather than the occupier.	Creates comprehensive new duties for manufacturers and suppliers of articles and substances for use at work.
4.	Sets minimum standards. The law is imposed from above and "policed". Prosecution and court order are the only available statutory methods of enforcement.	Systems and procedures: self-regulation, safety policies and safe systems of work involve all employees. Improvement and prohibition notices are additional new enforcement procedures which can produce results without resorting to the courts.
5.	Regulations for specific industries and processes: rigorous but difficult to keep up to date in the face of rapidly changing technology.	Specific regulations but couched in general terms and supplemented by approved codes of practice that are more easily updated.

(continued)

Table 9.1 (continued)

6.	Number of enforcing authorities and inspectorates in various government departments	Health and Safety Commission and Health and Safety Executive, under the Secretary of State for Employment, are responsible for all activities relating to occupational health and safety.
7.	Many requirements of the statutes and associated regulations are *absolute*.	Most requirements are qualified by *so far as is reasonably practicable*.

Robens Committee have been incorporated. (See Table 9.1 for a comparison.)

9.4.1 People v places

Although employment was a necessary prerequisite for the application of the "old" legislation, the primary criterion was the definition of the *places* to which it applied. Thus the Factories Act 1961 and the Acts relating to other types of premises define very carefully and precisely those places to which they refer. In particular, Section 175 of the Factories Act goes into considerable detail about what does, and therefore by omission does not, constitute a factory. This was the reason why, at the time of the Robens Committee, several million workers were not protected by any health and safety legislation whatsoever. They were employed in establishments, the definition of which did not fall within the ambit of the relevant section of the various enactments and included such large employers as hospitals, road haulage and education at all levels. This problem was addressed by concentrating on the people doing the job rather than the type of workplace. Thus the Health and Safety at Work Act applies wherever there is employment. Self-employment is included, the only exception is for domestic servants in private households!

9.4.2 The general duties

Sections 2–9 of the Health and Safety at Work Act are headed "The General Duties". They list comprehensively the duties of all those involved in any way with work activities. The majority of these duties fall to the employer. It is worth mentioning at this point that the Health and Safety at Work Act and the relevant statutory provisions form part of the criminal law; alleged breaches of them are criminal offences and may lead to trial in the Magistrates or Crown Courts. Compensation for injuries or disease sustained during employment is a separate matter pursued through the civil courts and will be discussed further in relation to liability for defective software in Chapter 10. Long before the Robens Committee had been convened, similar duties to those found in the Health and Safety at Work Act had already been established at common law by a series of decided cases in the Civil Courts, relating to compensation for injuries or disease contracted at work. The earliest reference to the standard of care expected between employer and employee is to be found in the case of *Priestley v Fowler* ([1837] 3 M & W 1): "The employer's duty is to provide for the safety of his servant in the course of his employment". Then some years later in *Cole v de Trafford* ([1918] 2KB 523) it was said that: "The master is bound to use reasonable care to provide safe premises and appliances for his servants to work in and with, and to use reasonable care to keep them safe".

The case of *Wilson and Clyde Coal v English* ([1938] AC 57) concerned a coal mine in Scotland in which English was working in a ventilation shaft off the main haulage way. As he finished work and emerged into the haulage way at the end of his shift, he was crushed by passing trucks. Another employee was operating the haulage system within shouting distance. The employers alleged that it was the plaintiff's fault; he should have looked out for haulage trucks as he was aware of their existence and was within calling distance of the operator. The court found in favour of English and in its judgement held that employers had the following duties:

> Provision of a competent staff of men, adequate material and a proper system and effective supervision.
> To take reasonable care and to use reasonable skill:-
> > (i) To provide and maintain proper machinery, plant, appliances and work.
> > (ii) To select properly skilled managers and superintendents.
> > (iii) To provide a proper system of working.

The duty of care of an employer to his employees was established in the civil courts by cases such as this and became well accepted. In many ways, the provisions of the Health and Safety at Work Act are an attempt to codify this duty as part of the criminal law regulating conditions in the workplace. Bearing this in mind, what are the duties actually required by the Health and Safety at Work Act? As previously stated the major responsibility falls to the employer and this is exemplified by Section 2(1): "It shall be the duty of every employer to ensure, so far as is reasonably practicable, the health, safety and welfare at work of all his employees".

This all-embracing duty is then amplified in the following subsections to include:

- provision and maintenance of safe plant;
- provision and maintenance of safe systems of work;
- ensuring safe use of articles and substances;
- provision of such information, instruction, training, and supervision as necessary;
- ensuring the workplace is maintained in a safe condition;
- provision and maintenance of a safe working environment and adequate welfare arrangements;
- preparation and revision as necessary of a written statement of safety policy and bringing it to the notice of all his employees;
- consultation with safety representatives;
- formation of a safety committee if requested to do so by the safety representatives.

In this it is easy to discern both the influence of the judgements at common law and the report of the Robens Committee. The above outlines the duties of an employer to his *employees* but, in addition, Section 3 of the Act requires both employers and the self-employed to ensure that persons *not* in their employment (i.e. the general public) are not thereby exposed to risks to their health and safety. This section also requires a self-employed person not to risk his own health and safety in the course of his business. Section 4 of the Act places a similar duty on persons in control of premises. This duty is to safeguard people who use the premises but are not employed there or whose employment is not based there. This section will apply, for instance, when outside contractors are at work, and will be in addition to the duties already required of their own employers by virtue of Section 2. It will also apply where equipment and/or substances are made available for use by non-employees. The Act also includes a requirement to use the best practicable means to prevent emission of noxious or offensive substances into the atmosphere, and to render harmless or inoffensive anything that is emitted and Section 5 places the same duty on persons in control of premises. Although the majority of the duties defined by the Health and Safety at Work Act relate to employers and those in control of premises, Section 7 places duties on employees. These duties are to take reasonable care for the health and safety of themselves and of others who might be affected, and also to co-operate with the employer in complying with the relevant statutory provisions. In addition, Section 8 contains a global requirement that no person, whether employee or not, adult or child, should deliberately interfere with anything provided to ensure health and safety.

9.4.3 Reasonably practicable

Many of the provisions of the Factories Act and similar legislation created specific and absolute duties, e.g. Section 14(1) of this Act: "Every dangerous part of any machinery *shall be* securely fenced", and Section 22(2): "Every hoist or lift *shall be* thoroughly examined by a competent person at least once in every period of six months ...". However, some of the requirements were qualified by the words *practicable* or *reasonably practicable*, e.g. Section 4: "... provision shall be made for securing ... adequate ventilation and for rendering harmless *so far as practicable*, all such fumes, dust ... as may be injurious to health", and Section 29(1): "There shall, *as far as is reasonably practicable*, be provided and maintained safe means of access to every place at which any person has at any time to work ...".

The majority of the duties in the Health and Safety at Work Act are qualified by these phrases. What do they mean? Unlike many other terms they are not defined by any of the relevant statutory provisions but have come to acquire their now accepted meaning through decisions in the courts. *Practicable* is usually taken as meaning "that which is physically possible in the light of current knowledge and invention"[6]. What of *reasonably practicable*? Clearly this cannot be such a strict standard as that denoted by the word *practicable* (or *all practicable steps* or *best practicable means*). The commonly accepted definition is that found in the judgement of Lord Asquith in the case of *Edwards v National Coal Board* ([1949] 1 KB 704):

> *Reasonably practicable* is a narrower term than *physically possible* and seems to me to imply that a computation must be made by the owner in which the quantum of risk is placed on one scale and the sacrifice involved in the measures necessary for averting the risk (whether in money, time or trouble) is placed in the other, and that, if it be shown that there is gross disproportion between them – the risk being insignificant in relation to the sacrifice – the defendants discharge the onus upon them. This computation falls to be made by the owner at a point of time anterior to the accident.

In other words, the greater the risk the more likely that it is reasonably practicable to go to substantial expense, trouble and invention to remove or reduce it. However, in arriving at this assessment the financial situation of the company is not taken as a relevant parameter but the degree of risk versus the cost of removing it (in all ways) is considered in isolation. This, then, will be the same whether the company is a large multi-national or merely has a few employees. In many ways, duties which are qualified by a phrase containing the word *practicable* present more of a problem than an absolute requirement where the duty is precisely defined. All qualified duties require employers, for instance, to consider carefully whether they are doing

---

6. See, for example *Lee v Nursery Furnishing Ltd* [1945] 61 TLR 263 and *Adsett v K. & L. Steelfounders and Engineers Ltd* [1953] All ER 97.

all that is *practicable*, or *reasonably practicable* or are using the *best practicable means*, in order to fulfil their obligations. Indeed, if any legal proceedings arise out of an alleged breach of a section involving such a qualification, the onus is on the defendant to show that it would not have been *practicable* or *reasonably practicable* to do otherwise[7]. In other words, there is a defence if it can be shown that all *practicable* or *reasonably practicable* steps had been taken to prevent such a breach.

9.4.4 Duties of designers, manufacturers and suppliers

One section which has not yet been referred to is Section 6. This section is concerned with the duties of designers, manufacturers and suppliers and has been left until last because it has wider ramifications than the preceding sections, particularly for software engineers. Prior to the Health and Safety at Work Act, there were few specific requirements on manufacturers etc. to ensure that articles and substances they supplied were safe. Section 17 of the Factories Act 1937, reproduced in the 1961 Act, made it an offence for a person to sell or hire out a power-driven machine for use in a factory on which certain specified parts were not effectively guarded. There were similar requirements in some regulations, e.g. those concerned with the construction industry. However, the parts specified were few and the consequent duty by no means onerous. In addition, there was no similar requirement for substances. This was not an entirely satisfactory state of affairs and there was some justification for the attitude of users of new machines or substances who, when asked to improve guarding or make additional precautions in use, considered that this responsibility should be shared with the manufacturer and/or supplier. Historically such problems had been acknowledged, at least in theory, and the Sale of Goods Act 1893 implied a number of conditions and warranties which related to the quality and fitness of the goods sold[8]. The basic rules of a supplier's liability to compensate persons who were not parties to the contract of sale were first propounded in the now celebrated case of *Donoghue v Stevenson* ([1932] AC 562). Donoghue had been taken by a friend to a café where the said friend bought her a ginger beer. Some of the ginger beer was poured out for her, which she drank, but on topping up her glass, a decomposed snail was found in the remainder of the contents of the bottle. The resulting shock and illness caused Donoghue to sue the manufacturer, Stevenson, even though there was no contract between Donoghue and any of the other parties involved (friend, café proprietor or manufacturer). She won her case in the lower court but Stevenson successfully appealed. Donoghue

---

7. Health and Safety at Work Act s40.
8. The appropriate statute is now the Sale of Goods Act 1979 as amended, most recently by the Sale and Supply of Goods Act 1994.

then appealed to the House of Lords where, in deciding for Donoghue, Lord Atkin said:

> A manufacturer of products which he sells in such a form as to show that he intends them to reach the ultimate consumer in the form in which they left him with no reasonable possibility of intermediate examination and with the knowledge that the absence of reasonable care in the preparation or putting up of the products will result in an injury to the consumer's life or property, owes a duty to the consumer to take that reasonable care.

By analogy, these words also apply to designers, suppliers and others who may handle goods on their way from the manufacturer to the consumer and have now been incorporated in industrial health and safety legislation by Section 6 of the Health and Safety at Work Act. This section has been amended by the Consumer Protection Act 1987[9], the main effect of which is to ensure that all those in the supply chain consider reasonably foreseeable risks during handling, maintenance, storage etc. as well as in use, and that they provide and update safety information and take account of non-domestic places other than workplaces to which they supply their products. These amendments also extend the scope of Section 6 to include the designers and manufacturers of fairground equipment. The duties placed on designers, manufacturers, importers and suppliers of *articles* for use at work are to:

- ensure articles are designed and constructed to be safe and without risks to health when being set, used, cleaned or maintained by a person at work;
- arrange for testing and examination to ensure safe design and construction;
- provide persons supplied with articles with adequate information about:
  - Correct use of the article;
  - Any conditions necessary to ensure safety during setting, using, cleaning, maintaining, dismantling or disposing of the article;
- provide persons already supplied with new information as it becomes available.

There is an additional duty on designers and manufacturers to arrange for research to discover and hence eliminate or minimize risks; but, there is no duty to repeat research where it is reasonable to rely on the results of others. Installers and erectors of any article for use at work have a duty to ensure that

---

9. For further consideration of the Consumer Protection Act and its application to products containing software see Chapter 10.

nothing about the way it is installed or erected creates hazards at any time. The duties of manufacturers, importers and suppliers of *substances* for use at work are in parallel with those of designers, manufacturers, importers and suppliers of articles. The duty to undertake research falls to the manufacturers. Clearly, Section 6, as amended, applies to the design, manufacture and supply of computerized equipment for the control of machinery and plant, but what of the software itself? Can it also be construed as an article for use at work and thus attract the legal duties imposed by Section 6? A starting point in finding the answers to these questions is to examine the definition of an *article for use at work* in Section 53 of the Health and Safety at Work Act:

(a) any plant designed for use or operation (whether exclusively or not) by persons at work, and

(b) any article designed for use as a component in any such plant.

Plant is further defined by the same section as including any machinery, equipment or appliance. Computers and data storage systems would fall within the above definition of *article* but the current legal opinion seems to be that it is unlikely that the programs themselves would be deemed to be articles in this sense. However, they may well be considered as *components* as in (b) above, especially where integral software (including firmware) is supplied with the hardware, and so the duties under section 6 could then be invoked. It is difficult to assess whether additional software and modifications to existing software fall within these definitions, but persons writing such programs would also have duties under Section 3 (to persons who are not their employees) and so the requirements would be the same, for all practical purposes if not from a strictly legal standpoint[10]. These duties, from whichever section they emanate, place heavy responsibilities on software engineers to ensure the integrity of their designs. Some problems in achieving this in safety-related applications are discussed in the next chapter.

9.4.5 Systems and procedures

As already mentioned, the Robens Report had identified apathy, and lack of motivation to consider safety, as factors which were just as likely to create hazards in the workplace as more obvious items like unsafe machinery and toxic fumes. Accordingly, the Health and Safety at Work Act was designed to provide a legal framework of obligations concentrating on changing attitudes and the establishment of appropriate organization, systems and procedures for achieving safety, rather than merely laying down detailed minimum

---

10. For further discussion of the legal arguments in relation to this Act and the Consumer Protection Act see Chapter 10.

standards in the manner of the previous legislation. This legal framework is intended to cause employers, employees and others concerned to think about health, safety and welfare at work and to plan their premises, processes, machinery, plant, work activities and work environment in such a way as to positively promote these objectives. It is also intended to encourage personal responsibility and to make individuals, as well as corporate bodies, accountable for their acts or omissions. We recall that amongst the duties conferred on employers by Section 2 of the Act are the following:

- Preparation and revision as necessary of a written statement of safety policy and bringing it to the notice of all employees.
- Consultation with safety representatives.
- Formation of a safety committee if requested to do so by the safety representatives.

These were new statutory obligations with respect to health and safety in employment and were designed to assist in achieving the objectives referred to above.

9.4.6 Safety policy

For firms employing more than five employees, Section 2(3) of the Health and Safety at Work Act requires employers:

> To *prepare* and as often as may be appropriate *revise* a *written statement* of general policy with respect to the health and safety at work of all employees and the *organization* and *arrangements* for the time being in force for carrying out that policy, and to bring the statement and any revision of it to the *notice of all employees*.

The italics have been added to emphasize the salient points of this requirement. A formal written safety policy to unify safe practice throughout the company is the first step on the way to improving safety standards; in many ways the fact that it is a legal requirement is the least important reason for producing it. Some other advantages created by the production of a safety policy are:

- It provides a statement of objectives, which is an important part of efficient management;
- It clarifies positions and roles and therefore helps establish responsibilities for safety;
- It provides a standard for measuring achievement;
- Formulation of the safety policy may highlight areas where the organization is deficient.

There is no fixed correct formula for producing a safety policy but each needs to be tailored to the particular company concerned. Following the pattern laid down in Section 2(3) produces a policy consisting of three parts, namely, a general statement, the necessary organization and the arrangements for implementing it. Depending on the type of industry and the size of the company, the statement of overall policy may be quite brief. It must, however, stress the company's commitment to health and safety. In order to underline this, it should be signed and dated by a member of senior management, usually the managing director or a director with overall responsibility for health and safety. Although safety may be regarded as a priority within a company, people do not go into business in order to be safe and so safety is not often listed as one of a company's objectives. There is no reason though, to treat safety in a different way from other objectives, such as productivity and profit. The safety organization should, therefore, normally reflect the management structure for achieving the other objectives. The organization should make it clear precisely where the responsibilities lie at all levels and how the chain of command is constructed. The following list gives examples of some points which would need to be considered:

- assumption of overall responsibility and leadership by top management;
- delegation – usually the initial responsibility is on line management at the appropriate level;
- use of job descriptions to identify duties and avoid overlap;
- all duties and responsibilities must be agreed with those concerned;
- the role of the safety officer/advisor and support from specialists where appropriate;
- consultation procedures;
- employees' responsibilities;
- safety budget – to show the commitment to safety in both money and time;

In establishing the arrangements necessary for putting the policy into effect, a complete hazard analysis would be necessary. The precise arrangements depend on the results of this and obviously differ between companies and between industries. Below are a large number of factors to be taken into account, but the list should in no way be regarded as exhaustive:

- safety: plant and machinery, cranes, hoists, lifts, etc., boilers, pressure vessels etc., fire, electrical matters, handling and storage of dangerous substances, handling of heavy weights, maintenance, transport, e.g. fork lift trucks, protective clothing, "housekeeping", off-site workers if any;
- health: control of noise, control of toxic substances, environmental monitoring, biological monitoring, disclosure of information, first aid;

- procedures: safety inspections, safety rules, safe systems of work, statutory inspections, accidents; reporting, investigation and analysis, emergencies, monitoring of safety performance;
- training and supervision;
- composition and remit of the safety committee;
- bringing the policy to the attention of all employees.

If relevant, all of the above need amplification in a real policy. Thus, a consideration of protective clothing, for instance, might include types available, areas where its use is mandatory, arrangements for issue and maintenance and instructions on use and training provisions, if these are not covered elsewhere in the policy. It might also include references to relevant legislation, e.g. Provision and Use of Work Equipment Regulations[11]. Use of breathing apparatus necessitates instructions on use, and training provisions, if these are not covered elsewhere in the policy. Safety policies will differ both in style and content, but should attempt to be as comprehensive as possible, and of a format sufficiently flexible to allow revisions to be incorporated easily. The role of a good safety policy in securing a safe working environment cannot be over-estimated. The very fact of producing one involves taking an objective look at the health and safety performance of the company and should include consultation with all levels of the workforce. This can be a very salutary experience and it is not unknown for the process to result in a complete re-organization of the factory!

9.4.7 Consultation

We have already mentioned consultation in the context of preparing a safety policy. We recall also that an employer has a legal duty, by virtue of Section 2 of the Health and Safety at Work Act, both to consult with safety representatives and to form a safety committee, if so requested. This obligation was formalized in the Safety Representatives and Safety Committees Regulations and the associated code of practice[12]. Under these regulations, recognized trade unions may appoint safety representatives, whose functions are defined in the regulations, and an employer must convene a safety committee if requested to do so in writing by at least two safety representatives. The provisions of these regulations did not mean that there could be neither employee representation nor consultation in non-unionized workforces but this was left as a matter for the individual enterprises. Rights of representation and consultation have now been extended to these workforces by the Health and Safety (Consultation with Employers)

---

11. SI 1992/2931.
12. SI 1977/500, now amended.

Regulations 1996[13]. Safety representatives, being selected to represent various sections of the work force, can play an important role both in raising awareness of safety issues and in motivating people to adopt safe working practices.

Their functions include, *inter alia*, inspections of the workplace and accident investigation. The purpose of their inspection may be to check that problems previously identified have been attended to, or to detect the problems in the first instance. Accident investigation can present problems due to the understandable trauma experienced by those at the scene of an accident. For all sorts of reasons it is difficult to build up an accurate picture of the circumstances leading to an accident. However, the most important reason why a safety representative should investigate an accident is to prevent a re-occurrence, not to apportion blame, so the *truth* does not particularly matter. What is important is to find out all the ways the accident *could* have happened, so as to prevent a similar incident by any of the uncovered routes. The period following an accident is a golden opportunity for instigating changes, when even the most indifferent person is likely to be more receptive. To assist safety representatives in the effective performance of their function, the regulations require an employer to permit safety representatives time-off with pay to conduct inspections and investigations, and to undergo any necessary training to assist in their role. It is important to realize that the functions of safety representatives are not the same as legal duties. Thus, by agreeing to a particular system of work, or by identifying a hazard, they do not incur any legal responsibility. The duty to ensure the safety of the workplace still rests with the employer.

9.4.8 Enforcement

Although the approach throughout the Health and Safety at Work Act is to foster improvement of standards by consultation and self-regulation, it would be unreasonable to expect that this would be effective in all cases. Accordingly, inspectors appointed under the Act are given wide-ranging powers of enforcement. These powers enable them to:

- enter premises at any reasonable time or, in cases of danger, at any time;
- make examinations and investigations;
- direct that premises be left undisturbed;
- make measurements, photographs, recordings;
- take samples of articles and substances[14].

---

13. SI 1996/1513. See also Section 9.4.11.
14. Where such samples are taken the inspector has a duty to consult an appropriate person, if necessary, in order to ascertain any dangers. When taking a sample of a substance, a portion of it should be given, if practicable, to a responsible person at the premises.

- take possession of articles and substances;
- cause testing and dismantling;
- question persons and take statements from them;
- require production of documents;
- require a person to afford facilities and assistance;
- take along a police constable, if serious obstruction is foreseen;
- take along any other person duly authorized, and any equipment required;
- issue improvement and prohibition notices;
- exercise any other power necessary for carrying into effect the relevant statutory provisions.

As already mentioned, the relevant statutory provisions are part of the criminal law, and prior to 1974 the only recourse available to an inspector faced with a recalcitrant employer was prosecution. The Health and Safety at Work Act introduced two new sanctions; the improvement notice and the prohibition notice, to assist in securing compliance with the safety standards. An improvement notice requires that certain matters be remedied within a specified time. A prohibition notice requires that a particular activity, deemed to involve a risk of serious personal injury, cease until the situation has been resolved. In many cases, notice procedure is more effective in improving standards than is prosecution, but the serving of a notice does not preclude legal proceedings. Failure to comply with a notice is, in itself, an offence.

In particular, prohibition notices may cause a company a great financial loss in terms of lost production, whereas, in general, fines imposed by courts for breaches of health and safety regulations have traditionally not been high. There are signs that this may be changing and that courts are becoming more willing to make use of the sentencing powers available to them. The average penalty is now about £6,000[15] having doubled since the mid 1990s, but this is not necessarily a significant figure when compared, perhaps, with an enterprise's annual turnover. Some guidance on appropriate penalties for health and safety offences has been given by the Court of Appeal in *R v Howe & Son (Engineers) Ltd* ([1999] 2 All ER 249) in which Scott Baker J said:

> Disquiet has been expressed in several quarters that the level of fine for health and safety offences is too low. We think there is force in this and that the figures which we have been supplied with support the

15. Average penalties discussed by Scott Baker J in *R v Howe & Son (Engineers) Ltd* [1999] 2 All ER 249 at 253. See also discussion in Frank B. Wright *Law of health and safety at work* (Sweet and Maxwell, 1997), chapter 6.

concern. ... The objective of prosecutions for health and safety offences in the workplace is to achieve a safe environment for those who work there and for other members of the public who may be affected. A fine needs to be large enough to bring that message home where the defendant is a company, not only to those who manage it but also to its shareholders.

The court went on to set guidelines to be taken into account in setting penalties in such cases, pointing out that death, failure to heed warnings and risks consequent on saving money should all be viewed as aggravating factors. On the other hand, prompt admission of responsibility, steps to remedy deficiencies and a good safety record may be seen as mitigating factors. The degree of risk and extent of the consequent danger together with the financial position of the defendant should also be considered as relevant. It is to be hoped that this detailed consideration by the Court of Appeal will have clarified the objectives and rationale of the imposition of penalties in this type of case and also serve as a stimulus to a more uniform approach to the problem from the lower courts.

As has already been pointed out, the Act is intended to encourage personal responsibility and to make individuals, as well as corporate bodies, accountable for their acts or omissions which result in contravention of the law. Thus it is not only companies who may be prosecuted for offences relating to their premises or to their status as designers or manufacturers. Individuals such as directors, managers, or indeed any employee, including software engineers may be held responsible for breaches in the law. This may lead to prosecution; in serious cases the fines are unlimited and imprisonment is a possibility. In addition, where personal liability is proved, there may be other sanctions available such as disqualification as a director under the Companies Acts. If this sounds alarmist, it is as well to remember that the objective is not punishment but the encouragement of all to take personal responsibility, as far as is within their power, to promote healthy and safe working conditions, and to safeguard others who may be put at risk by their activities.

9.4.9 Health and Safety Commission and Health and Safety Executive

The Robens Committee recommended the creation of a national authority for health and safety at work. This was reflected in the Health and Safety at Work Act by the establishment of the Health and Safety Commission (HSC) and the Health and Safety Executive (HSE), responsible to the Secretary of State for Employment.

The Health and Safety Commission

The HSC consists of a chairman and between six and nine other members appointed by the Secretary of State. These are drawn from the trade unions, employers organizations, and other relevant organizations such as local authorities and professional bodies. Among the Commission's primary function is the making of arrangements to secure the health, safety, and welfare of people at work and to protect the public from risks that may arise from work activities. To achieve this, the HSC proposes legislation, provides advice, information and guidance, and instigates and sponsors research. The aim is to produce a wide range of knowledge and expertise on matters relating to health and safety. It is assisted by advisory committees for particular industries who can provide specialist knowledge of individual processes. The Commission is also empowered to direct investigations and inquiries into accidents and other matters causing serious concern. Another important role is the approval of Codes of Practice[16].

The Health and Safety Executive

This consists of three members appointed by the HSC and is charged with implementing the powers of the Commission. It has special responsibility to enforce the laws relating to health and safety at work. A large number of the HSE's staff consists of the inspectors belonging to the five inspectorates that are now within the HSE, having previously been allocated to various government departments. The five inspectorates are: Agriculture, Explosives, Factory, Nuclear Installations, and Mines & Quarries. There are areas in which the relevant statutory provisions are not enforced by the HSE and in these the HSC has agreements with other bodies. Thus, for instance, the local authorities have responsibility for health and safety matters in premises such as offices, shops, and warehouses. Other such agency agreements are with the Railway Inspectorate of the Department of Transport and the Industrial Air Pollution Inspectorate. There are also the Pipelines Inspectorate and the Petroleum Engineering Division of the Department of Energy, which are responsible for monitoring the design and safety of on-shore pipelines and off-shore oil and gas installations. There had been debate over a number of years as to whether this was a desirable state of affairs and following a number of major disasters in areas for which the HSE was not the enforcing authority, all of these agencies were subsumed within the HSE. Another of the functions of the HSE is to represent the UK in discussions of health and safety at work within the European Union and

---

16. See Section 9.4.10 Regulations and Codes of Practice.

this role has increased in importance with the increase of legislative activity on health and safety within Europe[17].

9.4.10 Regulations and codes of practice[18]

Since the inception of industrial health and safety legislation, the relevant enactments have contained provision for the making of secondary legislation, or regulations, on specific topics. The procedure for producing such legislation, in the form of statutory instruments, is not so time-consuming as that for the primary legislation and so, in the area of health and safety, enables the law to react more quickly to newly-discovered or innovative processes or to update and amend legislation in the light of new knowledge, than would otherwise have been the case. Thus, throughout the twentieth century, many very detailed regulations were produced which applied only to specific types of workplace or to specific processes.

Following the advent of the Health and Safety at Work Act, the new philosophy was to try and replace the existing piecemeal legislation with a more coherent approach and to this end a programme of revocation of the "old" legislation, often by regulations, which although detailed, were of more universal application was embarked upon. This programme is still continuing. It was evident, however, that some detailed guidance on certain industries and processes was still both relevant and desirable, notwithstanding the new approach, and in such cases new regulations have continued to be made by statutory instrument or old regulations have been amended and brought up to date. However, just as the form of the Health and Safety at Work Act departs from that of the Factories Acts, for instance, so the form of these more recent regulations departs from that of similar pre-1974 legislation, which attempted statutory control of particular hazards and which are now also written in more general terms. Although, as mentioned above, statutory instruments are not subject to the same scrutiny as primary legislation, nonetheless, the formality of the necessary procedures can still inhibit the law's attempt to keep pace with technological advancement. In an attempt to ameliorate this situation, the Health and Safety at Work Act introduced the concept of the Approved Code of Practice[19].

---

17. See Section 9.4.11 EC Health and Safety Provisions.
18. See also *Health and Safety Regulations: a Short Guide* at http://www.open.gov.uk/hse/pubns/hsc13.htm.
19. In addition, as suggested by the Robens Report, there are also a large number of voluntary codes of practice in operation, produced by particular industries or industry groups, which represent good and expected working practices in those particular industries. Certain codes of practice are also produced by the British Standards Institution, for example BS 5515 (1984) *Code of Practice for the Documentation of Computer-based Systems* and BS 5304 (1988) *Code of Practice for Safeguarding of Machinery*.

Although *approved*[20], the Code of Practice does not form part of the regulations and can be amended and updated fairly quickly to keep pace with technology. The corollary of this is that, by keeping the regulations in general terms, the regulations themselves should never need amendment.

By way of example, the Control of Lead at Work Regulations[21] require an employer to provide, so far as is reasonably practicable, measures which will provide adequate control over the exposure of his employees to lead. The approved Code of Practice on the Control of Lead at Work then discusses such measures, based on good occupational hygiene practice, which can effectively control exposure to lead. Prior to the Control of Lead at Work Regulations there were numerous, very detailed, regulations relating to different industries and processes that use lead; these have now been revoked[22]. In addition, during the 1980s, a further variation on the new approach began to be seen as illustrated in, e.g. the Control of Substances Hazardous to Health Regulations (COSHH)[23]. These regulations, also supported by an Approved Code of Practice, have wide application and put the onus on employers to both assess and monitor the substances used in their workplaces. The approach contained in COSHH of assessment of risk, control of the hazard and monitoring or surveillance of the result is one which has far wider application than regulating the use of hazardous substances, and the influence of this type of approach can be identified in the European directives on health and safety and their implementing legislation[24].

9.4.11 EC health and safety provisions

At the beginning of this chapter we traced the origins of the regulatory framework for health and safety. This evolving framework has now been further modified and extended by the implementation in the UK of a number of EC directives on health and safety. It is, of course, in many ways artificial to separate out EC law from that originating in the UK, as if it were something which was merely added on to the existing regime; nonetheless it is convenient to consider it in this manner for both chronological and conceptual reasons. As we shall see, regulations which have been introduced in the UK, certainly since the Single European Act, as a result of EC directives have perhaps

---

20. By the Health and Safety Commission see Section 9.4.9 above.
21. The current regulations are the Control of Lead at Work Regulations 1998 (SI 1998/543) which revoke and re-enact with modifications the original 1980 regulations (SI 1980/1248).
22. Examples are The Lead Smelting and Manufacture Regulations 1911, the Lead Compounds Manufacture Regulations 1921, and the Lead Paint Regulations 1927.
23. The original COSHH regulations (SI 1988/1657 as amended) have been updated in 1994 and most recently in 1999. The version currently in force is the Control of Substances Hazardous to Health Regulations 1999 (SI 1999/437).
24. See Section 9.4.11 below.

marked a shift in the way health and safety legislation had begun to be formulated in the UK since the advent of the Health and Safety at Work Act.

The involvement of the European Communities in health and safety matters can be traced back to 1962 when the Commission established an Industrial Health and Safety Division but there was no really significant activity until the 1970s. At the beginning of 1974 the Council of Ministers adopted a Social Action Programme[25] which specifically referred to the *"improvement in safety and health conditions at work"* in its objectives. This was soon followed by the formation of the Advisory Committee for Safety, Hygiene and Health Protection at Work[26]. Whilst not referring directly to legislation on health and safety, the committee was given the following remit within its terms of reference:

> contributing towards the development of a common approach to problems existing in the field of safety, hygiene and health protection at work and towards the choice of Community priorities as well as measures necessary for implementing them.

Although the first European legislation relating to health and safety matters began to appear in the subsequent years[27], this was all based on the original article 100[28] of the Treaty which gave the necessary legal basis for measures which aimed to harmonize the laws of the Member States, where the laws of these States might create obstacles to the working of the internal market. There was no specific measure in the Treaty at that time which allowed the Community to create more general health and safety legislation. Nonetheless, a number of directives were made (and continue to be made) under article 100 and these started a pattern which was later to be repeated as Community health and safety legislation proliferated. This was to produce a general or "framework" directive which was then followed by subsequent "daughter" directives dealing with more specific topics within the area of the framework[29].

---

25. Council Resolution of 21 January 1974 [1974] OJ C13/I.
26. Established by means of Council Decision of 27 June 1974, (74/325/EEC, [1974] OJ L185/15).
27. E.g. *Council Directive of 25 July 1977 on the approximation of the laws, regulations and administrative provisions of the Member States relating to the provision of safety signs at places of work* (77/576/EEC, [1977] OJ L229/12) implemented in the UK by the Safety Signs Regulations 1980, SI 1980/1471.
28. The Treaty of Amsterdam which came into force in May 1999 has resulted in a renumbering of the treaty articles to rationalise the amendments made since the original treaty. Article 100 is now renumbered as article 94.
29. Thus *Council Directive of 27th November 1980 on the protection of workers from risks relating to exposure to chemical, physical and biological agents at work* (80/1107/EEC, [1980] OJ L327/8) was followed by individual directives on asbestos, lead and noise.

Further impetus was given to the development and improvement of standards of health and safety in the late 1970s and early 1980s by the adoption of two action programs on Safety and Health at Work[30] so that by the mid-1980s, the position and attitude of the Community with respect to safety and health at work was well established. Many areas had been identified within which action was a priority if the declared objectives of the EC were to be fulfilled. The ability of the Community to fulfil these objectives was then enhanced by the amendments introduced into the Treaty by the Single European Act 1986, which gave a specific legal basis for legislation on this subject. The amendment of primary importance introduced into the Treaty by the Single European Act was a provision which required the completion of the single internal market without barriers to trade by 31 December 1992. In addition to introducing this time limit, the Single European Act also, *inter alia*, created new articles 100a and 118a[31] which were ultimately to be the source of changes in the health and safety legislation. Of these, article 118a was to have the greatest impact on Community health and safety legislation. This deals both expressly and exclusively with the health and safety of workers and creates substantial additions to the provisions of the original article 118. Member States are required to encourage improvements, especially in the working environment, as regards the health and safety of workers, and to set as their objective the harmonization of conditions whilst maintaining the improvements made. To this end, the Council is enabled to enact legislation in the form of directives. Thus, for the first time, the Commission, in framing their proposals for legislation on health and safety, did not have to rely on stretching the concept of the functioning of the internal market to its limit, but were provided with an apposite legal basis. Accordingly, a large number of directives have been adopted since the Single European Act using this new legal base and dealing specifically with health and safety matters[32].

This new legal base introduced the concept of the "working environment" which has led the way to legislation based not just on the prevention of accident and disease but on risk assessment. On this model liability can arise not just as a result of defective equipment or process but because the risk has not been adequately assessed, avoided or controlled.

Although it is beyond the scope of this book to give a detailed discussion and analysis of the substantive law of the European Communities and the way in which it has been implemented in the UK, it is worth making some

---

30. *Council Resolution of 29th June 1978 on an action programme of the European Communities on Safety and Health at Work* ([1978] OJ C165/1: *Council Resolution of 27th February 1984 on a second programme of action of the European Communities on Safety and Health at Work* ([1984] OJ C67/2).

31. Now articles 95 and 138 post-Amsterdam, see fn 28.

32. For examples see, for instance, A. C. Neal and F. B. Wright, *The European Communities' health and safety legislation* (Chapman & Hall, 1992).

general points both about the nature of implementation of EC law and also about the structure of these particular directives as, independent of their subject matter, they are similar in ethos and style. Most EC legislation is in the form of regulations or directives. EC regulations (not to be confused with regulations made under the Health and Safety at Work Act and other statutes) are immediately binding in all Member States and do not require any further legislative activity at the national level. Directives, on the other hand, are binding as to the result to be achieved but leave the precise details of how this is to be done to individual Member States. As already explained the majority of EC legislation on health and safety at work is in the form of directives and in the UK these are usually transposed into national law by means of regulations made under the Health and Safety at Work Act.

Reference has already been made to the pattern of a general ("mother") directive followed by a number of more specific ("daughter") directives. This has proved a useful device and has enabled the general objectives, approach and ambit of the legislation to be set out in the mother directive, which has then been expanded on and applied to particular situations in the subsequent daughter directives.

The general duties which were to form the basis of EC law on health and safety at work were set out in the so-called framework directive[33]. This directive starts by setting out what could be regarded as the general principles of good safety management[34]:

- prevention of occupational risks;
- protection of safety and health;
- elimination of risk and accident factors;
- informing, consultation, balanced participation in accordance with national laws and/or practice;
- training or workers and their representatives.

Subsequent parts of the directive then deal with both employer's and employee's obligations. These obligations are probably most usefully discussed by comparison with the obligations under the Health and Safety at Work Act since the attitude of the UK to the EC directives on health and safety has been a minimalist one, based on the belief that the framework provided by the Health and Safety at Work Act was already in place and adequate to encompass and account for any additional obligations required by Community law.

---

33. *Council Directive of 12 June 1989 on the introduction of measures to encourage improvements in the safety and health of workers at work* (89/931/EEC, [1989] OJ L183/1).

34. *Ibid.* Article 1(2).

The approach of the directive is a proactive one and uses a similar philosophy to that which was introduced in the UK in such regulations as COSHH, of assessment, control and monitoring. This approach should produce a continuous cycle of self-regulation of safety matters as the monitoring and surveillance of the control procedures leads to a reassessment of the hazards.

The general duty found in the Health and Safety at Work Act is mirrored in the Framework directive[35]: "The employer shall have a duty to ensure the safety and health of workers in every aspect related to work". In addition there is an express provision[36] that the obligations placed upon the employer are in no way diminished by the obligations placed on workers something which is merely implicit in the UK legislation. It is submitted that, even though there are differences of detail in the directive and the Act, by and large these are not differences of substance. One exception to this may be those provisions which are concerned with consultation and participation. The directive requires that[37]:

> Employers shall consult workers and/or their representatives and allow them to take part in discussions on all questions relating to safety and health at work.

The UK requirement was originally contained in the Safety Representatives and Safety Committees Regulations[38] discussed in Section 9.4.7 above, which only gave *rights* of consultation to recognized trade unions. The requirements on consultation, and also provision of information, in both the framework directive and the daughter directives appeared to be much wider than this and the implementing regulations in the UK made no further provision for rights of consultation, other than those already contained in the Safety Representatives and Safety Committees Regulations. This situation has now been rectified with the Health and Safety (Consultation with Employers) Regulations 1996[39] which give rights of representation and consultation to employees not covered by the 1977 regulations. It could be necessary for an employer to consult under both regimes in the event of there being both unionised and non-unionized sections of the workforce.

The "daughter" directives take a similar approach but contain more detailed requirements in relation to their particular subject areas of concern,

---

35. *Ibid.* Article 5(1) cf. Health and Safety at Work Act s2(1).
36. *Ibid.* Article 5(3) "The workers obligations in the field of safety and health at work shall not affect the principle of the responsibility of the employer".
37. *Ibid.* Article 11(1).
38. SI 1977/500; see Section 9.4.7 above.
39. SI 1996/1513.

and this is reflected in the implementing regulations. The UK implementation of the framework and other European directives has incorporated familiar phrases qualifying the employer's duties such as *reasonably practicable*, the meaning of which has, as we have seen, been established and refined by the courts[40]. This is despite the fact that such qualifications do not conform to either the spirit or the letter of the directives. Although this might suggest that the UK is unwilling to implement the directives fully, safety is, necessarily, not an absolute concept and there will be occasions when it is impossible to remove all risks, despite the desirability of so doing. In such cases, a qualification of *practicable* or *reasonably practicable* may serve to make the law more accessible and hence more enforceable in practice. The problem, as far as Europe is concerned, is that the directives are intended to harmonize standards across the Member States which becomes difficult to achieve if individual States persist in clinging to particularly national concepts and approaches.

Additional concepts have also been introduced into the implementing regulations, incorporating certain other words and phrases from the directives. Examples of these are *effective and suitable* and *suitable and sufficient*. The interpretation of these phrases has perhaps not been tested in the courts to the same extent as *practicable* or *reasonably practicable* and, given their origin, it is likely that any litigation which depends upon the scope of these phrases will not be able to be completed without a reference to the European Court of Justice[41].

9.5 Human factors

This chapter has looked at the legal framework which has evolved in relation to health and safety at work. As we have seen, the current philosophy is one based on assessment of risk followed by the instigation of control and monitoring procedures. One risk factor which should not be ignored but which is not always so amenable to precise assessment is the human factor. Human beings are complex creatures capable of reacting in a variety of ways to a given situation and each individual's attitude to safety may be very complex and governed by a myriad of factors. How then is the contribution of human factors to the overall hazard level to be measured? There are two major categories of persons who may affect the safety of any system, one is those persons who design it, and their responsibilities are considered further in Chapter 10, the other category are those persons who operate or use the system and it is the contribution of the latter group which will be considered here.

---

40. See Section 9.4.3.
41. See Hendy & Ford, *Redgrave's health and safety* (Butterworths, 1998), par. 2.56.

It is frequently the case that such human factors only come to the fore following an accident; indeed, it is a common reaction following an accident of any magnitude to attempt to apportion blame, and to find a scapegoat. More often than not this seems to be someone who was actually involved in the incident directly, the pilot of the aircraft perhaps, or the operator of a machine. It appears that the most obvious cause of the Paddington rail crash in September 1999 was the driver of one of the trains involved failing to stop at a red signal. Apportioning blame to an identifiable individual may be therapeutic for all concerned (except of course the scapegoat) since it allows the trauma of the incident to be rationalized, and subsequently to be put to one side. The reality is not so simple. Accidents are rarely the result of a single causative factor but occur due to the simultaneous occurrence of several different events which by themselves may not have caused the incident. Whilst it is difficult to argue in the Paddington case that passing the signal at red was not a causal factor, the argument that it was *the* cause rather than *a* cause is rather more difficult to sustain. Although, at the time of writing, this incident is still under investigation, it appears that there was also evidence of the poor visibility of the signal in question. As one commentator remarked: "It was not so much that the driver failed the system as that the system failed the driver." Putting disasters down to operator error is usually overstating the case and is normally not very helpful in preventing a re-occurrence. This is not to deny the importance of human factors, but it is just as important to take these into account at the design stage as it is to consider all other risk factors. It is, therefore, important that designers, whether of control software, systems of work, or any other aspects of the process, take into account foreseeable human reactions, particularly in the case of aberrant behaviour of any aspect of the system. The usual guiding principle in safety engineering is that systems should always *fail safe*, i.e. refuse to operate in unsafe modes of operation. How can such a principle accommodate human factors so that safety can be achieved in practice?

The obvious answer is to provide safety rules and safe systems of work, but these will not produce the required results unless they are satisfactorily implemented and monitored and this will not be achieved unless the workforce, itself, is convinced of the necessity for and the integrity of the safety system. Safe systems of work may be disregarded for a number of reasons; the action may not be a conscious flouting of safety rules, but merely a reaction to the lack of perceived danger. Some hazards which are easily visible to an outsider's eye may not immediately strike those working in the area as being dangerous. Familiarity breeds, perhaps, not contempt but acceptance; this can be overcome by suitable instruction and training. On the other hand, safety rules are frequently seen, both by management and other workers, as slowing down the job, particularly where the work is paid by results (piecework). In some working environments, peer pressure may decree that taking safety precautions is only for the faint-hearted. Such tendencies can be eliminated by good design of the job and the workstation, including consideration of the appropriate ergonomic factors, to ensure that the quickest way of working is also the safest.

The most elusive hazards are frequent causes of accidents, and occur due to the juxtaposition of more than one event. Thus, dangers may only arise when, for instance, a machine jams during maintenance, when machines are being operated by untrained personnel, or when robots are being taught. The way in which people react to such events is particularly important as technology becomes increasingly complex. The normal situation in many automated plants involves little human intervention, but this increases in importance during abnormal circumstances, when personnel may need to react to out-of-the-ordinary events. Although these reactions can be modified by appropriate instruction and training, which will obviously be of paramount importance in the motivation of those involved to adhere to safe systems of work, the apathy identified by Robens is still in evidence and human attitudes are notoriously hard to change.

9.6 Financial considerations

Undertakings may have a number of objectives and in many ways there is no reason why safety should be treated any differently from any other business objective. Thus the established hierarchy for management and control can be used with good effect to manage safety matters for instance. But, of course, people do not go into business to be safe and so, in a number of ways, safety objectives will be seen as purely ancillary to more important objectives such as profit and productivity. One accusation frequently levelled at those that seek to improve safety standards is that safety is expensive and that, especially in times of recession, enterprises cannot afford to introduce such measures. This may be true when safety is not taken into account at the design stage but becomes an additional feature which is appended at a later stage. However, this will apply equally to any other changes in specification which are added at a later stage and not just to safety matters. Provided that safety considerations are specified in the initial stages, there is no reason why excessive expense should be incurred.

On the other hand, accidents and other incidents may prove very costly not just in terms of lost production, but also in terms of compensation which may have to be paid out to those injured and so may adversely affect insurance costs. A study by the HSE[42] has shown that in a number of case studies, the uninsured costs such as those which result from loss of goodwill or hiring and training of replacement staff often far exceed the insured costs. Indeed, for the cases under consideration, the uninsured costs exceeded the insured costs by a

---

42. *The costs of accidents at work* (HMSO, 1993).

factor of between eight and thirty six. Contrary to popular perception, therefore, safety can make economic sense as well as minimizing the potential effect on those who might be involved in accidents, whether employees of members of the public[43].

9.7 Corporate liability and manslaughter

Despite the extensive regulatory framework described, accidents at work and as a result of work still occur and are occasionally of disastrous proportions. Many are critical of a system which, even following multiple fatalities, can only deliver a prosecution for an offence under the Health and Safety at Work Act, especially in the light of the relatively modest penalties imposed to date. This has led to calls for companies to be able to be prosecuted for more serious offences such as manslaughter when their alleged mismanagement of safety issues results in death. As explained in Chapter 2, the fact of incorporation gives a company a certain legal identity and so it can, for instance, make contracts in its own name. Similarly it can be prosecuted in its own name for health and safety and other absolute or regulatory offences which do not require any proof of knowledge or intent. The law has, however, had difficulties in finding companies guilty of offences such as manslaughter where intent or other mental element needs to be proved due to the inherent problem of identifying the "controlling mind" of the company. This doctrine effectively means that the cumulative effect of bad safety management at all levels, even if it could almost be regarded as evidence of a reckless disregard for safety procedures in the company, is of no relevance. For a successful prosecution for corporate manslaughter there must be an individual of sufficient seniority to be identified with the company and who also fulfils the requisite requirements for a manslaughter conviction. This is an almost impossible task, especially for large enterprises, a fact which was very apparent in the well-documented collapse of the prosecution of P & O Ferries for manslaughter in the wake of the Zeebrugge disaster.

In response to these concerns, in 1996 the Law Commission published proposals[44] for a new offence of corporate killing which would be a more serious offence than those under the Health and Safety at Work Act. A company would be guilty of the proposed offence if a management failure by the corporation is the cause or one of the causes of a person's death and that failure constitutes conduct falling far below what can reasonably be expected in the circumstances. Although such an offence would be intended

---

43. A further study has looked at the wider effect on the economy of industrial accidents: Davies and Teasdale *The costs to the British economy of work accidents and work-related ill health* (HSE, 1994).

44. Law Commission No. 237 Legislating the criminal code: involuntary manslaughter (HMSO, 1996).

to provide a last resort when existing offences were deemed inadequate, the Law Commission report clearly suggests that adoption of the proposal would lead to an increase in prosecutions of companies for manslaughter, would respond to public concerns about fatalities arising from work activities and would cause business to think more carefully about the unacceptably high number of people who lose their lives in this way.

In July 1999, a further collapse of a prosecution of a company for manslaughter, that of *R v Great Western Trains*[45], led to the judge involved calling for new manslaughter laws. Scott Baker J commented on the failure to legislate on the issue and that there was little point in the Law Commission making recommendations if they were not acted upon. In response, a Home Office Consultation document *Reforming the Law on Involuntary Manslaughter: The Government's Proposals* was published in May 2000[46] which basically takes up the Law Commission's proposals for new offences. If changes in the law are now forthcoming it will be interesting to see what effect the existence of the new offence has on both attitudes to health and safety issues and on health and safety statistics.

9.8 Further reading

The text of most of the relevant legislation together with legal commentary is contained in J. Hendy and M. Ford, *Redgrave's health and safety*, 3rd edn (Butterworths, 1998).

For a discussion of the practicalities both legal and technical see, e.g. J. R. Ridley (ed.) *Safety at work*, 4th edn (Butterworth-Heinemann, 1994). F. B. Wright, *Law of health and safety at work* (Sweet and Maxwell, 1997) provides a detailed account and explanation of the existing regulatory regime.

The Health and Safety Executive web pages provide a useful range of material including health and safety statistics, guidance on regulatory requirements and consultation documents: http://www.open.gov.uk/hse/hsehome.htm

---

45. *The Times*, 2 July 1999.
46. http://www.homeoffice.gov.uk/consult/invmans.htm.

Chapter 10

Software safety
Liability and practice

10.1 Introduction

Throughout the last chapter it was stressed that in order to produce a safe working environment, safety should be the concern of all; is this also the way to ensure safe system design? If so, at what level does system safety begin? Can chip design, for instance, have any influence on the ultimate safety of the product into which it is incorporated, given that the chip designer may not be aware of all the multitude of applications for which it may be destined? It seems unlikely that safety considerations can be an influence at this stage. We suppose then that the system safety begins to be an entity when the proposed system is first postulated and the safety system specified. There is now no escaping the original question; who has the responsibility for ensuring the safety and integrity of the final product? There are two extremes; either everyone is responsible for safety or responsibility is delegated to a single person. In reality, neither of these options is perfect. In the first case, human nature being what it is, no-one does anything as they assume, falsely, that everyone else is doing it for them. The second case actively encourages others to take no responsibility for, and therefore no interest in, matters of safety. A judicious blend of the two would appear to be the optimum. While overall responsibility for the quality and integrity of the safety systems ought to be invested in one person, that does not preclude other personnel being aware of the safety ramifications in so far as they affect their own field of work. Such total responsibility may well be conferred on the quality manager of a software house. Since any mishap could result in personal liability, such personnel should be strongly supported by company procedures to assist them in this task. Whatever the personal liability, the company will retain a vicarious liability for the actions of their employees. This chapter will explore areas of legal liability and also other mechanisms for regulating these potentially hazardous activities as well as considering the factors which should be taken into account by software engineers engaged in producing software for safety-related applications.

No-one will deny that the design and construction of large software systems is an incredibly difficult task; how much more so when the failure of such systems may be costly in terms of suffering and human life. Nowadays, computer-controlled systems are to be found in a wide range of diverse applications such as:

- industry, e.g. flexible manufacturing systems; robots; process monitoring and control;
- medicine, e.g. intensive care monitoring; radiotherapy equipment; infusion pumps for drug administration;
- transport, e.g. automatic railway signalling; systems which are completely computer-controlled such as the Docklands Light Railway; fly-by-wire aircraft; the space shuttle;
- many military and defence applications.

These particular examples have all been chosen because they are all safety-related, a term usually taken to mean that failure of the system may result in physical injury to humans. It is also clear that many of the above are capable of causing extensive damage, producing anything from a single fatality to a major disaster with perhaps, gross environmental consequences. Such applications are termed safety-related or safety-critical. Sometimes these words are used interchangeably but safety-critical is frequently used to identify those systems to which there is, potentially, a high level of hazard attached. The software utilized in such systems, although highly complex, must be of the highest integrity and furthermore, high assurance is needed that such integrity has been achieved. The probability of failure demanded from such systems is very low, typically between 10^{-8} and 10^{-9}, which raises two questions:

- Is it possible to achieve such levels?
- Is it possible to show that such levels have been achieved?

The first question poses a design problem; are there techniques available to produce software of that reliability? The second question reflects the difficulty in designing tests to measure such low values. Whether or not there are such techniques and tests available, it is plainly a fact that there are already large numbers of safety-critical software systems in use, a fact whose increasingly high profile is attracting a corresponding public concern. Users of safety-related and safety-critical systems need and expect to have extreme confidence in the reliability and integrity of such systems; a confidence which may be damaged irrevocably by only one malfunction if it affects the safety of the system. In such cases, how do systems designers and software engineers satisfy themselves and their customers that they have fulfilled their responsibilities and their product is trustworthy? Furthermore how, if at all, is this area regulated and what sanctions, if any, can be applied if software failure does result in physical injury?

10.2 Regulatory issues

Although some accidents are predictable, many occur because of the juxtaposition of a number of factors, the probability of occurrence of each of which may appear to be unlikely. In addition, even where the correct modes of failure are identified and acknowledged, the requisite safety margin may still be contentious, as the perception of the risk involved may vary with the interest group involved. Thus manufacturers and designers are likely to see things in a different light from those who might be affected by any failure of the system. Historically, society has recognized the public interest factor in providing some assurance over the safety of potentially hazardous activities by imposing some sort of external regulation.

The success of such regulation in achieving its objectives depends on reconciling the technical problems of control with the sociological and psychological factors surrounding the individual and public perception of risk. Many of these issues are accentuated in relation to the safety of computer-controlled systems in comparison with those of "conventional systems" where failure modes may be well understood. The complexity of such systems means that, not only is it impossible to identify all possible failure modes, but also exhaustive testing in all conditions and environments is not feasible. In addition, the perception of the risk involved may be enhanced. Human beings are in some senses natural risk takers but with an important proviso, that they believe themselves to have some control over the risks incurred during a particular activity, whether it be hang-gliding or merely crossing the road. Where persons perceive that they have no control over the risk, such as passengers in a fly-by-wire aircraft, for example, they may be much less complacent about the risk involved. This individual view of risk may be compounded by the fact that, as technology has made more things possible, society now has high expectations of what can be achieved and expects that it will be achieved safely. However, methods of achieving safety have not always kept pace with technological advances and this has, at times, been exacerbated by the fact that the designers of systems are usually more concerned with what the system *will* do, whereas safety is more likely to depend on what the system must *not* do. Designers may well be more likely to concentrate on the former and their very familiarity with the system may also act as a bar to an awareness of the safety implications.

To be successful, any form of external regulation will need to take into account such opposing factors. The ultimate objective of the regulation of potentially hazardous activities is the protection of those who may be harmed if a hazard becomes uncontrolled, and the protection of society as a whole from physical and environmental disaster. Additionally, regulation may also provide the subsidiary function of giving a degree of protection to the system designers, who may be able to escape liability if they can show adherence to specified procedures. Regulation is most effective when voluntary, where those concerned recognize and accept the necessity for such measures. Nonetheless, the provision of suitable sanctions is a necessary requisite of any successful regulatory scheme, and an obvious corollary of this is that there must be an effective enforcement system. A number of systems containing software may attract the application of general legislation such as that relating to product liability or health and safety at work, but in the last few years there has also been much activity in drafting standards and certification requirements specifically for software for safety-related systems. The following subsections will examine and assess various methods available for regulation and discuss their application to software and system safety.

10.2.1 Standards

The use of appropriate standards is both a familiar and traditional technique for regulating hazardous activities and attempting to ensure the safety of a product and so, in principle, there is no reason why safety standards should not be developed for systems containing software[1]. The International Electrotechnical Commission (IEC) has defined a standard as a "document, established by consensus and approved by a recognized body, that provides, for common and repeated use, rules, guidelines or characteristics for activities or their results, aimed at the achievement of the optimum degree of order in a given context". In general, standards may be both difficult and time-consuming to produce, not least because of the need for consensus referred to in the above definition. Standards relating to the safety of systems containing software have proved to be no exception in this regard as will become apparent from the later discussion in this section. Relevant standards have been formulated by both specific industry sectors and international standards bodies.

One major problem has been to decide on the best approach, especially given the rapid rate of change of technology in this area. Design standards which mandate a particular method of design (and/or manufacture) are the frequent choice for safety standards, but these can have the effect of crystallizing the technology at a particular point in time with the result that other design methods, which may arise from improvements in technology, may not comply with the standard. In an ideal world, performance standards which

---

1. For a fuller discussion on the use of standards see D. Rowland, "Regulatory issues", in *Safety Aspects of Computer Control*, P. Bennett (ed.) (Butterworth-Heinemann, 1993).

govern what the product may or may not do may be preferable as they would allow new technological developments to be used during the design and manufacturing process without breaching the standards, providing the performance criteria were not compromised. Unfortunately, performance standards are much more difficult to implement and enforce and, for this reason, design standards are more usual.

Despite the technical problems involved in producing a workable standard for safety-related systems containing software, it was felt that, nevertheless, it was important to produce and publish such a standard, even if subsequent revisions soon became necessary, in order to cultivate uniformity of approach to the issue in different application areas. The existence of a standard would be expected both to enhance safety and have economic advantages. Without such a standard, the various industries involved might duplicate valuable resources in producing their own standards which could also lead to systems designers working to different standards for different applications, even for those with a similar level of risk. During the 1980s, the International Electrotechnical Commission (IEC) began work on draft standards encompassing, *inter alia*, the safety of systems containing software. These were to be design standards requiring the identification of the safety level needed taking account of the potential hazard, followed by the use of appropriate techniques intended to assist in achieving such a level.

The first draft international standard[2] was distributed to national standards committees, for comment, at the end of the 1980s and this was followed by a second draft IEC standard, entirely concerned with software[3]. This latter standard suggested a five point scale for levels of safety integrity, the idea being to match the required integrity level to appropriate design and development techniques. Even with this approach, there can still be no guarantee that there will be no faults in such complex systems. Interestingly, at this stage, the draft IEC standard did not make third party testing mandatory at any level, despite the fact that this had been a commonly accepted method of safety assurance for other hazardous activities[4]. It was, however, recommended for the higher integrity levels. Although intended to cover a wide variety of applications, including manufacturing and process industries, transportation and medical usage, these draft standards did not attempt to classify the safety integrity needed for any specific application which would still be a matter which had to be assessed by each industry. Producing these standards proved to be no easy task and no consensus emerged from the circulation of the original draft standards and so, at the beginning of the

2. *Functional safety of programmable electronic systems: generic aspects: Part 1: General requirements.*
3. *Software for computers in the application of industrial safety-related systems.*
4. See, e.g. G. Rabe, "Certification of safety-critical systems in Germany", in *Directions in safety-critical systems*, Redmill & Anderson (eds) (Springer-Verlag, 1993).

1990s it was decided to restructure the approach and produce new draft standards. The new proposal[5] was for IEC standards on the functional safety of safety-related systems covering the following areas:-

- generic requirements;
- requirements for electrical/electronic/programmable systems;
- software requirements.

Despite this it was not until the late 1990s that any real consensus began to emerge and, at the time of writing, four parts of a new system safety standard IEC 61508, the draft of which was published in 1998, have only recently been adopted covering general requirements, software requirements, definitions and examples of methods for determination of safety integrity levels. It is expected that the remaining three parts of this standard will also be granted official standard status in the near future.

This is not to say that there has been no guidance available for designers of software for safety-related applications in the interim. Certain sectors with a particular need for high-integrity software have led the way in standard setting and have been very influential in this area. A specific example is provided by the defence industry. Military applications have always needed to use high-reliability and high-integrity systems; indeed, the general topic of reliability engineering had its origins in the Second World War in the design and development of the V1 missile. As weapons systems increased in sophistication, so the reliability demands increased. By the time of the Atlas missile system containing some 300,000 components, the reliability of nine out of ten needed to be 99.99996 per cent. A reliability of 99.94 per cent, though good for most industrial uses would mean that the missile would never hit the target. Similar reliability demands are now being made on the software controlling weapons systems as on all safety-critical software. Weapons present a special case in that the potential hazard (to the user!) is not directly related to the reliability of operation. If the software is controlling detonation, then a fault could produce inadvertent operation with possibly escalating consequences. Leveson[6] cites the potential dangers which are required to be taken into account in the United States in any hazard analysis for nuclear weapon systems:

- inadvertent nuclear detonation;
- inadvertent pre-arming, arming, launching, firing or releasing of any nuclear weapon in all normal or credible abnormal environments;

---

5. See comment by A. Kemp, SCSC *Newsletter*, **2**(3), 8, 1993.
6. "Software safety: why, what and how", *Computing Surveys*, **18**(2), 125–163, 1986.

- deliberate pre-arming, arming, launching, firing or releasing of any nuclear weapon except upon execution of emergency war orders or when directed by a competent authority.

Whilst in one sense, it might be reassuring to find that these points have to be addressed in the design of such systems, it is to be hoped, for instance, that *all credible abnormal environments* are amenable to definition. Because of this necessary emphasis on high reliability and high integrity, many of the first standards pertaining to aspects of safety-critical systems were developed by defence bodies. The Ministry of Defence, as a major procurer of safety-critical software, produced two interim defence standards in 1991 relating to both software and system safety with which contractors were required to comply if they were to be awarded MOD contracts. These have subsequently been adopted as full standards. DEF STAN 00-55 (July 1997) covers the procurement of safety-critical software in defence applications and deals primarily with the technical aspects, while DEF STAN 00-56 (December 1996) is concerned with the safety management requirements for defence systems containing programmable electronics[7]. Of these, DEF STAN 00-55, generated much controversy because of its emphasis on formal methods for both specification and validation. This is, perhaps, an example of a standard attempting to stimulate technological advance by setting the standard at a higher level than could easily be achieved at the time of publication. There is no doubt that formally specified and validated programs are beginning to play an important part in the design of safety-critical software; a role which will expand, in all probability, as these techniques evolve. However, it is a moot point as to whether all safety critical systems could be designed in this way at present[8].

Another industry sector which has produced extensive guidance on software for use in safety-critical application is the aviation industry, to which the IEC standards will not apply. There has been close collaboration for some time between the equivalent organizations on both sides of the Atlantic to ensure that the same technical requirements were imposed in relation to the certification of software for use in aircraft[9]. This began in 1980 when both the European Organisation for Civil Aviation Equipment (EUROCAE) and the Radio Technical Commission for Aeronautics (RTCA) were in the process of producing documents establishing guidelines against which software-based airborne systems could be certified. They decided to work in concert and the result was the documents RTCA DO-178 and EUROCAE ED-12

---

7. The full text of all MOD standards is available from the MOD Directorate of Standardization web site at: http://www.dstan.mod.uk/home.htm.
8. But see also Section 10.5.
9. See also Section 10.2.2.

which appeared in 1982. The RTCA and EUROCAE documents have been the major guidelines used by the aeronautical industry throughout the world in assessing the software systems for use in aircraft and the current versions are RTCA DO-178B and EUROCAE ED-12B which are equivalent in technical content. These latest guidelines are complete revisions of the previous documents in response to changes in technology, particularly in the light of experience gained from the Boeing 747-400 and the Airbus A320.

Despite the fact that the above standards are applicable to different industry sectors and situations, there has been communication and consultation between those responsible for the individual publications, and their requirements are believed to be compatible with each other, even though their areas of application do not overlap. Thus RTCA DO-178B and the IEC standards both define a scale of integrity levels for software whose failure would compromise safety to different degrees. In addition, because of problems encountered in actually measuring the reliability and integrity of software, guidance, such as that to be found in RTCA DO-178B and EUROCAE ED-12B is a form of design standard and relies, at present, on specifying the methods to be employed in developing software for safety-critical applications. However, although it seems, intuitively, that there should be some correspondence between the various levels of integrity required and the methods to be employed, there is not yet a strong consensus amongst safety-critical practitioners and regulatory bodies over this relationship.

10.2.2 Certification and licensing

Certification and licensing are other examples of direct regulation which can be applied to both products and/or practitioners. They can also be used in conjunction with standards as when a product is certified against a particular standard. The terms certification and licensing are often used interchangeably but, strictly, certification requires that either the product or the practitioner conforms to some specified standard but there is no bar to the marketing of uncertified products or practising of uncertified practitioners. A licensing requirement, on the other hand, means that the product cannot go on the market at all, or the practitioner operate, unless the product is licensed or the practitioner in possession of the requisite licence. Licensing is, in a sense, therefore, a more severe form of certification[10]. Licensing is bound to have a restrictive effect on the market but this is usually considered to be justified in safety-related or safety-critical situations[11].

---

10. But note that this should not be confused with the familiar licence to use software.
11. For further discussion of certification and licensing in relation to safety-critical systems see, e.g. D. Rowland "Regulatory issues" in *Safety aspects of computer control*, P. Bennett (ed.) (Butterworth-Heinemann, 1993).

Those who support some form of certification or licensing[12] for safety critical systems argue that it is impossible for consumers and procurers to be in possession of sufficient information to assess either the risk or whether it is under control. Being able to choose either a product or a practitioner which conforms to a licensing requirement is a substitute for the procurer and consumer themselves having to evaluate the potential hazard, and should ensure that the end user is provided with the requisite safety level. It is often the case that those who belong to the profession in question, may be in the best position to appreciate the dangers in allowing unlicensed products or practitioners and, in situations where the potential consequences of the activity verge on the catastrophic, this may justify the imposition of the barriers to the market which are erected by licensing requirements.

Licensing requirements are often easier to enforce than some other forms of regulation, since the possibility of refusal to grant or renew a licence, or the threat of revocation can act as a very powerful sanction. Advocates of licensing for systems containing safety-critical software are usually assuming some form of licensing of practitioners, in addition to any licensing requirement or standards which pertain to the software itself. Such a premise assumes, necessarily, that there is a high correlation between the required qualifications for granting a licence and the end to be achieved. It must be remembered that this is only an assumption and, particularly where technology is changing rapidly, there must be some procedure built in whereby expertise can be shown to be maintained, if the licence is to retain its credibility. Even in the absence of formal licensing requirements, many of the existing documents of guidance take, as an initial premise, the presumed correlation between the quality, reliability and integrity of the end-product and the competence and qualifications of the practitioner[13].

A competence requirement ensures that general professional standards are maintained, which is a good starting point in relation to safety systems, but, beyond that, it is not clear precisely what factors are indicative of competence to produce safety-related systems or how such competence should be assessed. In particular, there is no defined route at present by which such practitioners can gain the requisite experience[14]. It may be that different licensing levels may be needed, perhaps related to the safety level of the system under development.

An alternative is to license the product rather than the practitioner, i.e. the product cannot be marketed unless it conforms to a predetermined standard. This has the advantage that it then becomes unnecessary to assess whether the developer's qualifications are adequate or appropriate; the question is purely

---

12. See generally S. G. Breyer, *Regulation and its reform* (Harvard University Press, 1982).
13. See also discussion of professional ethics in Chapter 1.
14. See also Section 10.4.

whether the product meets the appropriate standard. The problem of safety assurance is then transferred back to the adequacy of the standard used. Thus RTCA DO-178B and EUROCAE ED-12A are the standards against which the software for use in civilian aircraft is effectively certified.

10.2.3 Professional codes of practice

It is common for professional and trade associations to devise codes of practice[15] with which to govern their members. The subject matter of such codes may be general or more specific in nature but, in either case, they can perform a valuable regulatory function. Although they are a form of self-regulation which is not in itself legally binding, they are capable of producing legal effects if incorporated into the terms of a contract, and it may be that failure to comply with the requirements of a code of practice may, itself, be evidence of negligence[16].

It should come as no surprise that the software industry itself and the relevant professional bodies have become increasingly concerned about this problem not only because of the difficulties of the technology involved, but also from a legal standpoint. This has led to discussion about the standard of competence expected of software engineers involved with design and development of safety-critical software and about ways in which such competence can be assessed. In addition to general documents on professional accountability such as the BCS Code of Conduct, in the past few years other documents have been prepared and published that attempt to give guidance to software engineers on their responsibilities, specifically in relation to safety-related systems and risk issues, and on their presumed legal liability. The first such safety-related codes of practice were produced by individual organizations but these have been superseded by a more general and purposive approach. In 1993, the Engineering Council Code of Professional practice "Engineers and Risk Issues" came into force, which was of wide and general application. The particular recognition of the importance of safety-related engineering issues has also led to the major professional organizations in a number of engineering disciplines co-operating in the formation of the Hazards Forum[17]. This has resulted in the publication of *Safety-related systems: guidance for engineers*[18] although this is, in essence, based on an earlier professional brief produced by the IEE. The purpose of these publications seems to be to draw to the attention of those planning the development of such systems

---

15. See discussion in Chapter 1 and for approved Codes of Practice under the Health and Safety at Work Act see, Section 9.4.10.
16. See Section 10.3.2
17. http://www.hazardsforum.co.uk.
18. Hazards Forum 1995.

the factors which they have to consider if they are to avoid both failure and consequent legal liability. The Engineering Council Code sets out a ten point code of professional practice on risk issues that includes matters of professional responsibility, law, management, judgement and so on. However, within each heading, the responsibilities are couched in fairly general terms which may make compliance with it difficult to assess. The Hazards Forum publication, on the other hand, takes a different approach and attempts to provide a much more detailed exposition of the responsibilities incumbent on those involved with the design and development of safety-critical software. It includes background information, references to relevant information sources and a brief code of practice. It also includes a discussion on competence, an attribute of paramount importance but one which is not very amenable to practical definition; this matter will be discussed in more detail in Section 10.4. Suffice it to say that, there is no attempt to identify the levels of competence necessary for different applications other than to say that one factor evidencing competence is awareness of one's own limitations. Assessment of competence in individual cases is likely to be fraught with difficulties and complicated by other extraneous factors, especially where a lucrative contract might be at stake[19].

Activity by the professional bodies most closely associated with the software industry was supplemented by the establishment, in 1991, of a Safety-Critical Systems Club sponsored, initially, by the Department of Trade and Industry (DTI) and the Science and Engineering Research Council (SERC), although responsibility for management is delegated to the BCS and the IEE[20]. This organization has been instrumental in recent years in disseminating the latest information amongst those involved in developing safety-critical computer systems and other interested parties and clearly has an important role to play in raising awareness, not only of the central issues but also of the latest techniques available for addressing the problems raised.

The precise impact of professional codes as a method of safety regulation is difficult to assess, but, as with all methods of regulation, to be effective, a code must be carefully constructed, kept up to date and its operation monitored. This is where codes may enjoy advantages over other forms of regulation since their flexibility is compatible with a rapid updating to keep pace with technological change. Industry may also be more inclined to accept a negotiated code of practice, which they feel more adequately represents their views, than a legislative measure, notwithstanding the fact that there is bound to be a significant input from industry in formulating detailed technical legislation.

---

19. See, for example the discussion on the London Ambulance Service incident discussed in Section 10.4.

20. Day-to-day administration is carried out on their behalf by the Centre for Software Reliability, University of Newcastle upon Tyne.

10.2.4 Regulation by law

The law will also exert a regulatory effect[21] either directly, perhaps by requiring compliance with other forms of regulation such as standards and licensing or by incorporating similar requirements into statute, or indirectly, by exerting a deterrent effect because of fears of litigation if safety standards are breached. Law is frequently reactive rather than preventative and as such may be more concerned with providing a remedy after the event than with preventative measures. However, more recent statutes dealing with safety issues such as the health and safety legislation discussed in the previous chapter are couched in general terms leaving a certain degree of flexibility for individuals and enterprises to decide for themselves how to comply and allowing for a preventative role to a certain extent. This also helps to alleviate a further problem of legal regulation which is the way that the law is likely to lag behind the technology it is attempting to regulate. This can create serious consequences in areas such as computer control where the technology is advancing very rapidly. In some specialized areas, the practice is emerging of specifying that certain safety-critical functions can only be performed by "competent" persons[22] who are required to have certain qualifications. It remains to be seen whether this approach will be adopted for other industry sectors, but also raises important questions both in relation to the assessment of competence and the relationship between formal qualifications and practical ability. The whole issue of legal liability is discussed in more detail in the next section.

10.3 Legal liability

We have seen in the previous chapter that, as well as an obvious moral duty, systems designers and software engineers may have legal responsibilities under statutes such as the Health and Safety at Work Act to ensure that other people are not put at risk by their acts or omissions. Despite its apparently specific subject area, the general approach to safety matters contained in the Health and Safety at Work Act and associated regulations need not be confined to workplace safety. Indeed, the sequence – assess, control and monitor – found in the Control of Substances Hazardous to Health Regulations[23] and the "European" regulations is capable of application to

---

21. For a more detailed discussion of legal regulation in relation to safety-critical systems see D. Rowland, "Regulatory issues" in *Safety Aspects of Computer Control*, P. Bennett (ed.) (Butterworth-Heinemann, 1993).
22. See, e.g. Railways (Safety-critical work) Regulations 1994 SI 1994 No 299 and The Management and Administration of Safety and Health at Mines Regulations 1993 SI 1993 No 1897.
23. SI 1999 No 437; see Section 9.4.10.

the safety considerations necessary for a wide variety of practices. Specifically, where such regulations apply, then criminal penalties may be invoked in the case of breach as these rules form part of the criminal law. However, in addition, especially for cases of personal injury, there is likely, even in the absence of a criminal prosecution, to be a civil case to recover compensation for the damage caused.

The publications referred to in Section 10.1 are intended not only to help software engineers avoid failure of their systems, but also to avoid any consequent legal liability. On whom does the liability fall for defective software? And how can system failure and the consequent liability be avoided? This section will discuss the first of these questions and the second question will be considered in subsequent sections. The difficulty of keeping law relevant in the face of technological advancement has already been mentioned, but in relation to computer software this has been particularly acute. The problems have not merely been those consequent on technological progress but have included also difficulties of substance. Certain legal principles have had to be stretched to encompass this new entity and one of the major stumbling blocks has been how to define software for legal purposes. Is it tangible or intangible, goods or services, a product, an article for use at work? The problems these questions have posed for the law is summed up most appositely in the following comment in relation to the US Uniform Commercial Code[24]:

> Computer programs frustrate the law's traditional categories; they exhibit characteristics of both concrete property and abstract knowledge.

Although this was written some twenty years ago, it remains a relevant comment and the law is still struggling to come to terms with many of the issues raised by computer technology. It is beyond the scope of this chapter to expand fully on the various arguments, but the following outline is intended to explain the basic situation.

Problems surrounding the categorization of software from a legal point of view have already surfaced, usually in the commercial field and relating to whether supply of software can be properly classified as supply of goods or supply of services. Many of these have relied heavily on the technical classification of the software at issue, and there have been a number of attempts in relation to this "goods" v "services" debate to classify embedded software as "goods", on the grounds that it is mass produced and an integral part of a computer system which can be identified as the subject of a contract for the supply of goods. The situation is less clear cut with regard to applications software, and it is particularly felt that provision of one-off bespoke software

---

24. *Computer programs as goods under UCC* (1979) 77 Mich LR 1149.

for an individual customer can more aptly be described as a contract for services. Nonetheless, where applications software is mass marketed as off-the-shelf packages it would not be unreasonable to use the classification "goods"[25]. It may, however, be difficult to draw the line as to precisely when the transition from bespoke software to package occurs especially if the software is modified on the way.

Where the damage suffered due to defective software happens to a party to a contract for the supply of goods or of services, as appropriate, then there may be an action in contract[26] if the software had not been supplied to the correct specification or an action under appropriate legislation such as that relating to the sale of goods, if, for instance, the "goods" were not of satisfactory quality[27]. Suppose, though, that a robot arm makes an aberrant movement due to a defect in the control software and a person is injured, or the chip controlling the automatic braking system on a car fails, or a drug infusion pump in an intensive care unit gives a lethal dose because of a software fault. Such incidents may well result in injury to persons who have no contract with the supplier of the system whose failure led to the accident. In such cases there could be an action in negligences or in appropriate cases under the Consumer Protection Act 1987.

10.3.1 Product liability and the Consumer Protection Act 1987

Where there is no liability arising out of a contract, then compensation for damage suffered may be sought via an action in tort. This would frequently be for negligence in software design or system production (see later). However, in certain circumstances, the complainant may, alternatively and preferably, be able to bring an action under the Consumer Protection Act 1987 relating to product liability. In cases to which this legislation applies, it is unnecessary to show negligence, which removes a great burden from the person bringing the action. The only requirements are to show that the product was defective and the defect caused the damage. Liability can then be passed down the chain of supply to rest on the producer of the defective product or component. The application of the Act is limited to those actions involving consumers and, within that category, to defects which result in personal injury or physical damage to property.

25. See, for example, the reasoning of J. Rogers in *Toby Construction Products Pty Ltd v Computa Bar (Sales) Pty Ltd* [1983] 2 NSWLR 48 and the discussion on this point in *St Albans v ICL* [1995] FSR 686 (High Court) and [1996] 4 All ER 481 (Court of Appeal) discussed in a different context in Chapter 5.

26. For further consideration of liability in contract see Section 5.3.

27. See, e.g. N. Cameron, Fitness for purpose of the Pentium: "Excuse me this one has a chip in it", *Computers and Law*, 5(5) 22, Dec. 1994/Jan 1995.

One of the problems as far as the application of this statute to computer programs is concerned, is the question of whether software can be construed as a product, a term which in legal parlance usually relates to a tangible object, unless further specific provision is made. This brings the nature of software sharply into focus, and especially whether it is more accurately described as pure information, such as that which can be gleaned from a book, for instance, or whether it has also some of the attributes of tangible property in that, for some software at least, it is capable of performing actions which bring about perceptible effects in the real world. For real-time systems, therefore, there is perhaps some foundation in allocating a measure of tangibility to software. On the other hand, it would create inconsistencies if software in other systems were to be regarded in a different manner. Even for these though, the analogy with "pure" information can break down in that once a computer is acting on instructions contained in the software, an inevitable sequence of events is put into operation. In contrast, where data is extracted from books or other information sources, readers have the opportunity to decide for themselves whether or not to act on that information. Both the software as pure information and the combined tangible/intangible argument have their proponents[28] but which of these arguments will succeed in the courts is still a matter for speculation and the legal provisions themselves provide little direct clarification. "Product" is defined in s1(1) of the Consumer Protection Act 1987 as:

> Any goods or electricity and ... includes a product which is comprised in another product, whether by virtue of being a component part or raw material or otherwise

i.e. the components comprising a product are also treated as products in their own right.

For systems which contain both hardware and software, a naive analysis would suggest that, given the statutory definition of product, the software could be construed as a component of the product, so that a software house could attract liability in the same way as the producer or supplier of any other component.

The Consumer Protection Act was passed to implement the EC Directive on product liability[29] and the question of whether the definition of product might also include computer software has been the subject of a question in the

---

28. See for instance Scott (1987) 4 CL&P 133, who subscribes to the view that software has only intangible properties whereas a more circumspect approach is taken by Hirschbaek (1989) 5 CL&P 154.

29. Council Directive of 25 July 1985 (85/374/EEC) [1985] OJ. L210/29.

European Parliament addressed to the Commission[30]. The answer was unequivocal and said that as the term product was defined as all movables even though incorporated into another movable or into an immovable, the Directive also applied to software. It will ultimately be for the courts including the European Court of Justice, as the provisions of an EC directive will be at issue, to adjudicate on the correct interpretation, but the DTI statement above does not seem to be in accord with the intentions of the Directive. It should be pointed out that, despite the confusion surrounding this topic, the software industry and relevant professional organizations have taken the view that those concerned should operate as if software were indeed covered by the Act and the usual procedure is to ensure cover by product liability insurance. Whether or not software is a "product" as such will be of far more concern to the industry than to the consumers themselves as, in appropriate cases, there will always be an action possible against the manufacturer or supplier of the whole system.

10.3.2 Negligence

Even where an action under the Consumer Protection Act is not possible, there may still be grounds for an action in negligence. In simple terms, negligence may be established where the manufacturer or system designer has failed to take due care in the construction or design of the system, and this lack of care has resulted in failure leading to the injury. In addition, in order to assess whether any one individual involved in the design and development process has acted negligently, the law has developed certain guidelines by which it measures the behaviour of those in certain professions by reference to what is expected of the ordinarily competent practitioner of that profession[31]. Specialized case law relating to the attributes of certain professions has emerged during the twentieth century which attempts to set down guidelines for professional practice in particular subject areas. Because this has developed on a case-by-case basis, careful analysis is required to discern both general trends and specific principles which may be applied to the relatively new profession of software engineer.

In defending any allegation of negligence, the burden will be on the manufacturer or designer to show that they took all reasonable care to avoid such an eventuality and this is frequently done by showing that all relevant standards and codes of practice have been adhered to, hence the importance of documents such as those referred to in Sections 10.1 and 10.2. Such an approach has gained judicial approval, as for instance, in the case of *Bevan*

30. Written Question 706/88 [1989] OJ. C114/42.
31. See, for example McNair J in *Bolam v Friern Hospital Management Committee* [1957] 1 WLR 582, 586.

Investments v Blackhall and Struthers No 2 ([1973] 2 NZLR 45):

> A design which departs substantially from relevant engineering codes is prima facie a faulty design unless it can be demonstrated that it conforms to accepted engineering practice by rational analysis.

In other words, if standards and/or codes of practice are not adhered to, the onus will be on the designer/producer to explain the departure from the standards and demonstrate that what was done, in the event, achieved an equivalent or higher standard. Such an approach may work well in branches of engineering where there are well-defined standards and codes of practice, but as was discussed in Section 10.2.1, at the present time standards in relation to safety-critical software are only just emerging and, as yet, there are no generally well-accepted standards which can be used by software engineers developing software for use in such applications[32].

The cases relating to professional negligence seem to suggest that the professions fall into two broad categories:

- Those in which there can be no guarantees as to the results of their labours. Thus doctors cannot guarantee to cure the patient or solicitors to win the case. In such cases, the law has proceeded on a "best endeavours" basis guided by professional codes.
- Those, such as architects and engineers for example, in which the practitioners involved can be said implicitly to warrant to produce a particular result.

This latter is likely to be the category into which software engineers fall, especially as, in the usual case, they have a knowledge of the end result required. This implies the need for the software contractor to undertake a risk analysis of the application area and to select techniques for specification, design, development, and implementation that will achieve the appropriate level of integrity in the finished product. Whilst, in some cases, the client may be in a position to undertake the risk analysis, the responsibility for specifying and attaining the required integrity level ultimately falls upon the contractor, who has a duty to advise the client accordingly. Budgetary considerations are likely to provide no defence; it is the contractor's duty to advise of an inadequate budget rather than to provide a cut-price and inadequately safe product.

---

32. See also, for example R. Bell and D. Reinert, "Risk and system integrity concepts for safety-related control systems" *7th Symposium on Microprocessor Based Protection Systems*, Institute of Measurement and Control, London.

10.4 Competence, training and experience

It is clear from this discussion of negligence that the standard of a practitioner will be judged by reference to the standard of a *competent* practitioner of that discipline and competence is also a key word in the professional codes. There is frequently a tacit assumption that all those engaged in the design and development of safety system software are competent to perform the necessary tasks. The fact that there has been so much activity by the professional organizations in producing guidance on competence suggests that this may not be a reasonable assumption in all cases. Safety is not instinctive; it is an important and specialized subject and yet few software engineers are specifically trained in any aspects of safety technology. Most gain any relevant knowledge by experience, hopefully under the supervision of a more experienced person or as part of a suitably skilled team. Although the importance of this process should not be underestimated, in such a vital area it is nevertheless a rather haphazard method of ensuring a sufficient level of expertise.

As competence is the yardstick by which the professional is measured it is clearly crucial to have some comprehension of the meaning and scope of this term. The Hazards Forum[33] suggest that this "involves knowledge and the ability to apply that knowledge". Obviously factors such as training and relevant experience will have some bearing but there are a number of other components which are considered below together with the possible response of the competent software engineer. Professional qualifications may be obvious relevant factors, but it must be ensured that they are appropriate to the work in hand and, are, perhaps, made subject to continuing education requirements to ensure the level of knowledge is kept up-to-date. Although such credentials may provide a sensible starting point, it is not always an easy matter to correlate qualifications on paper with expertise in practice. It has been generally accepted that there seems to be a need for specialized training for those working on safety-critical systems development and there have been a number of recent developments in this respect. Professional examinations and continuing professional development (CPD) are familiar requirements of membership of a professional organization. The BCS professional examination has a new syllabus for safety-critical and real-time software due to be examined for the first time in 2001[34]. With respect to competency requirements there has been consultation on draft guidelines for those working with safety-related systems produced by the IEE and BCS and sponsored by the HSE. The final version is expected early in 2000[35]. It will be interesting to see whether such developments in training, qualifications and

---

33. See previous discussion in Section 10.2.3.
34. For details see http://www.bcs.org.uk/exam/syllabus/scrts.htm.
35. For further details see http://www.iee.org.uk/PAB/HandS/comp_pes.htm.

definitions of competence will strengthen the arguments in favour of certification of software engineers working on safety-critical systems.

One important attribute of a competent practitioner is to be aware of their own skills and failings[36] and this may demonstrate itself in the decision whether to accept a proffered contract in the first place. The procurers of safety-critical software may have a duty to engage a competent contractor, but in such a technical area, it is difficult for those not so qualified to assess whether the intended contractors are sufficiently experienced. It is possible that they may be assisted in this task if qualifications of the type referred to in the previous paragraph do become well-accepted. In addition, it is not clear who has the responsibility to identify that any particular system has safety implications. For many systems this will be obvious, and will be reflected in the specification, but, where it is not so clear that high-integrity software may be required, neither may it be so clear on whom is the onus to define the required system as safety-related. While the procurers may not be able to escape some responsibility, as they are the ones who ultimately define the requirements, this burden may also be shared by the contractor, who should be in possession of the relevant technical expertise to ensure that the system design and development is conducted using appropriate techniques to provide assurance of the necessary integrity.

Another subject with which both procurers and contractors will be concerned is the price of the proposed system. Design and development of software for safety-related systems is necessarily likely to be more costly than for other systems. This may well lead to conflict where the budget allowed is insufficient to accommodate such a high level of expenditure. Should the competent practitioner accept a contract when it is clear that the funds available are incapable of ensuring the required integrity of the system?

The problems which can be caused by both of these last two factors are well-illustrated by the incident involving the failure of the computer-aided despatch (CAD) system of the London Ambulance Service (LAS) in October and November 1992. A relevant aspect of the background to this incident, for the purposes of this discussion, was the fact that a previous attempt to implement CAD had been abandoned due to its high cost and because of the alleged inability of the contracting software house to understand the complexity of the requirements[37]. This might have been expected to start alarm bells ringing in relation to what could be achieved on the proposed budget. Any expenditure had to be in line with the Regional Health Authority standing financial instructions which required the lowest tender to be accepted unless there were "good and sufficient reasons to the contrary". It appears that no

---

36. See, e.g. BCS Code of Conduct, par. 21.
37. *Report of the inquiry into the London Ambulance Service*, South West Thames Regional Health Authority, February 1993, para 3046.

such "good and sufficient reasons" were identified in this case and the project was awarded to the lowest tenderer, despite the fact that, as it now appears, the full safety implications of the proposed system were never realized by either side[38]. Arguably, the LAS should have appreciated the level of safety requirements needed, especially in the light of the previously abandoned project, but, equally, the contractors cannot escape a share in the responsibility. Their proposal had suggested that they had experience in designing systems for the emergency services but, in fact, this related to administrative rather than "mission critical" systems[39], neither had the LAS been shown independent references casting doubt on the contractors competence in relation to a project of this type[40].

10.5 Factors affecting system safety

Most software engineers will have been trained to adhere to sound engineering practice and the first step is to ensure that systems are designed and developed on sound scientific principles. Applying these principles to safety-related systems means that safety should be made an objective at the first possible opportunity, i.e. at the design stage. This means not only that all foreseeable eventualities can be considered, but prevents safety issues from being marginalized, as safety mechanisms can be included as an integral part of the design process rather than as an afterthought. Nevertheless nothing can be made inherently safe and so any assessment of the safety of an object or process will depend on balancing a number of factors. As already mentioned, some accidents are completely predictable, but many occur because of the juxtaposition of a number of events which in themselves seem unlikely and it appears an even more remote possibility that they will act in co-ordination. Also, unfortunately for manufacturers and engineers, factors governing perceptions of safety are not all technical: sociological and psychological factors may also play a part and cannot be discounted.

When a computer system is used in a safety-related application then this must be borne in mind at all stages in the software life cycle, i.e. specification, design, testing etc. and it is the particular influence of safety requirements on each of these stages which we shall be studying in this section. All systems consist of both hardware and software and factors relating to both

---

38. Martyn Thomas, an acknowledged authority on safety related computer systems, quoted in *New Scientist* suggested the possibility that the London Ambulance system was never identified as being safety-critical: E. Geake, "Did ambulance chiefs Specify Safety Software", *New Scientist*, **136**, 5, 7 Nov. 1992.

39. *Report of the inquiry into the London Ambulance Service*, South West Thames Regional Health Authority, February 1993, para 3045.

40. *Report of the inquiry into the London Ambulance Service*, South West Thames Regional Health Authority, February 1993 paras 1007f) and g).

aspects will be considered, but especial emphasis will be placed on software. Most of the topics discussed will be familiar to the software engineer and the approach adopted is intended to heighten awareness of the pitfalls which may be encountered in producing a system of this type. It should be realized that this is an extremely complicated subject for which all of the necessary technology has not yet been developed and no apologies are made for over-simplification in some areas. The objective is to provide an overview of all the myriad factors which need to be taken into account. The problem for any systems designer lies in reducing the risk to an acceptable level and of course, the risk tolerated will vary between applications. Unfortunately, designing a system for any safety-related application will more often be found to be a matter of selecting an appropriate shade of grey rather than choosing the black and white options which would be preferable.

10.5.1 Hazard analysis

Before any further steps can be taken in designing a system for a safety-related application, it is necessary to arrange for a full hazard analysis to be undertaken to enable identification of all potentially dangerous situations. This can be a more difficult process in relation to computer-controlled systems than for "conventional" systems as acknowledged in the following quote[41]:

> It is essential that industry should be able to reap the enormous benefits computerization has to offer. But the sophistication and unfamiliarity of the new technology can conceal hazards, sometimes at the interface between man and the process, which could inhibit the rate of advance, *unless we learn to recognize them ...*" (emphasis added).

Such an analysis needs to include not only the obvious hazards, but also the more elusive contingent hazards which may arise due to unusual combinations of circumstances. If the hazards cannot be seen and identified in this way then clearly their potential effect cannot be removed or minimized. As the complexity of the system and the degree of hazard increases, formal techniques of hazard analysis become essential. The principles of these techniques may be based on inductive (i.e. bottom-up) or deductive (i.e. top-down) reasoning; principles which will be familiar to software engineers from their use in software design and testing. Briefly, fault mode analysis (FMA) begins at the component level. The various possible modes of failure are identified and the effects of these failures

---

41. J. D. Rimmington, Director-General, HSE, in the foreword to *Programmable electronic systems in safety related applications*, Vols 1 and 2 (HMSO, 1987).

on the next higher level of assembly are analysed. The probability of failure is estimated and the potential hazards can then be ranked according to criticality, i.e. the component failure producing the most serious effect and with the highest chance of occurrence is placed first and so on. The technique proceeds upwards until the effect on the entire system is evaluated. For real-time systems, it should be noted that the following modes of failure should not be neglected:

- premature operation;
- failure to operate at the prescribed time;
- failure to cease operation at the prescribed time.

On the other hand, fault tree analysis (FTA) begins with the definition of some undesired event, usually catastrophic, and analyses the sequence of events which could allow this to occur. It starts at the highest system level and continues through sub-systems until a specific component or functional failure is identified. The fault tree thus produced gives a graphical representation of the relationship between certain specified events and the ultimate undesired event. The initial, final and intervening events are portrayed and analysed by the use of logic diagrams. One benefit of FTA is that it can be used to consider all types of failure; hardware, software and human failures are equally amenable to assessment in this way. It is a well-accepted technique but can be unwieldy for large complex systems[42].

Another approach to hazard analysis which has been used in the process industries, most notably the chemical industry, for identifying hazards at the design stage is the use of hazard and operability studies (HAZOPs). This requires an interdisciplinary team to be assembled, based on the premise that even experienced and competent designers may sometimes make mistakes and that a multi-disciplinary team may identify points which might otherwise have been missed. This can enable potential problems to be identified much earlier in the design process thus also possibly producing financial savings. Essentially, the team are required to ask questions systematically throughout the design process, thus, in the early stages, the emphasis will be on identifying basic problems which will set the ground rules for the design. This allows for more concentrated and detailed checks of system design, assessment of operating procedures and so on in the later stages.

---

42. Further discussion and references to relevant methods of hazard analysis can be found in the booklet *Programmable electronic systems in safety related applications: 2 General technical guidelines* (HMSO, 1987).

There has been much discussion on the application of HAZOPs to computer-controlled systems (computer HAZOPs or CHAZOPs)[43]. In particular, defence standard DEF STAN 00-56 calls for HAZOPs in relation to both systems and sub-systems, but the only guide it was able to refer to originally was that for chemical process plant. This omission has now been remedied by the formulation and publication of interim defence standard DEF STAN 00-58 *Hazop studies on systems containing programmable electronics*[44].

10.5.2 Requirements and specification

Detailing the requirements is the first step towards ensuring that the correct end product is produced. For this to be achieved, it is necessary for the analyst, designer and implementor to fully comprehend the nature of the product. In many, if not the majority of cases, the user or customer, despite possessing detailed knowledge of the process or application, will not have sufficient understanding of the precise workings of the computer system to appreciate whether it is trustworthy or not. This is also true in reverse, the software engineer cannot be expected to be immediately aware of all the subtle nuances pertaining to the particular process or application.

This may be the case for both general and safety requirements. One prerequisite therefore for safe design is "full and frank discussions" between the customer and designer with a view to creating total understanding regarding both the nature of the product and the required safety performance. The objective is to incorporate an acceptable level of safety into the design before operation begins. In purely commercial terms, this will be a benefit to all concerned since any modifications necessary to enhance safety will invariably be cheaper to implement at this stage. The benefits to human life should be obvious[45]!

General difficulties which can arise are often due to the vagaries of natural language, which is notoriously imprecise. The use of technical terminology (jargon?) which may be more specific is often only partially understood by the non-specialist. Formal expression of the functional specification in mathematical terms may be useful for the software engineer but may further alienate the user who will inevitably find it more difficult to assess whether the proposed system is that requested.

---

43. See, e.g. P. Andow, *Guidance on HAZOP procedures for computer-controlled plant*, HSE Contract Research Report No 26/1991 and D. J. Burns & R. M. Pitblado, "A modified HAZOP methodology for safety-critical system assessment" in *Directions in safety-critical systems*, Redmill & Anderson (eds) (Springer-Verlag, 1993).
44. MOD July 1996. Text available from http://www.dstan.mod.uk/home.htm.
45. For an example of a system in which there had clearly been no such "meeting of the minds", see *Report of the inquiry into the London Ambulance Service*, South West Thames Regional Health Authority, February 1993.

In any event, even if the specification is expressed mathematically, this does not preclude it being incomplete. Incompleteness poses problems at all levels but particularly so for safety requirements. It would be unfortunate if conditions arose which could precipitate an accident and the code to deal with the consequent inputs was absent from the program because of omissions in the specification. Completeness with regard to the safety requirements should arise out of the results of the hazard analysis, but unfortunately this cannot always be guaranteed.

It is an advantage to have a separate specification for the safety requirements; at the least this will ensure that they have been given some consideration. While other aspects of the specification concentrate on what the system should do, many of the requirements of a safety specification will be concerned with what the system should not do. All systems are likely to fail at some time and in some way and an important part of the safety specification will be to ensure that the system fails to safety, i.e. refuses to produce in unsafe modes of operation. From a safety point of view, failure of the system may not be the most important factor but rather the consequences of such failure.

What should be covered in the safety specification? The initial consideration will be to identify the safety-related systems and the safety-related functions. It is of course possible for the safety of some computer-controlled plant to be adequately ensured by conventional means, but it is more usual for at least some of the safety-related systems to be also programmable. These may be either control systems or protection systems which are specifically designed to come into operation in the event of a mishap or malfunction. It is highly desirable that wherever possible, control and protection systems are separated. This has the advantage that the amount of software affecting safety is minimized and also ensures that failure of the control system does not precipitate a consequent failure of its own protection system. Leveson[46] suggests several software control faults that may adversely affect system safety:

- failure to perform a required function;
- performing a function not required;
- timing or sequencing problems;
- failure to recognize a hazardous condition requiring corrective action;
- producing an incorrect response to a hazardous condition.

The safety specification will need to elucidate how such faults are to be handled including a description of any necessary self-monitoring and built-in tests for malfunction together with the form of the user warning to be issued. Having identified the safety-related functions, the required safety level must

46. N. G. Leveson, "Software safety: why, what and how", *Computing Surveys*, **18**(2), 125–163, 1986.

be determined. This will be related to the desired reliability of the safety-related system and can be difficult to establish, especially for new or novel processes. Factors which need to be considered include the severity of the risk, the numbers of people exposed to that risk and so on. For any programmable system, the achieved safety level should be at least as good as that which can be achieved using conventional safeguarding.

The safety requirements must correctly reflect the critical properties of the environment in which the software is to operate. This is of importance since the software system may react differently in different environments and it is imperative to exercise the programs with representative inputs. In practice, general user requirements will change over a period of time and a necessary feature of the safety specification will provide for maintainability of the safety systems so that the achieved safety level is not compromised by future alterations.

The following example[47] shows how problems can manifest themselves. Note also that this mishap, in common with many others, arose because two unrelated events occurred concurrently.

The specification for a system controlling a chemical reactor included the requirement that in the event of a malfunction, an alarm would be sounded and all other variables would be kept constant. An incident arose when a signal was received by the computer indicating a low oil level in a gearbox. An alarm was sounded as specified, the operators checked for possible causes of the low oil level but found it to be normal and the warning false. That might have been the end of the matter but coincidentally, a catalyst had just been added to the reactor and to cope with the consequent heat generation, the computer had started to increase the cooling water flow to the reflux condenser. Because the system had responded to an apparent fault condition, this flow was subsequently kept constant instead of continuing to increase. The reactor overheated, the relief valve opened and the entire contents of the reactor were discharged into the atmosphere.

10.5.3 System reliability

Reliability is defined as "The probability of performing the intended purpose adequately for the period of time intended under the operating conditions encountered". Neglecting any human contribution, the overall system reliability can be considered as the product of the hardware reliability and the software reliability. Hardware reliability is determined statistically and is related to random failure[48] of individual components. To ensure that any

---

47. T. Kletz, "Human problems with computer control" *Hazard Prevention*, March/April, 24, 1983.

48. Failure can be defined as ceasing to perform the specified function, a definition which can be applied to both hardware and software.

hardware is sufficiently reliable for the purpose, we need to select components of an appropriate standard and combine them in appropriate ways. Even this may not be as straightforward as it sounds. Commercial microprocessors for instance may contain design errors at the silicon level, there may be slight changes in function between batches and in some cases the manufacturer's literature has been found to be ambiguous or even wrong. One such example is the error that was discovered in the floating-point division instruction of Intel's Pentium microprocessor[49]. It might be thought that such problems could be overcome by the use of formal methods and there are various examples where such techniques have been used to assist the design of reliable microprocessors but, as yet, there is always scope for errors to be found in commercially available microprocessors.

A standard method of increasing hardware reliability is to introduce redundancy. This gives the possibility of creating a more reliable system from less reliable components. Consider a very simple example where two components are connected in series as shown in Figure 10.1. Intuitively we can see that if either component 1 or 2 fails then the whole system will fail. Mathematically, if the reliabilities of the two components are given by R_1 and R_2 then the total reliability is given by

$$R = R_1 \times R_2$$

As nothing is totally reliable, both R_1 and $R_2 < 1$ and so this series construction has decreased the total reliability. If we introduce some redundancy simply by doubling up on components 1 and 2 as in Figure 10.2, then we can immediately see that this will be inherently more reliable than the original system. The total reliability is now given by

$$R = [1 - (1 - R_1)^2] \times [1 - (1 - R_2)^2]$$

Substituting numerical values will illustrate the dramatic effect this can have. Suppose we take $R_1 = R_2 = 0.95$, not a very auspicious value since it implies a failure rate of 5 in 100 operations. Without the redundancy the total reliability for the series connection falls to $0.95 \times 0.95 = 0.9025$ which is even worse. The redundant system, however, gives a total reliability of

Figure 10.1 Series connection.

49. See, e.g. C. Arthur, "Flawed chips bug angry users", *New Scientist*, **144**, 18, 10 Dec. 1994.

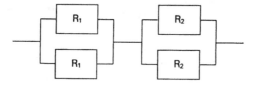

Figure 10.2 Introducing redundancy.

$$R = [1 - (0.05)^2]^2 = 0.995$$

which is obviously a vast improvement. Starting with more reliable components, say $R_1 = R_2 = 0.995$, we can produce a total reliability of 0.99995,
i.e. 99.995 per cent in this way. Further improvements may be made by
increasing the redundancy and/or introducing diversity in which case the
redundant components are not exact replicas. Software does not break
down or wear out in the same sense as hardware and so this approach is
not always relevant for software systems. Software may cease to perform its
correct function (i.e. fail) because of a misinterpretation, ambiguity or
inaccuracy in the specification. More insidiously, software failure may
occur when a particular combination of circumstances trigger an undetected bug. This may only arise after a long period of otherwise failure-
free operation. Such failures can be treated as random in analogy with
hardware since it is not possible to predict which combination of circumstances will cause the bug to surface. However, this is probably where the
similarity ends, as at the time of writing, although ways of expressing software reliability have been and are being researched, it is still very difficult
to arrive at any quantitative measurement of software reliability.

Even if we cannot assign a numerical value to the software reliability, this
does not prevent us from taking all possible steps to increase it. Formal
verification methods, which prove mathematically that the program meets
its functional specification, may be expected to increase the reliability.
Indeed, such methods are already used frequently in security applications
where the requirements are often simpler than safety requirements.
Although this may prove to be a way forward for the future, at present it
is only possible to prove relatively small programs. In addition, the problems
referred to in the previous section may be introduced.

Another line of attack is to design the software to be robust. Robustness is
defined as "The extent to which software can continue to operate correctly
despite the introduction of invalid inputs". Robust systems can thus prevent
dangerous values from being processed but clearly can only do this if the
dangerous values can be pre-defined, which returns the problem to the
hazard analysis and consequent specification details. It may be sensible in
safety-related applications to make use of reusable software where possible.

This should increase reliability as it will already have been exercised in working systems. One advantage might be that reusable components for safety-related applications may have been developed by safety systems specialists. A disadvantage is that even if a component has proved to be highly reliable in one situation, there is still no guarantee that undiscovered bugs will not be triggered by different circumstances in a new environment. We cannot assume that failure-free operation in the past will indicate failure-free operation in the future. Reliability should be improved by testing and debugging (see Section 10.5.7) provided no further bugs are introduced as a consequence of any corrections. Whilst comprehensive testing does appear to have this effect, real-time systems, including those which are safety-related, are complex and can never be completely tested nor are they ever entirely free of bugs. It should go without saying that the simplest design that meets the specification is the one that should be chosen.

10.5.4 Reliability and safety

Consider the definition of reliability already given above, namely "The probability of performing the intended purpose adequately for the period of time intended under the operating conditions encountered". Safety, on the other hand, can be defined as "The probability that no accidents will occur in a given length of time due to a system failure or malfunction".

This latter definition is an oversimplification since it takes no account of any human element which may be a factor. Although the reliability of a system is an important parameter, we must be careful not to confuse system reliability with system safety. Reliability is concerned with making the system *failure-free*, i.e. performing its specified functions correctly. It is perfectly possible for a system to be functioning correctly, i.e. as specified and yet for a mishap to occur as illustrated in the following example:

> An accident happened when an assembly robot jammed and stopped. The act of clearing the blockage caused the robot cycle to resume and the operator was injured. The control system was functioning reliably as specified but the design of the safety systems was at fault for allowing the robot to continue whilst the operator had access to the robot's workspace.

Safety is therefore concerned with making the system *hazard-free*. From a safety point of view, system failures can be tolerated, provided they fail to safety.

10.5.5 Design

Some elements of safe design have already been mentioned because of their relevance to reliability and we shall now discuss further design features which are specifically related to safety systems. For the purposes of this chapter, it is assumed that the usual methods of design appropriate to the development of a well-engineered product will be employed and there are a number of standards and other publications which provide general reference material for designers of programmable systems for safety-related applications[50]. The two booklets by the HSE discuss and give guidance on a number of salient points. They are directed particularly at industries which use such systems to control and monitor various types of equipment. Although they may have wider application, they are not adequate to deal with some safety-critical systems, nor are they intended to be. For those designing systems for use in higher-risk situations, the approaches taken by the defence standards, the RTCA and EUROCAE guidelines and the emerging IEC standards, discussed in Section 10.2.1 will be more appropriate.

The design approach chosen for the safety system will depend on the intended application but there are a few principles which can be considered. Basically these are based on the premise that hazards can either be prevented or they can be detected and treated. This leads to three possible design strategies:

- prevention or minimization of hazards, e.g. by monitoring and automatic control or provision of safety features such as interlocks, emergency and safety stops etc;
- use of automatic safety devices to control the hazard if it occurs;
- provision of warning devices, safe systems of work and suitable training to instruct personnel how to react in the event of a mishap.

These have been given in order of desirability but in practice, a combination may be required.

It is important also to keep the safety requirements firmly in view. There is no virtue in unnecessary over-complication of the design caused by the introduction of safeguards against hazards which will not be encountered, nor by an over-zealous pursuit of the elimination of one hazard to the exclusion of others which may be equally likely. Rather more contentiously perhaps for software engineers, there is no necessity to guard against hazards with software which might more appropriately (and probably more cheaply) be

---

50. For example: HSE *Programmable electronic systems in safety related applications* Vols 1 and 2 (HMSO, 1987). BS 5750: Quality Systems, Parts 1-6. BS 6739: Codes of Practice for Instrumentation in Process Control Systems: Installation, Design and Practice.

guarded by mechanical or conventional means. The proposed design should be studied to discover whether the failure of one single channel (of either hardware or software) will lead the system to malfunction to a dangerous state. If this is the case, then at least one additional method of achieving the required safety level should be introduced. For hardware this means either additional conventional safety systems or additional programmable hardware of a different design. If a software channel is involved, then this will indicate either extra conventional safety systems as before or diversification of the software. Usually, the latter option is only selected in those cases where the safety of the whole system depends on programmable safeguards.

In general, the higher the level of safety required, the more independent safety systems (programmable or non-programmable) must be provided. For all applications, the total number of programmable and non-programmable systems must not be less than the number of systems which would provide a satisfactory safety level in an equivalent conventional installation.

One area of the design which can cause a number of safety problems is the user interface. While this is perhaps more correctly an ergonomic problem, it is worth consideration here because of its potentially large effect on the overall system safety. The user interface can be considered as a surface across which information passes from system to user and user to system. The efficiency with which information is transferred across the interface will depend upon the visibility, legibility and intelligibility of the display and controls. In an otherwise well-engineered design, safety will be compromised if warnings do not receive the relevant response because of deficiencies in the user interface. All of the displays and controls should be assembled in a logical fashion and warning displays in particular should be clear, unambiguous and appropriate to the environment. Thus a flashing light rather than a sound signal may be a more suitable alarm where noise levels are already high. Two examples will illustrate these points.

In a chemical plant an operator caused serious interruption to processing by selecting the wrong control from a set of identical panels. On one side of the control room, the panels were arranged left-to-right but on the other side right-to-left. This confusing configuration had been used because it made the cabling installation easier[51].

A power blackout occurred in New York in 1977. It was initiated by separate lightning strikes which disabled two power lines causing heavy overloads on other parts of the system. The operator's response resulted in further power losses because it was based on the belief that a particular power line was still functioning. In fact it was also out of action but the flashing light and warning buzzer indicating this were in a different room.

---

51. *Human factors in industrial safety.* HS(G)48 (HMSO, 1989).

10.5.6 Testing and debugging

All large software systems will contain bugs. These may have been generated by coding or design errors or by faulty interpretation, ambiguity or incompleteness of the functional specification. Software testing is the controlled exercise of programs using sample input data. One of the aims of testing is to locate bugs and to remove them by debugging techniques followed by retesting to ensure that no further bugs have been introduced in the process. Testing and debugging will thus be undertaken many times in the software life cycle. It is also important to test thoroughly the effects of any modifications or maintenance which might be performed on the system at later date.

The testing of complex real-time systems should be comprehensive but it can never be complete. Exhaustive testing of software is out of the question; there are simply too many possible combinations of events. Selection of representative samples of conditions is therefore important and different aspects will need to be tested for the safety requirements than for other requirements. Testing and debugging also contribute to increasing the reliability of the system. For general reliability purposes, testing of typical situations is usually more important than testing boundary cases[52]. The converse is more often the case for safety-related and safety-critical systems since the ability of the system to cope with unexpected extremes of data will affect the ultimate safety level achieved. Many faults may be time-dependent and only manifest themselves when unusual combinations of circumstances occur. If such a combination only arises rarely but is capable of causing catastrophe, then the problem is obvious even if the solution is not! One of the major difficulties in creating a complete functional specification for a safety-related or a safety-critical system is to foresee all such potentially hazardous circumstances and one of the major difficulties in testing such a system is to ensure that the correct account has been taken of such circumstances.

Many faults will be discovered by routine testing but a fault could remain hidden for some time until triggered by a particular combination of inputs which may not have occurred before. On 15 January 1990, a software fault in a switch caused a massive failure in the AT & T telephone system in New York[53]. This fault had actually been introduced as a result of a routine software update in mid-December but had not come to light until triggered by an unusual combination of circumstances involving the failure of another component. The official report on the incident said that the new software had been rigorously tested in the laboratory but that the particular combination of events which led to the fault could not have been predicted and so the software was not tested against this eventuality. Once the problem had been

---

52. N. H. Petschenk, "Practical Priorities in System Testing". *IEEE Computer*, **2**(15), 18–23, 1985.

53. *Forum on risks to the public in computers and related systems*, **9**, 62, 26 Jan 1990.

observed it was able to be simulated in the laboratory and the fault eradi-cated. Communications systems do possess safety-critical properties in that they provide access to the emergency services, but such an incident could have had much more immediately serious consequences in some other safety application, if the event precipitating the failure was truly unforeseeable.

For most systems, acceptance testing involves testing the system with the real data which is destined to be processed. As just mentioned, safety systems will need to handle unexpected events, the consequences of which may be disastrous. It is apparent, however, that it is not possible to test the system in the actual environment for which it is intended. Extensive use of simulators is therefore required. Simulators are programs which can be used to mimic specific effects. They may simulate the effect of safety-critical failure or may simulate hardware devices for instance. The latter can prove very useful in testing software for many safety-related applications where there is potential for damaging the hardware. One drawback is that it is very difficult to ascertain whether the simulation is accurate or not.

Even after extensive testing there will be no room for complacency and a further precaution is to invoke third party testing. It is very common for producers of any article to be immune to its faults and software is no excep-tion. Third party testing may thus identify further faults. Such testing may be in-house, but the greater the risk, the more desirable truly independent test-ing becomes.

The stringent testing necessary for safety-related and safety-critical systems often constitutes a substantial proportion of the total development costs. This is not a suitable area for economizing though and cost can seem an insignif-icant factor when compared to the consequences of safety-critical failure.

10.5.7 Safety integrity analysis and risk assessment

The discussion thus far has concentrated on the way in which the develop-ment proceeds. Having rigorously completed all these steps, we now need to satisfy ourselves as to the quality of the product. With respect to safety requirements in general, we need *assurance* that the design is free from faults that could lead to danger and that the system is able to provide protection both against internal failures and from external factors. Assurance will be increased by comprehensive checking of all the procedural and engineering aspects of the system with a view to ensuring that a suitable quality level has been maintained throughout the design. Checklists may facilitate such an examination[54]. It will be a help if an established quality assurance system such as ISO 3000 has been used in the manufacture. Quantification of assur-

---

54. See, for example HSE, *Programmable electronic systems in safety related applications*, Vol 2 (HMSO, 1987).

ance suffers from the same inherent difficulties as quantification of reliability and development of both reliability and assurance metrics is one present line of research.

Risk assessment involves conducting a hazard analysis type of study on the finished product. A prediction of the likelihood of resultant injury compared to the potential severity of such injury can then be used to assess the risk. A further assessment can then be made of which safety systems are adequate for the task and those where further refinements are needed.

10.5.8 Documentation

Well-developed software should be described by comprehensive, intelligible documentation throughout the development process. It should include, *inter alia*, references to design methods, software tools employed and details of test plans together with results. Software maintainability has already been discussed and the documentation should also be maintained to respond to changes in the software and previous versions destroyed.

There may be a number of individuals who could be classified as users, e.g. operators, maintenance personnel, managers etc. and the user documentation needs to be relevant and intelligible to them all. There is a tendency among non-specialists to view computers as "black boxes". This view is not conducive to making optimum use of the system facilities and is unlikely to be alleviated by an incomprehensible user manual. Any process which will deepen understanding of the system will improve safety by improving the human reliability aspect.

Documentation of the safety requirements should include a description of the safety systems. It will need to detail when and how the system should be maintained, the safety precautions necessary before maintenance and the testing procedures afterwards, and describe methods of logging faults and failures. There should be well-defined safe systems of work for potentially hazardous occupations such as checking the system on-line. It is important that such safe systems of work are tailored to any existing safe systems of work which are relevant to the process. The documentation will also need to include explanation of any extra training necessary for operators or maintenance staff. Last but not least, it should contain a complete and easy-to-use index so that all the information is easily accessible to any level of user.

10.6 Practical approaches

It is very easy for problems to arise and mishaps to occur even in an apparently well-designed system. Where the system in question is safety-critical it is perhaps not really overstating the case to say that such problems should not be allowed to happen, as software failure could then lead directly to loss of life and major disaster. One approach is to recognize that even after taking all appropriate steps to produce a high integrity system, some residual faults will remain. If more than one computer is used to process the same information and the outputs are monitored, some of the problems which arise due to residual faults should be eliminated. This is similar in essence to the redundancy networks already discussed. Where only two computers are used for this purpose, it is necessary to specify the manner in which they will operate, i.e. are safety precautions initiated when both computers display a fault (known as two out of two or 2oo2) or when only one does (1oo2)? If only one system need detect a fault to instigate safety measures, spurious tripping, when no hazard is present, may occur, perhaps due to software faults. Thus, for reasons other than safety, the 2oo2 system is frequently selected. This is believed to be the way in which the safety systems on the Piper Alpha oilrig were operating before the disaster. It is understood that they have now been modified to 1oo2.

Usually the number of separate systems will increase with the perceived risk. When the number of computers is greater than two, the outputs are compared in a voting system. Thus in the Challenger space shuttle, four computers are used and their outputs monitored and compared by a fifth (the voter[55]). Frequently, the software for such computers is designed independently by different teams of software engineers using different algorithms and possibly different languages; so-called N-version programming. This was the approach chosen by the designers of the A320 Airbus, a fly-by-wire aircraft now in passenger service. It has five on-board computers, some of which are back-up systems and switch on in the event of a fault. Although N-version programming is an accepted technique, it is open to dispute as to whether the different versions of software so produced are truly independent, or can ever be so. Accepted procedures often dictate that problems are tackled in certain systematic ways and safety systems are no exception to this, nor should they be. The implication is however, that true diversity of software for the one application may not exist and, in any case, there is still the possibility that undetected software faults may precipitate overall system failure. Although in the A320 there are mechanical back-up devices for the pilot in the event of such failure, these offer only basic rudder and pitch trim and might not be sufficient to land the aircraft safely in adverse weather conditions. Although newcomers to civil aviation, fly-by-wire aircraft have been in military use for some time.

It might be expected that where very high integrity systems are mandated, as much use as possible should be made of mathematical methods. This has proved to be the case in some medical applications. Although the software controlling certain medical instrumentation may be safety-critical, the pro-

---

55. Failure of the voter is presumably not judged to be a problem; its function is much simpler than the others and it should therefore be easier to assure its high reliability.

grams involved are relatively small and the range of variables well-defined, making techniques using formal methods very attractive. New models of such instruments as heart monitors and defibrillators are currently being developed in which the software is entirely produced by formal methods. In contrast, in the United States recently, the manufacturers of gamma-ray scanning equipment were alleged to have caused the deaths of two patients. The scanning beam had two strengths and a shield protected the patient from overdose at the higher strength. An interlock was intended to prevent the high strength beam operating in the absence of the shield. In the cases in question, the software failed to check the state of the interlock and the patients received overdoses.

For some applications, external approval or certification of safety-critical software is a requirement as an intermediate step between the implementor and the user. It may well be that the approver has insufficient knowledge to understand the detailed workings of the system. In such cases, rather than relying on merely attempting to demonstrate the integrity of the system, a further third party involvement may be introduced to evaluate the software. For example, software for use in aircraft is effectively certified against the standard RTCA DO-178B or EUROCAE ED-12B, as discussed earlier in this chapter, and the Nuclear Installations Inspectorate (NII) of the HSE need to approve control systems for use in nuclear power stations. There has been concern voiced that the NII have insufficient resources to fulfil this role adequately, and that independent evaluation, by expert teams, of the software for the latest generation of nuclear power stations is called for. It must be remembered that whoever performs this function will need to have expertise not only in software engineering but also in the wider field of safety engineering.

It might be supposed that one major safety advantage of increased computer control would be a decrease in the numbers of human errors which are popularly considered to be the usual cause of disaster by the press. Unfortunately, the first indications are that the reverse may be true and that a high degree of automation makes users complacent and may compromise safety[56]. This may be due to failure to respond sufficiently quickly to alarm signals because of the sudden transition necessary from a passive monitoring role to an active fault finding or controlling role. Errors may also arise from input of incorrect data or ergonomic factors in the design. A further problem was identified in a report[57] on pilots using highly automated cockpits. Apart from similar factors to those just mentioned, problems which originated in design faults or incomplete specification were uncovered. For

---

56. N. G. Leveson, "Software safety: why, what and how", *Computing Surveys*, **18**(2), 125–163, June 1986.

57. NASA, Human factors of advanced technology (glass cockpit) transport aircraft, 1989.

instance, in such aircraft, the point where descent for landing begins is pre-programmed into the computer. If, for some reason, pilots wanted to start the descent earlier than this point, then they found that the only way to accomplish this was to input false information relating to tail winds. It should not be beyond the bounds of ingenuity to design a system which would cater for all the pilots' requirements without the need to resort to such actions.

10.7 Conclusions

Computer-controlled systems are here to stay; we need to ensure that they are not accompanied by an increasing number of disasters and catastrophes. There has been unprecedented activity on all sides during the last few years, in line with the importance and magnitude of the issue and, as we have seen, progress has been made in a number of different directions involving both the systems themselves and those working on them. Nonetheless, it will probably be apparent that for many of the points discussed in this chapter, more questions are raised than answers provided and these are just some of the problems in relation to safety-related and safety-critical software that the professional organizations and practitioners working in the area are trying to resolve.

The activity in respect of standards continues apace and the time must be approaching when there will be workable standards which can be applied to such systems. Until this occurs, the best approach at present seems to be to concentrate on the appropriate research and development and for the professional bodies to disseminate the results as widely and as rapidly as possible. Despite the standards activity, many subjects need urgent consideration such as methods of quantification of reliability and assurance, improved design methods and software tools, comprehensive testing of safety systems and above all, new methods of assessing not just software safety but system safety. As experience of safety-related and safety-critical systems is still in its infancy, there is as yet insufficient knowledge available as to all the possible failure modes of such systems. If safety system fault reporting was a legal requirement in the same way as the reporting of certain other defined dangerous occurrences is mandatory[58], then the data generated could be analysed as to the reasons for the system failure.

Another area which is in need of clarification is the place of formal methods in the development of software for safety-critical systems. Some applications where formal methods are being used have been mentioned, but it is still a matter of contention between experts as to whether their use can be extended to other more complex safety-critical systems at the present time.

---

58. The Reporting of Injuries, Diseases and Dangerous Occurrences Regulations 1995 SI 1995 No 3163.

Certification or accreditation of software engineers engaged in the development of safety critical systems has been suggested. Although this would undoubtedly be a step forward, given the innovative nature of the subject, it is difficult, at present, to imagine how it could be implemented. However, such a step would undoubtedly be brought closer if agreement is reached on professional qualifications for safety-critical software engineering.

10.8 Further reading

There are a number of specialized texts which consider in more detail some of the topics raised in this chapter. P. Bennett (ed.), *Safety Aspects of Computer Control* (Butterworth-Heinemann, 1993), discusses a number of general issues involved in the development of safety-related computer systems, including legal liability and regulatory issues. Redmill & Anderson (eds), *Directions in Safety-Critical Systems* (Springer-Verlag 1993), is the 1993 proceedings of the Safety Critical Symposium and contains a collection of papers on more specific aspects of the subject.

N. G. Leveson, *Safeware: system safety and computers* (Addison-Wesley, 1995) considers both general risk and safety issues before considering the subject in the particular context of safety-related computer systems. The book concludes with case studies of some of the more high profile systems failures. P. G Neumann, *Computer related risks* (ACM Press, 1995) details a large number of anecdotal accounts involving software and network failures before moving on to a consideration of the implications of these for the software industry and society in general.

More specific discussion of the relationship between professional codes and competence in the safety context can be found in D. Rowland & J. J. Rowland, "Professional competence in safety-related software engineering" *Software Engineering Journal* **10**, 43–49, 1995, and in D. Rowland, "Negligence, professional competence and computer systems", *Journal of Information Law and Technology*, Part 2, 1999, http://www.law.warwick.ac.uk/jilt/99-2/rowland.html.

Chapter 11

Computer misuse and the criminal law

The media and popular computing press abound with tales of multi-million pound computer frauds and of the dangers to commercial companies, governmental data banks, financial institutions and national security from the activities of computer hackers; and of paedophiles peddling pornography over the Web. There is nothing like a good scare story or scandal to heighten the interest of the public, and if it involves a new technology which has the potential to intrude into everyone's lives, so much the better. But how common are crimes involving computers? Is the fear of computer crime greater than the actuality? And, most importantly in the present context, how does the law regulate crimes perpetrated with the aid of computing skills? Is the law in its present form adequate to control abuses perpetrated with the use of a computer, or should the law be reformed, and if so how?

11.1 Computing and criminal activity

It is questionable whether the evolution of the computer has spawned a wholly new group of persons engaging in criminal activity, who without the advent of the computer would have led law-abiding lives[1]. Like the motorcar, the computer merely presents new opportunities and new horizons to those who, in the absence of the technological advance, would probably still be criminally motivated[2]. Furthermore, given that statistics on crimes involving a computer must have started from a base of zero in the not too distant past, it is hardly surprising that there has been a sharp rise in the number of crimes involving computing; and the Internet has undoubtedly created new security risks[3].

---

1. This probably applies equally to compulsive teenage hackers, hacking for kicks: see, e.g. *R v Bedworth* (1993), discussed further below.
2. Those inclined to view pornography would previously probably have been purchasing it under the counter, rather than downloading it from the Net.
3. See the Audit Commission survey of 900 public and private sector organizations at www.audit-commission.gov.uk/ac2/NR/LocalA/prgitm.htm.

Surveys show that, as in other areas, such as mugging and sexual assault, the fear of the crime outstrips the actuality. Furthermore, they show that crimes in which a computer is involved more often than not involve relatively small sums, and are committed by dishonest employees and sub-contractors rather than by a stranger hacking into the system from the outside, all in sharp contrast to the picture portrayed in the press. But as usual, statistics should not be taken just at face value. There are undoubtedly many crimes and misuses of computing systems which are not reported to the authorities. Indeed to counteract this there have been calls to make it compulsory to report computer crimes. These calls are unlikely to be acted upon, however, for it is important to ensure uniformity within the criminal law, and there is no duty to report other crimes, even the most serious ones of offences against the person such as rape and murder (although of course it is an offence actually to hinder the police in the course of their enquiries).

11.2 Reform of the criminal law

There has been much debate in recent years about the extent to which the criminal law adequately controls the misuse of computers and about the need for reform. Some see the computer as such a wholly different entity that it should be regulated by a completely separate set of laws, and argue that there should be a special Computer Crimes Act. This has happened in the United States of America, following the model of Florida's Computer Crimes Act 1978[4]. This is probably not the best approach, however. Firstly, Acts of Parliament governing areas of high technology rapidly become out of date as the technology advances, and as Parliamentary time is limited, it would not be possible to amend the law each time a change was needed. Secondly, although computers do possess very special characteristics in their ability to store, manipulate and transmit data, in many ways they are just like other pieces of equipment and do not warrant separate treatment by the law. For example, a computer may be damaged when a building in which it is housed is blown up by a terrorist bomb. Why should the destruction of the computer be treated differently from the destruction of the office furniture or a safe containing money? A computer may be used as a weapon, for example it may be programmed to cause an explosion at a power plant in circumstances where the death or serious injury to the employees of the power company is a natural and probable consequence. Charges of murder or wounding might be appropriate here, and the presence of a computer is largely irrelevant, as the legal conclusion would not depend on the means by which the offences took place. Also, the ownership, sale and distribution of pornography

---

4. There are computer crime statutes in all but three states; and at Federal level there is the Computer Fraud and Abuse Act 1986.

is already regulated by the law, as illustrated by the conviction in 1999 of the pop singer Garry Glitter after he pleaded guilty to possessing thousands of pornographic photographs of children, which he had downloaded from the Internet onto the hard disc of his computer. Glitter was caught because he took his machine to PC World for repairs. The material was spotted by a member of staff, who reported the matter to the police[5]. Catching those who purvey pornography on the Web is often more difficult and may need international co-operation, collaboration between the police forces of different countries, and the creation of specialist units to tackle crime on the Internet[6]. Attempts to censor the Net, or to make Internet service providers liable for the contents of Web pages have generally failed. In the US, the Communications Decency Act, which attempted to censor on-line material, was struck down by the Supreme Court as being unconstitutional[7]; and in Germany, the head of Compuserve had his conviction for purveying child pornography overturned by the Bavarian High Court[8].

The best approach to the reform of the law is to look at the extent to which the existing criminal laws regulate the misuse of computers. If this reveals gaps in the law which need to be filled, the first stage should be to consider whether the gaps can be filled by amendment of existing laws, e.g. by changing definitions or the conditions on which they operate. If this is not feasible, only then should wholly new offences be created. This is essentially the approach which has been taken by the Law Commission and the Scottish Law Commission in their studies of the criminal laws of England and Wales, and of Scotland respectively. New criminal laws should not be enacted without careful consideration.

The Home Office has drawn up guidelines which it said should be kept in mind by successive governments in proposing to Parliament the creation of new criminal offences. Firstly the behaviour in question must be so serious that it goes beyond what can properly be dealt with on the basis of compensation as between one individual and another; and regulation should also be in the general public interest. Thus, if we take the example of deliberately causing death to a person, this is not regarded as just a matter for the family

---

5. See *Independent*, 13 November 1999.
6. It was reported in the *Independent* on 26 October 1999, that a new national police squad is to be set up in the UK to tackle the problem of crime on the Internet. The unit will investigate a range of activities including fraud, pornography, paedophilia, spreading racial hatred, counterfeiting, hacking, software piracy, money laundering and sabotage involving computer viruses. For an illustration of EU activities and concerns, see the Communication to the European Parliament, The Council, The Economic and Social Committee of the Regions on illegal and Harmful Content on the Internet, available at www2.echo.lu/legal/en/internet/communic/html.
7. *Reno v ACLU*, discussed, with appropriate links, at www.epic.org/eda.
8. See *Independent*, 18 November 1999.

of the deceased to sort out with the perpetrator of the act. It is a wrong against society, warranting the intervention of the state and thus of the criminal law. Secondly, criminal sanctions should be reserved for dealing with undesirable behaviour for which other, less drastic means of control would be ineffective, impracticable or insufficient. This helps to maintain public respect for the criminal law. Thirdly, the new offence should be enforceable. Thus, if for example it was proposed to make it a criminal offence to tape record broadcasts of television programmes for the purpose of private viewing at home, this law would probably fall foul of the second and the third points, as there would be little public respect for imposing the full rigours of the criminal law, and the offence would be largely unenforceable. If it is to be controlled at all, it is best regulated by the civil law. (The issue of home taping and breaches of the civil laws on copyright is considered in Chapter 6.)

One proposal which could have a considerable impact is the proposal by the Law Commission[9] for a new offence of corporate manslaughter, which would punish a company that, through the failure of its management, caused or contributed to a person's death, where that failure fell far below what could reasonably be expected of a company in those circumstances. As a result of this, a company which implemented a defective safety critical system, causing death, could well be found guilty of corporate manslaughter, rather than a regulatory offence under the Health and Safety At Work Acts. This new offence would overcome current difficulties with the prosecution of companies for death caused by their acts or omission and would create a whole new area of computer crime[10].

11.3 Categories of misuse

In their study of the English criminal law, the Law Commission[11] highlighted a number of categories of misuse of computers. These were:

(a) computer fraud;
(b) unauthorized obtaining of information from a computer, which they sub-categorized into the following:

- computer hacking;
- eavesdropping on a computer;
- making unauthorized use of computers for personal benefit;

---

9. Law Commission, *Legislating the criminal law: involuntary manslaughter* (1996), Law Com. No 237, paras 1.10-1.21.
10. *Encyclopaedia of information technology law*, Chapter 12.
11. Law Commission, Working Paper No. 110 (1988); and Law Commission, Report No. 186 (Cm 819)(1989).

(c) unauthorized alteration or destruction of information stored on a computer;

(d) denying access to an authorized user;

(e) the unauthorized removal of information stored on a computer.

We shall now look at each of these in turn in order to assess the extent to which they are regulated by English law.

11.4 Computer fraud

The Law Commission defined computer fraud as conduct which involves the manipulation of a computer, by whatever method, in order dishonestly to obtain money, property, or some other advantage of value, or to cause loss. Computer fraud had previously been studied by the Audit Commission[12] in their attempt to assess the extent of crime involving computers. They had sub-divided computer fraud into three categories which they called input frauds, output frauds, and program frauds.

An input fraud occurs where a person dishonestly enters false data into a computer, or dishonestly suppresses or amends data as it is keyed in. This was found by the Audit Commission to be by far the most common type of fraud identified by respondents to their survey. This type of activity is not very sophisticated and is merely a variant on the type of false accounting which occurs regularly outside the field of computing and should be identified by appropriate internal auditing procedures. It might involve the creation of accounts for "ghost employees" or the misuse of credit cards.

Input fraud is often followed by output fraud, which involves the suppression or alteration of data which emerges from a computer. Output fraud is often used to try to conceal an input fraud, although the two do not always go together. For example, an accounts clerk who has misappropriated funds will commit an output fraud by suppressing the computer balance reports in order to hide the discrepancies.

Program fraud involves the dishonest alteration of a computer program. In practice, the Audit Commission thought that few such frauds actually occur, presumably because this type of fraud involves greater computing skills, but, on the other hand, as a higher proportion of the community become familiar with programming, the incidence of these frauds could be expected to rise. Program fraud includes the so-called "salami-slicing" of accounts. This occurs when a program is written which automatically "slices" small amounts of money from a number of accounts and transfers them to another account created for the purpose.

---

12. Computer fraud.

The main offences currently covering computer fraud are theft, obtaining property by deception, false accounting and common law conspiracy to defraud. It is not proposed to go into these offences in detail, but a few examples should suffice to illustrate their coverage. For example, under section 1 of the Theft Act 1968, theft is committed if a person dishonestly appropriates property belonging to another with the intention of permanently depriving the other of it. Therefore, someone taking a bank card belonging to another, then typing into an automatic bank teller machine that other's PIN number in order to obtain cash, can be charged with theft of the money. A second possibility is a charge of obtaining pecuniary advantage by deception, contrary to Section 15 of the Theft Act. If two or more people are involved they could be charged under the common law offences of conspiracy to defraud or conspiracy to steal.

The problem which arises with conspiracy to defraud, as with other fraud offences, is whether a machine, as opposed to a human being, can be deceived in order to found a charge. In the case of *R v Moritz* (1981) (unreported) the judge decided that only a human mind could be deceived, and not a machine. The case involved the submission of false VAT returns to the Department of Customs and Excise. Because the processing of returns was computer assisted it was not possible to say that a human had been deceived. The Finance Act has since been amended so as to define "intent to deceive" in terms of an "intent to secure that a machine will respond to the document as if it were a true document", but this change in the definition has not been carried through into other areas of the criminal law, such as the Theft Act, and with the increasing use of computers the problem is likely to grow. In order to overcome the difficulty the Law Commission in their Working Paper suggested that the definition of "deception" should be amended to include "inducing a machine to respond to false representations which the person making them knows to be false, as if they were true". The later Report of the Law Commission returned to the issue after consultation with interested bodies, and reaffirmed the need to amend the law relating to fraud. But instead of making recommendations in that Report, the Commission promised to look at it again in the context of their on-going and wider ranging review of the law relating to fraud. Proposals for reform can therefore be expected in that other context at a later date.

Another difficulty is in identifying where and when the offence takes place. In *R v Thompson* [1984] 1 WLR 962, Thompson was a computer programmer employed by a bank in Kuwait. He identified five accounts that were both substantial and dormant, i.e. no transactions had been made using those accounts for a long time. He opened five other accounts in his own name at various branches of the bank and transferred money from the five dormant accounts into them. To avoid detection, the program executing the transfer was designed not to run until after he had left the bank's employment and was back in the UK. His intention was that the program would erase itself and all records of the transfers after executing. Once back in the UK, Thompson opened accounts in UK banks and then wrote to the Kuwaiti bank requesting that the money in the five Kuwaiti bank accounts be transferred to him in the UK. It was then that his fraud was discovered and he was charged in England with obtaining property by deception. The main question was where the offence had been committed and whether the English courts had jurisdiction. The English court held that the offence was committed when the sums of money were received by the UK banks and when Thompson obtained ownership, possession or control of the money; and even though a computer and an electronic transfer was involved, the court was able to apply ordinary principles of law.

11.5 Obtaining unauthorized access to a computer

The second form of misuse identified by the Law Commission was unauthorized obtaining of information from a computer. As already stated, they subdivided this into three particular abuses:

- computer hacking;
- eavesdropping on a computer;
- making unauthorized use of computers for personal benefit.

We shall look at each of these in turn.

11.5.1 Computer hacking

Prior to 1990, when the Computer Misuse Act was enacted, it was difficult to convict anyone of computer hacking. There were two main issues: firstly offences regulating the penetration of the computing system; and secondly offences which dealt with the alteration or destruction of data by someone who has already gained access. The former had been the subject of greatest controversy. We shall look first at regulation of hacking by traditional offences, then at the 1990 Act.

One of the main lines of attack on the unauthorized obtaining of access to a computer was the offence in Section 13 of the Theft Act 1968, namely the dishonest abstraction of electricity. Originally intended to control the by-passing of electric meters in order to avoid payment, it was used against hackers for, in the current state of the technology, the unauthorized use of a computer causes the consumption of electricity. One problem here is that it might be impossible to quantify the amount of electricity used by a hacker, and indeed the amount may well be exceedingly small. The artificiality of the charge was highlighted in the Hong Kong case of *R v Siu Tak Chee* (unreported). Here the defendant had hacked into an electronic mail box system. He was charged with abstracting electricity worth less than one eighth of a Hong Kong cent, under a Hong Kong statute which reflects the main elements of Section 13 of our Theft Act. However, in view of the small amount of electricity involved, the magistrate said that no prosecution should have been brought. He discharged the defendant unconditionally and ordered that no conviction be recorded. In a case such as this, a prosecution is arguably an abuse of the criminal process and a waste of public money. It certainly does little to maintain the respect of the public in the criminal process and merely highlights the artificiality of the law, when no more appropriate charge can be brought.

Other traditional offences which may be relevant to someone who obtains unauthorized access to a computer, concern the misuse of the public telecommunications networks contrary to the Telecommunications Act 1984 and the Interception of Communications Act 1985. However, if a system other than a public system is involved, e.g. a private area network, no offences will be committed; and the 1985 Act will rarely apply because hackers generally initiate and receive communications, rather than intercept them, and it is only intentional interception which is covered by that Act. These offences were clearly inadequate to control computer hacking.

11.5.2 Computer Misuse Act 1990

The Computer Misuse Act 1990 enshrines proposals made in the Report of the Law Commission, a document produced after extensive consultation with interested bodies on proposals made in the Law Commission's Working Paper. In their Report, the Law Commission recommended the creation of three new offences, two relating to hacking, and a third concerning the unauthorized modification of data. We shall look at the latter when we consider the issue of criminal damage. For the moment we shall concentrate solely on the offences relating to hacking.

The first offence, called the basic offence, makes it an offence to obtain unauthorized access to computer material. Under Section 1 of the 1990 Act, a person will be guilty of an offence if:

(a) he causes a computer to perform any function with intent to secure access to any program or data held in any computer;
(b) the access he intends to secure is unauthorized;
(c) he knows at the time when he causes the computer to perform the function that that is the case.

It does not matter that the hacker is not aiming at particular programs or data; or at programs or data of a particular kind; or indeed at programs or data held in any particular computer.

The main purpose of Section 1 is to deter hackers. Unlike Section 2 (below) it does not require proof of an intention to commit a further crime and can be triggered by all forms of unauthorized access including "browsing" or "probing" a computer system. The offence is punishable with a maximum of six months' imprisonment or a fine of up to £5,000. It is the most likely vehicle for prosecution of the "benign hacker". Prosecutions are, however, likely to be few and far between. It will be difficult to identify hackers and juries seem reluctant to convict. For example, in *R v Bedworth*[13], Bedworth's hacking activities started when he was given a computer for his fourteenth birthday. By the time he was eighteen, he had hacked into an impressive array of computer systems. He was charged with computer hacking, contrary to Section 1 of the 1990 Act. His defence was that he was obsessed and unable to stop even though he knew what he was doing was wrong. Surprisingly, the jury acquitted him. It is doubtful, however, if a jury would be quite so understanding if his addiction was to smashing car windscreens.

The Court of Appeal in *R v Cropp*[14], confirmed that Section 1 applies to insiders who access computers, as well as to remote hackers, but the Act itself prevents criminalization of employees who out of carelessness or inattention obtain access to part of an employer's data or computer system without permission, or who inadvertently step outside the scope of their authority to use the system. A person will only be guilty of the offence if the intention was to try to gain access, knowing at the time of so doing that the access was unauthorized. The employee who is careless or inadvertent is more appropriately dealt with by disciplinary procedures at the workplace than by the criminal law. Furthermore it was confirmed in *R v Bignall*[15] that an employee who has authorized access, but who uses the information obtained for an improper purpose, is not guilty of an offence under Section 1, but is more appropriately dealt with by internal disciplinary procedures or, may be liable for prosecution under the Data Protection Act[16].

Persons who supply information useful to a hacker, such as a password, can be guilty of an offence under Section 44(1) of the Magistrates Courts Act 1980, if they know or deliberately close their minds to the fact that it might be used to gain unauthorized access to material held in a computer. This will catch, for example, persons putting information onto a hackers' bulletin board.

The second offence is more serious. Section 2 of the Computer Misuse Act makes it an offence to commit the basic unauthorized access offence outlined above, but with the intent to commit or facilitate the commission of a serious crime. It does not matter whether the further offence would involve the use of a computer or not; nor whether the further offence is in fact committed; nor even whether it is possible to commit the further offence (e.g. where the intended victim is already dead). The Law Commission in their Report gave the exam-

13. *R v Bedworth* (1993) (unreported), Southwark Crown Court.
14. *Times*, June 1992.
15. [1998] 1 Criminal Appeal Reports 1.
16. See further Chapter 12.

ple of a person who hacks into a computer in order to obtain confidential and personal information which he intends to use in order to blackmail someone. Another example might be access to a computer in order to alter data affecting the safety of a system with the intent to cause death or physical injury to another, or knowing that death or physical harm are natural and probable consequences. The seriousness of this offence is reflected in the maximum penalty which is five years imprisonment. Obviously, if the other serious offence referred to is committed, e.g. the blackmail or the murder, those offences will also attract the appropriate penalty, but the aim of the hacking offence is to catch someone in the early stages of the offence, perhaps before other laws on criminal attempts are able to bite.

11.5.3 Eavesdropping

Eavesdropping involves secret listening or watching. The name originally described those who stood outside a building, spying on its occupants, and who, presumably before the introduction of guttering, became wet from the dripping of water from the eaves. This is a far cry from those who now sit in vans containing electronic gadgetry outside the offices of commercial firms monitoring their computer screens, but the aim is the same, namely the acquisition of information.

English law does not yet recognize a general right to privacy (cf. US law)[17], and in the absence of burglary, damage to property or injury to the person, no criminal offence may be committed by surveillance by electronic or other means. This gap in the law is a cause for concern, but the concern goes wider than the issue merely of eavesdropping on computers, and arguably it would be wrong to regulate by the criminal law only this small aspect of the much larger problem. The Law Commission therefore made no proposals to reform the law relating to this particular aspect of computer misuse. They noted that at present it is not possible, except in the most favourable conditions and using sophisticated and expensive equipment, to listen effectively to emissions of electronic information from VDU screens, which is the typical case of electronic eavesdropping. But, as the technical position might alter, they said that it was worth keeping the position under review.

11.5.4 Unauthorized use of a computer for personal benefit

The Law Commission also made no specific recommendations for reform of the law concerning the unauthorized use of computers for personal benefit as such, although unauthorized access to computer material (which will of

---

17. The law will change when the Human Rights Act 1998 comes into force. This Act gives effect to the European Convention on Human Rights.

course be involved in unauthorized use) is covered by Section 1 of the 1990 Act (above). Most people who misuse computers for personal benefit are already in some form of legal relationship with the owner of the computer. They are often employees who have access for an authorized purpose, but who step outside that authority, for example in order to do private work. Here the most appropriate sanctions are the usual disciplinary ones under the contract of employment, and applying the full rigours of the criminal law might be like using a sledge-hammer to crack a nut, unless of course pecuniary advantage has been obtained by deception, or persons have been injured, in which case ordinary criminal offences will apply; and if the employee puts personal data about others (e.g. a club membership list) onto a computer belonging to an employer, there may be a breach of the Data Protection Act (see further Chapter 12).

In general, the unauthorized use of property belonging to another is not a criminal offence, unless the other is thereby permanently deprived of the thing, contrary to Section 1 of the Theft Act 1968. If A borrows B's lawn-mower in order to mow A's lawn, and returns it afterwards, no offence is committed. Borrowing does not amount to permanent deprivation and thus to theft. This can be illustrated by the case of *R v Lloyd* [1985] QB 829, where a film projectionist clandestinely removed films from the cinema for others to make pirate copies, with the result that the commercial value of the originals was diminished. An initial conviction for conspiracy to commit theft was quashed by the Court of Appeal, which held that there was no permanent deprivation of property in this case, for borrowing did not amount to permanent deprivation unless the property was returned in such a changed state that it had lost all practical value. This was not the case here, for the films could still be shown to the public at the advertised times.

If we apply this to computers or computing facilities, there is unlikely to be any permanent deprivation of property, unless discs or tapes are permanently removed, damaged or destroyed; and it is a question of fact whether any property which has been borrowed is returned in such a changed state that it has lost all practical value. Once again therefore, the unauthorized use of a computer is not a special issue, and it would be artificial to make changes solely in this area.

11.6 Unauthorized alteration or destruction of information

One of the main reasons for the growth in the use of computers is their ability to store, yet make readily accessible, very large amounts of data. However this has given rise to concomitant fears for the security of data, and to calls for appropriate sanctions against those who destroy or alter data without authorization. Two criminal offences currently cover this form of abuse: criminal damage and Section 3 of the Computer Misuse Act 1990.

11.6.1 Criminal damage

In *Cox v Riley* (1986) 83 Cr. App. R. 54, the defendant, a disgruntled employee, erased programs from a plastic circuit card which was used to run a computer-operated circular saw. He was charged, and convicted of criminal damage. Under the Criminal Damage Act 1971, a person commits criminal damage if he intentionally or recklessly destroys or damages property belonging to another without lawful excuse. The main issue in the case was whether erasing a program from a printed circuit card could constitute damage to property within the meaning of the Act, given that Section 10 of the Act defines property as "property of a tangible nature". The Court held that there was damage to property in this case, as the card itself had been damaged and it would require time and effort to restore it to its original condition by reprogramming. It should be noted, however, that the emphasis in *Cox v Riley* was on damage to physical property i.e. to the card, and not on the damage to or destruction of the information itself. Damage to something which is purely intangible will probably not form the basis for a charge of criminal damage. Thus, causing a break in the power supply in order deliberately to cause loss of information on a computer screen which has not been stored on any physical medium would not be criminal activity under the Criminal Damage Act, but inserting a virus or logic bomb into a program so as to cause loss of data stored on disc may well be covered.

11.6.2 Unauthorized modification of computer material

The Law Commission were not happy with the outcome of *Cox v Riley* in terms of the protection that that case afforded to computerized data. They therefore recommended the creation of a new offence, which now forms Section 3 of the Computer Misuse Act 1990. This provides that:

(1) A person is guilty of an offence if:
  (a) he does any act which causes unauthorized modification of the contents of a computer; and
  (b) at the time when he does the act he has the requisite intent and the requisite knowledge.

The requisite intent is an intent to cause a modification of the contents of any computer and by so doing:

1. to impair the operation of any computer; or
2. to prevent or hinder access to any program or data held in any computer; or
3. to impair the operation of any such program or the reliability of any such data.

The intent need not be directed at any particular computer; or at any particular program or data; or at a program or data of a particular kind.

The requisite knowledge referred to in Section 3(1)(b) above is knowledge that any modification he intends to cause is unauthorized.

As the Law Commission state in paragraph 3.65 of their Report, this offence is intended to cover several forms of conduct, the most important of which are:

- what might be called "simple" unauthorized modification, where a person intentionally and without authorization electronically erases or wipes clean programs or data contained in a computer's memory or on a storage medium, such as a disc or tape. The Law Commission specifically point out that the offence is not designed to cover physical damage to the computer or discs etc. which would remain within the general law of criminal damage;
- putting into circulation floppy discs which are "infected" with a virus, intending that that disc will cause some person somewhere to suffer a modification that will impair the operation of the person's computer;
- the unauthorized addition of a virus or worm to a computer's "library" of programs, intending thereby to impair the operation of the computer simply by using up its capacity;
- the unauthorized addition of a password to a data file, thereby rendering that data inaccessible to anyone who does not know the password.

It will also cover the case of a computer programmer who inserts a time bomb into a program which he has written, with the intention that the program will cease to run on a particular date, e.g. if he has not been paid for his work by that date; or the terms of a licence to operate his software have not been agreed by that date.

11.6.3 Forgery

The unauthorized alteration or destruction of data stored on a computer may also amount to forgery. Under Section 1 of the Forgery and Counterfeiting Act 1981,

> A person is guilty of forgery if he makes a false instrument, with the intention that he or another shall use it to induce somebody to accept it as genuine, and by reason of so accepting it, to do or not to do some act to his own or any other person's detriment.

Much will depend on whether a false instrument has been created. An instrument is defined in Section 8, most of which deals with written documents, but more importantly in the present context, an instrument can also be "any disc, tape, sound-track or other device on or in which information is recorded or stored by mechanical, electronic or other means". The key elements in this part of the definition are that information must be "recorded or stored", and it follows from the case of *R v Shifreen and Gold* [1988] AC 1063, that in order to be recorded or stored for the purposes of the Act, the information must firstly be held for an appreciable time and secondly it must be held with the object of subsequent retrieval or recovery.

In *R v Shifreen and Gold*, the defendants hacked into British Telecom's Prestel computer, using, without authorization, passwords which had been allocated to others. Typing in the passwords was alleged to amount to the making of a forged instrument. However, the problem was that the passwords were held only momentarily by the computer in order to check them as having been issued and not cancelled. As soon as this was verified, it allowed the hackers into another segment of the system and deleted the password from the first-mentioned part of its memory. Thus the passwords which the defendants had typed in were held for only a very short amount of time and not for the purpose of subsequent retrieval or recovery, and the prosecution failed. The Courts clearly did not regret this conclusion. Lord Brandon, giving judgement in the House of Lords, cited with approval the view of Lord Lane voiced in the Court of Appeal, that a prosecution on the facts of this case involved "a Procrustean attempt to force the facts . . . into the language of an Act not designed to fit them". The case does not, however, prevent the use of the statute in more appropriate circumstances, for example where an employee engaging in an input fraud alters computerized records.

11.7 Denying access to an authorized user

This can be illustrated by the Canadian case of *Re Turner* 13 CCC (3d) 430 (1984). Here, the defendants in Canada had accessed a data bank in America by telephone, and had spent ten and a half hours extracting and encoding accounts programs held in the data bank on behalf of two American companies. As a result of their activities, the two American companies could not access their data, as they did not know the key to the code. The defendants were charged with mischief, contrary to Section 387(1)(d) of the Canadian Criminal Code, which provides that a person commits mischief if he wilfully "obstructs, interrupts or interferes with any person in the lawful use, enjoyment or operation of property." It was argued by counsel that a prosecution under this provision must fail for there had been no damage to the tapes on which the information had been stored: the information stored on the tapes had merely been rearranged. The judge held that there was no need for damage to physical property in order to found a charge of mischief under the Canadian Criminal Code, for interference with enjoyment was sufficient, and this was established here, as on the facts of the case, the American companies were prevented from using their accounting records because they were unable to break the code.

English law has no general mischief offence along the lines of Section 387 of the Canadian Criminal Code, but the conduct illustrated by *Re Turner* falls within Section 3 of the Computer Misuse Act (above) as it involves the unauthorized modification of computer material. A charge of criminal damage might also succeed. In *Cox v Riley* (above), the fact that the owners of the printed circuit card had to spend time and money reprogramming the card was an important factor in finding that the card itself had been damaged. Thus, as the companies whose records had been encoded in *Turner* would have to spend time and money in trying to break the code, or in negotiating with the encoders in order to acquire the key to the code, a similar charge may lie.

Other examples of the denial of access to an authorized user can be given. A legitimate user might deliberately be denied access to a computer if all terminals or other means of access were being used by unauthorized users. Here offences such as abstraction of electricity, obtaining services or pecuniary advantage by deception, and improper use of a public telecommunications service and the new hacking offences might be applied to combat the abuse. The authorized user might also be denied access because an unauthorized person had tried to gain access to the system, but in so doing had triggered some security mechanism which had shut down the system. The basic offence in Section 1 of the Computer Misuse Act of unauthorized access to a computer would be relevant here; as might the offence in Section 2, but only if the hacker had the intention to commit or assist in the commission of a further more serious offence; and a charge might be brought under Section 3 for unauthorized modification of computer material, so long as there was the requisite intent and the requisite knowledge, as described above.

11.8 Unauthorized removal of information stored on a computer

This form of abuse may be controlled by the new offences in the Computer Misuse Act 1990, discussed above. They often apply, for in order to remove information stored on a computer it will be necessary to access the computer first. This is not the case of course if the information is stored, e.g. on a disc separate from the computer. The Law Commission in their formulation of the offences now in the 1990 Act referred specifically to unauthorized access to programs or data held in a computer, thereby excluding externally stored material. But there is a more fundamental issue at stake here, for the reforms also do not address the central question of the legal protection afforded to information as a commodity in its own right, i.e. aside from the protection of the medium on or in which it is stored, and, in particular, they do not address the question of whether the taking or misappropriation of information is theft, or is covered by some related crime, or whether some new offence should be created to cover gaps in the present law. We shall now look at some cases in order to illustrate the difficulties.

In *Oxford v Moss* (1979) 68 Cr. App. R. 183, an undergraduate improperly obtained the proof of an examination paper before the examination was held. He read the paper and then returned it, retaining the information for his own use. He was charged with theft, but was acquitted. Two reasons were given: firstly, for the purposes of the Theft Act 1968, information is not property, and only property can be stolen; and secondly, the university had not been permanently deprived of the tangible asset which had been taken, namely the piece of paper, and as we saw earlier, borrowing does not amount to theft. *Oxford v Moss* was followed in *R v Absolom* (*The Times*, 14th September 1983), where a geologist was acquitted on a charge of theft after he had obtained, and tried to sell to a rival company, details of Esso Petroleum's oil exploration off the Irish coast, information which was valued in evidence as worth between £50,000 and £100,000.

The problem which arose in these two cases was that in neither *Oxford v Moss* nor *R v Absolom* was the owner of the information permanently deprived of a tangible asset, such as a piece of paper. If this had been the case there could have been a successful prosecution for theft of that asset. But again the emphasis of the law was on the tangible asset, such as the storage medium. Information in itself is not protected by the law relating to theft, which concentrates on the nineteenth century notions of property and has not been adapted to protect the valuable intangible commodities of the computer age.

Should the unauthorized taking of information be a criminal offence? If I am sitting on a train, reading a draft of this chapter of the book, just having written it and before submitting it for publication, should I be able to request the prosecution of the person sitting next to me who also reads the draft over my shoulder and without my consent? What if the person sitting next to me on the train is a spy, who is reading a confidential memorandum on my company's secret processes? What if I am not in a public place, but sitting in my office reading information on a computer screen, and a spy is sitting outside in a van viewing the information on my screen using equipment for eavesdropping? As *Oxford v Moss* and *R v Absolom* show, in English law the misappropriation of information, without more, does not amount to theft.

Other jurisdictions view the issue differently. In the United States, the misappropriation of a trade secret is a criminal offence in at least 27 states; and in Canada, there have been proposals for reform. In the view of the present authors, English law should also be reformed. The Law Commission considered the matter but initially said that as the issue was a general one, not of concern solely in the area of computing, it was not for them on that occasion to make suggestions for reform.

There are various ways in which the criminal laws could be amended. One would be to amend the definition of property in the Theft Act, so that it encompasses either information generally, or specified categories of information, such as confidential information. But information is not property in the sense in which this term is used in law, which defines it very much in line with physical attributes which are just not appropriate to intangibles such as information. To amend the definition of property so as to include information, or even confidential information, would cause distortion of the concept and cause unnecessary complication. This issue was considered by the Supreme Court of Canada in *R v Stewart* (1988) 50 DLR (4d) 1, where the defendant was charged with counselling theft of confidential information. The Supreme Court, quite rightly in our view, refused to hold that confidential information was property, thus upholding the arguments put forward in the English cases of *Oxford v Moss* and *R v Absolom*, and quashing the conviction.

A second and preferable course for reform of the law would be to produce a custom-built offence circumscribing the misappropriation of those classes of information which it was felt deserved the protection of the law. This has already been done by the Official Secrets Acts in relation to governmental information and the Law Commission have now proposed that there should be a new offence relating to the misuse of a trade secret[18]. It is to be hoped that legislation will be forthcoming in the not too distant future.

11.9 Further reading

The Law Commission's working paper and its later report discuss the various practical problems of computer misuse, the extent to which they are currently controlled by the law, and make suggestion for reform. These documents are, however, written by lawyers for lawyers and they presume knowledge of law, but little detailed knowledge of computing. They should however provide useful background material.

>   Law Commission Working Paper Number 110, *Computer misuse* (HMSO, 1988).
>   Law Commission Report Number 186, *Criminal law: computer misuse*. Cm 819 (HMSO, 1989).

See also:

>   C. Reed (ed.), *Computer law*, 4th edn. (Blackstone Press, 2000), Ch. 8.
>   D. Rowland & E. Macdonald, *Information technology law*, (Cavendish Publishing, 1997), Ch. 8.

---

18. Law Commission Consultation Paper No. 150, *Legislating the criminal law: misuse of trade secrets, a consultation paper*, available at www.gtnet.gov.uk/lawcomm/homepage.htm.

Chapter 12

Regulation and control of personal information
Data protection, defamation and related issues

12.1 Introduction

At the end of the twentieth century there can be very few people who remain unaware of the dramatic impact which increasing computerization has had on the storage, processing, retention and release of information and data. Computerization has revolutionized the handling and processing of information to such an extent that the data itself has now become a commodity which possesses commercial value and can be traded on the market in the same way as any other commodity. The value to businesses is also enhanced by the fact that data can be transferred around the globe with great ease. On the other hand, increasing use of the Internet, predicted to have up to 200 million users over the next few years, drawn from both academic and commercial sectors, has resulted in a profligate transfer of personal data which may or may not be for commercial purposes. As with all technological advances, the benefits may be many but there will, inevitably, be potential for abuse. It is difficult to estimate how much of the data which is constantly and routinely being transferred around the world by means of global computer networks is of a personal nature. In 1988 it was estimated at only c. 2–5 per cent of all trans-border data flows[1], but it seems likely that, given the explosion in the use of this medium, the proportion may have increased. In any event, given the massive total of on-line information available, this still gives rise to fears of the abuse and misuse of data which could involve invasions of privacy, use of the data for unauthorized and unexpected purposes and so on. Where false information is communicated about a person this could also lead to the possibility of an action in defamation (see Section 12.7 *et seq.*).

Whoever we are, whatever our status, age or calling, it is likely that there will be many organizations and businesses who hold data on us. This may be for central government reasons such as the issue of passports, driving licences

---

1. M. Briat in P. Hansen *et al. Freedom of data flows and EEC law* (Kluwer International, 1988) – although the criteria on which the assessment was based was not made clear.

or eligibility for benefits, for local government reasons such as council tax administration or educational reasons, for reasons related to employment, health care, banking and finance, mail order and marketing etc[2]. Prior to the widespread use of computers for manipulating information, information which was held on persons was kept in manual files which were only likely to be accessed occasionally by the user, except in exceptional circumstances. In addition, there was unlikely to be any correlation of the information held by various people and organizations on particular individuals. The advent of computers has changed all this. In particular, it has made the correlation of data held by different people, in different places, for different purposes a practical reality and there is the consequent apprehension that the whole picture may appear greater than the sum of the parts. It is perhaps worth noting at the outset though that the technology is not, of itself, the cause of the problems. Whether or not privacy is invaded or is perceived to have been invaded is an issue for people not computers. Personal data has been collected and held for a multitude of purposes throughout history with the consequent possibility of inappropriate or unauthorized use or disclosure. To quote Earl Ferrers, "(T)he collection of personal data is as old as society itself. It may not be the oldest profession but it is one of the oldest habits"[3]. A number of strands of concern emerge – the potential for abuse of organizational records, the incidental and often unwitting transfer of personal data. It is the issues raised by these factors which will form the subject matter of this chapter.

Such potential for abuse raises issues about the correct way to respond to the problem and whether the solution should be located in the realms of law, politics or management or a combination of these[4]. A common response amongst those who have such concerns is to lobby for or pass legislation and this has been the preferred option in many jurisdictions faced with the threats posed to individuals' privacy by data mismanagement. The United States stands in isolation on this as being the only major jurisdiction with no generic data protection legislation (although that is not to say that the area is entirely unregulated) and with major actors still unconvinced of the need for such a step[5]. On the other hand, in Europe, Directive 95/46/EC (see Section 12.6 *et seq.*) could be regarded as setting a standard for good information practices

---

2. See also Lord Hoffman in *R v Brown* [1996] 1 All ER 545 at 555 and Lord Williams of Mostyn *Hansard* HL Vol. 585 Col. 436 2 February 1998.
3. Earl Ferrers, House of Lords, *Hansard* HL Vol. 549 Col. 37 11 October 1993.
4. This chapter will focus, for the most part, on legal responses – for sociological and political implications see, e.g. C. Raab, "The governance of data protection", in *Modern governance*, J. Kooiman (ed.) (London: Sage, 1993) pp. 89–103.
5. A report on Internet Privacy by the Federal Trade Commission requested by the US Congress in 1998 and published on 13 July 1999 suggested that "legislation to address on-line privacy is not appropriate at the present time"; see http://www.ftc.gov/os/1999/9907/pt071399.htm.

and requiring the relevant states to incorporate this into their national legal systems. In the presence of legitimate concerns about potential invasions of privacy and the need to balance both the rights of the data subject and the data user/holder, it is worth considering also some of the characteristics of different regulatory schemes and these are discussed in Section 12.4.

12.2 Data protection and privacy

The discussion thus far has tacitly assumed that the reader is aware of what is meant by data protection and its relationship and interrelationship with the concept of privacy – a term even more elusive of definition[6]. Since the first formulation of best practice at the beginning of the 1980s, many of the existing guidelines seem to either assume a connection or appear to use the terms interchangeably. Thus the Council of Europe Convention ... whose declared object is to "strengthen data protection" then sets out in article 1 that the purpose of the Convention is to "secure [the] right to privacy with regard to automatic processing of data". On the other hand the preface to the Organization for Economic Co-operation and Development (OECD) guidelines suggests that the guidelines are necessary to help "harmonize national privacy legislation" and only introduces the phrase "data protection" in the explanatory memorandum on the grounds that it is a recognized term in European jurisdictions. More recently, article 1 of the Data Protection Directive 1995[7] sets out the objective of the directive as being to "protect ... [the] right to privacy ... ".

Such an apparently close relationship between data protection and privacy seems to have created a stumbling block in the legislative consciousness of the UK because of the lack of legal protection for privacy *per se* in this jurisdiction. There is protection for what could be viewed as particular facets of privacy (an example is the action for defamation for the protection of reputation discussed in Section 12.7 *et seq.*) but privacy has not otherwise been a legally recognized concept. Historically, this can be explained, in part, of course, by the lack of a written constitution and declared Bill of Rights, although the existence of such instruments does not, of itself, guarantee privacy protection[8]. Thus the situation with regard to privacy protection in the

---

6. The seminal article on privacy remains S. Warren & L. Brandeis, *The right to privacy* (1890) 4 Harv L Rev 193. See also, e.g. A. Westin, *Privacy and freedom* (Bodley Head, 1967) R. Wacks, *Personal information: privacy and the Law* (Clarendon, 1993). For an accessible article in the context of the present discussion, see F. G. B. Aldhouse, *Data protection, privacy and the media* (1999) 4 Comm L 18.

7. Directive 95/46/EC. See Section 12.6.2.

8. This situation may be different in the future in the UK with the enactment of the Human Rights Act 1998 to incorporate the European Convention on Human Rights. At the time of writing this statute is not yet in force.

United States, a country with a strong constitutional tradition has been likened to a patchwork quilt[9] and, as Bennett has pointed out "(T)he approach to making privacy policy in the US is reactive rather than anticipatory, incremental rather than comprehensive, and fragmented rather than coherent. There may be a lot of laws but there is not much protection"[10]. In the UK there has been resistance to the notion of a "privacy law", as such, and a particular anathema to the thought of "privacy legislation by the back door" which is one slant on data protection. Hence Viscount Astor's comment during the second reading of the Data Protection Bill that "(W)e need to protect the rights of individuals to privacy but we do not want a back door privacy law"[11]. Consequently there have been a number of attempts to divorce the twin concepts of data protection and privacy notwithstanding the fact that, as the earlier discussion suggests, they can otherwise be regarded as closely related. Although one of the antecedents of the data protection legislation in the UK, the Report of the Younger Committee on Privacy[12], conceded that increasing computerization could threaten privacy, the subsequent report of the Lindop Committee on Data Protection[13] attempted to distinguish the two whilst at the same time agreeing that data protection could perhaps be equated with "information privacy". Interestingly, it appears that the notion of data protection is a European invention and US commentators appear to give no significance to possible nuances of meaning. Thus Cavoukian and Tapscott merely remark "Privacy or data protection as it is called in Europe ..."[14], while Gellman suggests with rather more detail and precision that data protection is "a useful European term referring to rules about the collection, use and dissemination of personal information. This is an important subset of privacy law"[15].

The extent to which the Data Protection Act 1984 protected privacy is debatable[16] but, nonetheless, judicial comment and interpretation of that statute has acknowledged the link between the two. In a case which was appealed to the House of Lords, Lord Hoffman said[17]:

---

9. R. Gellman, "Does privacy law work?", in P. E. Agre & M. Rotenberg (eds) *Technology and privacy: the new landscape* (Cambridge Mass.: MIT Press, 1997).

10. C. J. Bennett, "Convergence revisited: towards a global policy on the protection of personal data?", in P. E. Agre & M. Rotenberg (eds) *Technology and privacy: the new landscape* (Cambridge Mass.: MIT Press, 1997) p. 113.

11.. *Hansard* HL Vol. 585 Col. 445 2 February 1998.

12. *Report of the Committee on Privacy*, Cmnd 5012 (HMSO, 1972).

13. Cmnd 7341 (HMSO, 1978) paras 2.03–2.07

14. A. Cavoukian & D. Tapscott, *Who knows. Safeguarding your privacy in a networked world* (New York: McGraw-Hill, 1997) p. 179.

15. *Op cit*, p. 194.

16. See Section 12.6.1 below and D. Rowland and E. Macdonald *Information Technology Law* Cavendish 1997 pp 297–301.

17. *R v Brown* [1996] 1 All ER 545 at 555. See also later discussion in Section 12.6.1.

> English common law does not know a general right of privacy and
> Parliament has been reluctant to enact one. But there has been some
> legislation to deal with particular aspects of the problem. The Data
> Protection Act 1984, with which this appeal is concerned, is one such
> statute.

and in a recent decision of the Data Protection Tribunal it was said that
"(A)n underlying purpose of the data protection principles is to protect
privacy with respect to the processing of personal data"[18] – a verbatim
quote from article 1 of the Data Protection Directive. Further, both holders
of the post of Data Protection Registrar to date have viewed their role as
primarily one of protecting individuals' rights. In 1994, the first Data
Protection Registrar, Eric Howe, said in his final report: "... data protection
legislation is about the protection of individuals rather than the regulation of
industry. It is civil rights legislation rather than technical business legislation"[19], a declaration which might have seemed almost heretical in 1984. His
successor, Elizabeth France, has never denied, indeed has actively espoused,
the link between data protection and privacy and has formulated the following mission statement: "(W)e shall promote respect for the private lives of
individuals and in particular for the privacy of their information by: implementing the Data Protection Acts, influencing national and international
thinking on privacy and personal information"[20].

The matter might have been finally resolved with the implementation in
the UK of the EC Directive on data protection but, notwithstanding the
tenor of article 1 of that directive, the Data Protection Act 1998 never actually makes mention of the word "privacy" and it is clear from a number of
debates in Parliament during the passage of the legislation that the connection between data protection and privacy is not accepted by all sides of the
debate. Interestingly enough, Lord Wakeham who has been a vigorous opponent of "back door" privacy legislation in the context of the Human Rights
Bill[21] felt that "... the Data Protection Bill does not introduce a back-door
privacy regime. it is entirely in line with the Government's stated commitment to self-regulation and their opposition to a privacy law". It is a moot
point whether the absence of the word "privacy" from the Bill (and subsequent Act) had any bearing on this view.

---

18. *British Gas Trading Ltd v Data Protection Registrar* (1998), see Appendix 6, *14th Annual Report of
    the Data Protection* (HMSO, 1998) available at http://www.open.gov.uk/dpr.
19. *Tenth Annual Report of the Data Protection Registrar* (HMSO, 1994).
20. See http://www.open.gov.uk/dpr.
21. See, e.g. *Hansard* HL Vol. 583 Cols 771–4, 24 November 1997.

12.3 The impact of the Internet

The original challenge of data protection law was to provide a suitable mechanism for dealing with the perceived threat to individual privacy of large centralized data banks and with abuses of information management made possible by techniques such as data matching. This was very much in the context of the increasing storage, manipulation and correlation of personal data by large organizations whether public or private[22]. In contrast, in the 1990s and beyond, it is the individual's personal interactive use of the advantages of global networks which pose the major challenge for the law on data protection. It has been suggested that "(T)he development of global information networks has changed and intensified the character of the privacy protection problem"[23]. The question which is inevitably being asked is whether the original formulation of data protection law is capable of controlling the amorphous decentralized activities which occur through the medium of the Internet and World Wide Web. In contrast to the situation for which data protection law was developed, this medium has no identifiable "data controller" in whom responsibility for safeguarding privacy can be invested.

Of particular concern is the traceability of operations performed via on-line services together with a lack of general principles relating to the dissemination of information and protection of personal privacy[24]. One central feature of the development of global networks such as the Internet is that a number of common features such as the ability to leave "navigation trails", the existence of privileged websites, the use of "cookies" to capture and retain information about users and so on may effectively replicate other data matching processes. The possibility of retaining and collating trace information from successive Web searches may prove very useful for personal profiling purposes. In addition, it is possible that access/service providers may hold personal details about their clients, transactional information such as the types of site visited, connection times etc., and even, perhaps, the content of private communications such as e-mail.

Although it was originally developed in the context of military and defence use, once adopted for civilian purposes, the initial ethos of the Internet was centred in ideals of free speech and empowerment of the individual. To a large extent this is still evident amongst users – a feature of the Internet being open accessibility, multiple use and multiple users. However, since the poten-

---

22. Indeed the threat was seen in many jurisdictions to emanate primarily from branches of government rather than from the commercial sector and in some countries data protection only applied to the public sector.
23. Bennett, *op cit.*, p. 103.
24. See further *On-line services and data protection and the protection of privacy*, vol. 1, Annex to Annual Report 1998 of the Working Party established by art. 29 of Directive 95/46/EC (EC Commission, 1999).

tial for marketing on-line has been realized by the business world there may be a tendency for network users to be at the mercy of "operators whose commercial objectives run counter to the "community" spirit of the network pioneers"[25] as the Net/Web is hijacked from a collective information forum to a free market place.

A further issue, as in many other branches of information technology law, is that of jurisdiction. Where the issue is one of correlation of personal data between organizations within the same jurisdiction, this may be dealt with appropriately by existing data protection legislation. The fact that data protection legislation usually contains provisions prohibiting trans-border data flow under certain conditions may also be useful in situations where the organizations are in different jurisdictions. However this situation is far more complex in relation to the Internet for which the accepted geographical concepts of jurisdiction become meaningless.

12.4 Factors influencing the regulation of data processing

From the European or UK perspective, it is easy not to question the use of conventional legal devices to regulate this area. Legislation imposing sanctions backed up by action in courts and tribunals has, for a number of reasons, been the method chosen or imposed on these jurisdictions. This does not, however, mean that it is the only available mechanism for regulation of such activities and the fact that a major power such as the US relies heavily not on statutory intervention but on self-regulation should, at least, give some food for thought. How should or can data processing be regulated? There is by no means a straightforward answer to this question, complicated as the issues are by rapidly advancing technology, the global nature of the activities to be regulated and the variety of possible regulatory approaches to be found in the various legal traditions within the world. As pointed out succinctly by Raab:

> Formidable problems of policy and implementation are presented by the attempt to regulate systems and practices that are technologically advanced, widely dispersed, rapidly changing and employed by powerful economic and government interests[26].

---

25. *On-line services and data protection and the protection of privacy*, vol. 1, Annex to Annual Report 1998 of the Working Party established by art. 29 of dir. 95/46/EC 1999 p. 15.
26. C. D. Raab, "The governance of data protection", in *Modern Governance*, J. Kooiman (ed.) (Sage: London, 1993), p. 89.

In addition, regulation will be completely ineffective if not suitably implemented and supported by the availability of relevant and appropriate sanctions. The reader will recall in the chapters on health and safety the concept of risk assessment and legislating to balance risks, i.e. comparing the likely outcome if the risk remains uncontrolled with the measures needed to effect that control. In many senses the situation is no different in relation to the "risks" of data processing. Regulation needs to be able to reconcile the risk to an individual's privacy if the activity is not controlled with the measures needed to be put in place to control that risk. In other words, data protection measures can be considered as risk management devices[27]. In relation to privacy such a concept is more often discussed using the rhetoric of rights – balancing the right to privacy of the individual against the need for a free flow of information/data or the rights of the data subject against those of the data user and the majority of international legal instruments in this field present the issues in this way[28]. Whichever conceptual framework is chosen, the practical problems and potential solutions are identical.

Returning to the risk assessment approach, a further advantage of visualizing the problem in this way is that it may assist in the design of data processing systems. In Chapter 10 it was pointed out that safety should not be seen as an "optional extra" bolted on to a system afterwards but should be considered from the inception of the system design. Such an approach is capable of bringing efficiencies in both cost and operation. In a similar fashion, building in good data management practices from the beginning can turn the necessities and imperatives of data protection to advantage. Data subjects' confidence in the administration of both public and private organizations may be considerably enhanced by the transparency of their data management practices and the internal administrative efficiency of such organizations can also be improved by implementation of the procedures made necessary by data protection such as the deletion of obsolete material, correction of inaccurate data etc.

Taking such factors into account, which regulatory strategy will be the most effective – the "top-down" approach of legislative intervention or the "bottom-up" approach of sectoral self-regulation? The use of such terminology implies conflicting philosophies, but it would, in fact, be misleading to imagine that these apparently opposing mechanisms are entirely mutually exclusive. Although self-regulatory mechanisms are frequently invoked as a substitute for, or an avoidance of, legislation, they may also play a valuable role in both implementing and supplementing framework legislation by pro-

27. See also C. D. Raab, "Trust, technology and privacy", *Ends and Means* (the Journal of University of Aberdeen Centre for Philosophy, Technology and Society) 3(1), Autumn 1998, available at http://www.abdn.ac.uk/cpts/rab98.htm.
28. See, e.g. OECD guidelines, treaty 108, Directive 95/46 etc.

viding particular rules for specific sectors and/or purposes. Compare, for instance, how a general framework for maintaining privacy might be put into effect in relation to e.g. direct marketing as opposed to the management of health records. In each of these cases, the risks and consequences of inappropriate processing are very different. Codes of Practice (a common form of self-regulation) can be very effective at filling in the necessary detail to enable the framework requirements and guidance to be complied with in specific cases. The disadvantage, of course, is that too great a reliance on self-regulatory codes may result in divergence between the sectors which, in turn, can lead to fragmentation at the implementation level. This effect may well not be apparent at the higher legislative level where technological equivalence has resulted in broadly similar principles being adopted by otherwise different political and legal traditions and where "... a cross-national policy [has] coalesced around a shared concern for the privacy problem and a desire to emulate the policies of other jurisdictions"[29].

Thus far there has been little mention of making use of a technical solution such as the use of cryptographic techniques for what is frequently viewed as a technical problem. It is certainly true that some such advances may play a part and may even form part of the necessary regulatory mix. It may be, for instance, that a correct application of accepted data protection guidelines relating to the necessary level of data security will require the use of encryption under certain circumstances and for certain purposes[30]. It seems clear though that without an appropriate legal framework for their use "privacy-enhancing technologies cannot be a substitute for public policy"[31].

12.5 Convergence of data protection practices: the formulation of fair use guidelines

The previous section highlighted some of the factors that are of relevance in the development of data protection regimes. As mentioned, it is an observed fact that, at the level of international agreements and national legislation, the requirements imposed by this particular type of technology have resulted in a convergence of the rules made to ensure good data management. A recurring example in this respect is the emergence of data protection principles or fair use guidelines which have created a harmonizing effect on national legislation on data protection.

---

29. Bennett, *op cit.*, p. 99.
30. For further discussion of the role of cryptography in data protection see, e.g. S. A. Price, "Understanding contemporary cryptography and its wider impact upon the general law' *International Review of Law, Computers and Technology*, **95**, 108 *et seq.* (1999)
31. Bennett, *op cit.*, p. 117.

Arguably, one of the first formulations of such principles can be found in the Younger Report (*supra* n.12) which suggested 10 principles against which good data management could be measured. These are set out in Table 12.1.

The OECD Guidelines of 1980[32], although covering essentially the same ground as the Younger principles, reduced the number to eight and identified them by a description of the content, rather than merely numerically, as shown in Table 12.2.

Although the OECD is an intergovernmental organization rather than a supranational organization and, as such, it is for individual member countries to adopt or reject these Guidelines, the recommendations accompanying the Guidelines suggest that member countries take into account in their domestic legislation the principles concerning the protection of privacy and individual liberties contained in the Guidelines and co-operate in their implementation. Given the fact that, currently, there are 29 different states which are members of the OECD, there could be a dramatic effect if all were to comply.

Table 12.1 Younger principles.

1.	Information should be regarded as held for a specific purpose and should not be used without appropriate authorization for other purposes.
2.	Access to information should be confined to those authorized to have it for the purpose for which it was supplied.
3.	The amount of information collected and held should be the minimum necessary for achievement of a specified purpose.
4.	In computerized systems handling information for statistical purposes, adequate provision should be made in their design and programs for separating identities from the rest of the data.
5.	There should be arrangements whereby the subject could be told about the information held concerning him.
6.	The level of security to be achieved by a system should be specified in advance by the user and should include precautions against the deliberate abuse or misuse of information.
7.	A monitoring system should be provided to facilitate the detection of any violation of the security system.
8.	In the design of information systems, periods should be specified beyond which the information should not be retained.
9.	Data held should be accurate. There should be machinery for the correction of inaccuracy and the updating of information.
10.	Care should be taken in coding value judgments.

---

32. *Guidelines on the protection of privacy and trans-border data flows of personal data,* available at http://www.oecd.org/dsti/sti/it/secur/prod/priv-en-htm.

Table 12.2 OECD Guidelines

Name of Principle	Requirements of Principle
Collection Limitation Principle	There should be limits to the collection of personal data and any such data should be obtained by lawful and fair means and, where appropriate, with the knowledge or consent of the data subject.
Data Quality Principle	Personal data should be relevant to the purposes for which they are to be used, and, to the extent necessary for those purposes, should be accurate, complete and kept up-to-date.
Purpose Specification Principle	The purposes for which personal data are collected should be specified not later than at the time of data collection and the subsequent use limited to the fulfilment of those purposes or such others as are not incompatible with those purposes and as are specified on each occasion of change of purpose.
Use Limitation Principle	Personal data should not be disclosed, made available or otherwise used for purposes other than those specified in accordance with the Purpose Specification Principle except: (a) with the consent of the data subject; or (b) by the authority of law.
Security Safeguards Principle	Personal data should be protected by reasonable security safeguards against such risks as loss or unauthorized access, destruction, use, modification or disclosure of data.
Openness Principle	There should be a general policy of openness about developments, practices and policies with respect to personal data. Means should be readily available of establishing the existence and nature of personal data, and the main purposes of their use, as well as the identity and usual residence of the data controller.

(continued)

Table 12.2 (continued)

Name of Principle	Requirements of Principle
Individual Participation Principle	An individual should have the right: (a) to obtain from a data controller, or otherwise, confirmation of whether or not the data controller has data relating to him; (b) to have communicated to him, data relating to him: within a reasonable time; at a charge, if any, that is not excessive; in a reasonable manner; and in a form that is readily intelligible to him; c) to be given reasons if a request made under subparagraphs(a) and (b) is denied, and to be able to challenge such denial; and d) to challenge data relating to him and, if the challenge is successful to have the data erased, rectified, completed or amended.
Accountability Principle	A data controller should be accountable for complying with measures which give effect to the principles stated above.

The Council of Europe Convention[33] which was the major catalyst leading to the first data protection legislation in the UK did not enunciate principles in quite the same way but treaty articles corresponding to the various OECD labels can be located. These labels can similarly be applied to the provisions of the Data Protection Directive. Unlike the other instruments, this latter measure, having been adopted by the legislative body of a supranational organization, the European Union, must be implemented in the domestic legislation of 15 Member States and failure to do so may lead to enforcement action at the European level. Thus a qualitative difference can be noted in the legal effect of the Data Protection Directive as opposed to the earlier documents from the OECD and Council of Europe. Although these latter might be influential and persuasive amongst the member countries of those organizations, the documents, of themselves, are not capable of producing legal effects unless incorporated into the law of each individual country. This is not the case with the directive whose provisions have to be taken note of and acted upon once the date for formal implementation is past, regardless of whether any specific national provisions to deal with the issue have been put in place.

---

33. For text see http://www.coe.fr.

12.6 Data protection in the UK and Europe

Against the background of the factors and issues discussed in the preceding paragraphs, this section will consider the evolution of data protection law in the UK and in the European context and then will move on to a discussion of specific problems in applying the existing regime to the Internet and World-Wide Web.

The origins of the UK data protection legislation are often traced back to the Report of the Younger Committee on Privacy but, as can be seen from Table 12.3, it was still some years before the first Act was passed. In the end it was the Council of Europe Convention, referred to in the previous section, which finally precipitated action in the UK. The UK signed the Convention later in 1980, but could not ratify until the domestic legislation had been enacted. A prime impetus was that it was becoming apparent very rapidly that it was vital for Britain's international trade that the UK should have data protection legislation. Without it, there was a very real risk that the UK would be categorized by other countries as unsuitable to receive data on the grounds that, due to the lack of regulation, the rights of individuals to safeguards on the processing of their personal information could be prejudiced. This would have had catastrophic consequences for business and commerce in this country.

The Government's intention to legislate on data protection was announced in March 1981, when the Home Secretary announced that the Government would be introducing legislation to provide statutory protection for personal

Table 12.3 Development of data protection legislation.

Report of Younger Committee on Privacy, Cmnd 5012	1972
White Paper: Computers and privacy, Cmnd 6353 and Suppl Cmnd 6354	1975
Report of Lindop Committee on Data Protection, Cmnd 7341	1978
Council of Europe Convention on Protection of Personal Data	1980
White Paper: Data protection; the government's proposals for legislation, Cmnd 8539	1982
Data Protection Act	1984
Original proposal for a directive on the protection of individuals with regard to the processing of personal data COM (90) 314 final – SYN 287 [1990] OJ C 277/3	1990
Amended proposal for a directive on the protection of individuals with regard to the processing of personal data COM (92) 422 final – SYN 287 [1982] OJ C 311/30	1992
Directive 95/46/EC of the European Parliament and of the Council on the protection of individuals with regard to the processing of personal data and on the free movement of such data, [1995] OJ L 281/31	1995
Data Protection Act	1998

information handled automatically. This would follow the European guidelines and allow the Convention to be ratified.

A White Paper entitled *Data protection: the government's proposals for legislation*" followed in 1982[34]. This confirmed that the Younger principles would be embodied in the legislation and also contained the text of the Council of Europe Convention. The central feature of the new legislation was the registration requirement and all data users whether in the public or private sectors would be required to register in the same way. In the event the first Data Protection Bill was lost due to the dissolution of Parliament in spring 1983 and it was not until July 1984 after extensive and protracted debates and many amendments that the Data Protection Act finally received the Royal Assent, 14 years after the Younger Committee had been formed. The legislation which resulted only accorded protection to information held on computer and did not extend to data stored manually, although this was permitted by the terms of the Council of Europe Convention.

12.6.1 Brief overview of the 1984 Act

Although by the time this book is published, the implementation of the Data Protection Directive will mean that the 1984 Act will have been superseded by the Data Protection Act 1998 (see Section 12.6.3), a brief description of its provisions and application of this first statute regulating data processing in the UK is in order. Some major changes have been effected by implementation of the directive but, nevertheless, certain key concepts remain unchanged.

The underlying objectives of the 1984 Act were to protect individuals from three potential dangers; the use of personal information that was inaccurate, incomplete or irrelevant, the possibility of personal information being accessed by unauthorized persons and the use of personal information in a context or for a purpose other than that for which the information was collected. The fundamental conception was the provision of a regulatory framework within which a user would supply details of source and type of personal information to be processed, purposes of processing, those to whom disclosure would be made and so on. Such users would then process this data in accordance with the rules of good data management laid down in the data protection principles (see Table 12.4). All data users were thus required to register their particulars with the Data Protection Registrar who had the responsibility for overseeing the resultant register and for enforcing the data protection principles.

The Registrar had powers of enforcement to assist in this process and could serve notices requiring compliance with the data protection principles. The

---

34. Cmnd 8539.

Table 12.4 Data Protection Principles 1984.

OECD "label"	Data Protection Act 1984
Collection Limitation Principle	First Data Protection Principle. The information to be contained in personal data shall be obtained and personal data shall be processed, fairly and lawfully
An aspect of the Purpose Specification Principle	Second Data Protection Principle. Personal data shall be held only for one or more specified lawful purposes
Aspects of the Purpose Specification Principle and the Use Limitation Principle	Third Data Protection Principle. Personal data held for any purpose or purposes shall not be used or disclosed in any manner incompatible with that purpose or those purposes.
An aspect of the Data Quality Principle	Fourth Data Protection Principle Personal data held for any purpose or purposes shall be adequate, relevant and not excessive in relation to that purpose or those purposes.
An aspect of the Data Quality Principle	Fifth Data Protection Principle. Personal data shall be accurate and where necessary be kept up to date.
An aspect of the Data Quality Principle	Sixth Data Protection Principle. Personal data held for any purpose or purposes shall not be kept longer than is necessary for that purpose or those purposes.
Individual Participation Principle	Seventh Data Protection Principle. An individual shall be entitled (a) at reasonable intervals and without undue delay or expense (i) to be informed by any data user whether he holds personal data of which that individual is the subject; and (ii) to access to any such data held by a data user; and (b) where appropriate to have such data corrected or erased.
Security Safeguards Principle	Eighth Data Protection Principle. Appropriate security measures shall be taken against unauthorized access to or alteration, disclosure or destruction of, personal data and against accidental loss or destruction of personal data.

service of such notices could be appealed to the Data Protection Tribunal in the case of dispute. In addition, the Act created certain criminal offences which could be tried in the magistrates' courts. These included offences for failure to register and for some acts, such as knowingly or recklessly using data other than for purposes registered, which paralleled some of the requirements contained in the principles.

One major loophole which emerged in the enforcement of the Act was that the Data Protection Registrar had no power to enforce the data protection principles against a user who had not registered. All that could be done in such a case was to prosecute for non-registration. The majority of prosecutions which were brought under the Act were for this offence.

The Act only applied to personal data, i.e. that relating to an identifiable individual and in a form that could be processed by equipment operating automatically, in other words, by computer. It did not apply to information kept by other means such as in filing cabinets. No distinction was made between different types of personal information. The Council of Europe Convention suggested that "sensitive data" i.e. that relating to race, health, religion, sexual life etc. should not be processed unless appropriate safeguards were in place. The 1984 Act gave a power to the Secretary of State to make special provisions for such data but this power was never utilized.

In addition to the powers invested in the Registrar for the purposes of enforcing the provisions of the Act, a number of rights and safeguards were given to the data subject. The first of these was the right to be informed on enquiry whether the data user held personal data on the data subject and, subject to certain provisos, to be supplied with a copy of that information. The Act also provided a number of possible remedies for the data subject whose rights had been infringed. These included compensation for holding/processing inaccurate data in cases where the data subject suffered loss or damage as a result and compensation for loss or unauthorized disclosure. In certain circumstances, application could be made to the court for an order for rectification to correct inaccurate data or for erasure in cases of unauthorized disclosure.

Although, in principle, the Act applied to all data users whether in the public or private sectors, there were also a number of data processing applications which were exempted from some or all of the requirements of the Act. Applications are usually exempt for variations on one of two reasons. Either they do not pose a particular threat to privacy, so that applying the full rigour of the law would pose an unnecessary burden on that class of data user, or it is felt that the interests of the State mean that exemption is required on the grounds of national security, administration of justice and detection of crime, or the collection of taxes.

A body of case law has gradually developed in relation to the interpretation and application of the 1984 Act and, in so far as they relate to certain key concepts which remain unchanged in the 1998 Act, some of the decisions of the courts and Data Protection Tribunal will remain of relevance. The first data protection principle (see Table 12.4) required that data should be obtained and processed fairly and lawfully. The adjudication of what constituted "fair obtaining" was considered by the Data Protection tribunal in *Innovations (Mail Order) Ltd v Data Protection Registrar* (1993)[35]. The case arose out of an appeal against an enforcement notice served on Innovations Ltd by the Registrar. The company, which ran a well-known mail-order business, generated a substantial amount of its income from "list rental" making its lists of customer names and addresses available to other companies for direct marketing purposes. It included a notice of this practice in its catalogues but not in individual advertisements placed in a variety of media outlets. In some cases, therefore, customers did not learn of the possibility that their data could be used for this purpose until after they had made an order, i.e. after their information had been processed. The decision of the Tribunal was that data could not be deemed to be *fairly obtained* unless the data subject was aware of the potential purposes of processing at the <u>time</u> the data was collected and not at some later time. Compare this outcome with the Purpose Specification principle in the OECD guidelines in Table 12.2. Further, in *Linguaphone Institute Ltd v Data Protection Registrar* (1995)[36], the Tribunal also pointed out that it could equally be a violation of the first data protection principle if the "opt-out" box, commonly used to allow data subjects to indicate their refusal to have their data processed for other purposes, was so small as to be easily missed.

Having <u>obtained</u> the data fairly it must then be <u>processed</u> fairly. This latter requirement was considered in *CCN Systems Ltd and CCN Credit Systems Ltd v Data Protection Registrar* (1991)[37]. It had been common practice amongst credit reference agencies to process requests for information concerning the credit-worthiness of individuals merely by comparing addresses against which bad debts were recorded, rather than using a combination of name and address. This led to a number of complaints from those whose applications for credit had been refused because of bad debts recorded against another or previous occupant of the same address with whom the current applicant had

---

35. Case DA/92 31/49/1; see *Tenth annual report of the Data Protection Registrar* (HMSO, 1994). Salient extracts from this decision are extracted in D. Rowland & E. Macdonald, *Information technology law* (Cavendish Publishing, 1997), pp. 276–8.
36. Case DA/94 31/49/1; see *Encyclopaedia of data protection*, Vol. 3 (Sweet and Maxwell, 1988–1998), paras 6-514–6-518.
37. Case DA/90 25/49/9 relevant paragraphs of the decision are extracted in Rowland and Macdonald, *op cit.*, pp. 280–1.

no connection. The Tribunal found this to be an example of unfair processing.

The meaning of adequate, relevant and not excessive in the fourth data protection principle (see Table 12.4) was considered in a number of cases originating from the administration of the community charge or "poll tax" at the end of the 1980s. In essence this was merely a *per capita* tax levied on each adult person residing at a particular address. A number of complaints were received that many Councils were demanding far more information than appeared to be compatible with the collection of this tax. This might include detailed questions about the type of property inhabited or the subject's date of birth (which should have only been needed in the case of exemptions). In a number of cases the Data Protection Tribunal confirmed that only information which was directly necessary to the purpose of processing could legitimately be obtained from a data subject[38].

As will be appreciated after the consideration of the provisions of the 1998 Act in Section 12.6, the standards required for obtaining and processing information form the basic building blocks of data protection and these decisions are likely to remain important and influential. On the other hand, the only case under the Data Protection Act 1984 to reach the House of Lords, *R v Brown* ([1996] 1 All ER 545), although containing some authoritative statements about privacy and data protection is unlikely to remain of direct relevance. The central issue in the case was the meaning of "use" in the context of unauthorized use which was a criminal offence by virtue of the provisions of Section 5(2)(b), and was also in the third data protection principle (see Table 12.4). In contrast, the criminal offences in the 1998 Act no longer contain this construction and neither is it a feature of the new data protection principles.

As mentioned, one of the major reasons for introducing legislation in 1984 was to protect the interests of business against the effect of potential prohibitions on trans-border data flow from other jurisdictions. It is arguable that the resultant statute was not able to provide significant protection to individual information privacy. The main reasons for this were the paucity of control given to individuals over processing of their data as long as that processing is carried out in accordance with the terms of the registration which are, in the main, self-defined by the data user. Neither was this situation helped of course by the inability of the Registrar to enforce the data protection principles against unregistered users.

---

38. See, e.g. Cases DA/90 24/49/3, 4 and 5 *Community Charge Registration Officers of Runnymede Borough Council, South Northamptonshire District Council and Harrow Borough Council v Data Protection Registrar* on property type and Case DA/90 25/49/2 *Community Charge Registration Officer of Rhondda Borough Council v Data Protection Registrar* on date of birth, both extracted in Rowland and Macdonald, *op cit.*, pp. 286–7.

12.6.2 The Data Protection Directive[39]

Although the Single European Market in goods and services had been envisaged since the inception of the European Community, it was not until 1987 that the Single European Act set 31 December 1991 as the date for its intended completion. This led to a flurry of legislative activity at the European level and the adoption of many harmonizing directives in all sectors of the free market economy designed to remove the remaining barriers to trade[40]. Despite the phenomenon of convergence of data protection rules noted in Section 12.5, it was apparent that discrepancies in the protection offered in different jurisdictions could lead to problems with data flow between Member States. In turn this could have an inhibiting effect on the exploding European market in data and information services. In addition, there was an increasing tradition of the protection of fundamental human rights in the European Community, in parallel with that provided by the European Convention on Human Rights, and it is clear from the preamble to the directive that this aspect had an equal importance with business efficacy when the directive was drafted.

The original proposal for the directive was made in 1990[41] but the final form of the directive was only adopted in 1995. The delay was the result of protracted negotiations during the various legislative stages and the final form of the directive was a much amended and augmented version of the original proposal containing a total of 72 recitals in the preamble.

The scope of the individual protection offered by the directive is greater than that provided by the Data Protection Act 1984 in a number of significant ways. The practical effects of these changes will be considered in the discussion on the Data Protection Act 1998 which implements the directive in the UK. A summary of the major differences is given below.

- The directive applies, not only to data processed automatically, but also to manual data provided it is contained in a "relevant filing system" or "accessible record". It is perhaps something of an irony that this has become a legal requirement at a time when computer records are much more the norm. The UK was concerned at the potential implications and impact of the inclusion of manual records and negotiated a long

---

39. Directive 95/46/EC of the European Parliament and of the Council of 24 October 1995 on the protection of individuals with regard to the processing of personal data and on the free movement of such data. [1995] OJ L281/31. Full text can also be viewed at http://europa.eu.int/eur-lex/en/lif/dat/1995/en_395L0046.html.
40. See also in this connection the discussion in Section 9.4.11.
41. COM(90) 314 final – SYN 287 [1990] OJ C 277/3.

transitional period for many records of this type before the new legal
regime is fully applicable.

- Except under certain conditions, the consent of the data subject is needed
before processing can take place (article 7). More stringent conditions are
placed on the processing of so-called sensitive data and the directive gives
Member States the option of prohibiting the processing of this type of
data altogether (article 8).

- The rights of data subjects are expanded. In addition to the right of
subject access, rights in relation to automatic decision taking, rights to
prevent processing likely to cause damage and distress, to prevent processing for the purposes of direct marketing, to compensation in the case
of damage, and to take action to rectify, block, erase or destroy inaccurate data are included.

- The scope of the directive is also greater than that of the 1984 Act in that
a number of crucial definitions are expressed in wider terms including the
definitions of personal data, data controller (user in 1984 nomenclature)
and processing.

- Registration is replaced by notification which concentrates on the fact of
processing rather than the purpose of processing. In the absence of universal registration, oversight of the provisions is given to a Data
Protection Commissioner.

- In broad terms the exemptions are similar to those familiar with the
1984 Act but an important new exemption is contained in article 9.
This is designed to balance the right to privacy of the data subject with
the right to freedom of expression. Locating the appropriate balance
between competing rights is never an easy task and the directive leaves
it to individual Member States to achieve a suitable compromise
between the different interests involved, a process which is likely to
be influenced by the distinctive cultures and traditions of the different
Member States with respect to both privacy and the freedom of the
press.

12.6.3 The Data Protection Act 1998

Article 32 of the Data Protection Directive required that the terms of the
directive be implemented not later than three years from the date of adoption, i.e. by 24 October 1998. The Data Protection Act[42] received the Royal
Assent in July 1998 but was not brought into force until 1 March 2000 due to
the need for approval of a number of crucial pieces of secondary legislation.
The new Act retains the same basic structure as its predecessor and a state-

---

42. Full text available at http://www.hmso.gov.uk/acts.

ment of data protection principles (see Table 12.5) remains of central importance. A comparison of Tables 12.4 and 12.5 shows that there are some significant changes in wording and some renumbering, but that the text of a number of the principles remains unchanged.

The statute itself is a lengthy and convoluted document and the complexity of the new regime can be further appreciated when it is realized that this text merely provides the framework and that many of the important practical details are contained in the secondary legislation referred to above. The main differences in definition between the 1984 and 1998 Acts are summarized in Table 12.6 for those familiar with the terminology employed in the previous enactment.

The lacuna in the 1984 Act has been filled, in that the new data protection principles will apply independently of registration/notification. In other words, a data controller will be required to comply with the principles independently of whether the fact of processing has been notified or whether, indeed, notification is required in the particular case. Notification of registrable particulars is still likely to be the norm in the majority of instances but there may be some exceptions. It seems likely, also, that certain processing applications (so-called "assessable processing") which could potentially exhibit a high capacity for damage of the data subject's interests will need some type of prior permission or risk assessment from the Data Protection Commissioner. The precise details of the notification process including provisos and exemptions are contained in secondary legislation[43].

As already mentioned, it can be seen that the scope of the definitions of some of the key concepts is wider that that under the corresponding definition in the 1984 Act. Thus the definition of both data and personal data are expanded. The definition of data controller has also a rather broader ambit than the comparable definition of data user which it replaces, especially when taken in conjunction with the wider definition of processing. It is difficult to imagine anything which could be done with data which does not fall within the new definition of processing. In particular, it should be noted that the meaning of processing in the new Act also includes the initial obtaining of the data.

The first data protection principle contains the requirement that personal data shall be processed fairly and lawfully. Given the inclusion of "obtaining" in the amplified definition of processing, this is essentially the same requirement as that contained in the 1984 Act. The cases of *Innovations*, *Linguaphone* and *CCN Credit Systems* discussed in Section 12.6.1 above are thus likely to remain of relevance. The principle then continues

---

43. The Data Protection (Notification and Notification Fees) Regulations 2000 SI 2000/188. See http://www.legislation.hmso.gov.uk/si/si2000/20000188.htm.

Table 12.5 1998 Data Protection Principles.

OECD "label"	Data Protection Act 1998
Collection Limitation Principle	First Data Protection Principle. Personal data shall be processed fairly and lawfully and in particular shall not be processed unless (a) at least one of the conditions in Schedule 2 is met [consent etc.] and (b) in the case of sensitive personal data, at least one of the conditions in Schedule 3 is also met [explicit consent etc.].
Purpose Specification Principle	Second Data Protection Principle. Personal data shall be obtained only for one or more specified and lawful purposes, and shall not be further processed in any manner incompatible with that purpose of those purposes.
An aspect of the Data Quality Principle	Third Data Protection Principle. Personal data shall be adequate, relevant and not excessive in relation to the purpose or purposes for which they are processed.
An aspect of the Data Quality Principle	Fourth Data Protection Principle. Personal data shall be accurate and, where necessary, kept up to date.
An aspect of the Data Quality Principle	Fifth Data Protection Principle Personal data processed for any purpose or purposes shall not be kept for longer than is necessary for that purpose or those purposes.
Individual Participation Principle	Sixth Data Protection Principle. Personal data shall be processed in accordance with the rights of data subjects under this Act.
Security Safeguards Principle	Seventh Data Protection Principle. Appropriate technical and organizational measures shall be taken against unauthorized or unlawful processing of personal data and against accidental loss or destruction of, or damage to, personal data.
	Eighth Data Protection Principle. Personal data shall not be transferred to a country or territory outside the European Economic Area unless that country or territory ensures an adequate level of protection for the rights and freedoms of data subjects in relation to the processing of personal data.

Table 12.6 Comparison of the Terminology and Provisions of the Data Protection Act 1984 and the Data Protection Act 1998.

Data Protection Act 1984	*Data Protection Act 1998*
Data – information recorded in a form in which it can be processed by equipment operating automatically in response to instructions given for that purpose.	Data – as 1984 Act plus data which form part of a *relevant filing system* or part of an *accessible record*, i.e. applies also to manual records.
Personal data – consisting of information which relates to a living individual who can be identified from that information (includes opinions but excludes intentions).	Personal data – as 1984 Act but includes both opinions and intentions.
Data User – one who "holds" data, i.e. controls its contents and use.	Data Controller – one who determines the purposes for which and the manner in which any personal data are, or are to be, processed.
Computer Bureau – one who provides other persons with services in respect of data.	Data Processor – any person (other than an employee of the data controller) who processes the data on behalf of the data controller.
Data Subject – an individual who is the subject of personal data.	Data Subject – as 1984 Act.
Processing – amending, augmenting, deleting or rearranging the data or extracting the information constituting the data and, in the case of personal data, means performing any of those operations by reference to the data subject.	Processing – obtaining, recording or holding the information or data or carrying out any operation or set of operations on the information or data, including – (a) organization, adaptation or alteration of the information or data, (b) retrieval, consultation or use of the information or data, (c) disclosure of the information or data by transmission, dissemination or otherwise making available, or (d) alignment, combination, blocking, erasure or destruction of the information or data.
Data Protection Registrar	Data Protection Commissioner
Registration – all data users and computer bureaux must register and holding of data by unregistered persons is prohibited. Registration is a prerequisite for application of the other provisions of the Act	Notification – all provisions apply independent of notification, but notification of registrable particulars will still be required in the majority of cases.

by placing certain constraints on processing namely that, except in certain defined cases detailed in Schedule 2 of the Act, the consent of the data subject will be required before processing and where the data in question is "sensitive data" then, in most cases the explicit consent of the data subject will be required. The only exception in this latter case is for certain fairly tightly defined situations detailed in Schedule 3 of the Act. Consent is not defined by the Act but article 2(h) of the directive gives the meaning as "any freely given specific and informed indication of his wishes by which the data subject signifies his agreement to personal data relating to him being processed". What can be deemed to constitute consent? It seems clear that a blanket consent valid for all time will certainly not suffice. The use of the word "informed" and the phrase "signifies his agreement" are of particular note. It will not be just a question of the data subject having allowed the controller to have his or her data but of that permission being linked to a particular reason or purpose. Even without further clarification, the word "informed" suggests some knowledge on the part of the data subject of the possible consequences of processing. Thus consent given without a clear knowledge of the potential purposes may still not result in fair processing. Where the information has been provided by the data subject, he or she must be provided with the identity of the data controller, the identity of any representative nominated for the purposes of the Act, the purpose or purposes of processing and any other information which is deemed necessary to ensure fair processing. This could include those to whom it might be disclosed and for what reasons for instance. It may be that there is a need for some positive act signifying consent which cannot be inferred from such ambiguous events as the failure to return an opt-out form or to tick a box. The standard used in the directive itself is one of "unambiguous" consent, something which has not survived the transposition into domestic law.

Although consternation was expressed in some quarters at the potential impact this provision could have on data processors, in many cases it should not be at great variance from existing good practice. The Data Protection Tribunal in the *Innovations* case in 1993 (see Section 12.6.1) made the point that where data subjects could not be informed of a potential use of their data at the time of obtaining that data, such as where existing data is used for a new purpose, for instance, then "the obligation to obtain the data subject's positive consent for the non-obvious use of their data falls upon the data user". A later case, that of *British Gas Trading Ltd v Data Protection Registrar* (1998)[44] arose out of complaints from British Gas customers that their data was being used for marketing purposes and not just in connection with the supply of gas, albeit that each

---

44. *Supra* n. 18.

customer was sent a circular allowing them to opt out of processing for such purposes. The tribunal discussed the issue of consent within the circumstances of this case in some detail and concluded that positive consent could not be inferred from the failure to return a leaflet and that, notwithstanding the difficulties of obtaining consent, it would be possible to both notify and obtain the consent of customers, prior to processing, of the potential (and non-obvious) uses of their data.

The above discussion refers to what could perhaps be referred to as "ordinary" data. Where the data fall within the definition of the term sensitive personal data then the starting point is the need for explicit consent. This suggests a higher standard of consent than that required for "ordinary" data which would be likely to require detailed and clear information about the purpose of processing, likely disclosures etc. Whereas it may be possible in relation to ordinary data to accept implied consent, provided that it is deemed sufficiently clear and unambiguous, it is extremely unlikely that this would suffice for sensitive data.

With regard to the second data protection principle, there has been a change to a two-stage test consisting of (i) declaring the specified process (via the notification process or in information provided directly to the data subject) and then (ii) not doing anything further which would be incompatible with that purpose. This requirement also assists in ensuring that once data have been obtained they should not be processed in a cavalier fashion incompatible with the original reason for collection.

There has also been some strengthening of the provisions in the security safeguards principle in the seventh (previously the eighth) data protection principle. What security measures are appropriate will depend, not only on the nature of the personal data concerned, and the potential harm that could result from access, alteration, disclosure, loss or destruction, but also on the place where the personal data are stored, the security measures programmed into the relevant equipment and on the ascertainment of the reliability of the staff with access to the data system. Security measures must extend beyond the hardware of the system to include also the administrative measures regulating physical access. This may indicate the introduction of vetting procedures for personnel involved with data processing. The decision as to which combination of methods of ensuring the security and integrity of the system, and to what extent it is implemented, must depend on the type of personal information being processed and the potential for harm in the event of any of the other data protection principles being violated. It may well be different levels of security might be appropriate depending on the type of personal data being processed.

The level of security necessary must be balanced with the harm that might result, taking into account factors such as the present state of the technology, cost, reliability of personnel, cost-benefit analysis etc. In relation to processing done by a data processor (previously computer bureau) on behalf of the data controller, it is the data controller's responsibility to choose a suitable one and the processing must be done under contract evidenced in writing. Such a contract must require the data processor to act only on instructions from the controller and to comply with the same obligations regarding security as imposed on data controllers by the seventh principle.

As mentioned above, in relation to the directive, there are an increased number of rights conferred by the Act on individual data subjects which, as would be expected mirror those detailed in the directive. It is too early at this stage to be able to predict how these will work out in practice, but it is important to distinguish the general right of subject access and the need to provide information which enables the data subject to make informed consent in relation to the first data protection principle. The new access right is a similar but more detailed form of the right of subject access provided by the 1984 Act and fees are still permissible and expected. The difference in the 1998 Act is that, at least where the data is derived from the data subjects themselves, it would be expected that a substantial amount of information relating to intended processing etc. would be available to the data subject at the obtaining stage. In any case information will be provided by the Data Protection Commissioner as to what must be given in response to a subject access request.

In order to ease the changeover to the new regime, the Act, in line with the directive, provides certain transitional periods and arrangements for different types of data and processing. The first transitional period is between 24 October 1998, the date by which the directive should have been implemented and 23 October 2001. Data for which processing is under way immediately before 24 October 1998 need not comply with the new provisions until the end of this first transitional period. If new systems, procedures, purposes etc. are introduced then they will immediately be subject to the new regime which may mean the operation of a dual standard. These dates originate from the directive, itself, and so are unaffected by the fact that the Act was not finally brought into force until 1 March 2000. Also during the first transitional period, some of the 1984 exemptions, e.g. mailing lists etc. will continue in so far as they are concerned with eligible data. In addition eligible manual data are also exempt from the primary requirements of the Act during the first transition period – the only exceptions are that the data controller must still comply with the right of access and any problems relating to inaccuracy[45].

---

45. Some manual records may still be subject to transitional relief during the six years following 23 October 2001, designated as the second transitional period. For details see *The Data Protection Act 1998: An Introduction* available at http://www.open.gov.uk/dpr.

12.6.4 Implications of the implementation of the Data Protection Directive

One of the key objectives of the data protection directive was the harmonization of data protection rules throughout the member states of the European Union. For a number of reasons many commentators are of the view that its influence may be felt even beyond these jurisdictions. Bennett[46] has suggested that the "Data Protection directive now constitutes the rules of the road for the increasingly global character of data-processing operations" and Mayer-Schönberger[47] predicts that the directive will assist the drive to homogeneity of approach on a global scale. Whether the effect of the directive turns out to be as wide reaching as this remains to be seen but, without doubt, non-Member States are unlikely not to be affected by the provisions of the directive because of the prohibition on trans-border data flows in certain circumstances detailed in articles 25 and 26.

One potential area of anomaly may be the way in which data protection laws are applied to on-line services such as those provided via the Internet or World-Wide Web. Some of the challenges for data protection legislation raised by the increased use of on-line services have been discussed in Section 12.3. Can the provisions of the 1995 directive, which may perhaps be regarded as the current "state of the art" as far as data protection legislation is concerned, meet these challenges? The difficult issues are not so much the cases where the data subject is aware that data has been collected and used or even where this information is made available on the Internet since this is, arguably, the type of activity for which data protection law was designed. Rather the problems, as explained in Section 12.3, are more likely to arise as a consequence of the traceability of operations on-line in situations where the potential data subject may not be aware that data is being collected and retained.

How can the provisions of the directive be applied in such cases? Although this collection and retention of data may be an inevitable consequence of the use of the Internet for many purposes, the correlation of that data with a specific identifiable individual may not be straightforward. Whether such a correlation can be made may be crucial for the application of the directive. Although directives are legally binding as to the result to be achieved, they leave the choice of form and method for achieving that result to the individual Member State. Notwithstanding the fact that the Data Protection Directive is intended to harmonize data protection provisions throughout all Member States, there is thus the propensity for a certain divergence of approach. Given that the directive is not explicit on its application to the

---

46. *Op cit.*, p. 111.

47. V. Mayer-Schönberger, "Generational developments of data protection in Europe" in P. E. Agre & M. Rotenberg (eds) *Technology and privacy: the new landscape* (MIT Press: Cambridge Mass, 1997), p. 223.

Internet, the manner in which data protection law has developed in the different jurisdictions may be crucial.

One anomalous area which has already been identified is in the interpretation of what constitutes "personal" or "nominative" data. Many jurisdictions, including the UK, require a close link between the data and the individual for data protection law to apply. However, the definition of nominative data has been construed rather wider in France, for example, than most other jurisdictions in the EU. This difference in scope may be sufficient to bring, for example, the information gathered by "cookies" within the ambit of data protection law in France, whereas this seems unlikely elsewhere because the connection between the data and an identifiable individual in such a case may be tenuous[48]. Given that the objectives of the directive include not only the protection of the individual but also the removal of obstacles to the free flow of information and the harmonization of the relevant national provisions, this is clearly a problem which cannot be ignored.

These issues are under consideration by the various parties involved and the Working Party on the protection of individuals with regard to the processing of personal data (set up by the Data Protection Directive) adopted a working document *Processing of personal data on the Internet* in February 1999[49]. The matter has also been discussed in the Council of Europe and the OECD whose original guidelines were instrumental in the development of data protection law. The Working party has also set up an "Internet Task Force", which has amongst its objectives a consideration of the way in which the provisions of the directive can be implemented in an homogeneous way in relation to data protection on the Internet, particularly in relation to e-mail and related applications.

The Working Party and other groups consider not only the application of the relevant law but also a variety of non-legal solutions which might assist in the resolution of some of the difficulties. Problems with the divergence of definition of personal data may be resolved if identification of specific individuals is never possible from data traces, i.e. the promotion of anonymity on the Internet. An earlier recommendation of the Working Party[50] had suggested this as a way forward for remedying privacy concerns surrounding the

---

48. Nonetheless, it is clear that, in some situations at least, the use of cookies and similar tools raise privacy concerns not only because of the data collected but also because that collection may not be apparent to the subject. For suggestions on good practice see *Recommendation 1/99 on invisible and automatic processing of personal data on the Internet performed by software and hardware* available at http://europa.eu.int/comm/dg15/en/media/dataprot/wpdocs/wp17en.htm.

49. WP16 (5013/99/EN/final) available at
http://europa.eu.int/comm/dg15/en/media/dataprot/wpdocs.

50. Recommendation 3/97 see
http://europa.eu.int/comm/dg15/en/media/dataprot/wpdocs/wp6en.htm.

use of the Internet. One of the main conclusions put forward by the Working Party in this document was that "the ability to choose to remain anonymous is essential if individuals are to preserve the same protection for their privacy on-line as they currently enjoy off-line". Only a moment's reflection should reveal that the reality is not so simple and that anonymity is neither feasible nor desirable in many situations. Although the traceability of on-line activity on the Internet may facilitate unnecessary invasions of privacy, it is likely to be of positive advantage in the attempt to deal with unlawful activity on-line. Any successful solution needs therefore to find a satisfactory compromise between conflicting public policy objectives. These concerns were recognized in further conclusions of the Working Party that any legal restrictions should be "proportionate and limited to what is necessary to protect a specific public interest in a democratic society" and should be in line with any similar balance found to be necessary in relation to traditional technologies.

12.7 Defamation and the protection of reputation

Data protection is only one aspect of privacy which may be compromised by the increasing use of computers and computer networks. As discussed above, whereas anonymity on the Internet may be a positive asset in the protection of informational privacy, it may also provide a perfect shield for more scurrilous activities. Even without the cover of anonymity, the various methods available for the dissemination of information on computer networks provide fertile ground for the propagation of opprobrious material about others. The unique characteristics of computer networks in being able to communicate information to large numbers of people in different geographical locations almost instantaneously may well lead to the Internet becoming, if not quite a safe haven, at least the preferred choice for such activity.

What redress is available for those who feel that untrue and unwarranted statements have been circulated about them? In the physical world, publication of such material might attract an action for defamation – such actions are not uncommon against newspapers and other sections of the media. Although there may be some differences of degree and substance, most jurisdictions provide some form of remedy for injury to a person's integrity or reputation[51]. The precise scope and nature of the legal wrong may be modified by the effect of constitutionally protected rights, such as freedom of expression, but, despite such points of distinction, there is a remarkable degree of coherence between jurisdictions. Actions for defamation can be regarded as another facet of the protection and control of personal information[52] but, as we shall see in the

---

51. For a summary of the law relating to defamation in most of the world's jurisdictions see P. Carter-Ruck & H. Starte, *Carter-Ruck on libel and slander*, 5th edn, Chs 27–31 (Butterworths, 1997).
52. See, e.g. T. Gibbons, *Defamation reconsidered* (1996) 16 OJLS 587 at 589.

context of the Internet, raise opposing interests and issues to those raised by the data protection debate. The action for defamation in English law has been developed over several hundred years but, nevertheless, it may still not always be clear what the law regards as defamatory. The law on this subject can appear rather technical in places and the various components need to be examined and understood if the issues raised in relation to global computer networks are to be appreciated fully. It is also worth noting that, at common law, libel may also be a crime. Whether or not a prosecution is likely to ensue will depend on the severity of the action – "the essential feature of a criminal libel remains the publication of a grave not a trivial libel" (*Greaves v Deakin* [1980] AC 477 at 495 per Lord Scarman). Criminal prosecutions for libel are rare and usually reserved for serious cases which raise issues of public interest.

12.7.1 The ingredients of defamation

Defamation is divided into libel and slander. The obvious distinction is that libel applies to written statements whereas slander is relevant to the spoken word. More precisely, it is clear that an action for libel may be used for that which is written and permanent and slander for that which is audible and transient. It is evident that not all statements are made available via media for which such a categorical definition can be made. Material disseminated over the Internet might be written but can it be regarded as permanent? Clearly information held on computer networks can be given a degree of permanence but perhaps more importantly, its effects are capable of being felt just as much if not more than those of the conventional written word. To date the courts in relevant cases (see Section 12.7.2) have all proceeded on the basis that the ingredients for libel have been made out. The difference is not merely academic – libel is actionable *per se* whereas slander requires proof of damage for an action to succeed. For a statement to be classified as defamatory it needs to satisfy the three criteria discussed below.

Is it defamatory?

In 1840, Parke B. (*Parmiter v Coupland* (1840) 6 M & W 105 at 108) said that a defamatory statement was one "which is calculated to injure the reputation of another by exposing him to hatred, contempt or ridicule". Some jurisdictions include the requirement of falsehood in the definition. This is not the case in the UK but truth or justification does provide an absolute defence to an allegation of defamation. Lord Atkin (*Sim v Stretch* [1936] 2 All ER 1237 at 1240) thought that the test of exposure to ridicule etc. was too narrow and suggested instead that the appropriate question to ask was whether the statement was one which would tend "to lower the plaintiff in the estimation of right-thinking members of society generally". Although this test has been described as a "very fair guide"[53], at the beginning of the twenty first century the term "right-thinking members of society" sounds rather archaic and, in any case, who are the members of such a class is not immediately capable of precise definition.

A specific ambiguity is the question of what constitutes the relevant society. To quote Gibbons[54], the use of this test "reflects the idea that an external assessment has been made of the person's behaviour and characteristics, and that it represents the views of a group or a community of interests, for example, neighbours, colleagues, clientele, customers or the public at large". Where reputations are at issue, whether professional or social, the likelihood of damage from a defamatory statement is far greater if communicated to other members of that profession, neighbourhood etc. Does the society in question need to be defined in each case or is the issue to be judged against the views of society in general? The decisions in the courts on this issue are ambivalent and so provide little real guidance but the question may be a crucial one with respect to defamation on the Internet. Application of the above definition to the dissemination of derogatory or vituperative statements on bulletin boards and news-groups where "flaming" is commonplace, indeed might be expected in response to provocative statements or abuse of "netiquette", could create difficulties. It is only necessary to browse a selection of newsgroups to appreciate that, in some of them at least, vituperative language is common currency. Where such a mode of expression in the norm does this make defamation more difficult to establish or is the test the objective one based on generally accepted standards? The latter test would seem to suggest that, in theory, some consensus of opinion could be identified but, in practice, this may be an impossibility in a modern pluralist society. In a global society, such as that encountered on the Internet, such an evaluation verges on the meaningless.

Does it refer directly to the person concerned?

Defamation is a particularly personal kind of wrong and the person allegedly defamed is the only one who can bring an action. Neither can such an action succeed unless it is clear that the offending statement refers directly to him or her. In other words there must be no confusion over the subject of the statement. Obviously if the statement names the person then this aspect is in no doubt, but even in the absence of a name, identification of the subject may be possible because of the way in which he or she is described or, more controversially, because of other information well-known to the reader. Difficulties also arise when a statement is not obviously defamatory of itself, or does not

---

53. Carter-Ruck and Harvey Starte, *op. cit.*
54. *Op. cit.*, p. 589.

obviously refer to the plaintiff, but might do so when considered in conjunction with other information. A definitive test for use in such cases has proved elusive. It has been pointed out on a number of occasions that the relevant issue is whether the words convey a defamatory meaning to the "ordinary man" and as pointed out by Lord Devlin (*Lewis v Daily Telegraph* ([1963] 2 All ER 151 at 174) a rule cannot be made about that. In similar vein in the same case, Lord Reid ([1963] 2 All ER 151 at 154) discussed the fact that the ordinary man "can and does read between the lines in the light of his general knowledge and experience of worldly affairs" and that such inferences could also be regarded as a component of the ordinary and natural meaning, whether or not this would be the case as a matter of pure legal construction. This is of particular significance in the context of defamation for as Lord Reid expressed it, "sometimes it is not necessary to go beyond the words themselves ... but more often the sting is not so much in the words themselves as in what the ordinary man will infer from them". It is clear, though, that the words, themselves, must be the starting point even if an inference is then drawn as a result of additional knowledge. On the other hand, if the adverse inference is drawn purely from other information then the material cannot be defamatory.

Publication

Finally, for a successful defamation action, the statement must have been published to at least one other person – it is this communication to third parties which gives rise to the legal remedy and without which there cannot be a successful defamation action. Publication is such an essential ingredient because damage to reputation has no real significance except in the context of the opinions of others and so the fact that at least one other person is aware of the defamatory statement is vital. Insults, however vituperative and unmerited, will not be defamatory if only received by the person concerned. So if a person sends an e-mail to another which contains many personal insults and unfounded accusations the recipient will not be successful in obtaining a legal remedy. If, however, the person copies the e-mail to another recipient there will be the requisite publication. To develop this scenario further, it may be that this latter recipient then forwards the e-mail to several others who in turn forward it to others. The offending message can thus be "published" to many destinations for a fraction of the effort that would be involved in circulating the same number of people with hard copies.

Of course, some publication over the Internet is more akin to other conventional forms of publishing. Examples are web pages, bulletin boards and newsgroups etc. How many of those who act as the conduit for this information could be liable for publication in the event of the material having defamatory content? The general rule is that all those who have participated in the dissemination, be they editor, printer etc. could be implicated in the defamation. However, anyone who is not the originator, but merely a distributor, of the defamatory statement may be assisted by the defence of "innocent dissemination". In essence this defence will protect intermediaries who did not know that the information was libellous, nor was likely to be and that this lack of knowledge was not due to any negligence. In such a case the distributor is deemed not to have "published" the libel. In the UK, such a defence has always been part of the common law but has now been supplemented by a similar statutory defence contained in Section 1 of the Defamation Act 1996. This Act provides that the defence is not available to an *author, editor or publisher* (s1(1)(a)), these terms being defined and explained in s1(2) and (3). In particular, the term "publisher" refers to a commercial publisher and no one shall be considered to be an *author, editor or publisher* if only involved in, *inter alia*, "processing, making copies of, distributing or selling any electronic medium in or on which the statement is recorded, or in operating or providing any equipment, system or service by means of which the statement is retrieved, copied, distributed or made available in electronic form". Those who wish to rely on this defence must show that they did not fall into one of the categories defined above, that they took reasonable care in relation to the publication (s1(1)(b)) and that they neither knew or had reason to believe of their contribution to the publication of a defamatory statement (s1(1)(c)).

12.7.2 Defamation and the Internet

During the 1990s, the courts in a number of jurisdictions have adjudicated on a number of defamation cases involving the Internet as the medium of publication[55]. Some of the hearings in the US have concerned the liability of service providers. There are frequently inherent difficulties in identifying or tracing those who are the original authors of allegedly defamatory material published on the Internet or other computer network, perhaps because of the use of anonymous remailers etc. or because those concerned are in another jurisdiction. This can make service providers very vulnerable to defamation actions, being both easily identifiable, likely to be solvent and also perceived as part of the general process of publication. A crucial issue in determining whether there is liability in such cases will be an analysis of the precise nature of the functions performed by the service provider in question. In the first of these cases in the US, that of *Cubby Inc. v Compuserve Inc* (776 F Supp 135 (SDNY 1991))[56], which involved a service provider that provided access to a

---

55. See, e.g. T. Arnold-Moore, Legal pitfalls in cyberspace: defamation on computer networks" *Journal of Law and Information Sciences*, 165 5 (1994), and F. Auburn, *Usenet news and the law* [1995] Web JCLI http://webjcli.ncl.ac.uk.
56. Extracted in Rowland and Macdonald *Information technology law* (Cavendish, 1997).

bulletin board which was subject to independent editorial control, the court likened the function of the service provider to that of news vendor or book-store. In other words it only had the responsibilities of a distributor and, provided it "neither knew nor had reason to know" of the alleged defamation, there could be no liability. The court was of the view that imposing any higher standard than would be expected of a traditional distributor would "impose an undue burden on the free flow of information".

A different outcome resulted in the later case of *Stratton Oakmont Inc. v Prodigy Services Co.* (NY Sup Ct Nassau 1995, 1995 WL 323710, 63 USLW 2765) because the court, whilst not disagreeing with the decision in *Cubby*, found in the particular circumstances of the case that Prodigy, in fact, both held itself out as exerting control over the contents of bulletin boards and used an automatic software screening programme for the purpose. There are now statutory provisions in the US intended to prevent service providers being treated as primary publishers and becoming liable for information originating from a third party making use of the service[57].

In the UK, the precise functions of the service provider may still be crucial in ascertaining liability for defamation. Neither is the avoidance of liability simply a matter of refraining from editorial intervention because the nature of the defence available to distributors requires that they neither knew, nor had reason to know, of the existence of the defamatory material. When the Defamation Act 1996, referred to above, was passed, it was widely believed that service providers were excluded from the definition of *author, editor or publisher* in Section 1 (see above) and would, in consequence, be able to escape liability. But such an exclusion always depends on the proviso that reasonable care was taken and that there was neither knowledge nor reason to believe that there was any contribution to the publication. The service provider was unable to rely on this defence in *Godfrey v Demon Internet Ltd*[58]. The facts were that a contribution to a newsgroup purported to come from the plaintiff but was a forgery. Its contents were obscene and defamatory. The plaintiff there-fore informed the managing director of Demon that he had no responsibility for the posting and asked that it be removed from the Usenet server. Although Demon did not deny receiving this request, the offending material was not removed until it expired due to the usual time limit. Morland J pointed out that, in this case, the role of the service provider was more than merely passive – they received postings, made them accessible and deleted them. In particular, Demon could not rely on the defence in the Defamation Act 1996 s1 as they had clearly been made aware of the contents of the offending posting.

---

57. See, e.g. *Zeran v America Online* [1997] 129 F3d 327.
58. [1999] 4 All ER 342 and see http://www.courtservice.gov.uk/godfrey2.htm.

An added nuance was that it appeared that the plaintiff had provoked the libel by himself issuing provocative postings to newsgroups and that he had acted in a similar fashion on other occasions and in other jurisdictions. However, this had no bearing on the issue of liability but only on the damages which he might expect to recover. In contrast, in a similar case in the US[59] where an offending message purported to come from the plaintiff, the service provider was held not liable in the absence of proof that they knew the statement to be false.

12.8 Concluding remarks

This chapter shows that there are a number of issues and concerns for the protection of individual privacy and integrity arising out of the use of computers and computer networks. In relation to privacy and data protection, a detailed regulatory framework has evolved in the European Union and also in a number of states which, though not members of the EU, are members of the Council of Europe or the OECD. In contrast to this the US has, at present, no generic data protection legislation, as such, but instead relies on sectoral self-regulation by means of codes of practice and similar instruments.

Despite the existence of such legislation and self-regulation, there are still a number of difficult issues which need to be resolved in relation to the perceived to threat to individual privacy posed by the use of global computer networks such as the Internet. This medium has also made the dissemination of defamatory and other scurrilous material especially easy and any developments in the law and regulation of the Internet need to be able to balance the right to privacy against the need to make those who perpetrate unlawful acts accountable for their actions. An important part of this balancing act is to apportion to the service provider only such part of the responsibility as is fair and reasonable in the circumstances.

12.9 Further reading

There are now a number of specialist texts on information technology and computer law all of which include chapters on data protection law and issues. Examples are D. Rowland and E. Macdonald, *Information Technology Law* (Cavendish, 1997), I. J. Lloyd, *Information Technology Law*, 2nd edn. (Butterworth, 1997) and D. Bainbridge, *Introduction to Computer Law*, 4th edn. (Pitman Publishing, 1999). For specific detail on the latest regulatory regime see *Blackstone's Guide to the Data Protection Act 1998* and the web pages of the Data Protection Registrar (soon to be termed Commissioner) at http://www.open.gov.uk/dpr.

---

59. *Lunney v Prodigy Services* [1998] WL 999836 (NYAD 2 Dept).

The books by Rowland and Macdonald and by Lloyd also consider defamation on the Internet as does Edwards and Waelde (eds), *Law and the Internet: regulating cyberspace* (Hart, 1997).

Appendix: The British Computer Society Code of Conduct

Rules of professional conduct

As an aid to understanding, these rules have been grouped into the principal duties which all members should endeavour to discharge in pursuing their professional lives.

The public interest

1. Members shall in their professional practice safeguard public health and safety and have regard to the protection of the environment.
2. Members shall have due regard to the legitimate rights of third parties.
3. Members shall ensure that within their chosen fields they have knowledge and understanding of relevant legislation, regulations and standards and that they comply with such requirements.
4. Members shall in their professional practice have regard to basic human rights and shall avoid any actions that adversely affect such rights.

Duty to employers and clients

5. Members shall carry out work with due care and diligence in accordance with the requirements of the employer or client and shall, if their professional judgement is overruled, indicate the likely consequences.
6. Members shall endeavour to complete work undertaken on time and to budget and shall advise their employer or client as soon as practicable if any overrun is foreseen.
7. Members shall not offer or provide, or receive in return, any inducement for the introduction of business from a client unless there is full prior disclosure of the facts to that client.
8. Members shall not disclose or authorise to be disclosed, or use for personal gain or to benefit a third party, confidential information acquired in the course of professional practice, except with prior written permission of the employer or client, or at the direction of a court of law.

9. Members should seek to avoid being put in a position where they may become privy to or party to activities or information concerning activities which would conflict with their responsibilities in 1–4 above.

10. Members shall not misrepresent or withhold information on the capabilities of products, systems or services with which they are concerned or take advantage of the lack of knowledge or inexperience of others.

11. Members shall not, except where specifically so instructed, handle client's monies or place contracts or orders in connection with work on which they are engaged when acting as a private consultant.

12. Members shall not purport to exercise independent judgement on behalf of a client on any product or service in which they knowingly have any interest, financial or otherwise.

Duty to the profession

13. Members shall uphold the reputation of the Profession and shall seek to improve professional standards through participation in their development, use and enforcement, and shall avoid any action which will adversely affect the good standing of the Profession.

14. Members shall in their professional practice seek to advance public knowledge and understanding of computing and information systems and technology and to counter false or misleading statements which are detrimental to the Profession.

15. Members shall encourage and support fellow members in their professional development and, where possible, provide opportunities for the professional development of new entrants to the Profession.

16. Members shall act with integrity towards fellow members and to members of other professions with whom they are concerned in a professional capacity and shall avoid engaging in any activity which is incompatible with professional status.

17. Members shall not make any public statement in their professional capacity unless properly qualified and, where appropriate, authorised to do so, and shall have due regard to the likely consequences of any such statement on others.

Professional competence and integrity

18. Members shall seek to upgrade their professional knowledge and skill and shall maintain awareness of technological developments, procedures and standards which are relevant to their field, and shall encourage their subordinates to do likewise.

19. Members shall seek to conform to recognized good practice including quality standards which are in their judgement relevant, and shall encourage their subordinates to do likewise.

20. Members shall only offer to do work or provide service which is within their professional competence and shall not lay claim to any level of competence which they do not possess, and any professional opinion which they are asked to give shall be objective and reliable.
21. Members shall accept professional responsibility for their work and for the work of subordinates and associates under their direction, and shall not terminate any assignment except for good reason and on reasonable notice.
22. Members shall avoid any situation that may give rise to a conflict of interest between themselves and their client and shall make full and immediate disclosure to the client if any such conflict should occur.

Index